ANNALS OF LABOUR

ANNALS OF LABOUR

Autobiographies of British
working-class people
1820–1920

Edited by John Burnett

INDIANA UNIVERSITY PRESS
BLOOMINGTON & LONDON

First published in the United States by
Indiana University Press.

Copyright © 1974 by John Burnett

Library of Congress catalog card number: 73-19584

ISBN: 0-253-30745-7

Printed in Great Britain

Let not ambition mock their useful toil,
Their homely joys, and destiny obscure;
Nor grandeur hear with a disdainful smile
The short and simple annals of the poor.

'Elegy Written in a Country Churchyard,'
Thomas Gray

CONTENTS

Contents

PREFACE
AUTOBIOGRAPHIES AS HISTORY

'If one should desire to know what life in England was like a hundred years ago, he could scarcely do better than make a study of the contemporary diarists. There are plenty of them, and variety enough to suit all tastes.'[1] Few social historians would quarrel with James Aitken's first statement, though they might doubt his second. The remarkable thing about his edited extracts from twenty-two published English diaries is that they contain only one from anyone who might remotely be considered 'working-class', and that from the well-known *Rural Rides* of William Cobbett, himself the son of a small farmer. Similarly, when Arthur Ponsonby published his *English Diaries* in 1922 he felt compelled to admit that 'no diary of a professional manual worker was discoverable',[2] though in a second volume published a few years later he was able to include one extract from the diary of a foreman rivetter working on the Uganda Railway between 1898 and 1901.[3]

The almost total absence of published working-men's diaries applies nearly, but not quite, as much to autobiographical material. For many years historians have made use of a handful of autobiographies of working men,[4] the majority of whom played some important part in the development of trade unions or the labour movement, and more recently these have been added to by as many again which have come to light subsequently.[5] But it remains true that the direct, personal records of working people have not so far been regarded as a major historical source, and that the whole area of such material remains largely unexplored territory.

It has too readily been assumed that working people of the nineteenth century left too few accounts for any meaningful picture to be drawn. The most usual explanation for this is that until the advances in elementary education after 1870 the great majority of the working classes were too illiterate and inarticulate to leave behind written records: their main medium of communication, it has been supposed, was an oral one, in which folklore and personal memories were handed on to succeeding generations in the harvest-field or around the winter fireside. These assumptions ignore the important effects of 'self-help' agencies of education long before 1870, and the growth of literacy among large sections of the working classes, from at least the 1820s onwards, if not before. The

volume and quality of working-class literary remains in the early
and mid-nineteenth century suggest major cultural changes outside
the mainstream of formal education, which probably had its greatest
effects on the children of unskilled workers who had been beyond
the reach of self-help or voluntary agencies. Again, it has been
supposed that the lives of ordinary men and women were too dull
and of insufficient importance to merit recording, or that they had
too little time or energy left after a long working day for literary
exertions. The last may well account for the relative scarcity of
regularly kept, day-by-day diaries of working people, though inter-
mittent journals, and autobiographies written over a period of years
and, often, towards the end of life, are common enough. In the
main, working people who wished to write found time and energy
to do so – late at night, on their Sundays and rare holidays, in
periods of unemployment and in old age.

For such reasons, real or imagined, social historians interested in
working life and conditions in the last century have drawn their
evidence very largely from two sources: first, the Parliamentary
Papers, Reports of Royal Commissions, and Committees of Inquiry
in which the period is so rich, and, second, the surveys of private
investigators and researchers of which a long and distinguished line
extends from David Davies and Sir Frederic Eden at the end of the
eighteenth century to Charles Booth and Seebohm Rowntree at the
end of the nineteenth. The mass of detailed evidence which these
inquiries threw up must remain among the social historian's major
sources, but it is important to recognize that they are at a stage removed from the individuals with whom they deal. They necessarily
represent a bias, one way or the other, of the investigator who decided what questions were to be asked, and framed them in his own
way; witnesses were led – sometimes consciously, more often unconsciously – to make responses to particular, selected questions
which were the most important to the observer but not necessarily
to the witness.

The chief value of autobiographies and diaries is, therefore, that
they are direct records of the person involved in the situation from
which he or she writes at first hand. There is no intermediary re-
porter or observer to change the situation. The writer himself and
alone selects the facts, incidents and events which are to him most
important, and in doing so he also unconsciously reveals something
about his own attitudes, values and beliefs. These may not be what
the historian, sociologist or psychologist expects, or even 'wants' to
find, but they will have a personal integrity and authenticity which
responses to prepared questions may lack, especially when, as is

usual, the questioner has very different cultural, educational and social-class origins. The same comment will apply to the recent technique of tape-recording the memories of old people born at or before the beginning of this century. However skilful the interrogator, he necessarily places the respondent in the position of an actor playing out a role, and being led and prompted along particular lines of thought or recollection which may not be those the witness would have chosen.

What, then, are the difficulties in the use of such material? Not its scarcity. The careful researches of W. Matthews have revealed some 6,500 published British autobiographies and over 2,000 diaries covering the sixteenth to the twentieth centuries[6] and he would be the last to claim completeness for his inquiries; to the published works must be added a huge but quite incalculable mass of unpublished material, some of it in the form of treasured family papers, much of it possibly unregarded attic lumber. It is, of course, true that working people have not been among the most numerous autobiographers. In the nineteenth century the list was headed by politicians and statesmen, followed by the clergy (especially the nonconformist clergy), missionaries, doctors and soldiers, while in more recent times authors and journalists and stage and screen personalities have joined the ranks. But the records of working people of many kinds – skilled men, factory workers, domestic servants, farm labourers, navvies and even tramps – are still sufficiently numerous to constitute perhaps not a sociological 'sample' but at least a cross-section of many different occupations, geographical regions and standards of living.

Yet the chief defect of the use of diaries and autobiographies as a source must be the self-selectivity of the 'sample'. To keep a daily journal or to write the story of one's life is, and was, at once atypical, especially for working people to whom writing did not usually come easily. Often there was a particular motivation behind such memoirs, most commonly the author's belief that he had some important message for others which it was his duty to communicate. In the Victorian age this was often his personal triumph over difficulties and misfortunes, the classic account of a rise from humble origins to a position of honour and respectability through hard work, self-education, thrift and a concern for the betterment of mankind. Equally commonly it was the story of redemption from early sin, profligacy or drunkenness by divine grace, often experienced as a sudden act of conversion or salvation at a revivalist or temperance meeting. More recently, a main motivation has been to leave for one's children or grandchildren a record of a different age and society which, despite its material privations, had compensations which contemporary society seems to lack. Whatever his reasons, it is necessary to recognize that the autobiographer or diarist was engaging in an activity which set him apart from the majority of his fellow men, and that to this extent he was not a strictly representative figure.

Similarly, although the extent of working-class literacy in the mid-nineteenth century was clearly greater than has sometimes been supposed, literacy was still differential, and varied widely between different occupations and strata within the working classes. This is reflected in the surviving literary remains. There are more memoirs of skilled workers than of unskilled, more of upper domestic servants than of lower, more of school-teachers than of farm labourers, for the obvious reasons that they had not only more education, but more leisure and more opportunity to think of things other than the daily struggle to survive. Occupation also tended to determine literary involvement in that people who worked at dull, repetitive jobs were less likely to write about them than those who did unusual, exciting or dangerous things; thus, there are more accounts of miners, sailors, soldiers and steel-workers than of labourers, factory workers, house-maids or dress-makers.

A further question has to be asked about the trustworthiness of this kind of evidence. It could be argued that diaries, which are kept daily or, at least, at fairly regular intervals, provide a much more reliable record than autobiographies written after the events, and often towards the end of life. All human memory has its failings: it may forget events, sequences or whole periods of time, it may unconsciously edit and refine, it may erase particularly unhappy memories so that in the distance of time life seems to bear a mellower complexion than when first experienced. There are certainly suggestions of such editing in some autobiographical accounts, though in general it seems that it is the highlights of life that are best remembered – the especially bad as well as the especially good times – and that memory tends to sift out the merely uninteresting rather than the unpalatable. Whether in old age there can be 'total recall' of early life is a debatable theory, but it is certainly the case that a great many autobiographers write in vivid detail of their childhood, school-days, and their first entry to work and the adult world which was evidently for many a traumatic experience. Selectivity there must be in any autobiography, but the unconscious selection by the author may itself be a signal to the historian about the aspects of life which, in retrospect, the author thought most significant. More serious are the deliberate omissions or 'improvements' which may creep into an autobiography intended for publication or for the edification of future family generations; the tone and style of the writing may sometimes suggest such treatment, though there can be no guarantee that the reader will not be deceived.

For these reasons it would be a mistake to rely too heavily or exclusively on this kind of material as a historical source. Its importance is as a valuable supplement to existing contemporary records, which can offer direct evidence not only of life and work but of the attitudes and aspirations of the author. These may modify in important respects some of the received views about working-class life in the nineteenth century.

The first and most obvious characteristic of working-class autobiographies and diaries is the generally high quality of the writing itself, especially when it is remembered that most of it comes from largely self-educated men and women or, in the later nineteenth century, from the products of the often-maligned elementary schools where children typically had three or four years of formal grounding in 'the three Rs', often at the hands of a young pupil-teacher. The language they employ is usually simple, direct and unadorned, and has a limited vocabulary, but it makes its points well, clearly and concisely: even when it is ungrammatical (as in Emanuel Lovekin) the meaning is not in doubt. Evidently there existed a working-class literary form, which was quite distinct from 'polite' literature. What its origins were, how it was transmitted and how widely it diverged from vernacular speech can only be guessed at. Occasionally it is partly derivative – as in the mannered style of John Robinson, the butler, or William Lanceley, the house-steward, where these upper servants reflect the language as well as the attitudes of their employers; in the diary of John O'Neil his avid reading of the daily press is clearly a major stylistic influence, while Lucy Luck has to some extent modelled hers on the penny novelettes she must have read. For others, the Bible, the Prayer Book and the English Hymnal were major influences on thought, imagery and vocabulary (Emanuel Lovekin) and the language of scripture becomes the language of everyday affairs as it did for some Chartists, trade unionists and socialists. But obviously derivative writing is exceptional. Most of the authors use a form which is their own, which has been cultivated (sometimes, as in William Tayler, the keeping of a journal is explicitly part of the process of self-improvement), but which bears so close a resemblance to writings from quite different regions and occupations as to suggest common cultural roots. There are no undiscovered literary gems in such writing, nor would one expect them, but not uncommonly it is deeply felt and moving, if only because of its naïveté. Occasionally it is poetic, as in Thomas Jordan's description of his mining village; in one instance – that of George Sturt, the wheelwright – it is pure idyll, though Sturt was being educated for a profession before he inherited the family business and became a practising craftsman.

One of the most remarkable characteristics in much of the writing is the uncomplaining acceptance of conditions of life and work which to the modern reader seem brutal, degrading and almost unimaginable – of near-poverty and, sometimes, extreme poverty, of over-crowded and inadequate housing accommodation, of bad working conditions, periodic unemployment and generally restricted opportunities, and of the high incidence of disease, disablement and death. Yet most of those who experienced such conditions are not, in their writings at least, consciously discontented, let alone in a state of revolt. There is a sense of patient resignation to the facts of life, the feeling that human existence is a struggle and that survival is an end in itself. Especially is this so in relation to the early death of wives or children – a fatalistic attitude that 'God gives and God takes away', and that although one may mourn, one does not inveigh against the Fates which, to us, seem to have treated some so cruelly. Such resignation was, in part, the product of a long history of deprivation and suffering by which, for generations past, working people had been accustomed to poverty, personal tragedy and limited expectations; for some it was reinforced by the religious teaching that this world was, in any case, a vale of tears, and that happiness could only be expected in the life to come. These attitudes are true of the great majority, though not of all. In a few who are politically motivated or involved in trade union activities (the 'old potter', John O'Neil, Winifred Griffiths, Rosina Whyatt) the resentment against misery and exploitation is open and expressed, and it is noticeable that a more critical tone develops over time, the writings of the early twentieth century (T. R. Dennis, Jean Rennie) being more outspoken than those of the mid-nineteenth. But even here, the dislike is turned against particular individuals rather than against the system itself, and on the evidence of this admittedly very small sample one is led to conclude that working-class discontent was not only much less widely diffused than might be supposed, but that it was almost always limited to demands for improvement within the existing system rather than attempts to overthrow it.

Such attitudes on the part of the British working class are well known to students of labour history, and need cause no surprise.

What is more remarkable is that workers wrote so little about their work. The twenty-seven autobiographical extracts which follow have been selected principally in order to illustrate working conditions and attitudes towards work in the nineteenth and early twentieth centuries, yet they have been chosen from five or six times as many which pay little or no attention to the subject. Work, it seems, was not a central life-interest of the working classes. For most it was taken as given, like life itself, to be endured rather than enjoyed; most were probably glad enough to have it at all, and to expect to derive satisfaction or happiness from it was an irrelevant consideration.

It is true and predictable that this attitude varies with different types of occupation and work-task, and that skilled workers were able to derive notably more satisfaction from their work than semi-skilled and unskilled. Thus George Sturt can write lovingly about his work with timber, Arthur Gill about his very different, but creative, sign-writing; T. R. Dennis has evident pride in the way that, as an apprentice cabinet-maker, he was able to make a kidney dressing-table from 'a sweep of [the employer's] hands, a swear-word or two to impress', while the stonemason, Henry Broadhurst, takes a self-effacing pleasure in the fact that remains of his carving are still to be seen in Westminster Abbey, the Albert Hall and the Guildhall. Where craftsmen were fashioning and creating things which were satisfying and perhaps beautiful, such emotions are easily comprehensible; they appear to extend also to less skilled workers who had charge of their work-situation and discretion over the way the task was done, such as B. L. Coombes, the miner at the coal-face, or Winifred Griffiths, the 'first hand' shop assistant. But these were the minority of workers in the nineteenth century, as now; the factory hands and workers in sweated trades, the domestic servants, farm workers, navvies and labourers did not, if their writings are to be trusted, either think very much about their work or derive a sense of fulfilment from it. Work was a means to an end, not an end in itself, and the end was survival in a hostile world which often seemed to deny even this modest ambition. In this, there seems to be some parallel with the attitudes of the contemporary car-workers analysed by Goldthorpe, who also see their work primarily as a means to an end and regard having satisfying work-tasks as low on their list of priorities;[7] the supposed alienative nature of assembly-line work has little significance for them, and probably had little for their nineteenth-century counterparts, because work itself was not a central, dominating influence.

Although the actual details of work seem to have been of relatively
small importance to most autobiographers, the search for it was
often a major concern, and the writings of nineteenth-century
working people suggest that occupational and geographical mobility
was much greater than has sometimes been supposed. The 'tramping' of skilled workers has already been well-documented by Professor E. J. Hobsbawm,[8] but frequent movement between jobs was
by no means limited to them, or impelled by the driving force of
unemployment. Some skilled workers, like the compositor Paul
Evett, clearly chose to spend at least their earlier years on the move,
broadening their professional experience and at the same time enjoying the variety of fresh places and faces; Thomas Wood, the
engineer, and Henry Broadhurst, the stonemason, both covered
considerable distances in the search for work, while Charles Newnham, the carpenter, and Emanuel Lovekin, the mining butty, were
constantly moving within more restricted areas. At the other end of
the scale, the anonymous navvy had no settled occupation until
middle life, and even after his marriage was always travelling, com-
bining farm work at harvest time with railway labouring and tunnelling, as did Patrick MacGill at a later date.[9] Again, upper domestic
servants frequently moved for promotion or change of scene, while
many women servants regarded the occupation as almost casual,
and migrated easily into sweated trades, shopwork or, later, factory
work. Clearly, some occupations were much less mobile than others,
coal-mining perhaps being the extreme instance of a hereditary
expectation to follow one's father, while Lancashire millwork, at
any rate for men, offered few alternative employments. But the
massive overseas emigration of the later nineteenth century, and the
relative ease with which a ribbon-weaver like William Andrews
left Coventry to search for work in Cologne, Heidelberg, Baden,
Basle, Saint-Étienne, Lyons and Paris in 1860–61[10] suggest that
many English workers did not regard themselves as being tied down
to their native towns and villages. Perhaps the most highly skilled,
and therefore sought-after, workers moved less and even regarded
tramping as not quite respectable, while at the other end of the
scale, some farm workers were imprisoned by their own ignorance
and shiftlessness, but between the two extremes large numbers of
working people were frequently moving, changing jobs, being
promoted, becoming unemployed, seeking their fortune in London
or Manchester, periodically returning home and settling temporarily or permanently elsewhere. Only a few, like Lucy Luck, were
blown hither and thither by the wind of circumstances; most made
conscious choices based, often enough, on inadequate or false infor-

mation, but nevertheless viewing themselves as free agents in control of their own destinies.

But, for most working people, what mattered most was not work itself or the search for it, but personal relationships – with their families and friends, with their workmates and social acquaintances, and, above all, for some, with their God. To stand well in the eyes of friends and neighbours, to be trusted and respected, to be loved by one's children and grandchildren and to know, in old age, that they were making their ways honourably in the world are the ambitions which dominate the writings of working people, and are accorded much more importance than mere material acquisitions. They are intimately linked with standing well in the eyes of God. Although formal religious observance declined markedly as the century advanced, the values and beliefs of the majority of working men and women continued to be religiously determined: many of the contributors were regular church- or, more often, chapel-goers, and some were lay preachers or dignitaries of their connection, but whether they were formal 'believers' or not, their frames of reference, values and aspirations continued to be intrinsically Christian. Behaviour, both personal and commercial, was judged explicitly or implicitly by such standards, and many of the workers who had suffered much in this life looked forward to another world in which sins and pain would be washed away and they would be reunited with their loved ones.

Life outside work was clearly of greater importance for most people, and particularly involvement with other people – with individual friends, with family and with group activities. For some, like Emanuel Lovekin, the centre of this network was the extended family; for others it was the chapel which at once fulfilled spiritual and social needs. John O'Neil found his social relationships in trade union activities and the Mechanics' Institute. From the prominence which is given in autobiographical writings to Sunday School outings, to the firm's annual 'wayzgoose', to visits to fairs and markets, to village sports, excursions into the countryside or simply to walks with friends, interpersonal relationships were of paramount importance in working-class life. About courtship, marriage and marital relationships most writers are predictably reticent (Lucy Luck and the 'navvy' are exceptions). Perhaps they were too deeply felt to be recorded except in the sorrow of death; most seem to have held to the view that matrimony was a blessed, if not a holy, state, and at a higher level of experience that everyday affairs. Although sexual attraction clearly played a part in courtship, married love is written of in totally unphysical terms: a good wife is a support and a helpmate, a wise counsellor, an economical housekeeper and a devoted mother but not, if the writings are to be believed, a responsive sexual partner. This would accord with the Victorian view that a dutiful wife was sexually submissive but not co-operative, and with the fact that, in the absence of artificial methods of birth-control until late in the century, unrestrained sexual intercourse could have disastrous consequences on the frail standard of life of the working classes.

The picture which emerges from these writings is of men and women who are materially very poor by contemporary standards, who are uncomplaining in their poverty, who lead lives of hard work but rarely expect to find fulfilment from it, and for whom the family, interpersonal relationships, and relationship with God are centrally important. Their intellectual and cultural horizons are strictly limited: very few concern themselves with national events or politics, even with local trade union or labour movements; they are uninterested in material acquisition or achievement as such; they are not socially mobile and barely conscious of class beyond a recognition that the 'masters' constitute a different order of society into which they will never penetrate. Their aspirations are modest – to be respected by their fellows, to see their families growing up and making their way in the world, to die without debt and without sin. Such happiness and satisfactions as life has to offer are to be found in social contacts within groups – the family, the work-group, the chapel or, for a few, the public house; here meaningful relationships can be made, experiences exchanged, joys and sorrows shared.

Within what seemed a closed and rigid social structure the working classes constructed their own exclusive world, remote from the acquisitive, accumulative impulses of the Victorian economy. In part, it was an escape from the harshness of the real world, in part an attempt to create community in the anonymity of the industrial town. Ultimately, through the growth of education and democracy, improvements in living standards, working conditions, housing, food and dress, the working classes became, to a degree, participant members of society, but for most of the period covered by these writings they were both excluded, and excluded themselves, from public life. Behind the great public institutions and images of the Victorian age the working classes inhabited an inner, secret life which perpetuated traditional values and patterns of behaviour, essentially of rural origin, into the new urban industrial society. In past times almost the whole of life, including work, had gone forward within the circle of the family; increasingly, as the nineteenth century progressed, though much less quickly than is commonly supposed, work became separated from the family and the home, and the new cult of work sought to erect it into the centre of human existence. The working classes, it seems, for long rejected this unpalatable and alien notion.

Of the autobiographical extracts which follow, more than half are previously unpublished. They came, together with nearly a hundred more, in reply to letters in the press, and the response suggests that a much larger quantity of such material remains untapped. If this publication reveals more, or encourages others to commit their memories to paper, it will have achieved an important objective. The other extracts are from works previously published, though usually out of print or in out-of-the-way sources often unknown even to specialists. Together, the twenty-seven extracts cover most important occupations of working people, stopping short of professional occupations such as clerical work and school-teaching: they span the hundred years from the 1820s to the 1920s, ending where human memory can still easily reach. They have been given deliberately short head-notes designed to set the writer in his place and time. The extracts speak for themselves, and at different levels: most of them tell a story which has its own interest, but beyond this it is the intention that the historian, the sociologist, the psychologist and the general reader should draw their own conclusions.

My sincere thanks are due to all those who answered my request for material, and who have borne patiently with me over the three years this book has been in preparation; those whose contributions appear have the unexpected pleasure of finding themselves in print, but I, at least, have learned as much from the many others which are not included. I acknowledge with gratitude permission from the publishers to reprint extracts from their works.

Lastly, I wish to thank Fenner Fraser and Annemarie Maggs for their intelligent and uncomplaining typing of unfamiliar manuscripts as well as the more familiar difficulties of my own.

PART ONE

The Labouring Classes

INTRODUCTION

Historically and traditionally, those who earned their living by manual work fell into two broad, distinct categories: the skilled and the unskilled. In the centuries before the nineteenth this distinction was a fairly easy one to make, since, with a very few exceptions, it rested on apprenticeship: the skilled man was one who had 'served his time' in an organized craft, proceeding from apprentice to journeyman and, perhaps, to small master, while the unskilled was the man who had no formal training, no 'calling' and, usually, no organized association for his protection until the expansion of trade unions in the later nineteenth century. Although some industries were traditionally associated with skill, and others with the lack of it – wheelwright's work, for example, was predominantly skilled, while farm labouring was regarded as unskilled – the distinction did not rest solely on occupation. Within many occupations there was a hierarchy of skill, with labourers working alongside craftsmen, fetching and carrying, mixing up materials, doing the rough, preparatory work and other jobs for which muscle, rather than skill, was the main requirement.

This well-understood relationship defined not only role and status, but earnings, for in many trades the craftsman had received wages half as much again as the labourer over long centuries of time.[1] It was gradually broken by the intrusion of factory production from the late eighteenth century onwards. Factories, it is true, required a kind of skill to manipulate the new machines, but it was a skill which could often be learned in weeks rather than years, by women and children as easily as by men, and, usually, without formal apprenticeship. To this rule the engineering shops formed an important exception, but in the cotton-mills which were the prototypes of the new form of power-production 'apprenticeship' survived only in the wretched bondage to which pauper children were sometimes subjected by penny-pinching poor law administrators. In the cotton-mills, and in the later hosiery, clothing, shoe and furniture factories, the machines themselves provided much of the skill which had formerly been supplied by the hand, the eye and the judgement of the worker: in economic terms, they made mass production and the mass market possible, and very largely accounted for the industrial predominance of Britain in the nineteenth century.

The effect of the growth of factory production on the hierarchy of labour was twofold. First, it interposed a new class between the artisan and the labourer which, in Victorian times, was usually referred to as 'the factory operative' or 'the less skilled labour class', and which today is most commonly described as 'semi-skilled'. Second, it had important effects on the composition of the other two classes, since it both overtook, and eventually overwhelmed, some existing occupations and created some new ones. The classic victims of technological change were the handloom weavers, who, at the beginning of the nineteenth century, were among the highest-paid and most independent of all craftsmen, but who, by the 1840s, had been reduced by the development of powerloom weaving to starvation earnings of one penny an hour. Their sufferings were paralleled by those of framework knitters, ribbon-weavers and other hand workers as the century advanced. Those who, often for good reasons, clung obstinately to their crafts, were gradually pulled down in status and earnings to the level of the lowest-paid unskilled or casual workers, their misery heightened by the affluence they had once enjoyed. But the new factory trades were not recruited only, or mainly, from the downward mobility of former craftsmen and their descendants, For many of the unskilled 'labouring poor' factory work held out new opportunities of a higher standard of living than the traditional employments of agricultural labour and domestic service could ever offer, and a majority of its recruits came as a result of positive attraction rather than negative dispossession. For young men and young women from the country villages which had been the homes of some 80 per cent of the English population in 1801, work in the factory and life in the town seemed to open up new visions of material progress, cultural advancement and recreational opportunities which, perhaps, only our own generation has begun to question.

At first, the new factory operative was a phenomenon of the North of England, localized almost entirely in the cotton and woollen areas of Lancashire and the West Riding, but as mechanization advanced he came to be found in the metal industries of Birmingham and the Black Country, the hosiery trades of the Midlands and, later still in the century, in the myriad consumer industries ranging from furniture- and shoe-manufacture to tobacco and food industries. But although the factory came to typify British industry in the nineteenth century, it is important to remember that very large groups of workers remained outside it for many years, carrying on their trades at home or in small workshops in much the same way as in pre-industrial England. The handloom weavers probably numbered not fewer than 200,000 persons in the 1840s, and formed one of the largest occupational groups after agricultural workers and domestic servants. The framework knitters of Nottinghamshire, Derbyshire and Leicestershire formed a similar group, unmechanized until long after the application of steam-power to hosiery in 1845: thousands of ribbon-makers, silk-weavers and lace-makers still plied their hand trades in various parts of the country into the 1860s and 1870s, while straw-plait-making and glove-stitching continued throughout the whole century. These and similar trades made up a vast army of semi-skilled workers, predominantly, though not exclusively, women, who fought a losing battle against new techniques, new materials and new fashions. Their lineal descendants, by the end of the century, were the 'sweated trades' of domestic dress-makers, tailors and shirt-makers, match-makers, box-makers and button-stitchers, which formed the last refuge of many near-destitute women and children in London and other cities throughout the country.

For male workers without skill industrialization probably had smaller effects. The labourer's heavy tasks have been little changed by mechanical aids until very recent times, and in the last century he worked in much the same way as his predecessors had for centuries past: as Professor J. F. C. Harrison has reminded us, 'A vast amount of wheeling, dragging, hoisting, carrying, lifting, digging, tunnelling, draining, trenching, hedging, embanking, blasting, breaking, scouring, sawing, felling, reaping, mowing, picking, sifting and threshing was done by sheer muscular effort, day in, day out.'[2] In 1851 over a million of these men laboured on farms, and still formed the largest single occupational group in the country. A quarter of a million building labourers assisted nearly as many craftsmen bricklayers, masons, plasterers and joiners to build the houses and shops, the factories and offices of Victorian England, while others dug out the docks of London and Liverpool, loaded and unloaded cargoes and carried goods about the country on roads, rivers and canals. The new railways opened up another, generally more remunerative, field of labouring, employing by 1851 some 200,000 'navvies' in the construction of the iron way. So the decline of agriculture as a staple employment was compensated, in part at least, by the vast growth of building and constructional work. Although his work was more arduous and more dangerous than field labour the navvy in good times might earn up to 25 shillings or more a week; in bad times, or at harvest, he might return to the land

to work in the peripatetic gangs which increasingly supplied the
farmer's need for occasional labour, or to a new building-site where
hundreds of hands were suddenly needed. The labourer was necessarily more mobile, more migratory than the factory operative or the
domestic worker whose job opportunities tended to be localized by
geography, custom and personal relationships.

A labourer of a very special kind – more akin, in some respects,
to the skilled worker – was the miner. In the hierarchy of labour he
defies classification; his earnings sometimes equalled those of the
craftsman, in sturdy independence of thought and action he had no
superior, yet down to 1914 the physical labour required of him was
more intense, and the working conditions more dangerous, than in
any other trade. The raw material of industrialization was dug out
of the earth by the muscles of men aided only by pick and shovel,
and as the demand continued to grow more and more men found
their livings below ground. In the first reliable Census of 1851 coal-
miners, at 216,000, were ninth in the occupational order: copper-,
tin- and lead-miners added another 53,000, and iron-miners 27,000.[3]
By 1881 the colliers numbered 382,000, and by 1911 they had reached
their peak at 877,000 – as many now as the agricultural labourers; in
that still prosperous year they raised the record total of 273,000,000
tons, and coal made up more than one-tenth of the value of all United
Kingdom exports.[4]

But just as typical of the age of industrialization as factories and
coal-mines were shops. In 1801 only 20 per cent of the population had
lived in towns over 5,000 inhabitants, 80 per cent in villages and on
farms, but by 1851 half the population was urban and by 1911 80 per
cent had become town-dwellers. Meanwhile, the whole population
of England and Wales had quadrupled, from 9,000,000 to 36,000,000.
Townspeople, unlike their rural predecessors, were necessarily
dependent on professional producers and retailers for many of their
daily needs – for their bread, meat, milk and groceries, their clothes
and shoes, their tobacco, newspapers, beer and spirits. Precisely
how many people served these multifarious needs is impossible to
know. Very many of them were small, independent shopkeepers who,
by convention, were not usually identified with the 'working class'
though they worked as hard as, and probably longer than, most and
had no assistants other than their wives. Public houses, of which
there were no fewer than 82,466 in England and Wales in 1831, or
one to every 168 persons,[5] needed their barmen and barladies, and
in the latter half of the century the size of many shops – whether
'multiple' grocers, drapery houses or co-operative stores – grew
to the point where a dozen or so assistants behind the counters was

a necessity. By the end of Victoria's reign the rapid growth of restaurants, cafés and tea-shops was adding another large category to the denomination 'shop assistant'. In total, the number of those engaged in the distributive trades in 1911 was 930,000, three-fifths of them male, two-fifths female.[6]

These groups together – the factory and domestic workers, the miners, labourers and shop workers – made up the largest category in the hierarchy of Victorian labour. The statistician Dudly Baxter's well-known calculation of 1867 placed the total male working class of England and Wales at 7·7 millions; of these, 1·1 million were the 'skilled labour class', 3·8 millions the 'less skilled labour class' and 2·8 millions 'agricultural workers and unskilled labour class'.[7] Baxter's calculations were for men only, and to them have to be added some 2·7 million women and girls over the age of fifteen who were gainfully employed in 1861; they represented 26 per cent of the whole female population, a proportion which remained remarkably constant through the later Victorian decades.[8] Very nearly half of these were to be found in domestic service, an occupation so distinct and important as to warrant separate treatment in the next chapter; the rest were employed mainly in the textile factories, in millinery, 'sweated' and 'out-work' trades, and very few would have found a place in the 'skilled' category.

Semi-skilled work not including domestic service or agricultural labour, therefore, occupied at least five million adults or near-adults in the mid-Victorian period – probably two in every five occupied persons. Since then, the general trend has been towards a 'filtering-up' of labour as mechanization has advanced, new skills been created, and a greater proportion of the labour force has passed from primary production into distributive, clerical and professional functions. In 1911 the divisions still looked much the same as they had to Dudley Baxter, with 39·5 per cent of all occupied persons in the semi-skilled category; by 1951 the class had fallen to 32·6 per cent.[9] Though smaller than it was, and with some of its more painful employments removed by mechanical progress, semi-skilled work remained, and still remains, the lot of most British wage-earners.

The source of this growth of semi-skilled labour, the great 'reserve army', which was constantly tapped as old occupations expanded and new ones were created by the impulses of industrialization, was the land itself. The nineteenth century transformed England from a rural to an urban society, from an agricultural to an industrial economy. In 1801 four out of every five people lived on farms, in hamlets or in villages: a hundred years later four out of every five lived in towns and cities and earned their livings in ways increasingly unconnected with the now decaying English agriculture. But it was from peasant stock that most of the new town-dwellers had come, some, it is probable, forced off the land by technical and tenurial changes which were consolidating holdings and making the position of the small independent farmer increasingly difficult, but most attracted into the cities by the possibilities of higher earnings and wider horizons of life. Of all the adult inhabitants of English towns in 1851 nearly two-thirds were first-generation town-dwellers, and even at the end of the century only a minority could point to urban grandparents.

The distinction between country and town was not, of course, the same as that between agriculture and industry. Many people in the nineteenth century who lived in the countryside worked at industrial occupations connected with the land–blacksmiths, wheelwrights, carpenters, cobblers, millers, builders and village shopkeepers, to list only a few. The numbers of those directly engaged in farming are not precise in the early censuses, since they counted families rather than individuals, the 1831 Census giving 961,100 families so employed, or 28 per cent of all the families in Great Britain. Of these 144,600 were occupiers who employed labour, 130,500 occupiers who did not hire labour, and 686,000 were labouring families.[10] A farm labourer who did not have at least one son at work was an unusually unfortunate man, and many would have two or three, at least for a few years of their lives, besides a wife who worked at hay-making, bean-setting and harvesting; the figure of 686,000 labourers' families therefore suggests a total population of agricultural labourers of not less than a million and a half, and perhaps as much as two million. From 1851 onwards the statistics are more reliable and the trends are clear. In that year, taking England and Wales only, there were 965,000 agricultural labourers, not counting farm bailiffs or foremen (10,500), or farmers, graziers and their relatives. For the next decade, during the so-called 'Golden Age' of agricultural prosperity, the numbers of labourers grew by 20,000, but from 1861 the decline began, and for the last thirty years of the century 100,000 workers left the land in each decade to swell the populations of towns and colonies. By 1911 the agricultural workers had fallen to 643,000, and the whole agricultural population to 972,000.[11] The mobility of the labourer, once imprisoned in his parish by poverty, Poor Laws and ignorance, had been greatly aided by the coming of railways, and by the schemes of migration and emigration which trade unions began to develop from the 1870s onwards. Already by then farmers were complaining of the unwillingness and inefficiency of their workers, and of the

fact that as the strong and ambitious left the land the quality of
those who remained constantly degenerated. Half-hearted attempts
at cottage-improvement and the provision of allotments could not
arrest the decline, and ultimately the labourer was the chief instrument of his own improvement, both by leaving the land which
would not yield him a reasonable living and by forming effective
trade unions for those who stayed behind.

All the contemporary evidence indicates that the agricultural
labourer had the lowest standard of living of any large occupational
group in the century, his food coarser and less plentiful, his living
accommodation more overcrowded and insanitary and his wages
lower than any regularly employed town worker. Generalizations
about his economic position tend to be misleading, since it varied
so much in different parts of the country, at different seasons and at
different phases of his life, the *Seven Ages of a Village Pauper* (1874)
already identifying the 'poverty cycle' through which he would pass
between childhood and old age. A Parliamentary Report of 1824
revealed wages as little as 3s. a week for a single man and 4s. 6d. for
a married man in some southern counties depressed by the Speen-
hamland 'allowance' system; in other parts of the south they were
typically 8s. or 9s., but still compared very unfavourably with 12s.
in Oldham and up to 15s. in Cumberland, where they were forced
up by alternative industrial employments.[12] With wages still at 8s. or
9s. a week in the dear 1840s, when the half-gallon loaf of bread was
1s. or more, many labourers existed at near-starvation level, and
were fortunate if they had children old enough to bring in another
2s. or so a week.

The abject poverty of the labourer was not alleviated, and even
then only slightly, until towards the end of the century. A careful
survey by James Caird in 1850–51 found wages which varied from
6s. a week in south Wiltshire to 15s. a week in parts of Lancashire:
the average for the whole country was 9s. 6d., 8s. 5d. in the south
and 11s. 6d. in the north.[13] The extensive employment of children
from the age of seven or eight upwards, and of women, often organized into migratory 'gangs', were inevitable consequences, common until at least the 1870s when the expansion of schooling and the
statutory regulation of 'ganging' began to limit those evils. In 1872
an official inquiry put the average labourer's wage at 14s. 8d. a week,
though in Devon and Somerset 8s. and 9s. was still common, and it
was still the higher northern wages which pulled up the mean.
There was little change in money wages subsequently, 14s. or 15s.
remaining general up to the outbreak of the First World War, but
some improvement in the standard of life had come with lower

prices, especially of imported food, shorter hours, more education and more effective labour-organization.[14]

Traditionally regarded as an unskilled occupation, farm work in fact demanded many and varied kinds of skill, acquired not by formal apprenticeship but by equally long experience. This was reflected in many variations of pay. A foreman or a head man in charge of a department of agricultural work on a large farm – the stock, the plough-team or the dairy – an expert mower or hedger-and-ditcher, or merely a hard-working and reliable labourer, could always command more than the average wage, had more security of tenure, could expect a better cottage and more generous 'allowances' of beer and cider, and perhaps turf or a potato-patch. As good men became scarcer towards the end of the century such inducements became more common, and the lowest wages were increasingly reserved for those who had no special accomplishments, for older workers and for the many who became 'crippled up' with rheumatism by exposure to the cold and the wet. For an exceptionally able and intelligent young man like Joseph Arch farm work could offer rewards and satisfactions which would have been hard to find in factory work in a town. Born in Barford, Warwickshire, in 1826, he began work at nine as a crow-scarer, earning 4d. a day for twelve hours' vigilance, 'But if those days spent in the field were rather monotonous, they were at any rate wholesome, and I throve apace.' After two or three years of this he graduated to plough-boy at 6d. a day, and at twelve could drive a pair of horses and plough his own piece: 'It was a proud day for me when I drove my first pair and got eightpence a day wage.' At fourteen he was picked out by a wealthy banker and J.P. in the village and made a stable-boy at 8s. a week, as much as his father was then earning, and at a time when his mother took in washing and 'we seldom got a taste of fresh meat more than once in the seven days'. But at sixteen Joseph Arch learned a new type of hedge-cutting which had been introduced, started to enter hedging competitions and at the third attempt won the first prize and the title 'Champion Hedgecutter of England'. He now left home and began moving around England and Wales, getting 'very good money, and . . . in great request'; before he was twenty he was organizing gangs for mowing and other farm work, 'and had almost invariably a gang of from twenty to twenty-five men under me in the field'.[15]

A man like Arch, untypical as he was, clearly derived pride and satisfaction from his specialized kind of farm work. How far the great majority of agricultural labourers – poor, over-worked, ignorant and dependent – did so is difficult to know. Their work was often monotonous drudgery, carried on in all weathers and, at some seasons, for immensely long hours, and with very little aid from machinery until late in the century; on the other hand, they lived in village communities, worked with a measure of independence, spent their days in the open air and were part of a social system which provided an ordered and structured life. The relatively few agricultural labourers who have left autobiographies tend to write freely about the injustices of their employers and the poor rewards of their work, but affectionately, even lovingly, about the nature of the work itself. Especially, like Fred Kitchen, they write about the happiness they found in tending the farm animals,[16] or, like Frank Wensley, the pride and pleasure they had in driving and caring for a team of fine horses,[17] but even the regular farming operations like ploughing, sowing, reaping and mowing could bring satisfaction if men were not overburdened with poverty or fatigue. Like domestic service, farm labouring gradually sank during the course of the century into a low-status occupation, and the more ambitious men, who may have liked their work well enough, felt almost obliged to get away to the town, the army or the colonies in case they were thought to be shiftless yokels. Their transference was responsible for one of the important transformations of British society in the nineteenth century.

Textile workers

Although agriculture continued to occupy such an important place throughout the nineteenth century as an employer of labour, and landownership continued to be a major determinant of social and political status, rural England and all that it stood for gradually came to be increasingly anachronistic in the new civilization of factories, mines, iron-works and great cities. By 1850, perhaps even by 1830, the economic centre of gravity of England had already moved from the land to industry, and with the repeal of the Corn Laws in 1846 the nation took a conscious decision to live by its exports of manufactures and to buy its food in the cheapest markets of the world, even if this meant the sacrifice of agricultural prosperity. And in 1846 exports meant, overwhelmingly, exports of textiles and, pre-eminently, of cotton textiles. The new industry of the eighteenth century had established itself as the prototype and the pace-setter of the Industrial Revolution, the classic example of large-scale organization, the use of power-driven factory machinery and the minute division and intensive exploitation of human labour,

male and female, adult and child. Both contemporaries and subsequent historians have been struck by the rapidity of its growth and
its importance in the national economy. 'It is to the spinning jenny
and the steam engine that we must look as having been the true
moving powers of our fleets and armies,' wrote the statistician G. R.
Porter in 1847,[18] and proceeded in the next seventy pages to pile
table upon table illustrating the growth in the numbers of workers,
power looms, imports of raw cotton and exports of finished cloth.
Professor W. W. Rostow, the historian of economic growth, has
recently described the cotton industry as 'the original sector in the
first take-off',[19] while J. A. Schumpeter has stated that 'English
industrial history [in the period 1787–1842] can be almost resolved
into the history of a single industry'.[20]

The cloth industries were already old by the nineteenth century.
Since the Middle Ages the weaving of woollens, not only for use but
also for sale at home and abroad, had been England's staple industry.
Controlled at first by the guilds, it had passed in the fifteenth and
sixteenth centuries into the merchant capitalist stage in which
'clothiers' supplied the yarn to weavers working in their own homes,
paid piece-work wages on the basis of output, bleached, dyed and
marketed the finished cloths; some masters employed thousands
of workers spread over several counties, a few congregated hundreds
together in sheds, workrooms and disused monasteries. Thus, a
capitalist system of organization was already well-established in
many parts of the woollen industry, and the independent master
weaver was already a dying phenomenon, well before the advent of
the Industrial Revolution, while in other hand-textile industries
such as the framework knitting trade of Nottinghamshire, Derbyshire and Leicestershire, and the silk and ribbon industries of
Coventry, Macclesfield and East London, the same trend towards
control by middlemen and reduction of the worker's status to wage-
labourer was also apparent.

What was new in the eighteenth and early nineteenth centuries
was the application of mechanical invention to an industry which had
depended on the spinning wheel and the handloom. The long list
began with Kay's 'flying shuttle' of 1733 and Paul's carding machine
of 1748, but the crucial innovations came in the spinning process
with Hargreaves's 'spinning jenny' (patented 1770) which, by the
end of the century, could spin up to 120 threads at once, and Ark-
wright's 'water frame' (1769), which could spin a yarn strong
enough to serve as warp as well as weft, and so made the manufacture
of pure cotton cloth possible in Britain for the first time. Unlike the
jenny, the water frame was a powered machine which demanded the

factory system, the original motive-power, water, being gradually replaced by steam after 1785 when the Boulton and Watt engine was first used in a spinning-mill. The whole character of the industry changed rapidly as spinning came to be concentrated in factories where men could be taught the new mechanical processes in a very short time, and women and children could assist in carding, roving and a host of ancillary occupations. Spinning was the first mass production industry of the modern kind, the first to involve minute structural differentiation of labour,[21] and the first to harness men, machines and capital together on a scale which delighted some and terrified others.

Mechanization of weaving was a much slower process, Technically, it was more difficult to simulate than spinning, and thousands of handloom weavers drawn in from agricultural work and, later, from Ireland, could for the time being cope with the increased output of the jenny and the water frame. Cartwright's powerloom (1787) was imperfect in many respects, and it was not until after the end of the Napoleonic Wars that improved versions by Horrocks and others slowly came into use. Power weaving ultimately triumphed in the decade 1830–40, though more than 250,000 handloom weavers continued to drag out a miserable existence in competition with the new form of production. 'It is earnestly to be desired,' wrote the contemporary Edward Baines, 'that the whole number would be transferred to other branches of industry, as they have no prospect from continuing toil at the handloom but increasing misery and degradation.'[22] Theirs was the classic case of technical obsolescence. At the beginning of the century handloom weavers had ranked among the aristocrats of labour, with earnings of 30s to 35s. a week and more; in Carlisle in 1842 fully employed weavers could earn only 7s. 2½d.,[23] a mere penny an hour for what had once been regarded as a skilled and honourable trade.

Already by 1812 cotton had outstripped the woollen industry in national importance, and accounted for between 7 and 8 per cent of the national income of Great Britain. In 1815 exports of cotton textiles accounted for 40 per cent of the value of British exports, woollen goods for another 18 per cent, while by 1830 cotton made up more than half the total value of our exports.[24] Between the 1780s and the 1840s the imports of raw cotton, mainly from the Levant and the southern states of America, increased fifty times. As technical improvements continued in mid-century the industry became increasingly concentrated geographically and dependent on factory production: it is likely that by the early 1840s the number of powerloom weavers exceeded the number of handloom weavers for

2

the first time, and thereafter the decline of the latter was rapid. Of
the new factory workers, only a minority were men. Many of the
operations could be performed equally well, if not better, by women
and children whose wages might be only a third or a quarter those
of adult males: thus, in 1835 only a quarter of operatives in cotton
factories were men over eighteen, half were women and girls, and
13 per cent children under fourteen.[25] With an abundant and cheap
supply of labour wages remained low, and virtually stationary, in
no way reflecting the rapid expansion of the industry and the
accumulation of entrepreneurial capital and profits.

Up to the 1840s the development of the cotton industry was the
most spectacular achievement of the Industrial Revolution. Thereafter, its growth was less rapid, and its place as a 'pace-setter' was
gradually taken over by newer industrial enterprises – the railways,
steel-making and engineering. Between 1845 and 1870 the cotton
industry's output doubled, but this was a rate of growth only half as
rapid as that of the preceding twenty-five years. By the decade of
the 1880s it was clear that the growth both of the cotton and woollen
industries had fallen off sharply: there was increasing concentration
into South Lancashire and the West Riding of Yorkshire, and, as
new capital began to flow from the joint stock companies the size
and mechanization of mills grew, but small and inefficient firms were
finding it hard to exist in conditions of growing competition.[26]
Although in the 1880s cotton and wool still provided 46 per cent of
British exports, their great period of predominance in the economy
was already coming to an end.

Yet the decline was a relative, not an absolute one, and due
primarily to the fact that in the process of continuing industrialization the rank order of different industries necessarily changed at
different stages of their development. In 1871 textiles and clothing
still employed more people than all other manufacturing industries
together in England and Wales, and the value of the output of
cotton alone was greater than that of any other industry. But by
the time of the 1907 census of production coal-mining was far and
away the greatest contributor to national wealth with a net output of
£106 million; engineering was in second place with £50 million,
cotton in third with £45 million and wool much lower down with
only £18 million.[27] But the belief in cotton died hard. In a minor
boom period between 1905 and 1907 ninety-five new mills were
built in Lancashire – the significant fact was that the looms installed
were mainly of an old pattern which required some manual operations
by the weaver, and in 1914 Britain had only 15,000 fully automatic
looms in use as against 400,000 in the much smaller industry of the

United States. Technical stagnation, already apparent before the First World War, became a major problem in the 1920s and 1930s in the context of declining world markets and intense competition from newly industrialized countries like Japan. Britain never recovered the 40 per cent share of world trade which she had still enjoyed in 1914, and cotton, and to a lesser extent wool, gradually sank into the status of 'problem' industries with surplus capacity. By 1937 – by no means the worst of the inter-war years – exports of cotton piece-goods were a mere third of the volume of 1913.

The other textile industries of the nineteenth century – hosiery, silk, lace and linen – were much later to be mechanized, and economically much less important than cotton and wool. The framework knitting of hosiery had been a staple industry in parts of Nottinghamshire, Derbyshire and Leicestershire since the seventeenth century, and in the first half of the nineteenth it still remained in the same condition of a domestic, out-work trade in which the entrepreneur supplied the material and, very often, the frame itself at an extortionate rent. In circumstances of declining demand and increasing exploitation, the framework knitter and his family sank into a degradation as abject as that of the handloom weaver until the industry was rebuilt on the basis of powered machinery and the factory system. This only began after 1845 when a Belgian invention, the 'roundabout' frame, became available; by the 1860s hosiery factories were spreading rapidly, and the industry moved 'from its dilapidated base to a new level of prosperity'.[28]

The English silk industry has a different history. Since Tudor times it had had a sheltered life, protected behind tariff barriers which gave English manufacturers a 15 or 30 per cent edge over French imports; more importantly, the power weaving of silk had developed more rapidly in Manchester and Macclesfield in the 1840s than it had in Lyons and its neighbourhood. The industry survived by the great ingenuity and diversity of use to which silk was put – the handloom trade of Spitalfields, the ribbon-making industry of Coventry, the waste-silk industry (for velvets) of Manchester and Glasgow – which enabled it to weather even the ending of protection which came with the Cobden Treaty with France in 1860. Coventry was, undoubtedly, very hard hit, as the autobiographies of William Andrews and Joseph Gutteridge make plain;[29] many of the skilled hand weavers on Jacquard looms became unemployed, some emigrated, almost all lingered on through vicissitudes of fortune, the 'last really good spell of business' at Coventry being enjoyed in the late 1880s.[30] By then, the industries of the city were, fortunately, becoming diversified in the light-metal and engineering trades.

Because of their spectacular development, their importance to the economy, their early use of powered machinery and, not least, their extensive employment of women and children in factories, the textile industries in general, and the cotton industry in particular, gave rise to much contemporary comment. Both then and since the factory system has had its critics and apologists, its defenders and abusers. Much depended on the convictions of the observer and the particular time, locality or mill that he selected: new mills were almost always better places to work in than old ones, large mills better than small ones, well-regulated ones cleaner and healthier than badly managed ones. Thus, William Cooke Taylor could describe in 1842 the homes of the workers at Ashworth's model mill near Bolton as built of stone, consisting of four to six rooms, each with separate lavatories, and containing mahogany tables and chests of drawers, clocks, barometers and collections of books: none of the wives here worked, and the employees were 'not merely contented with their situation, but proud of it'.[31] Leon Faucher commented similarly in 1844 on the 1,500 employees of Thomas Ashton of Hyde, who rented good houses at 3s. to 3. 6d. a week, kept them clean and warm, and furnished them with sofas and pianos.[32] Even the factory children – whose hours of work had been shortened to eight (at nine to thirteen years) or twelve (at thirteen to eighteen years) in 1833, could be likened to 'lively elves . . . always cheerful and alert, taking pleasure in the light play of their muscles – enjoying the mobility natural to their age'.[33]

By contrast, there were many who condemned the cruelty and injury to children's bodies, minds and morals which, they believed, the factory system imposed, the slavery of working with the tireless machine for twelve or more hours a day, six days a week, the unventilated and insanitary atmosphere of the mill, the cruelty, even bestiality, of some masters and overlookers, and all this suffered for the merest pittance of a wage. William Dodd in 1842 wrote of the factory girl awakened at 4.30 A.M. to be at the mill by 5.30; with only short pauses she would be there until 7 P.M., and would then return home and 'throw herself into a chair exhausted'. 'This young woman looks very pale and delicate, and has every appearance of an approaching decline. I was asked to guess her age; I said, perhaps fifteen . . . Her mother . . . told me she was going nineteen . . . She is a fair specimen of a great proportion of factory girls in Manchester.'[34] Others, like Engels, claimed that the factory system had broken up the pre-industrial family by forcing father, mother and children out into separate employment; it demoralized children, it unfitted girls for marriage or domestic life, sometimes it even reversed sexual roles by turning the wife into the chief breadwinner and making a housekeeper of the husband. 'Factory servitude . . . confers the *jus primae noctis* on the employer. If the master is mean enough . . . his mill is also his harem.'[35]

Much of the contemporary criticism was based, explicitly or implicitly, on an idealized and romanticized view of the domestic system of industry which preceded the factory age, but, at least, the congregation of great numbers of workers into factories where conditions became exposed to public attention and concern had the good effect of bringing about increasing state regulation and control. From 1833 onwards factory acts began to protect first child and juvenile workers, later women workers, and to introduce measures of compulsory schooling, cleanliness and safety. By 1847 the Ten Hours Act laid down a maximum working day of ten hours (not including meal-breaks) for the age-group thirteen to eighteen, and for women of any age, and because many machines required the combined attentions of adult and child workers, the Act implied a similar restriction for adult males too. It seems certain that by mid-century the factory acts were bringing perceptibly better working conditions to the textile-mills than those experienced by workers in the unregulated workshops and sweated trades where children of any age could still be employed for any length of time. Gradually the application of the acts was tightened and extended – to prevent the shift-working of children, to cover smaller factories and workshops (1867) and to raise the minimum age of employment to ten (1876). But increasing state regulation was not the only ameliorating influence. Since at least the 1820s the growth of factories had encouraged the growth of labour organizations among the workers, and further reductions in hours for adults came, in part, from the pressure of increasingly powerful trade unions. By 1874 the nine-hour day and the fifty-six and a half-hour week had become general, and the textile workers were up with the engineers and other skilled trades; thereafter, further improvement was less rapid, the Factory Act of 1901 cutting only one more hour off the week to fifty-five and a half.[36]

The earnings of textile workers are meaningless as an average. Although the industry was conventionally classified as semi-skilled (or 'less skilled') it contained, in fact, many varying degrees of skill, and some earnings as high as those of craft workers; the low average level of earnings is largely accounted for by the high proportion of child and women workers, which tends to obscure the fact that an adult male in a cotton-mill could earn twice or three times the wage of an agricultural labourer. Again, it is important to remember that, at least in the earlier part of the nineteenth century, wages were part of family earnings, that, as far as possible, the father of a family employed his own children as 'scavengers' and 'piecceners' in the factory, and so perpetuated some of the work characteristics and familial relationships of the pre-industrial system. As the size of factories grew and the tasks became more and more differentiated, this became increasingly difficult from the 1830s onwards, though by no means unknown even at the end of the century.

In the 1830s children up to the age of thirteen or fourteen would work usually as piecceners (or 'piecers'), watching and joining together manually any broken threads which the spinning machine missed; the usual wage for this was 2s to 3s. a week, increasing with age and skill. Older girls and women were employed as throstle spinners in the cotton industry and as power loom weavers, and would earn from 5s. to 10s. a week. An adult male spinner in Lancashire or Yorkshire could expect from 14s. to 22s. a week, but much more if he were a skilled man working on 'fine counts', with a wage-level rising to 36s. or so. To some extent the weaver's wage was under his own control, since he was paid by the number of looms minded – usually two, sometimes three, occasionally even four. Fifty years later, in 1885, Leone Levi gives 40s. a week for fine male spinners, 11s. for piecers, 5s. 6d. per loom for weavers, 35s. 6d. for tacklers and 35s to 38s. for mechanics. Women's wages had improved more materially than men's, and by the 1880s a woman minding two pairs of looms could earn 23s. a week, out of which she would have to pay a 'tenter' 5s. 3d. Few women anywhere in the country would have earned so much for fifty-six and a half hours' work in what was still stable employment.[37]

Until 1914 textile wages continued to hold their level, and to fare better than those in some other industries during the inflation period after 1896. This has generally been put down to the Brooklands Agreement of 1893, marking the end of a twenty-weeks' strike in the previous year which had successfully resisted the employers' demand for a 5 per cent cut in wages;[38] thereafter, textile wages enjoyed an unusual stability for the next twenty years. Starting work as a fourteen-year-old piecener at the beginning of the new century Ellen Gill worked from 6 A.M. to 5.30 P.M. with one and a half hours for meal-breaks.

My wages were 2s. 6d. per week while I was learning, which turned out to be until somebody either left or died. Consequently, I was there over a year before there was a vacancy, when I was given a place at the bottom of the mule at 7s. a week. We moved up in the same way, and when I left at 21 years I had 9s., waiting for someone to leave, have a baby, or die.

The highest-paid job was at the head of the mule, when you had to 'mind the chain' for 10s. a week . . . When I left the mill I had 9d. a week pocket-money, which continued until I married.[39]

At the same period, in 1900, J. B. Cumberlidge began work as a 'half-timer' at the age of eleven, having passed the Labour Examination; when he worked mornings he earned 5s. 9d., when afternoons 5s. 3d. There followed two years of very interrupted schooling until thirteen, when he started full-time work at 11s. a week. During a boom period (1905–7) he moved to a new weaving-mill in which very up-to-date machinery had been installed, and was quickly earning 20 per cent more than his father, who was still employed on old looms.[40]

In some respects there had been real improvement in the conditions of factory life and work in the latter half of the nineteenth century. Already in 1868 an observer could report favourably on the progress of the past twenty-five years – the practical disappearance of bodily deformities, the reduction of hours from thirteen to ten, the Saturday half-holidays, the light, well-ventilated rooms of the new mills, 'the lavish provision of public parks, pleasure grounds, baths and free libraries in all the larger Lancashire towns'. But in 1868 the child could still begin work 'half-time' from the age of eight until thirteen. At that age, if in weaving, he became a 'tenter' assisting the adult in charge of the looms until, at fifteen or sixteen, he would be given a pair of looms to mind himself at a wage of 10s. to 12s. a week. An adult weaver in charge of four looms could expect 22s. to 25s. Marrying often at eighteen to twenty, and almost always another weaver, he might then earn 30 shillings or more a week until the birth of a family would depress his standard of life until the age of dependency was past. Rowntree's 'poverty cycle' was already well known in 1868. 'Finally, as his sons and daughters marry off . . . the operative, if still alive, lapses into penury – perhaps, if his children prove ingrates, falls to the parochial officers, and so ends the story.'[41]

Textile-factory work offered an acceptable standard of life, much superior to that of an agricultural labourer, while health and strength lasted. Its outstanding disadvantages lay in the nature of some of the work-processes and organization – the punctuality of mill life and the monotony imposed by the tireless machine, the task system which fixed a minimum production quota for each machine and penalized a worker who fell behind it, the fines for imperfect work and the deductions suffered by piece-workers from poor materials or faulty machines. These pressures imposed strains which some found it impossible to endure and produced, in a minority, 'an inveterate repugnance to factory work, and a constant desire to get away from it'.[42] As machinery constantly became both more sophisticated and more reliable later in the century, and productivity per worker constantly rose, these pressures increased rather than diminished. For women and girls such conditions were perhaps more bearable, since mill work did not normally continue after marriage, but for men a lifetime of such routine work must often have had harmful physical or psychological effects. It was this aspect of the factory system which most struck a woman weaver in 1924:

Work inside the factory is much harder than it used to be owing to the great speeding up of machinery. The toil is now almost ceaseless; the machinery demands constant attention. Thirty years ago this was not the case; the machinery ran very much slower and the operatives had a little leisure during working hours, but all this has been abolished. Production has increased without the corresponding increase in hands, showing that machinery has largely superseded human labour. Whether spinner or weaver, the textile operatives are on their feet from the first turn of the wheel in the morning till the last turn in the evening. Their feet are never still, their hands always full of tasks, and their eyes always on the watch. For 48 hours a week year in and year out one is expected to keep up to the great machine monsters. While the machinery runs the workers must stand; it cares nothing for fatigue or weakness or worry, and must not be interfered with by human pain or woe.

Were it not for its effect upon human beings, a textile mill would be a splendid monument to man's skill. The marvellous and complex machinery that seems to work with hands, feet and eyes, that acts almost as if it had a conscious brain, is startling in the almost human, though automatic, perfection it has reached. One looks with wonder at the automatic looms of today which stop just at the right moment and dispose of the empty shuttle, pick up a full one and re-start as though possessed of magic power. One is inclined to think 'what a boon to the worker', but this is not the case, because a weaver of ordinary looms tends two, but an automatic weaver tends four with very little difference in wages. This is one of the many cases where invention exploits the worker.[43]

Coal-miners

In a real sense, coal-miners were at the heart of Britain's industrial expansion of the nineteenth century. The industry itself was already old-established, stretching back to the commercial exploitation of coal-resources at least three hundred years earlier; its techniques were primitive and strangely unchanging until very recent times;

it exhibited few of the characteristics of mechanization, specialization and structural differentiation which made the cotton industry the prototype of the Industrial Revolution, and in many respects it had more in common with the old pre-industrial ways of life than it had with the new factory system. Yet coal, above all else, was the raw material of industrialization. It fed the steam-engines which powered the factories and workshops; it drove the locomotives and steamships; in the form of coke it smelted the iron and steel which were the other essential material requirements of industrial growth; with coal the English people warmed their homes, lighted their streets and buildings and paid, at least in part, for the imported food on which a rapidly growing population was fed. Coal, it could be argued, rather than cotton, was king of the nineteenth cenury.

In round numbers, and allowing for some uncertainty in the statistics of a commodity that was not easily reckoned, coal-production grew from 5,000,000 tons a year in 1780, to 10,000,000 in 1800, 100,000,000 in 1865 and 200,000,000 in 1897.[44] The peak – 273,000,000 tons –was reached immediately before the outbreak of the First World War, when demand, both at home and overseas, was still at its height; by the decade of the 1920s depression had reduced the yearly average to 251,000,000,[45] and the industry was already entering into the period of troubles which, in one form or another, have marked its history in the last half-century. A Royal Commission of 1925–6 discovered that there were 1,400 colliery undertakings in Britain with 2,500 mines, many of them too small and too inefficient for successful existence in the new conditions of declining demand and increasing foreign competition. The most aggressively individualistic of all British industries became sucsively subjected to subsidy, General Strike, massive unemployment, wartime control and, ultimately, in 1947, nationalization, and in recent years has also had to adapt to the competition of new sources of power which are, in some respects, more efficient and flexible.

The mining industry was, of course, geographically localized by the accessibility of the coal measures. Historically, outcrops of coal had simply been cut from the surface and followed into the earth whither they led, but by the nineteenth century practically all coal had to be 'got' (or 'won', the other technical term) by mines in England or adits in Wales. When most coal still came from a hundred or so feet below ground, seams were worked until they gave out and the pit was then closed; experimental shafts would be sunk elsewhere, based on the local, empirical knowledge of small masters who could divine coal almost as some could divine water. Men like Emanuel Lovekin, who successfully opened up many small pits

2*

in Staffordshire in the 1840s and 1850s, had no book-learning, and
brought only experience to a task in which they themselves suffered
much disappointment, injury and financial loss.[46] But by mid-century mining was starting to become a more professional business,
and owners were turning to geologists and mining engineers to follow
the coal measures into new and unsuspected regions. Northumberland and Durham, the home of the industry which, in 1830, produced more than a quarter of the coal of England and Wales, was
coming to be rivalled by the Lancashire coalfield, where pits of
1,400 feet at Pendleton and 1,200 feet at Wigan were regarded as
very nearly the limit of profitable working; even in Staffordshire,
famous for its shallow pits, it had been discovered that another seam
could be reached by driving down 1,000 feet through beds of old
sandstone. As the demand continued to grow, and new techniques
of haulage and ventilation made deeper working possible, new areas
were constantly opened up – in Yorkshire, Derbyshire and Nottinghamshire, under the North Sea, eventually, in the 1890s, in the
unlikely 'garden of England', Kent, where coal lay beneath the
chalk. Earlier fears that our natural asset was being quickly exhausted were dispelled by the discovery towards the end of the century
of vast resources of concealed coal.

In law, the owner of the surface land owned the coal beneath.
The great landed families who possessed so much of the soil of
England sometimes exploited the new wealth that lay below their
farmlands themselves; more often, they sold or leased the land to
entrepreneurs, who took the real risk of guessing how much lay
below; sometimes, as in the Midlands, they contracted with a
'butty' who engaged with the proprietor to deliver the coal at so
much the ton, himself hiring the labour and using his own equipment. In such arrangements the mine-worker often became exposed
to the petty tyrannies of indirect employment. His wages and conditions of work were constrained by the 'charter' which the butty
had contracted with the proprietor; one could always be pleaded
against the other, neither was responsible for accidents because
neither would admit to being the employer. Thus, the miner's
position exhibited a strange contrast between a high degree of independence which he enjoyed at the coal-face and the constraints
which restricted him above ground. The extreme form of such restriction was the 'yearly bond', almost a relic of feudalism, which
persisted in the Durham coalfield until 1872, when the mining
union took advantage of a particularly prosperous period to bring
it to an end and substitute fortnightly agreements.[47]

To most Victorian observers coal-miners represented a strange, almost half-human, stratum of the working class, pugnacious, brutalized by their lives of grimy toil, inhabiting isolated communities which, in leisure time, became dens of drunkenness and savage sports. A few praised the miner's courage and resourcefulness in a dangerous occupation where accidents were a daily ocurrence, and the plight of women and young children in the mines early aroused humanitarian concern. The employment of women and of boys under the age of ten below ground was statutorily forbidden by the Coal Mines Act of 1842 after the horrible disclosures of a Royal Commission led by Lord Shaftesbury, and raised to the age of twelve in 1860, but difficulties of administration, ease of evasion and the unco-operativeness of many parents themselves prevented effective enforcement for a good many years. In 1851 there were 32,000 boys under fifteen reported in English and Welsh mines and still 26,000 thirty years later;[48] boys were essential to the economy of the mine, as were the 'pit-brow' girls and women who sorted and graded coal at the surface, though after 1842 they were rarely found dragging tubs along the underground roadways as in earlier years.

But Tom Mann, the later labour leader, remembered clearly enough doing such work in 1866, when he was only ten years old:

> I started work down the mine in the air courses. A number of men and boys were always at this work: the duties were to make and keep in order small roads or 'courses' to convey the air to the respective workings in the mines. These air courses were only three feet high and wide, and my work was to take away the 'mullock', coal, or dirt that the man would require taken from him as he worked away at 'heading' a new road, or repairing an existing one. For this removal there were boxes known down the mine as 'dans', about two feet six inches long and eighteen inches wide and of a similar depth, with an iron ring strongly fixed at each end. I had to draw the box along, not on rails; it was built sledge-like, and each boy had a belt and chain. A piece of stout material was fitted on the boy around the waist. To this there was a chain attached, and the boy would hook the chain to the box, and, crawling on all fours, the chain between his legs, would drag the box along and take it to the 'gob' where it would be emptied. Donkey work it certainly was. The boys were stripped to the waist, and as there were only candles enough for one each, and these could not be carried, but had to be fixed at the end of the stages, the boy had to crawl on hands and toes dragging his load along in worse than Egyptian darkness. Many a time did I actually lie down groaning as a consequence of the heavy strain on the loins, especially when the road was wet and 'clayey' causing much resistance to the load being dragged.[49]

The anonymous author of *Our Coal and Our Coal-Pits* (1853) found a little boy trapper who was certainly not above seven years

old, and may have been only six. 'He told me his father was killed
in an explosion, and that he was very much afraid that if any accident should happen he would never get out of the pit alive. "For,"
said he, "I go in very far bye [far in] and it is very hot there." '[50]
Their work was to open and close the ventilation-doors, placed so
as to regulate the direction of the currents of air necessary to maintain oxygen in the workings; it was a lonely, immobile job for a
small child, crouched in a dark corner by the doors which he pulled
open by a cord when the trains of coal wagons came through. They
normally worked for twelve hours – in two shifts when a mine was
in full production and the miners themselves worked in three of
eight hours – and the usual trapper's wage in mid-century was 10d. a
day, or 5s. in a very full week.[51]

Older boys, usually from twelve upwards, worked as 'putters'.
Their job was to push (or 'put') the trains of coal from the places
where the hewers filled them to the crane where they were hoisted
on to wagons for transporting to the shaft; this last part of the
journey was along the main roads underground, and the wagons
were usually pulled by horses or ponies. Thus, the effort required
of putters was a rather brief, but extremely strenuous one, an observer commenting that 'next to the hewers they are the hardest
labourers in the pit, and in some few places their labour is even
harder'.[52] The average weight of the loaded tubs dragged by the
putters was six to eight hundredweight, the greatest ten hundredweight; the putters generally worked in gangs consisting of a 'heads-
man' assisted by 'half-marrows', 'foals' and, on steep slopes,
'helpers-up'. They were paid by the number of tubs put, the daily
wage varying, with age and strength, from 1s. 3d. to as much as
3s. 6d.

Notwithstanding the severity of this toil, it does not commonly injure
the boys' health very materially, if they be naturally strong boys. Such
boys feed well and drink water in large draughts down the mine ... They
stop to 'bait' at fixed times, and then devour huge hunks of bread and
cheese, with a bone or so of meat, drinking at that time cold coffee or milk
out of tin canteens. When at home after work they eat as much as they can
get, and they generally get fat meat or bits of 'singing hinnies' which are
rich, kneaded cakes that sing with their exuding fat when baking on a
girdle or gridiron.[53]

At the coal-face itself worked the hewers – always a minority of
those employed about a coal-pit, the key men of the whole system,
whose picks and shovels tore the coal from the seams whose thickness varied, in different mines and different parts of the country,
from about three feet to ten feet or more. Their shift in mid-

century was already usually only eight hours, though in a job where payment was by results, and a hard or awkward seam was unrewarding, it often extended beyond this: a statutory eight-hour day, which included the time spent in getting to the face, was not won until 1908. In pits free of fire-damp, gunpowder charges helped to free the coal from the surrounding rock; otherwise, the hewer used only his short pick, standing, kneeling, lying on one side or on his back according to the position and thickness of the seam. In his 'stall' he was usually alone, and his degree of discretion was great, though sometimes he worked with a younger assistant who loaded the tubs: in some pits he propped the roof with timber as he proceeded, or left uncut pillars for the purpose.

The best hewers have learnt to do their work in quick time, and it is curious to watch them shifting their postures and strangely adapting themselves to the exact form or figure required to bring down the coal with advantage and speed. I have never seen any labour like it: but its duration and voluntary extent must be measured against its intensity.[54]

In mid-century, the hewer's daily wage, depending on the locality and his output, varied from 3s. to 4s. 6d. and probably averaged 3s. 9d. If he used gunpowder, this was at his own expense; he would need a pound of candles a week, costing 6d., and his half-dozen or so picks and other tools had to be kept in repair and replaced when need be. A suit of coarse flannel pit-clothes cost about £1 at the 'slop' shop, less if made at home. But in most mining villages a cottage was provided by the owners rent-free, and free coals were available for the miner's enormous fires of which all contemporary observers spoke: the value of these two perquisites might be another 5s. a week in winter and hardly less in the northern summer. The wage-rates were extremely sensitive, in an increasingly steam-ruled world, to trade fluctuations and general movements in prices, and so could vary significantly from one year to another. But the greatest difficulty in assessing miners' actual earnings lies in estimating the number of days worked. Unlike the factory, where the working week was carefully controlled because it was linked to powered machinery, the mine permitted a more flexible system of working which allowed a man to choose, within conventional limits, when he would work. A mine in full production would be working sixd ays a week, but early nineteenth-century estimates – like present-day ones – suggest that four and a half days a week was the average actually worked,[55] and on this basis a weekly wage of 17s. to 20s., plus allowances, is indicated. Many, perhaps most, earned more at some seasons, but long-continued working for six days a

week was probably neither physically possible nor socially acceptable in the small mining communities where deviance from the
norm would be eccentric and unpopular. Four or five days' work a
week was normally sufficient to provide for the miner's unsophis-
ticated range of wants; two or three days of 'play' were sometimes
voluntary, sometimes obligatory in slack periods, but they were
probably necessary in an occupation which made men old by their
forties.

Like most other fully employed workers, miners shared in the
general prosperity of the mid-Victorian 'Golden Age', their real
wages probably advancing by around 20 per cent between the
1850s and the 1880s;[56] if this was less than the gains of agricultural
labourers and building workers, the miners started from a higher
base. But in a bad decade (1878–87), when export prices of coal
fell by around 30 per cent, the miners' unions were obliged to
accept a sliding scale of wages and the principle that 'wages should
be based on the selling price of coal'. Condemned as a 'sell-out'
to the commercial values of a capitalist society, the sliding scale
greatly increased the status and authority of the unions, and at
least provided a living wage. In Durham in 1884 winders were
earning 4s. a day, surface workers 3s. 9d. and underground hewers
4s. 9d.; Manchester hewers were averaging 26s. 3d. a week, colliery
engineers 32s. 6d., draymen 21s. 2d. and carters 18s. 2d.[57]

After the bad decade of the 1880s, the coal-mining industry
apparently returned to something like prosperity. The numbers of
miners doubled between 1881 and 1911, and on the eve of the war
coal accounted for 10 per cent of the value of British exports. But
this prosperity was not reflected in miners' earnings, which dipped
into a trough after 1900 and, even by 1911, were 11 per cent below
the level of the beginning of the century; meanwhile, prices had
reversed their previous direction, and had risen by at least 9 per
cent by the later date.[58] The abundance and cheapness of labour in
the mines was now beginning to act as a brake on technical developments, and although productivity was starting to fall seriously only
7 per cent of British coal in 1914 was cut by machine compared
with over 50 per cent in the United States. Strikes, labour unrest
and unemployment characterized the years immediately before 1914,
though the miners' interests were strongly represented by the
Miners' Federation and by the young Labour Party which, in 1912,
succeeded in passing what was referred to as a statutory minimum
wage but what was, in fact, an act to establish district conferences
to determine local minima by arbitration. In 1906 the average
yearly earnings of coal-face workers were £112; in 1924, after war-

time inflation, they were £180, but in 1935, in the depression, they had slumped to £149.[59]

Although coal-miners were never highly-paid, and never ranked among the aristocracy of labour élite, it seems clear that from the last quarter of the nineteenth century until the outbreak of the Second World War their economic position and their status were in decline compared with most other workers. Such an easy generalization requires immediate qualification, since mining was an industry which embraced many distinct occupations and gave, at least to the coal-hewer, some discretion to regulate his own earnings. A strong young miner like B. L. Coombes could sometimes earn up to £3 and £4 a week in 1913 when the minimum rate was 7s. 4d. a day;[60] on piece-rate earnings much depended on whether the coal was cutting easily, the generosity of the current price-list and – ultimately – the state of the trade. By this time much was changing in the formerly isolated mining communities of the mid-nineteenth century, whose remoteness from the town had carried advantages as well as disabilities. 'Free' (i.e. 'tied') cottages which had once been a necessary device for attracting labour were, by the end of the century, coming to be replaced by rented accommodation provided by the speculative builder; on the other hand, payment of wages in 'truck'; which had been rife in some of the coalfields, as it had in navvying, nailing and the iron industry, was almost extinct by 1872 except in South Wales and West Scotland,[61] and the miners' unions were fighting a series of successful battles against 'long pays', false weighing of the hewer's output, and other sharp practices of the employer.

The effect of such changes was to establish free labour in the coalfields by the closing years of the century, at least in a legal sense. But for social, economic and geographical reasons coal-mining remained a highly in-bred, hereditary occupation in which the normal expectation of a son was to follow his father down the mine as soon as he could escape from school. Very often there was no local alternative anyway, and the pressure to hold the family together as an insurance against the death or incapacity of the chief breadwinner was immensely powerful. Yet, despite its dirt and danger, its liability to unemployment and short time, mining had its positive attractions as a manly occupation which gave a good measure of independence at work and could yield good earnings; the risk and uncertainty may, indeed, have been part of the attraction for men to whom sport and gambling were important facets of life. In their autobiographies miners also write with feeling of the beauty of the countryside which could transcend the ugliness of pit-workings and slag-heaps,[62] and of the intimate life of the mining community where work and leisure, birth, marriage and death all occurred within a kind of extended family group with a network of relation-ships. To this extent the mining community re-created much of the social pattern of the pre-industrial village, and provided satisfactions which were often lacking in the anonymity of the industrial city.

Sweated Trades

There is a modern myth to the effect that until quite recent years the vast majority of women devoted themselves exclusively to home-making and the bearing and rearing of large families, and that only a few engaged in gainful employment. What has, in fact, changed is that more married women and more middle-class women now work than formerly. Given the huge size of the Victorian work-ing class (at least 80 per cent of the population if we take the 'manual' definition of class), the demographic consideration that because of the unequal sex ratio one in three women were 'doomed' to spinster-hood anyway, and the fact that the wages of many semi-skilled and unskilled male workers were so low or so uncertain that they would not support a family unless supplemented by the earnings of wives and children, it cannot be doubted that a high proportion of Victorian women, both single and married, regularly engaged in paid work.

Victorian women provided a vast reservoir of labour, necessary for an expanding though immature economy whose fluctuations demanded additional workers at one time, fewer at another. The precise size of the female working population is impossible to know since the Census returns almost certainly underestimated it; the numbers of women factory workers may well have been more or less accurate, domestic servants probably rather less so, but thousands of milliners and seamstresses, washerwomen, framework knitters, nailers, straw-plaiters and women workers in the score or more of 'sweated' trades where they worked in their own homes, sometimes whole-time, sometimes part-time, must have escaped the Census investigators, especially when it was feared that penalties might follow from a full declaration of income. The Census of 1851, the first to attempt to count occupations in any detail, gave a total of 2·8 million women and girls over the age of ten in employment out of a female population of 10·1 millions, forming a proportion of 30·2 per cent of the whole labour force. (In 1901 they composed 29·1 per cent and in 1931 29·8 per cent of the labour force, though compulsory schooling to fourteen by the latter year has to be taken into account.) Domestic service took by far the greatest number in 1851 – 905,000, not including 145,000 washerwomen and 55,000 charwomen: milliners, dress-makers and seamstresses were in second place, with the enormous number of 340,000; third, cotton-workers at 272,000, then women workers in agriculture 227,000, woollen-workers 113,000 and silk-workers 80,000; there were 56,000 women linen-workers, 54,000 in the lace industry, 31,000 women shoe-makers and 30,000 hosiery workers.[63] Outside these big occupations were the statistically much less reliable groups of domestic workers – 28,000 straw-plait workers, 25,000 glovers, 18,000 tailors and 10,000 nailers. The dependence of women workers at this period on domestic service and on the stitching and washing trades is out-standing; from this long list only the cotton and woollen industries as yet offered opportunities of factory work.

Similarly, we cannot be at all certain about the numbers of married women who worked for wages. The 1851 Census counted 3,462,000 wives in Great Britain, of whom 2,630,000 entered themselves as being of no specified occupation; of those stating an occupation the largest group were predictably wives of farmers, inn-keepers and shop-keepers and, less predictably, of shoe-makers. Of 795,000 widows, 605,000 specified an occupation. The diffi-culty with the wives' statistics is that in all probability they only returned themselves as employed if they engaged in whole-time work, while those who helped their husbands, took in some washing, worked at millinery or a sweated domestic trade when other duties allowed did not so describe – or regard – themselves. To guess that half a million wives came into this category would hardly be an exaggeration, and if we add them to the 800,000 who declared themselves as workers, we have 1·3 million wives who 'regularly' worked out of a total of 3·5 million – a fraction of about two-fifths. But the statistics also make it clear that, despite the myth to the contrary, it was unusual for a woman to continue to work in a cotton-mill after her marriage. Two-thirds of the women cotton-workers of 1851 were under twenty-five years of age, and a mere 19,000 were between the ages of thirty and thirty-five.

There is no precise definition of the 'sweating' trades. They were not, as might be supposed, jobs which demanded hard labour and great physical strength; on the contrary, most 'sweated' work was light in terms of muscular effort. The term was certainly in use by the 1830s to describe a system of sub-contracting in the tailoring trade, where journeymen who had failed to set up as master tailors acted as agents for their successful colleagues, supplying bespoke or ready-made clothes either by their own labour or by employing out-workers in their own homes.[64] Orders were obtained by offering the lowest possible prices and constantly under-cutting their rivals by reducing the wages paid to the out-workers to barest subsistence levels. Many of these were women and children, augmented by unemployed men and, in the later half of the century, by Jewish immigrants from Russia and Eastern Europe; the wages paid were almost invariably piece-rates for the garment, and the 'sweating' arose from the immensely long hours which had to be put in to achieve anything like a living wage, and the savage exploitation of workers, mainly female, who were too poor and too scattered to organize effective associations for their own protection.

Sweating was particularly associated with the stitching trades – tailoring, millinery, seamstressing, glove-stitching and boot- and shoe-making – though not restricted to them. Any work which could be done at home without elaborate equipment, which was repetitive and mechanical, and which needed only a fairly simple and easily-acquired skill was subject to sweating, and a long list of such trades would also include nail-making, straw-plaiting, box-making, match-making, brush-making and framework knitting, silk-weaving and ribbon-making in their periods of decline. By common usage the term was also extended to small workshops, or 'sweating-dens' where the employer had direct control over a group of workpeople who might range from two up to twenty or so: they were, again, especially common in dress-making and tailoring, and grew rapidly in London and other towns from the 1860s onwards when the use of the sewing-machine introduced more expensive equipment into the trade. Since they did not use steam-power, workshops were outside the purview of the factory acts until 1867 (and those employing fewer than five persons until later still), and the public concern that rightly resulted in the regulation of hours and conditions of work in textile mills could have been invoked even more appropriately on behalf of the wretched workers in sweat shops. The Committee on the Employment of Women and Children in 1843 reported that:

In some of what are considered the best-regulated establishments during the fashionable season, occupying about four months of the year, the regular hours of work are fifteen. In many establishments the hours of work during the season are unlimited . . . very frequently they work all night. These conditions are worse than in the worst-conducted factories . . . There is no ventilation by day or night, and the work-girls are crowded one upon another in dark rooms.[65]

Twenty years after this John Williams, the editor of a union journal which was struggling to bring association to the London tailors,

described a visit to out-workers in Petticoat Lane. He told of a journey to evil-smelling hovels where Jewish immigrants worked and
slept cheek-by-jowl, without sanitary arrangements, washing facilities, light or air; in these conditions of dirt and disease they were
making fashionable garments at a price which demanded that every
moment not actually spent in sleep was spent at work. One was
making a black Whitney Chesterfield coat, for which he would get
4s., less trimmings and thread; he worked eighteen hours a day.
Another was making a Highland cloak, double-stitched all round,
for 2s. 6d., and some women at sewing-machines were making a
heavy brown Melton overcoat, with lapped and double-sewn seams,
edges double-stitched, four outside pockets with flaps and a velvet
collar for 3s. 6d., less trimmings.[66]

By the 1880s more details of the earnings of sweated workers
became available. The statistician Leone Levi reported in 1885 that
in the domestic glove trade

Men can cut 14 to 25 dozen per week, and they may earn on an average
26s. The general average, however, is 16s. to 20s. A woman can make [i.e.
stitch] when she employs all her time on it 1½ dozen or 2 dozen per week;
but few persons work at it all day, having household duties to attend to.
The average wages are 5s. to 7s. per week, but a good hand will earn
double that of a common hand . . . A good sewer can make 30 or 36 pair
per week, and get 3s. 3d. per dozen pairs . . .[67]

It is clear from his account that dress-making and shirt-making were
now beginning to pass into the factory – or, at least, the workshop
stage, where powered sewing-machines were operated by women
machinists at 18 shillings a week. As elsewhere, the larger employers usually provided much better conditions of work and wages
than the smaller. One of the best dress houses paid its women
managers £150 per annum with board and lodging, each manager
having several 'first hands' under her at from £40 to £70 a year,
again with board and lodging; a 'first hand' had charge of a room
with about twenty seamstresses, the women earning 16s. to 18s. a
week and the girls 10s. to 12s. (living out in both cases). The hours
of labour were from 8.30 A.M. to 7.30 P.M., half an hour each being
allowed for dinner and tea.[68]

Levi's somewhat optimistic account was based largely on the new
dress-making factories rather than the still large out-work trade.
Charles Booth's great survey, *London Life and Labour*, begun in the
1880s, drew evidence also from the lower strata of partly employed
and casually employed women – the finisher of shirts who was
'generally elderly, infirm, penniless and a widow . . . she is nervous

and timid, and takes work at whatever price it may be offered to her' and the young wife of the clerk who 'takes sealskin capes home from the warehouse where she worked as a girl'.[69] Out-work wages for a full week ranged from about 8s. to 16s., with the wretched fur-workers lower still. In 'the season' (Easter to August) a first-class hand might earn 20s. a week by immensely long hours, but over the year her average was probably 12s. to 14s. The hopeful sign was that the number of out-workers was now beginning to contract as work passed into the better-paid factories, where 16s. to 18s. a week was typical – out-work was more and more the last refuge of the old, the halt, lame and widowed, for many of whom poor relief acted as a depressant on wages.

Autobiographies of the late nineteenth and early twentieth centuries can usefully illustrate the conditions of the millinery trade at this time at both its better and lower ends. Louise Jermy, born in 1877 the daughter of a foreman stonemason, was apprenticed at fourteen to a small dress-maker at Dalston for 3 guineas to serve for two years as an 'improver' at 3s. a week, and then, fully trained at seventeen, was taken on at 5s. a week, rising by increments of 1s. and 6d. as her experience grew.

Walking home one day with the head skirt-hand I began to talk to her about the wages and she said, 'Well, if your people wanted you to earn a good screw they should have put you into something very different, for you'll never get it at dressmaking. The head bodice-hand here gets 12s. 6d. weekly, and the others are paid less. I get 10s. 6d. as head skirt-hand. But you know, dearie, it is not how much you earn that matters, but what you do with it . . .

The most that Louise Jermy ever earned as a dress-maker was 10s. a week during 'the season'; she eventually left for domestic service, and had saved £100 by the time of her marriage in 1911 to a farm labourer.[70]

At what was probably one of the largest and most fashionable 'Court Dress-makers' and department stores outside London, Kendal, Milne and Company of Manchester, Margaret Penn had a far happier experience. After an abortive apprenticeship with the local village dress-maker, who required her to spend half the day in domestic chores, she managed to get a place in 1910 in the work-rooms of Kendal, Milne and Company. The normal apprentice-ship here was for three years without pay, but by special pleading she was taken on as an errand-girl at 5s. a week to do odd jobs for the head buyer, to go out 'matching' and be generally useful; she would receive some instruction, and if she showed aptitude would com-

plete an apprenticeship in four years. Hours of work were from
9 A.M. to 7 P.M. (2 P.M. on Saturdays), with three-quarters of an hour
for meals; there was a dining-room for the staff in the basement
where food could be heated up and cups of tea or cocoa bought for a
halfpenny. Coming from a small village fourteen miles from Manchester, she found the 'young ladies' of the workroom immensely
smart and sophisticated, reading the latest novels, visiting the
theatre and talking so quickly and animatedly that she could scarcely
understand them.[71]

In 1900 Olive Malvery, a middle-class Anglo-Indian who had
trained as a singer at the Royal College of Music and had become
disillusioned with 'musical society' in London, became deeply
interested and concerned with the state of the poor; for several
years she lived and worked with costermongers, street sellers and
buskers and worked in factories, shops and sweated trades in order
to gather first-hand evidence of conditions and attitudes. In a cardboard box-making factory employing eighty women and girls the
average piece-work wage after a year's experience was 6s. a week
and the most skilled hand, who worked with 'incredible speed',
earned 14s.; work began at 8.15 A.M., but the box-maker with whom
Miss Malvery lodged had to employ a 'knocker-up' at 4d. a week
to wake her at 6 A.M. for a long train-journey. In a jam factory,
where very rough casual workers were taken on in the season, 7s. a
week was the average wage, and 'Saint Monday' was still widely
observed. A home match-box-maker and her four children earned
up to 14s. a week, being paid at the rate of $2\frac{1}{4}$d. per gross, or 2d.
an hour: work began at 6.30 A.M., the children returning to it
at dinner-time and after school. The making of the boxes was
broken down in great detail so that even the smallest children
could help – one glued, one made the 'drawer', another pasted on
the sandpaper while the youngest fitted the 'drawer' into the
'cover'. In the out-work dress-making trade she found one woman
stitching petticoats for 4d. each. Each one required hundreds of
yards of stitching, three button-holes and two drawing-ribbons
which she provided; they were sold in West End shops at prices
from 15s. to 30s.[72]

By the beginning of the new century the problem of sweating had
been fully exposed and was exciting keen concern as a national evil.
After a *Daily News* exhibition of sweated goods in 1900 had been
visited by many politicians, titled ladies and the general public, a
National Anti-Sweating League was formed to campaign for a legal
minimum wage on the model of the Australian Wages Boards; the
Liberal government of 1906 appointed a Select Committee of

Inquiry into Home Work, and the Wages Board Act resulted in
1909.[73] The Act empowered the Board of Trade to establish boards
to regulate wages in any trade where they were exceptionally low,
each board to consist of employers' and workers' representatives
and independent members. They concentrated first on women
workers in nail- and chain-making, cardboard-box-making and
machined lace, turning later to the tailoring and dress-making
trades. The boards were, in effect, fulfilling the main function of a
trade union for workers who had been unable to form effective associations for themselves, and the very conception of such boards
represented a major change in philosophy from the time, still recent,
when trade unions themselves had borne the taint of illegality. The
early boards experienced great difficulties in negotiating fair rates
between the opposing parties, and even more, in enforcement of the
rates when agreed. It was easier to fix time-rates than piece-rates,
easier to inspect factories than out-workers. Yet by 1915 the wages of
half a million workers were regulated and, after the impetus of the
war, extensions of the Act in 1919–21 brought the total to sixty-
three boards covering nearly three million workers.[74] Sweating was
not dead in the 1920s, and in conditions of growing unemployment
it had some revival, but changes in women's fashions, the growth
of multiple tailoring firms based on factory-made clothes and the
vigilance of Board of Trade inspectors meant that it never again
approached the scale or the inhumanity of Victorian times.

Anonymous navvy*

The anonymous author was born about 1820. The editor states that 'this paper is exactly what it professes to be – the story of a navvy's life, taken down from his own narration, facts and sentiments together, just as they come'. Like many other agricultural labourers, this man left home in the 1840s to 'tramp', working on railway-construction and tunnelling when it was available, combined with harvesting and odd jobs; in the winter he was often out of work, or only casually employed. By middle age, and under the influence of a thrifty wife, he had adopted temperance and had become adjusted to settled life and work in London.

Struggles for a livelihood

I was born at Wimbush, near Saffron Walden, in Essex. My father was a labouring-man, earning nine shillings a week at the best of times; but often his wages were reduced to seven shillings.

There was a wonderful large family of us – eleven was born, but we died down to six. I remember, one winter, we was very bad off, for we boys could get no employment, and no one in the family was working but father. He only got fourteen pence a day to keep eight of us in firing and everything. It was a hard matter to get enough to eat.

One very cold day, that we had nothing at all in the house, my mother called me. 'Bill,' says she, 'you must go out and beg a few turnips for dinner today, for we have nothing to eat.'

I took a bag, and presently I lit on a farmer, and said to him, 'I've come out to ask for a few turnips, sir, if you'll please to give 'em me.'

'You can go down the field,' he says, 'and pull some, if you can get 'em up.'

I went; but the ground was so hard, I was forced to cut 'em out with a bill-hook. When I brought them home we had to thaw them before the fire before we could pare them for boiling.

At last, mother she went off to the church parson, and stated the case to him how she was situated. He put his hand in his pocket and pulled out a shilling, and ordered her to go to a woman as kep' a little shop, and get half a bushel of bread baked. She got besides a lap-ful of broken victuals, that the cook looked up for her; and, when she came home, she found us still cooking the frozen turnips, and little expecting such a dinner! Before we'd cleared the table father come in; and mother sat down

* 'Autobiography of a Navvy', *Macmillan's Magazine*, Vol. v, 1861-2.

as soon as we had all finished and read us a chapter in the Book – where it says the Lord will provide for us; and that is what made me remember about it.

Mother still goes on, to her old age, reading a chapter after she's had her food – let it be breakfast or dinner; and I don't suppose anybody ever sees her now, but what she's a-murmuring something over to herself as she goes along. She is a real good woman, and knows her Bible well. My younger brother, Benjamin, took after her; he was a very religious man, and my mother's favourite son. He lived foreman to a man in Kent for three years. He was just married then, and he had three births and three deaths in those three years. Then he buried his wife; and at the end of the three years he died himself. He now lies buried at Saffron Walden; and mother can see his grave out of her window. She will never leave the place as long as she is alive, and when she dies she must be buried there beside him, in a plot of ground she has bought on purpose; for she can't get over the loss of 'her Benjamin', as she used to call him. I don't think mother has ever forgotten that it was me as 'ticed Benjamin away from home, to go rambling about the country for work. She never can help bringing it up against me. Let me come home when I will, she always opens her Bible at the verse where Jacob says, 'If mischief befall him by the way, then shall ye bring down my grey hairs with sorrow to the grave.' She does not mean it unkindly, but somehow it always seems to come over her to read that whenever she sees me again.

The first work ever I did was to mind two little lads for a farmer. I drawed them about in a little cart, for which I got my breakfast and a penny a day.

When I got older I went to tending sheep. I was about seven year old then. My mistress was a very gay woman, fond of company and dress, and going about; and this often caused them to fall out . . .

I stopped in that place, at Farmer G—'s two years. Missis would still keep going on with her parties and company, o'rum o'minding her farm and her dairy; and this brought them at last to poverty. Last time I lit on 'em, he was a-mending a barrow in the streets of Lincoln. I took him into the 'Red Lion' and gived him two or three quarts of ale and the change out of half-a-crown.

'Mr G—,' I says to him, 'I should think some of them crusts you used to chuck away, and never give to a poor person, would come in rather handy now?'

'Yes, Bill,' he says, 'they would; but I little thought then I should ever have come to this.'

But it was all caused by his wife's idle extravagant ways.

Matrimonial speculations

My father used to work at times for Squire G—; and, when I was a little boy, they used to have me up to clean the knives and run of errands.

The Squire was a young man then, not of age yet. He used to have a friend from London to go out shooting with him. Let the young Squire go out a-shooting when he would, he'd always have me to go along with him. It used to be their fun to set me on a horse, and then fire the gun and start off the horse to run away. I used to cling on tight by the horse's mane, and that amused them.

When I was about twelve years old I went to live with Farmer S—. He was a very honest, respectable man. When he was young, he fell in love with one of his father's servant-maids, which made the family very angry. They would give him no money, nor nothing to settle upon; so he hired himself as a labourer on his father's farm, ploughing and doing his work just like a servant; and out of his own wages he sent the young woman to a boarding-school, and paid for her education for two or three years. When she returned from school he married her, and took a little one-horse farm; he used to get on by dealing in pigs and sheep. He never had but one price. What he'd say his pigs was worth, he'd have it. He'd never bate a halfpenny; but then he was always fair and honest. All the dealers could trust his word, and a poor man would go and buy a pig on him . . .

I often think of his words, and I did as he told me in one respect. 'William,' he'd say to me, 'if ever you choose a young woman, look out for one whose hair lies straight on her head, for she'll be sure to have a good temper.'

'Look at your missis,' he'd say, 'look at her hair, and be sure you try for a poor servant girl,' says he. 'I'm married to a servant, though my father turned me out of the house for it, and see how I am off now.'

When I got a little older, I used to keep looking out for all the young women with straight hair. I fixed upon one in my own village, but she was all on for us to get married, and I wanted to stop till we was older; so we fell out and she went to service. When her twelvemonth was up she married the cow-man. She sent me a letter to say she did not think no more about me, but had got married to someone else. 'Thank the Lord for it!' I sent her word back, 'I only hope you'll have a happy husband.'

I soon began to keep company with another young woman, whose name was T—. Her father had nineteen children; but he would not have any of them christened; he would call them anything that come up – sometimes Betsy, sometimes Sarah, just as it happened. I used to call this girl 'my little mouse', because she worked hard all the summer, and laid by a store for the winter. She used to work in her father's brickfield, for he was a brick-maker; but the end of it was, she killed herself with it.

She was the only woman ever I knew killed herself by hard work. She used to do just the same as a man, and she was nearly as strong.

She had a sister who was stronger than a man; she still travels the country as a show. Just before she was born, her father had some ferrets. He was nearly caught with them one day, and he ran home thinking he was followed, and threw the ferret into his wife's lap, telling her to hide it under her apron; but she was frightened, and fell right down on the floor, and the ferret ran away.

Soon after, she had this little girl born, with red eyes, as red as flames, and white hair, as white as snow.

She is married now, and gets a lot of money by going about to fairs. She is so strong, that she can lift a blacksmith's anvil up by her hair. She also lies down and has the anvil placed on her chest. Anybody may take up the anvil and satisfy themselves that there is no deception in it. She generally goes about the north parts of England, and I have met with many who have seen her scores of times.

After I lost my poor 'little mouse', I felt very uneasy in my mind, and I did not rightly get over it for about two years.

In the meantime I quarrelled with my master through going to the public house. I had often made up my mind to run away from home, and had even started a few miles on the road, but the thoughts of my mother always brought me back again. However, this time I really did go; and a brother of 'the mouse' came along with me for company.

On the tramp

After I left home, I started on the road 'tramping' about the country, looking for work. Sometimes I'd stop a few weeks with one master and then go on again, travelling about; never long at a time in the one place. I soon got into bad company and bad ways, and at times it would come over my mind that I thought more about the devil than I thought about my Saviour; but still I kept wandering on in that long lane and found no end to it.

This is the way we used to carry on. Perhaps I'd light of an old mate somewhere about the country, and we'd go rambling together from one place to another. If we earned any money, we'd go to a public house, and stop there two or three days, till we'd spent it all, or till the publican turned us out drunk and helpless to the world. Having no money to pay for a lodging, we had to lie under a hedge, and in the morning we'd get up thinking, 'What shall we do?' 'Where shall we go?' and perhaps it would come over us, 'Well, I'll never do the like again.'

We'd wander on till we could find a gang of men at work at some railroad or large building; sometimes they would help us and sometimes they would not. Once I travelled about for three days without having anything to eat. We'd always sooner take a thing than ask for it, and the devil kep' on tutoring me to steal, till at last, seeing some poor labouring man's victuals lying under a hedge, I jumped over and took them. I thought to myself at the time, 'I'll never get so low again, but always keep a shilling in my pocket, sooner than get to this pitch.'

I came away, till I got some work in Sussex, as a 'tipper'. I got four shillings a day, working Sundays and all. I bid there eleven weeks till I had saved nine pounds, and then I left to come to London by the train. There I got along with bad company, and spent three or four of my pounds, and then turned towards Derby, where I spent the rest of my money, and had to lie again in a stable. From there I walked into Yorkshire.

While I was in Yorkshire I met with a young gentleman who had a fine house of his own, but would spend all his time in the beer-shop. One day he saw me there and called out, 'Well, old navvy,' he says, 'can you drink a quart of ale?'

'Thank you, sir,' says I.

'I dare say now you could sing a good song about shooting, could not you? and hunting, and all?' he says. 'Can't you tell us a good tale?'

'Yes, sir. I don't sing much, but I can make a noise about anything you ask me.'

'Well, if you will stop along of me, I'll keep you in drink, as long as you like to sing me songs,' says he.

'Master,' says I, 'I'll have you! I do like my beer.'

I stopped at the public-house with the young gentleman, holloing and shouting and drinking, and up to all sorts of wild pranks. He could not abide to be left alone, because of the 'blue devils', as we call them. He had been drunk every day for three months; so he would do anything to get someone to keep him company.

I stopped with him a fortnight drinking Yorkshire ale at 6 pence a quart, while he drank rum and brandy, and soda water between whiles. But at the fortnight's end I had to run away. I could not stand it any longer. He'd have killed me with it if I'd gone on.

Then I went to work at Bradford, where I stayed about six or eight weeks. Here an engine was to start upon a new line; and the contractor gave us a load of beer (about four barrels) for the opening. I was not satisfied with the way the man drawed this beer; and so, as soon as his back was turned and the crowd all round us, so as he could not see, three of us got hold of a barrel and rolled it down the hill and over the hedge, knocked in the head of it, and drank out of our hats, which we dipped into the cask.

Not content with all this, we must still go to a public house and have some more; and there I bid, till the landlord throwed me out in the road, where I laid till morning, while the rain poured down, and the water ran off both sides of me . . .

It was not long after this that I got sent to prison. I was working at Hastings, when we struck there. The ganger he came up and reckoned three or four on us, and then he upped with his fist and knocked me down; and as fast as I got up he hit me down again. Says I, 'Well done, old chap! you're going it gradely; but you've got a rum 'un to deal with this time,' I says; 'you ain't a-going to serve me as you have some of the drivers – leathering on 'em just when you like.'

Another makes answer, and says, 'Go it, Black 'un,' he says (they used to call me 'Black 'un', when I was young), 'Go it, Black 'un, I'll come in and help you,' and he comed up and caught hold of the ganger while I horse-whipped him, for I was a driver then; and another of them joined us. They come and ta'en us the next day, and had us locked up in Lewes Gaol; two on us got two months, and the other one month. We was all very happy and comfortable there, though we were kept rather short of victuals. There they learnt me to spin mops, and it was there that I got hold of most of my scholarship. I learned to read from the turnkey – a very nice man. He come and stand by my cell door and help me to a word whenever I asked him, and a church parson used to preach to us every morning of the week – and very good it was! It did me a deal of good going to prison, that time – it learned me to be a scholar and a better man. Another of the three with me in prison got run over by a wagon soon after we came out; they took him to the hospital, but he only lived three weeks afterwards. He used to send for his mates to come and see him, and talk to us so that we could not bear to hear him.

'Look at me,' he'd say, 'what a fine young man I was, when I went out to work that morning, and now see how I am cut down, like the grass. Never be so wicked no more as you have been, but remember those sarmints what was preached to us in Lewes Gaol.' He'd send such beautiful letters to our hut before he died, that I could not stop to listen to them, they made me cry so. It was a blessing for him, poor chap, that he died when he did, for I believe he went the right way; but it was all owing to his being sent to Lewes Gaol, for before that, he was a wicked one as ever lived, and he came out from there an altered man, and kept so till the day he met with his accident.

These things kind of made an impression upon me, and kept me straight for some time; and then maybe they'd go out of my head again, when I got along with bad company. It made me feel very bad when my little favourite sister died, and wanted to see me, and mother did not know where I was. My brother Benjamin at last found me out, and brought me word; but then I could not go home, for I'd been drinking and pawning my clothes, and I was ashamed to go and see them all. But I took this very much to heart. I thought it was a judgement on me! She was so much younger than I was, and yet she was called off first.

And then my brother Benjamin was taken the next. I used often to walk seven miles to see him when he was ill; and he would talk to me, and tell me how to behave better. He was a real pious man. Then I got hold of a parson in Herefordshire. I broke my ankle, and he used to come and sit with me, and I could talk to him and ask him questions. I found out more from him than from any other since I came out of Lewes Gaol.

When a working man don't hear anything but swearing, and jeering, and laughing all the week round, for month after month, he can't hardly get it out of his head again rightly; but, if somebody will come on the works at dinner-time, and read, or talk to us, the men will mostly like it, and be glad to listen. It always does some good, if it is only the being spoken to, now and then, like as if we was the same flesh and blood with other people. We are wonderful tender-hearted, too. A 'navvy' will cry the easiest thing as is. If you'll only talk a little good to him, you can make a navvy burst out crying like a child in a few minutes, if you'll only take him the right way.

My wife

When I was at work at Baldock, in Hertfordshire, about ten years ago, I lodged at a public house. Just opposite, lived a young woman, a straw-plaiter, who I used to notice many a time, though she did not so much as know me by sight.

It was six years since Caroline had married, and I had never seen any one I cared about in all that time. Now I made up my mind to marry this girl.

I used to say to my young landlady, 'That's the girl I'll have for my wife, if I ever have a wife at all; her hair is so nice and straight.'

'Why, and so would my hair be nice and straight, Bill,' says my young landlady, 'if I like to put it so.'

'Ah, but you've got a bad temper,' says I; 'I won't have nothing to say to you.'

Well, I left Baldock after a bit, and had never spoken to Anne but once, and that was one evening when I chanced to meet her taking a walk. 'So you're out for a walk, young woman?' I says to her.

'Yes, I am,' says she, and that was all that passed between us; but I have watched her times after times a-sitting in her father's house, plaiting straw and singing the while. She was the cleanest-looking girl, as I thought, in all the town, and fresher-coloured than she is now. I then went to Barnet, where I bid three months. I lived as steady as possible all the whole time, and saved up £4 15s. on purpose to marry upon, though I'd never even asked her about it . . .

So then I took up to her and kept on walking with her for about five weeks, and we settled to be married the next fair-day – and so we were. It was a very quiet wedding; but they came with a drum and an old tin-kettle to give us the rough music. Some people tell you it's unlucky to marry; but all I can say is that it's the luckiest day's work that ever I done in my life.

And now, perhaps, you'd like to hear the way I was broke of drinking. When first I married I used to sit and look at my wife plaiting till the blood run out at the ends of her fingers; and, when she'd done a good bit I'd say, 'Now, old gal, go and sell that plait and get me a pint of beer.'

She'd say, 'Bill, you ought not to go on like this;' but still she'd sit and plait and give me the money. Sometimes I'd say – 'Well, I'll try and get better some day; but some money I want and some money I must have.'

'Now, Bill, it's of no use my trying to get on and you a-trying agen' me all the while; we shall always be bad off,' she'd say; 'we should both pull one way.'

'If we put the sheet over the beam, and both pull the same way, we shall soon pull it in two in the middle' – that was an old saying as I had heard. 'Never mind, old gal! I'll alter some day.'

'I don't know when, Bill; but I am afraid you won't alter till the Lord Almighty alters you.'

One day I went as usual to the public house, where I was in the habit of spending seven or eight shillings a week in drink.

'Good evening, Mrs W—.'

'Good evening, Bill.'

'What fine caps you always have on your head, Mrs W—. How do you get them?' says I.

'Why, take them out of fools like you, to be sure,' says she.

'Thank you, Mrs W—; I hope that's done me good,' I says; and I went straight home and off to bed without saying a word to anybody. Then I considered about what Mrs W— had called me. I says, 'It's done me good; she shall never call me fool again,' and from that I spent no more money at her beer-shop. . . .

Our last tramp

We went on to Oxford, where I started to work for about two months, and stopped all that winter at Moreton-in-the-Marsh. There was no work to be got; but we had made enough in the harvest to keep us through the winter. In the spring time, when our money was gone, we came on to Warwick, where we bid a few days, while our two or three shillings lasted us. On the Saturday morning we found we'd got nothing left, and no victuals for the next day.

Says I, 'Whatever shall us do, old gal?'

'I'm sure I don't know, Bill; I thought "Brommy" would have been to see us, or Abram Baxter,' she says. 'I made sure they'd have seed us and given us a shilling or two. I'll bet a guinea,' she says, 'if that "Brommy" don't come now, I'll never give him nothing no more."

We stopped at our lodge to see whether he'd come, but he never come nigh us. We set all day talking of it over, one to another. It is not our way, don't you see, to ask any one to help us, unless it's one of our own sort. We don't mind taking a few shillings from people like ourselves, so as we can do the same for them another time; but we never begs of anybody else. It's against our rules.

At last evening came. 'I'll tell you what, old gal, you'll have to go out and sing in the streets' (for my wife was a most beautiful singer, and knew a 'most every tune you can name, unless it is that one about 'Boney going over the Alps'; she never could rightly manage that one; but ask her for anything else and she'd sing it to you directly).

'Oh, Bill,' she says, 'I don't like; I'm 'shamed, Bill,' says she.

But by a deal of 'suading I got her to go along of me, and in about an hour she'd made four and ninepence. The ninepence she got all at once for one tune, that a man wanted very particular; and he was so pleased with the way she sung it, that he gave her the ninepence down.

'There! Let's leave off now, Bill,' she says, 'at the hour's end. 'Tain't worth while to keep on when we've got enough.'

'Well, we'll go home, then. We can do till Monday morning, anyhow';

and so we went home; and, thank God, we've never had to come back to her singing in the street again, and I hope we never shall.

When we left Warwick on the Tuesday morning, we went to Birmingham and stopped till harvest time came round again. We went to Coventry on purpose to show my missis 'Peeping Tom' (it is an old image stuck up in the corner of the street), and then we came back to Birmingham. From thence we travelled to Wolverhampton, Stourbridge, Worcester, and Malvern, walking from thirty to thirty-three miles a day. We have done thirty-six sometimes.

At Ross we bid a twelvemonth; and from there my wife and I set off on a tramp of more than four hundred miles, stopping every night, and walking all day. It took us a month and three days. We never did a bit of work all the time. It was a bad harvesting, and we had saved money enough to keep us till we came home to my mother's in Essex, where we stayed with the old lady three days. After that we went to Stratford for one twelvemonth, and saved money to carry us into Kent and keep us through a good bit of the harvest, by which we made ten pound, and came to Chatham. There my wife was taken ill with the fever, and I had to wait upon her day and night. She was ill very nigh a twelvemonth altogether; and I had to nurse her as best as I could, and clean the house, and cook, and make her gruel and everything, for we could not afford to pay a woman to help us. We did not get to work again till next harvest, when we had to sleep in a barn, and we both of us got the ague together; and I could not do much work then. When we got a little better, a man took pity upon me, and put me watchman over two houses. I was there about three weeks, and then he got me another little job, and we got a few shillings together and took our things out of pawn. From that I went to work up at Rochester Bridge; and, when winter came on, I got in a tunnel at Ford Ret, for about three months. It is rather chokey kind of work, all done by candle-light, and the smoke makes the air thick and misty. Once, when I was in Dorsetshire, I was in a tunnel that fell in at both ends. There was only one man and me and some horses buried in it, and he drove a hole through the ground (he was about eight hours doing it), and then he and me got out, and left the horses in for three days and nights. We had to lower corn and water to them through the hole, till we could dig them out again; but we were none of us hurt. When I went away I left my wife at Chatham, and used to send her five shillings a week; and she saved money out of that! I was away nine weeks, working at different places, and went down to see mother. From Essex I walked to see my sister, who was in service in London, forty miles in one day, and she paid my fare to return home to Chatham; and a man came after me to go to work in Chatham Dockyard, for Mr R—. I staid there two years and a half, and then Mr R— sent me up to London, where I have lived ever since, working at different places under different masters.

Ever since then things have seemed to go the right road with me.

Tom Mullins
*farm labourer**

These records of farm labouring in the 1870s were recorded by
J. H. Ingram when he worked on Tom Mullins's farm at Wincle,
Macclesfield, in 1941. 'It was while working together in the fields
and woods that he told me the details I have written down. He was
a fine story-teller, full of old tales and proverbs and country lore.'
Mullins was born about 1863, and the district he describes is known
as 'the Moorlands', a landscape of high hills and deep valleys
isolated from the nearest town of Macclesfield by a steep ridge
impassable in a snowy winter. Mullins died some time in the
1950s and is buried in the hamlet of Rushton Spencer.

His description of farming in Staffordshire in the 1870s indicates
that the 'agricultural revolution' had not progressed very far in this
part of the country; many of the practices described were still
almost medieval.

When I was seven I started as half-timer at a rope-works in Leek, and
earned 1s. 6d. a week by turning the handle of the rope-winding machine.
I liked the job and remained a twelvemonth. My stepfather was a hasty-
tempered man, and once when I showed him a half sovereign which I
had found, he declared it was one which he had lost and whipped me for
stealing. Afterwards he found his coin in the seam of his trousers, but he
did not give me my half sovereign back. I saved my pocket-money and
bought a bicycle for 2s. 6d. It had a wooden frame and handlebars, but
no chains or pedals, you simply pushed it along the ground with your feet.

I wanted to be a blacksmith and had just started learning the trade
when my parents moved to a village near Burton-on-Trent. When I was
ten I left school to work on a farm for £3 a year and my keep; later I got
£5. As a carter's lad I helped drive the horses, and when there were two
I had to walk between them while leading and often got trodden on.
Harvest was later in those years and when the snow came early in October
much of the corn was buried and was never got in. I was always hungry
at that place, but after a year I moved to a bigger farm where the living
was better.

Before bridges were built we often had difficulty in getting our horses
and wagons across flooded streams. Often my clothes were quite wet when
I took them off at night and still wet when I put them on again next
morning. On Sundays I walked ten miles home to have dinner with my

* From unpublished autobiography.

parents, and then walked ten miles back to start milking. One stormy night my Mother and I crossed a stream when it was breast-high, and I was nearly swept away. We still had five miles to walk through the dark. There were many toll-gates on the road and it cost a penny a mile for a wagon to pass them. When I was eleven the under-carter was taken ill, so I was given two horses, and after a little instruction, was told to start ploughing.

I then went to work on a farm belonging to Michael Bass. He was an easy man to talk to and you did not realize he was titled. I often went to his house for the hot soup, meat and dripping which were distributed free to the poor of the parish; at Christmas there was a bigger distribution of eatables. The Bass family was well thought of in the neighbourhood.

One of my jobs was to take the letters to the post-box, and this I did not like doing for the lane ran alongside a dark wood where rough men wandered about. When I was thirteen I milked and tended seven cows single-handed. I used to watch where the master got his best apples and then go and help myself. It puzzled him to discover how his apples kept disappearing, but I was never caught.

There was a public house attached to the farm and as I had a good singing voice I used to sing there at nights. I could have had a barrel of beer if I had wanted, but I was never that way inclined. About this time somebody discovered that feeding wet barley grains to cows made them give more milk, so one of my jobs was to take the horse and cart to Burton for a load of grains and maltcombs. Before that our beasts were fed on horse-beans ground into meal, and on roots, rye and crushed oats. There was no Indian meal in those days.

I worked on a milk-round in Leek for a year, and then went to work at a farm in Rusholme, Manchester, but the family lived like pigs and expected me to exist on bread and dripping, so at the end of the first week I left. About 1880 I started as a carter at a seventy-five-acres farm called Weathercock, near Leek, where I remained seven years. When not ploughing I carried coal from the pits. Coal was 3d a hundredweight at the pit-head, and they would throw in an extra hundredweight or so for good measure.

It took a team of three horses to carry a load of thirty hundredweight or two tons, and you'd be at it from six in the morning until nine at night. One winter's day my team fell down on the ice coming from Biddelph, and I had to remove their shoes and take them to a smith to be sharpened before I could get my load back to the farm.

There was little farm machinery used in those days. 'Hand work is best work,' my master used to say, and he did not like to have even a horse in the field. Corn was cut with a short 'badging' hook and hay was cut with the scythe. A man could cut half an acre of corn a day and bind it into sheaves, but usually the farmers banded themselves together and worked in groups of from twelve to twenty.

Each man had a distance of so many yards to cut, known as a 'natch'. He would take hold of the corn stalks and hold them with his left hand

and sever them near the base, holding them until he had collected enough to make half a sheaf, which would be laid at the end of the 'natch'; by the time he had worked his way back again he had cut enough to finish the sheaf, which was then tied with a straw 'bant'. Men would follow one behind the other, sometimes twenty in a line; they could soon clear a field. Gangs of 'paddies' contracted at so much a field. They used a sickle with a thin curved blade a yard long, having teeth like a bread knife, which would cut nearly half a sheaf at one stroke.

How country folk laughed when the first machines appeared. A few mowing-machines had already reached Staffordshire. Some had reaping-gear fixed to them and were used as reapers, with a dozen men following behind binding. There were a few threshing machines also, but corn was mostly threshed by flail. Men were paid sixpence a 'threap', or bundle of twenty-four sheaves, and had to make their own straw 'battens'. Tedding-machines came next, before swathe-turners. Beans were threshed (after being cut by machine) earlier by hand, by a threshing-machine driven by water. We tried ploughing using a long wire and two stationary steam engines; it made a rough job but was quicker.

Little artificial manure was used. Cows' water was collected in tanks and carted out into the fields in barrels, where it was spread with a long-handled ladle. Contractors used to collect night-soil from the towns and sell it to the farmers. Good money was made at this job, and at least one man I know saved enough money to buy his own farm. Women earned is. 6d. a day by following the horses grazing in the pastures and breaking up the dung with a long fork.

Little wheat bread was eaten. We lived mainly on oatmeal which was made into flat, sour cakes shaped like gramophone records. A cream-stean filled with oatmeal and water with a little sour dough to start it fermenting was left to stand for twenty-four hours. Every house had its 'bakston', a brick fireplace with a circular iron top, standing beside the kitchen range. When the iron top was hot it was greased with a little fat, and enough oatmeal mixture to make a thin cake was poured on it.

They cooked in about three minutes, and usually enough were made at one baking to last a week or ten days. By that time they would be covered with a green, furry mould, which would be scraped off so that they could be toasted before the fire and eaten with butter or cheese. There was nothing better you could wish for. Oatmeal was also made into porridge known as 'lumpty-tums', made by stirring the meal into boiling milk; this was eaten with salt.

Our cattle were fed on oatmeal, for there was little corn imported, and also on turnips and cabbage. Kale did not come into use until later and was thought little of. A great many beans were grown and ground into meal; they made strong food for cattle. Pigs were not killed until they reached fifteen or twenty score. We had little meat in those days, for fewer beef cattle were kept, but there was often pork and we were never without bacon. Hams were not smoked, but after being hung up to dry for two or three weeks they were put in the 'meal ark', a great oak chest nine feet long and a yard wide, in which the oatmeal was kept. The hams were buried out of sight in the meal, and were thus kept airtight until required.

When we needed extra meat we shot rabbits, and almost every farm had a fishpond where trout and pike could be caught. Rhubarb and gooseberries were the fruits most grown, and wines were made from damsons, cowslips, sloes and elderberries. There were few eggs, for few hens were kept. About 1890 wheat flour started to come into favour. Few houses had an oven, and the women used to make their own dough and take it to the bakehouse; baking cost a halfpenny per quartern loaf.

When I was seventeen I earned £16 a year and my keep, the highest wage a man could get. Though wages were low people managed on them and also saved a bit. Ten shillings went a lot further then than now. Bread was 3d. the quartern loaf, milk 3d. a quart, tobacco 3d. an ounce (what a cry went up when it was raised to 3½d.), while beer was 2d. a pint, the best was 3d.

The year's work ended at Michaelmas, when all farm workers took a week's holiday, and then went to the Hiring Fair, about October 10th. But I never needed to hire myself out, as I always had more jobs offered than I could undertake. Pity I couldn't have spread myself a bit! Farmers were always wanting lads, and some lads would take the shilling hire-fee, and then never turn up. Other holidays were May Day and Well-dressing.

When I was twenty-three I married and a year later I rented a small-holding of seven acres for £15; an extra five acres brought the rent to £20. I remained there fourteen years. My wife managed the holding and our three cows, while I worked as labourer for neighbouring farmers. When idle between hay-making and harvest I broke stone in the parish quarry with box and 'scrat'. Rates were 6d. a ton for large stone, 1s. 6d. to 2s. a ton for small. A man could break four tons a day if he worked hard.

Sometimes I cleaned 'dyches'. The pay was 8s. a week or 2d. the rood of eight yards; I preferred the latter rate. I also did carting and pig-killing. Once a week I walked six miles to Leek market with a basket containing two hundred eggs on one arm, and another basket with twelve pounds of butter in it on the other.

In 1902 I was able to move to my present farm, which I rented for twenty years and then bought.

Lucy Luck
*straw-plait worker**

Mrs Luck was born in 1848 and died in 1922 aged seventy-three;

* From 'A Little of my Life', *London Mercury*, edited by J. C. Squire, Vol. XIII, No. 76, November 1925–April 1926.

her husband died two years later, aged seventy-eight. Her memoirs were written towards the end of her life; her daughter says, 'Mother used to sit and write it at night when she couldn't sleep.' She had a particularly unfortunate childhood in the workhouse, was orphaned early in life and had a succession of wretched jobs until she became skilled at straw-plait work; her married life in London, where she had seven children, was a happy, though still busy one. The account is emotional, in the style of a Victorian novelette, though there is no reason to doubt its accuracy.

I, L.M., was born on May 25th, 1848, at Tring, Herts. I was one of a family of four, the eldest a girl, nine years old at the time I take you back to; she was a cripple with a diseased hip; the next, a boy between six and seven, and myself, a girl between three and four; the youngest, a baby in arms, a boy. My father I will sum up in a very few words. I had been given to understand he was an experienced brick-layer by trade, but was a drunkard and a brute. After bringing his wife and children to poverty and starvation he deserted them and left my mother to face the world alone as best she could with her family, and she never heard of him again.

What could my mother do but apply to the parish? – which she did, and the answer they gave her was, 'You must go to the workhouse, and the Guardians will find your husband.' (But they never did.) There was nothing else for my mother but to go there.

Now the workhouse belonging to Tring was five miles away, and some sort of conveyance was provided for my crippled sister, but my mother had to get there as best she could with us others. She started to walk there, but as I was very young (not four years of age), I don't remember much of that. I remember there was a man with a heavy cart going down the road, and he took us part of the way, until he turned up another road and then we walked on until we got to a school not far from the Union. There my mother sat down on the steps with one of us on each side of her, and one in her arms, crying bitterly over us before she took us into the Union.

I must tell you here, my mother had not been well since her youngest baby's birth, through neglect and trouble. Well, I don't remember much of what passed during my life in the Union. My sister was ill a long time, and was obliged to keep to her bed. Sometimes ladies would visit the Infirmary and give her dolls to dress as she sat in bed, but after a time (I don't know how long) she passed away. I was allowed to follow her to the grave. I seem to see her now, being carried on the shoulders of the Union men.

Well! Time passed on, and my brother might have been nine years old (not any more). I know he was sent back to Tring, with another lad, to work in the silk-mills. Both were put to lodgings with the man who used to ring the mill bell.

There were two of us left in the Union then with my mother. I was sent to school; the same school where we had sat upon the steps previous to going to the Union, and going there seemed to press that one thing on my memory.

I cannot tell much more of what passed while I was there, except just one or two childish things. As I said before, ladies would visit the place, and once or twice give a threepenny piece to the children. Oh! how pleased we were. And weeks before Christmas we would cut pieces of paper in fancy shapes to put our Christmas pudding on when we got it. Another time, which I think was Good Friday, I was going out of the gates of the school, when a girl stood in the pathway with a basket of buns on her arm. She said to me, 'Do you want any buns?' and I said, 'Yes, please.' She then asked me for the money. I said, 'I have not got any,' and she answered. 'Then you can't have any buns.'

How disappointed I was! I quite thought she was going to give me one, and I cannot tell how many times I have thought of that Good Friday. And again, we used to have tin mugs for our gruel or milk, whichever we had, and wooden spoons. One morning my mug was half full of dry crumbs and the half-cold gruel did not wet it. I leave you to guess what it was like when I stirred it up. I have thought of it a great many times, particularly when I see paperhangers' paste. You may think this a lot of foolish talk, but it is the truth . . .

. . . Well, I was not quite nine years old, when I was sent back to Tring with another girl to work in the silk-mills. Now I had got my mother and brothers to see sometimes, but this other poor girl had not got a living relation, so you see she was worse off than I. We were sent to live with a Mr and Mrs D—, who had a son about thirteen and a daughter about fifteen years of age.

The first day I went to work I was so frightened at the noise of the work and so many wheels flying round, that I dared not pass the rooms where men only were working, but stood still and cried. But, however, I had to go, and was passed on to what was called the fourth room.

I was too little to reach my work, and so had to have what was called a wooden horse to stand on. At that time children under eleven years of age were only supposed to work half-day, and go to school the other half. But I did not get many half-days at school, as Mr D— was a tailor by trade, so I had to stop at home in the afternoon to help him with the work. But I have never been sorry for that, for I learned a lot by it. Neither was I eleven when I had to work all day at the mill.

I can fancy children now at that age, having to work from six o'clock in the morning until six at night. Every morning at half-past five the bell would ring out, 'Come to the mill; come to the mill'. But still that would not have been so bad if we had a good home. But I was a drunkard's child, and the 'relieving officer' had found us a drunkard's home.

Mr and Mrs D— lived a most awful life, drinking, swearing and quarrelling. The son and daughter led us two girls a wretched life. We never had enough to eat, and I think everything that could be thought of by those two they did to worry and torment us. I don't think Mr D— ever struck us, but I cannot say that of his wife. She was a most horrible woman, both in ways and looks, for she had a broken nose which disfigured her very much . . .

[After being turned out of the house] So you see what sort of a home the Parish found us; two poor girls cast out of home at three o'clock in the morning. God only knew where we were to lay our heads that night, for we did not. We wandered about until the old bell rang out, 'Come to the mill'. Well, we went to the mill, and started work at six o'clock, and breakfast-time came; we had no home to go to now. There were a great many mill-hands who lived too far away to go home to breakfast, so boiling water was provided for each room. It soon got spread about how we two were placed, and one and another gave us to eat and drink, and we found we had more than enough. So you see there were kind hearts even there. Dinner-time came at two o'clock on the Saturday, the time we left off for the day, no home to go to.

We wandered on with the rest of the mill-hands, not knowing where we were going, but someone saw me, and told me I was to go and live with Mrs H—, a poor but respectable widow with three sons and a daughter. It was a far better home than I had been turned out of. Mrs H— was a good woman. Now my money at the mill was only 2s. 6d. a week up to the time I left, and the Parish made this money up to 3s. 6d., and that was all anyone had for keeping us parish children, as we were called. How could anyone properly feed hungry children upon that? So, to add to it a little more, I had to make five yards of straw plait every night after I had done work at the silk-mill. But I had a very good time there. I don't ever remember one of them raising a hand to strike me. The Parish supplied my clothes; fairly good of the sort. I never remember having anything but cotton dresses, the old-fashioned lilac print capes like our dresses in the summer; and shawls in the winter; good strong petticoats and thick nailed boots, both summer and winter; big coal-scuttle bonnets, with a piece of ribbon straight across them. I leave you to guess what we looked like. I only remember having one plaything and that was a big doll that my sister had left me when she died. Soon after I had gone with Mrs H— to live, I was taken so ill in church one Sunday, I did not know how to get home. I could not eat anything all day, and on Monday morning I could hear the bell, 'Come to the mill, come to the mill'. I did not know how to raise my head from the pillow to go to work that morning. I managed to get there somehow, and the master of my room was very good to me. He saw how ill I was, and knew how I was placed, and sent me to lie down at the top of the 'alley' as it was called. Now every day the overseer would go in each room, just before breakfast-time, dinner-time and evening. He would walk very slowly up the room, stop at every few steps, and then come back again, and then would be gone. The master would tell me to stand to my work until he had gone. This went on for a week, and I lost three quarters during that time, but that poor widow had to be the loser of that money. How I went to work that week God only knows . . .

Now, I had been with Mrs H— until I was thirteen years of age, and

'Black Garner', as he was called (the relieving officer), came to see her one day and said, 'Fanny, I am going to take your girl away.' She said, 'Be ye, Mr J—, and where be ye going to take her to?' He said, 'I am going to take her to St Albans, to service. It is about time she was off our hands. Get her ready by next week.' Yes! It was time I was off their hands, for I was costing then 9d. a week, besides clothing, and when I was obliged to go to him to ask for anything to wear, or to have my boots mended, he would treat me like a dog. A time or two, the boot-repairer could not mend them the same night, and he would lend me a pair. It did not matter about the fitting. Once he lent me a pair of button boots. I never had such a thing on my foot before . . .

The next week Mr J— came and said he would take me to St Albans himself. I had had a very good home with Mrs H— (and always visited them in after years). They bid me good-bye, and gave me a penny, then Mr J— and I started. When we got to Watford we had to change and wait some long time for the St Albans train; so he told me I could walk with him up the town a little way, and when we got to a restaurant he went in to lunch, but gave me a penny to wait about outside . . .

Well, we reached St Albans at last, and the place of service he had found for me was a public house. What did it matter? I was only a drunkard's child. But if they had found me a good place for a start, things might have been better for me. But there I was, cast upon the wide world when I was only thirteen years old, without a friend to say yea or nay to me. Whichever way I took, I had only God above to guide me. The parish people sent me a parcel of clothes; no box to put them in. They had quite done with me now. The place where Mr J— took me to was very near the old Abbey. It was a double-fronted house, a shop and beer-house combined. Mr and Mrs H—, who kept it, were elderly people and had only been there one month themselves. They kept something of a general shop on one side of the doorway and a taproom the other. I know they had a cow, and a donkey, and I used to make butter and sausages, and sometimes serve in the taproom, and sometimes go out with milk. I know I was not much of a servant, for I had never been taught to do it. Mrs H— always had a charwoman in once a week, and this woman often told me her 'wipes' were better than my 'scrubbing', and I don't doubt it. I always went to the Abbey on Sunday mornings.

My money was 1s. 6d. weekly, but my mistress spent it for me in getting me a few more clothes, and gave me a box to keep them in. She was very good to me, but after they had been there twelve months they were obliged to give the place up, and took a small cottage in a village between Watford and St Albans, and she could not afford to keep me; so I was obliged to make another shift . . .

[After two years in service in Kent and the death of her mother.] My mother died on Wednesday, August 5th 1863, and was buried on Saturday, August 8th, with only the three of us to follow her. I was now turned fifteen years of age, just the time when a girl needs a mother's care the most. Well, at my new place the mistress was very good to me, but the master was one of the worst who walked God's earth. Always fighting with his wife; the pots and glasses would go flying through the glass doors and windows, and he would beat that woman shamefully. On one Sunday night I had my new mourning dress torn from my back, through trying to part them when fighting. But that was not the worst of him. That man, who had a wife and was a father to three little children, did all he could, time after time, to try and ruin me, a poor orphan only fifteen years old. He would boast to me, and even tell me the names of other girls he had carried on with. God alone kept me from falling a victim to that wretched man, for I could not have been my own keeper. It was impossible for me to stop where he was, and whilst I am writing here, I will tell you of his end. Some time after I had left, his poor wife died, and I was told he had shot himself.

By now I had begun to bitterly hate service, and a fatherly old man who used the public house where I had been, told of a place in Luton where they wanted a girl to learn the straw-work and help in housework. Although this was another public house, I thought it was a chance to learn a trade, so I went there. By the way, I stayed with this man's wife until I was ready to go. He was what was called a packman in the country, one who travels to different parts of the country with a pack on his back; that was how he came to hear of the place at Luton. As I said before, I went there, and the place was very well and they were very good to me, but they did not keep to their promise. They would not pay me more than 2s. a week, but said they would teach me the straw-work. You may think it strange, straw business going on in a public house, but it was so, and I think the reason was, part of the business belonged to a sister and daughter. I sometimes did housework, sometimes served in the bar, and other times did the finishing of straw hats. They never attempted to teach me the making of them, but I was determined to learn, and would get a piece of straw and sit up half the night trying to do it. Now a girl with whom I had been out a few times told me of a woman who wanted two girl apprentices for six months, and would supply food, but no money. I went with her to see this woman, and it was agreed that we two girls should go there. I did not know if I was doing right or not, but as I had been some time at my place, and the money so little, and they had not shown me how to do the work, except the finishing-off (lining and wiring); I wanted to make the hats, so I made up my mind and left. I had a good lot of clothes, but not much money, and so I started right into the straw trade.

Hats were very different then to what they are now. I thought I was going to do wonders, but I think my real troubles had now begun. I liked the work very much, and was quick at it. I could do the two leading shapes of the season in a fortnight. but this woman set us a task every day which was impossible to do. I have sat up all night sometimes, in bitter cold weather, not daring to get right into bed for fear I should get warm and lay too long. I have even been obliged to do the work on Sunday, and then perhaps not finish the amount, and whatever quantity I was short she reckoned I was so much money in her debt. As I say, it was impossible to do in the time what she gave us, and so my little money went, and when that was gone she had my clothes just for my living. I don't wish to boast, but I had kept myself respectable so far, and now this woman took in two other girls who had a most filthy disease, to sleep in the same bed as myself. Time went on like this for five months; at the end of this, the work began to get very bad. Mrs P— came back one morning in a shocking temper, because she could not sell the work, and brought home a new-shaped bonnet which she gave me to do. The first time I did it, it was wrong. I did it again; it was wrong. I did it a third time; it was still wrong. The day was more than half gone, and I had not done half or a quarter of my day's work. I had only been taught just the two leading shapes, and it took much longer to do this new shape. But the season was over, and she had taken from me all I had got, and now she did not want me any longer. I threw the work down, and told her I would do no more, for I had got to that state of mind I did not care what became of me. That woman had taken all I possessed because I could not do the amount of work she set me, just for my food. I started out of that house that day, after having only been there for five months, with nothing but my mother's Bible and a few little things tied up in a handkerchief. The season was over, and I was homeless, penniless, and with only the clothes I walked in. She had turned the other girl away, who went there with me, some time before, because she was rather slow at the work. What to do or which way to turn I did not know. Some people would say it was my own fault; I should have kept to service. Well, perhaps it was, but remember I was never put to a decent place at the beginning.

I wandered about; I did not care what became of myself that day. I had had no dinner, and I had nowhere to go, but towards night I thought I would try to find the other girl who had been there with me. I found her at last, with an aunt and uncle, and I told them how I was placed, and they, although strangers to me, took me in. This man said he had an order for work that would last for two or three weeks, and I could stop there and help to do it, and he would pay me what I earned. So you see, a home was again provided for me before night. I stayed there and worked as long as they had any to give me, and even after that, when there was nothing to do, I was allowed to stay, although they had not much room.

The work was very bad everywhere at this time, and I wandered about, trying for work, sometimes getting just enough to get some food; but I could not get any more clothes, and my boots were almost worn from my feet, often causing me to get wet-footed. How often I was tempted to lead a bad life, but there always seemed to be a hand to hold me back. I don't want you to think I boast of myself, for I was not my own keeper, neither was I without faults; far from it. After a time, I got some work in a workroom, but I wanted a lot of improving before I could do it properly. So a woman in the same room undertook to see that I did my work correctly, and in time I was able to earn fairly good money now and then. I went to live with this woman, and on Saturday she would take my money and

3*

pay herself for looking to my work, and on the way home would meet two or three others, visiting different public houses. Often when I got home quite half of my money was gone . . .

Well, it happened again that there was not enough work at the room where I was, so I started out again to find more. I wandered about for some time, and at last I saw in the window of a very respectable house, 'Good sewers wanted'. I went there, and the woman looked at me rather straight, and asked me several questions; where I lived, and where I had worked. I told her the truth, and she said she would give me work if I left that house at once, and would give me a home until I could find respectable lodgings. I went back to my place, and told them I did not owe them anything, for I had been earning very good money, but had not been able to do any good with it. They swore at me awfully, but the storm did not last long, as I had not many things to get together, and so I left bad company.

The first week I was at my new place, Mrs L— got me some new boots, and had one of her own dresses altered for me, got me other things, and I paid her something each week. I had plenty of work and a good home, but of course I was given to understand she could not keep me there, as there was not room. That woman was a true friend to me. I believe it was her who saved me from going quite to the wrong. When I had been there some two or three weeks (there was still plenty of work, and the card still in the window), a young woman called in answer to the card. She had come from a small farm just outside Luton, and Mrs L— gave her work. I asked this young woman if she knew where I could get lodgings, and she said, 'I wish my mother would let you come to our house, for it would be company night and morning. I will ask her.'

Next morning she came with the answer that I could go there to live. I did so, and we went together to this same place to work as long as they could give it to us. I was now pretty comfortable, and began to get some good clothes; but after about three months, Mr and Mrs H— (the young woman's parents) left the small farm they were managing, and went to live in a village about three miles out of Luton. They wished me to go with them, so I did. We could not go into the workroom now to work, as it was too far away from Luton, but we had our work out to do, and used to take it in two or three times a week to Luton. Mrs H— as well as her daughter Sarah used to do the hat-work in the season, they were also both good straw-plaiters and would do that work in the dull season; but I was not much of a plaiter, and so would get what hat-work I could, or make children's clothes for the village people . . .

While I was living with Mrs H— a young man who lived very near often came in to see Mr H—. He had driven a plough for him when a lad, but at this time he worked at a farm called Eaton Green, a farm between Luton and the village in which we lived. I leave you to guess whether this young man called mostly to see Mr H— or myself, but I had to put up with a lot of sneers from Sarah and her mother. It set me bitterly against him, and I told him I would not have anything to do with him; but one day when

I was alone with Mr H— in the house, he put his hand on my shoulder and said to me, 'My girl, you have poor Will; he will make you a good husband, and he will never hit you. Never you mind what Sarah or her mother says, you have Will.' . . .

After this, I began to think a little more kindly of W— L—. Soon after there was some unpleasantness between me and Mrs H— about my work, and she said some bitter things to me. I had sat night after night at work until eleven or twelve o'clock, using a rushlight candle, and my eyes had begun to get so bad that I could hardly see. It was about harvest-time and Will came as usual, and asked me plainly about getting married. Then I consented. He had been a steady, saving chap; if he had not got a few things together I could not have done so; so we settled it to be married about Christmas time. His master had a cottage to let at 2s. a week, so he took it a few weeks before Christmas and got as much furniture as he could afford. I could not realize having a home of my own; I could not have thought more of it if it had been a palace.

I had been with Mrs H— now for nearly three years, and I left there on the Friday night as we were to be married next day. W— and myself went to Luton that night to do some shopping. It was a lovely night, although the snow laid thickly on the ground; the moon was shining beautifully. I went to my home (that was to be) for that night, as I had odd jobs enough to last me nearly all the night. My future husband and his brother, who was going to church with us, went off to bed, and a young woman, his cousin, sat with me until two o'clock, then went to her home and I sat in a chair and slept for a little while. That was how I spent my last night before marriage.

At five o'clock on the Saturday morning the weather changed; it began to rain fast and never ceased all day, and we had to start from home by eight o'clock to walk all the way to Luton. No carriage for us, as everyone looks for at the present time. I have often heard it said, 'Happy is the bride that the sun shines on.' Well, it did not shine on me that day, for the rain poured down, and the snow was sloshing under our feet; it was an awful day. To add to this misfortune, when we arrived at the church, we found all the doors closed. There had been some mistake, so we had to stand by while my brother-in-law-to-be went for the clerk. So don't you think I had reasons to remember my wedding-day, which was on Saturday, December 21st, 1867?

After we were married, we went to a certain hotel where my brother-in-law was ostler, and went to his harness-room, where there was a good fire and something to eat and drink. After we had dried our clothes a little we started for home, a place I could now really call my own home. God alone knows how proud I was of it. My husband's money was only 12s. a week, and at that time bread was 8d. a quartern-loaf; also meat, tea and sugar, and other things, were very dear. He had to be up every morning soon after three o'clock, as he had to walk two miles to work. I worked on as hard myself as ever I had done, so we got along very well, adding a little more to our home whenever we could.

My first baby, a girl, was born on January 7th, 1869. Things went on in a general way, living happily together but working very hard, and we found it difficult to keep things straight, and as time went on I had three little girls; the third one died at eight months and a fortnight old. That was a great blow to us. She was buried in the chapel grounds at a village called Brache Wood Green. It would be strange to see a burial like that now, for we had six little girls to carry her to the grave. Soon after that we left that part of the country, and my husband went as ploughman to a farmer in the Dunstable road, near Luton. We had to live in a cottage belonging to the farm; there were four ivy-covered cottages standing by the side of the road for the workmen. It was there where my first boy was born; but he was very delicate, and when he was eleven months of age, there was an agitation among the farm-labourers for miles around, about the wages. Most of the farmers had agreed to give their men a little more; but not so with the farmer where we were. My husband's money was only 13 shillings a week, and out of that 2 shillings went for rent, leaving 11 shillings, with three little children to keep. So he asked for a rise, as other farmers were giving, but the master soon told him if he were not satisfied, he had better take a month's notice and go. He did so, which meant getting out of the cottage as well. There was the worry then as to where we should go, or what we should do, but he had thoroughly made up his mind to go to London, and try to get work there . . .

Well, when our month's notice was up, we could not get a house anywhere that we could afford, so we parted with a few things and packed the others up. I went to my brother-in-law's with the three children till we could see what we were going to do, and Will, my husband, went to London to find work. He made his way for the Edgware Road, to a young man who had been groom at the same farm that we had left. He was at an hotel at work, and told Will of different places to go to for work. The first night he spent in London, he slept in a manger, and the rats ate part of his food which he had in his pocket while he slept. The next day he got lodgings near Paddington Green. It was on November 2nd when he went to London and on the 5th he got work as horse-keeper for a railway company, and I came to London a fortnight later, so that we were settled down in our home before Christmas, and so had our first Christmas dinner in London.

I have reason to remember that dinner, for we had to have it by lamplight. It was a shocking day. I shall never forget my first two or three months in London. I think I cried most of the time, for my husband was on night work, and I amongst strangers and thinking of my poor child I had so recently buried. I would have given anything to have gone back to the country. I still kept on with my straw-work, as the person I worked for sent it up from Luton once a week, and I would send it back to the warehouse. Some months after, they forgot to send thread with my work on one occasion, which threw me in a great fix, as I could only obtain it in the City, and I did not even know for certain what shops or what part of the City. I was told by someone that they were sure I could get it at

Whiteley's, but I tried and could not, and went to Owen's but could not get it there, although I was told by them I could get it at the shop opposite, as they did the work for Owen's. I went there, and saw the lady herself. She obliged me with the thread, and wanted to know a lot about Luton work, and told me if I would work for her she would pay me far better than I was being paid. So I finished up with Luton and worked at the shops in Westbourne Grove for thirteen years. I was in the workroom part of the time, and had my work at home the other part. My eldest daughter also worked for them for ten years. I should have stopped with them longer but the lease was up, and the shops passed into other hands that did not do that kind of work.

After that I went to another place in the West End, where I worked for one gentleman for twenty years. I always liked my work very much and although I had trouble with it when I first learnt, it has been a little fortune to me. I have been at the work for forty-seven years, and have never missed one season, although I have a large family. I have had seven together not earning a penny-piece. In my busy seasons I have worked almost night and day. I don't like to talk of what I have done, but I generally bought up what I could at sales, and made up my children's clothes in my dull season, and I don't think I have paid away 30s. for any kind of needlework.

The straw-work is very bad, as a rule, from July up to about Christmas. During that time I have been out charring or washing, and I have looked after a gentleman's house a few times, and I have taken in needlework. This was before any of my children were old enough to work. I have done my best to bring them up respectable.

I met a woman quite lately, whom I got to know soon after I first came to London. I had not seen her for many years, and of course she wanted to know how we were getting on. I told her, and she said, 'I suppose you have got a black sheep amongst them?' 'I am pleased to say I have not,' I said to her, and the woman seemed surprised. I have had my troubles with them, as any mother would have with a large family, but not one of them have brought us any sorrow or disgrace.

John Ward (O'Neil)

*weaver**

In 1947 this diary was picked off a heap of rubbish by a labourer who was feeding the furnace at the Clitheroe destructor. It was

* From *The diary of John Ward of Clitheroe, weaver, 1860–64. Transactions of the Historic Society of Lancashire and Cheshire for the year 1953.* Vol. 105, 1954, pp. 161 et seq.

written in a cash-book containing 142 pages, and covers the years 1860–64, including those of the cotton famine caused by the American Civil War.

The author has subsequently been identified (*Transactions of the Historic Society of Lancashire and Cheshire for the year 1968*, Vol. 120, p. 89) as John O'Neil, born in Carlisle in 1810, who married Margaret Ward some time in the mid-1830s. He left Carlisle in 1854 through unemployment, and eventually found work as a power-loom weaver at Garnett and Horsfall's factory, Low Moor, Clitheroe. He died there in 1876.

O'Neil was clearly an intelligent man, well-informed of public events and with wide interests. He was a lifelong liberal, an ardent supporter of Reading-rooms, Mechanics' Institutes and trade unions, of which he was frequently a delegate or committee member. The extracts describe the ending of a lockout at Low Moor Mill in 1861, and the effects of the cotton famine from 1862 to 1864. The original spelling has been retained.

April 1861

1st All the mills in Clitheroe commenced work this morning. At Low Moor there is a great many off. There is above a hundred looms standing. It has been a fine day and I feel very tired after being out so long.

2nd Another very fine day. Some odd weavers got to their work today.

3rd Another fine day. The weavers' committee have chosen their arbitrators and sent them in to the solicitor.

4th Another fine day. The arbitrators met at the Swan Hotel and elected the Rev. Mr Fielding umpire. They had some discussion and adjourned to this day week, when they hope to settle it.

6th Another fine day. I went up to Clitheroe to a committee meeting, when it was decided to have a public meeting after the decisions of the arbitrators was known.

7th This has been a very fine day. I cleaned myself and had a walk up to Clitheroe and saw the newspapers. There is a very good article in the Preston paper upon the arbitration case.

11th Another fine day. The arbitrators met today and after a long dis‾cussion they came to no decision, because the Masters' arbitrators would have 5 per cent for local disadvantages. They made their statement and would have nothing else, nor would they listen to anything else, although the weavers' arbitrators could prove to them that their statements were false and that there was no disadvantages whatever; but they would listen to nothing but what they stated themselves. But as the other side would not agree the umpire had to be called in, but he said before he gave his decision he would like a number of the operatives and Masters to be present so that they could all hear his decision. After some little delay a number of operatives and Masters was got together, when he delivered judgement. He said that he had been inquiring into the question, and from the best of his information there was a difference of $2\frac{1}{2}$ per cent between Clitheroe and Blackburn, but he did not think the weavers should pay it all, therefore he decided that the Masters should pay 1 per cent and the operatives $1\frac{1}{2}$. The Masters was greatly enraged at this decision because they were bent upon having 5 per cent. At night we had a public meeting. John Wood was in the chair, when Mr Banks and Mr Heaton, two of the arbitrators, gave an account of the whole proceedings, when a motion was made and carried that we accept the decision until we can mend ourselves. A vote of thanks to the arbitrators and to the umpire and the chairman was passed and the meeting broke up.

12th This has been another fine day. We got the list of prices this fore-noon what we have to be paid for the future. There was a deal of grumbling among the narrow weavers because they have taken a farthing a cut too much off them. There was a turn-out among them at noon, and one of the committee men, John Wood, was discharged of the ground as being a ringleader, although he was innocent of the crime, but they seem determined to get rid of every committee man, both at Low Moor and Clitheroe, as all the blame is attached to them for resisting the reduction of 10 per cent; so we all look for nothing else when they can find an opportunity.

13th Another fine day. We had a committee meeting tonight to consider how those men should be dealt with that was made victims to the tyranny of the Masters. It was agreed that they should have 15s. per week until they get work again, and that each member be called upon to pay a penny per week towards a fund to be called the victim fund.

14th This was a fine day. I sat in the house all day reading the newspaper. I have not had much time since the lockout to see any papers, but the news is not of much interest, except that there is a probability of a civil war in the United States.

17th Another fine day. This was our quarterly meeting tonight and my term of office as President expired. It was strongly [pressed] upon me to take it again for another year but I would not, but they were determined not to do without me so they elected me a committee man for six months, and Robert Garner our secretary told the meeting that he had lost his work that afternoon for being a committee man, as he knew of nothing else. It was then put to the meeting that they should be supported, and all that might be made victims, and was carried unanimously.

19th Another fine day. They came round tonight collecting for the victim fund. They got 5d. in our house.

20th Another fine day. I went up to the committee room, and the collectors got more money than they expected for the victim fund, so it was agreed they should only go once a fortnight . . .

27th It has been cold and stormy all day and a great deal of snow has fallen. I went up to Clitheroe and saw the newspaper. Civil war has broke out in the United States and Fort Sumter has been captured by the secessionists . . .

November

16th Cold and frosty all day and a great deal of snow has fallen. I went up to Clitheroe. It was snowing very fast and there was very little to be seen. I read the newspaper but there is nothing fresh from America nor any word from the naval expedition that has gone to the south. There is great distress all through the manufacturing districts; they are all running short time through the scarcity of cotton.

21st It has rained all this day. Ribble is so high that we had to stop half an hour sooner for backwater.

22nd Another very wet day. We commenced working at half past eight this morning and stopped at four o'clock – an hour a day less time.

23rd This has been a fine clear frosty day. All the hills are again covered with snow. I went up to Clitheroe and read the newspaper. Things are much about the same, but a rebel privateer captured and burned a steamship belonging to the Federals in the English Channel yesterday . . .

26th It was very wet and stormy all night, and Ribble was so high with the flood that we could not start to work until the afternoon.

30th Cold and wet again. I went up to Clitheroe and saw the newspaper. There is a great deal of excitement owing to a Federal warship boarding a British steamer and forcibly taking the two rebel commissioners and their secretaries. England has sent a Queen's messenger to Washington to demand restitution and reparation.

December

2nd A clear frosty day but now tonight is raining. I have joined the Low Moor Mechanics' Institute and Reading-room. It is a penny per week, so I will see a daily paper regular. They have put me on the Committee.

3rd This has been a very wet dark day. We commenced to light gas tonight and have gone on full time, but there is nothing but weavers to work full time . . .

7th Ribble was so high this morning that we had to give over for three hours before we could make a start. The latest news from America this day says that the people in the Northern states are filled with joy at the capture of the rebel commissioners, but still there seems to be a doubt about the legality of the proceeding . . .

10th It has been a little better today, but cold. The news from America is all about the taking of the rebel commissioners out of the British steamer *Trent*. There seems to be great rejoicing through the States.

12th A cold dark day. The newspapers is filled with accounts of great preparations making for war. Very large reinforcements are to be sent out to Canada and a great number of ships of war to be sent to the American coast . . .

14th A clear cold day. The papers is all taken up with the preparations for war with America unless the rebels' commissioners are not given up and every reparation made. The Guards should have gone this week, but the Prince Consort, who is their Colonel, could not review them as he is confined to his chamber with a severe cold.

15th A dark misty day. There is a rumour tonight that the Prince Consort is dead.

16th It is true that Prince Albert is dead. The newspapers are all in mourning. There was no one expected such a sad calamity, he being a young man and had only a slight cold. Every one has got a shock by it being so sudden . . .

21st Another clear frosty day. There is nothing fresh in the newspapers. I went up to Clitheroe to get some things for Christmas day, but it was very cold and I did not stop long.

23rd As this is the day that the Prince Consort is buried the mill was stopped all day, so I took the opportunity and whitewashed the house.

25th Christmas day, and the finest I ever seen. It was as warm as some summer days. I spent the day very pleasant. I had plenty of currant cake and whiskey but I kept myself sober and did not go to any public house.

26th Another very fine day, but now tonight is very frosty. The news from America is very scanty. The papers are all taken up discussing the *Trent* affair . . .

31st The last day of the year and a cold damp day it is, and no news from America. Now as the year is finished I must say that I am not so well off as I have been for several years, owing to so much short time and a prospect of war with the United States.

January 1862

1st We are beginning the New Year under very poor prospects. Bad trade, short time, and a prospect of a war with America, which, if it should take place, will be worse than ever, as we will get no cotton from it. Every one is anxious for the arrival of the next mail, which is expected every day. We have been working all day – it has been cold and damp.

2nd Another dark soft day, and the news from America is better than we expected as it is of a peaceable kind; but we must wait for the answer to the despatches sent by our Government before we can rely upon anything.

4th A fine clear frosty day, and later news from America is of the same peaceful tone. My daughter was married today* at the old church in Clitheroe. It passed off very quietly and nobody got drunk . . .

8th Another wet cold day, and owing to the scarcity of cotton we are working such rubbish as I never saw in my life. We cannot do the half work that we used to do.

10th A dark wet day, and the latest news from America states that the rebel agents are to be released . . .

17th Dark weather, bad yarn and short time answers very badly. A great number of weavers have given up their odd looms [i.e., third loom] as they cannot keep it on, the yarn is so bad.

20th We started full time this morning. It has been snowing all forenoon, but now tonight it is raining . . .

22nd A clear day but cold. The newspaper is filled with an account of a coal-pit that has closed and buried 220 human beings near Newcastle.

23rd A dark dull day, and very bad for us poor weavers with rotton cotton.

24th There is no later news from America, and we stopped at half past four this afternoon again.

25th They have got the debris cleared away from the shaft of the Hartley coal-pit near Newcastle upon Tyne, but every one was dead, having been suffocated with gas . . .

30th Wet again today. The Confederate commissioners, Slidell and Mason, who were taken out of a British ship by a Federal warship, has arrived in England.

February

2nd It has been very mild and calm all day, just like a spring day. I had a walk after dinner and home again . . .

9th Another hard frosty day. I cleaned myself up and had a walk round by Clitheroe to look at the Co-operative mill which is getting on very fast. They are now at the cock loft . . .

21st A fine day. I had a very narrow escape with my life this morning. The shaft above my head broke and fell just as I was coming from under it. As it is it broke a deal of yarn . . .

March

1st A very fine day. The news from America confirms the taking of Ronoake Island, but the loss of the Federals was not more than 350 men.

2nd This has been a very fine day. I had a walk round by Clitheroe to look at the Co-operative mill which has just got the timber on . . .

18th Another fine day. We had a break down this morning which is likely to last all week.

---

* His daughter Jane, aged twenty-five, married Bernard Knowles, of Low Moor, widower, aged thirty-four, spinner.

19th Another fine day. We have stopped tonight for all week.

21st Another very bitter cold day. I had thought to have a walk out in the country but 'twas so cold. The news from America contains a message from President Lincoln recommending the emancipation of the slaves.

22nd There was a hard frost last night and it has been very fine all day. I had a walk in the country round by Waddington and Clitheroe and saw the newspapers, but there is nothing of importance in them.

26th Another very cold day and we have stopped today for all week.

27th It has not been so cold today. My daughter was confined this afternoon with a very fine son.

28th This has been a very fine day and I went and gathered some sticks for kindling fires. There is great news from America. The rebel army has retreated from the Potomac and the Federals have got possession of all their strongholds and another battle was fought in Missouri, when the rebels was routed with the loss of 1500 men, and there has been a great naval battle fought in James's River, when the rebel steamer *Merrimac* attacked the Federal fleet and destroyed two frigates and blew up three gun-boats. She is mail-clad, so that none of them could hurt, but next morning a Federal iron steamer *Monitor*, not half its size and only two guns, attacked the *Merrimac*, and after five hours fighting the rebel was glad to run back disabled, while the *Monitor* was not in the least injured.

30th This has been a fine day. I had a walk in the evening round by Waddington and Bashall Eaves [eight or nine miles].

31st We started at half past eight this morning and stopped at half past four, and things are likely to get worse if cotton gets no cheaper . . .

April

8th Another cold day and it seems our Government is taking alarm since the American fight with iron steamers, and have given orders that no more wooden ships of war are to be built, but that a fleet of iron ships be built as soon as possible.

13th Another hard frost last night and the hills all round Clitheroe are covered with snow. I went to Church this morning, it being Palm Sunday, and after dinner I had a walk with my son-in-law round by Hodder bridge and Hodder House and home by Mitton [about eight miles]. It was a fine day but cold . . .

20th Easter Sunday. This has been a very fine day. I had a good deal of walking this afternoon . . .

May

2nd A cold windy day. We stopped at noon and won't start until Monday morning. The news from America is much about the same as last mail . . .

10th A fine day but rather cold. I feel very poorly myself. It is a bad cold I have got.

11th I have been very poorly all day and never been out of the house.

13th Another very fine day. The news from America tells of the capture of New Orleans by the Federals without a blow.

14th Another fine day. It seems that the siege of Yorktown is going on favourably.

15th Another mail from America confirms the capture of New Orleans and of Baton Rouge, the capital of Louisiana.

16th This was a fine day, and as I had nothing to do I went a gathering sticks and heard the Cuckoo several times . . .

22nd Another fine day, and we stopped this forenoon for all week.

23rd Another fine day. I have been playing cards nearly all day.

24th Another fine day. I have been reading nearly all day. I went up to Clitheroe in the evening and saw new potatoes for the first time. They were 4d a pound . . .

June

4th Another wet day and the news from America says that the Federal army was within seven miles of Richmond, but that the rebels would make a stand there and fight to the last, and also that the blockade was raised in New Orleans, Port Royal and Beaufort.

7th This has been a very cold day. I went up to Clitheroe and stood awhile in the street and my feet and hands got as cold as if it had been midwinter.

8th This has been a very wet day and I have never been out of the house all day.

[The Diary breaks off here in the middle of a page, and resumes on the next page with:]

April 1864

10th It is nearly two years since I wrote anything in the way of a diary. I now take up my pen to resume the task. It has been a very poor time for me all the time owing to the American war, which seems as far off being settled as ever. The mill I work in was stopped all last winter, during which time I had 3s. per week allowed by the relief committee, which barely kept me alive. When we started work again it was with Surat cotton, and a great number of weavers can only mind two looms. We can earn very little. I have not earned a shilling a day this last month, and there are many like me. My clothes and bedding is wearing out very fast and I have no means of getting any more, as what wages I get does hardly keep me, my daughter and son-in-law having gone to a house of their own during the time I was out of work. I went twice to Preston to see my brother Daniel, but him and his family were no better off than myself, having nothing better than Surat to work at, and it is the same all through Lancashire. There has been some terrible and bloody battles fought in America these last two years . . . The principal reason why I did not take any notes these last two years is because I was sad and weary. One half of the time I was out of work and the other I had to work as hard as ever I wrought in my life, and can hardly keep myself living. If things do not mend this summer I will try somewhere else or something else, for I can't go much further with what I am at.

17th I have had another weary week of bad work. I have just earned 7s. 3½d. off three looms and there are plenty as bad off as me, and if any one complains to the Master of bad work he says, if you don't like [it] you can leave. He wants no one to stop that does not like it, and that is all the satisfaction we can get . . .

May

1st There has been some little rain today, the first we have had for three weeks. It is much wanted . . . I have given up my odd loom as I cannot keep two looms going, and last week I had only 5s. 1½d. after a very hard week's work, but they have promised us better work as soon as the cotton is done that they have on hand. They have promised so often that we can hardly believe them.

8th We have had a very fine week of sunshine and showers, and everything is growing very fast in fields and gardens, and markets are coming down very fast . . . The work at our place is beginning to mend. I have got two beams in, the best I have had for twelve months, but they are for shifting the looms out of our shop into a new shed that is ready for starting, so I hope to get better on than I have done this last winter. In Denmark the Danes are retreating and the Austrians and Prussians are advancing. There is a conference sitting in London on the war, but how it will end there is no one knows.

15th Whitsunday. It has been very hot all day and I have been out walking nearly all afternoon. The news from America gives an account of the defeat of the Federal army under General Banks on the Red River with the loss of 4000 men and twenty pieces of cannon, and in the course of another week we may hear of one of the greatest battles that ever was fought . . . At home things are much about the same. I have been shifted into the new shed and got two very bad looms and bad work in them, so I am no better off than I was. We are to have a holiday tomorrow, but I am too poor to go anywhere so I must stay at home.

22nd It has been very hot all this week, with some thunder showers. I have been walking all this afternoon, and everything looks well in fields and gardens, with every prospect of a good fruit year . . . In Denmark all is quiet just now, and the Polish inserection is over and many hundreds of families are sent to Siberia; and at our mill things is likely to get worse. The spinners turned out, and a deputation waited upon the Masters, wanting them to mend the work as it was so bad they could scarce get a living. The Masters said they would not mend it and if they did not like it they could leave, so they had to go work again.

29th Another week of bad work. It is as bad now as ever it was, and no signs of it mending . . .

June

19th It has been fine growing weather this last week, and hay harvest has commenced . . . In Europe the Danish armistice [is] prolonged another fortnight, and if nothing definite is come to, there will be war again; and at Low Moor things are as bad as ever. I went up to Clitheroe last night. There was a great temperance demonstration and procession which passed off very well. New potatoes were selling at two pound for 3½d.

26th There has been a great deal of rain this last week and today is very cold and boisterous . . . There was a great battle fought last Sunday morning off the French coast near Cherbourg between the Federal war steamer *Kearsa[r]ge* and the Confederate cruiser the *Alabama*, which had burned and destroyed one hundred merchantmen belonging to the United States. The fight lasted an hour and ten minutes when the rebel ship was sent to the bottom. The captain and some of the officers escaped on board an English yacht that came out of Cherbourg with her. They had eleven killed and twenty wounded, and about ten or a dozen were drowned, along with the surgeon; while the *Kearsage* was very little damaged and had only three men wounded. They picked up sixty-eight men from the sinking ship . . . In Clitheroe last night new potatoes were selling five pounds for 6d., so I got some for my dinner and came home again.

July

10th It has been very fine warm weather since Wednesday, and a great deal of hay has been got in in good condition . . . In Denmark the Prussians are taking every place they come to, the Danes offering very little resistance. In Parliament the Tories brought forward a motion for a vote of censure upon the Government for the way they have treated the Danish question. The debate lasted all week, and on a division the Ministers had a majority of eighteen. There is no other news of importance this week . . .

August

14th This has been a fine warm week and we stopped yesterday as the engine wanted repairs, so I whitewashed and cleaned the house and today I am very stiff and tired. The latest news from America shews that Sherman has not captured Atlanta but that he has invested it with a view to make it surrender; and General Grant has blown up a fort at Petersburg with a rebel regiment and had taken the outer line of defences. There is nothing else of importance . . . At our mill we have had two turn-outs for bad work. It has been getting worse all summer until we could stand it no longer, and the last time we were out we stopped out all day, when the Master told the deputation that waited upon him that he would work his present stock of cotton up and then he would buy better sorts and have as good work as any in Clitheroe. It is shameful the work we have in at present. I had only 6s. this last week with very hard work, and there was some had less than me; and then our machinery is running very slow owing to the great drought as Ribble is very near dry. We have had frosty nights and warm days this last fortnight, and harvest has been commenced. There were thirty mills stopped in Blackburn this last week for want of water, and will not start again until wet weather sets in. I don't know that there is anything else of importance.

September

11th We have had a week of very wet weather which was much wanted . . . Things are much about the same at Atlanta and Mobile, but the principle news from America just now is the coming election for President, because it depends upon which of the candidates is chosen whether there will be peace or a continuance of the war, and as the position of the parties are about evenly balanced there is no knowing yet how things may be, because if there should be peace, then the price of cotton must come down 2s. per pound, and that is the reason why the cotton trade is so bad just now. The merchants will not buy cloth, as they expect the price will come down one half, and the Manufacturers will not buy cotton for the same reason. There are several mills in Lancashire begun to run short time and some are stopping altogether. At our mills the cotton was done last Tuesday and no signs of any coming. There is none working now but weavers, and if no cotton comes, why then, we must stop next, so everything has a black look – and winter coming on!

18th Another wet week and bad prospects for trade. We got as much cotton last week as kept the mill running two days and a half, and as cotton has come down 4d. per pound it is thought we may get some more . . . The Chicago convention have met and have put General M'Clellan in nomination as President in opposition to Abraham Lincoln, so now both sides are fairly at work, and as the election comes off on the fourth of November the cotton trade in the meanwhile will be greatly depressed until the result is known.

25th We have had some fine weather these days, and harvest is nearly over . . . The cotton trade is getting worse every day. There is no market whatever, and mills are closing every day. The weft we have had this last week is worse than ever, but we are forced to put up with it, as we don't know how soon we will have to stop altogether.

October

2nd It has been very fine all week and things are looking very bad. At our mill they are all working three days a week, except the weavers, who are yet on full time; but as the material is very bad they make very little wages. I have given up my odd loom and I find that two is as many as I can manage with such bad weft. There is a complete stagnation in trade, both in the cotton and cloth market, and nothing doing . . .

9th Another fine week and very little doing. There has been nothing but the weavers working at our mill this week. All the rest are doing nothing, but they have got some cotton which will last three days, and all have to start tomorrow morning . . . There is great distress all through Lancashire at present owing to so many mills stopping, and Clithero will soon be as bad as anywhere else.

16th We commenced short time last Monday, and on Thursday we stopped altogether and does not know when we will start again. The cotton that was bought last week – about forty bales – fell a penny a pound about two hours after he had bought it and he will buy no more until the market settles. I should have gone to Preston this morning but it was so wet, but I shall go tomorrow if all be well . . .

23rd We have been stopped all week and likely for stopping a little longer as there is no cotton bought yet, although it has fallen 2 pence per pound last week, but in the cloth market there is nothing doing whatever. I went to Preston last Monday but only to find that my brother and family had left last Whitsuntide owing to the mill they were working in stopping. They have gone to Dolphinholme near Lancaster and never sent me word. I saw McMurray and family, who gave me all the information, so I found it was no use stopping there so I walked all the way to Blackburn [ten miles] and took the train to Clitheroe. It has been very stormy all week and we have had little pleasure. I applied with several others to the Relief Committee yesterday and got 3s., and our Masters gave every hand 2s., so we are not so badly off this week, whatever they may do next week. It was the great fair yesterday, and a very poor one it was owing to the stormy weather and so many people out of work. The news from America is much about the same as last week, very little doing on either side. The friends of Mr Lincoln say they are sure of winning the election by a large majority.*

30th We commenced work last Thursday and started full time, as our Masters have bought a large supply of cotton which will last a few weeks; and the cloth market is a trifle better this last week and it is thought that it has got a turn for the better . . . The public mind is taken up with the Presidential contest, both sides say they are sure of winning, but in a week or two we shall know all about it. There is nothing else of any importance.

November

6th The weavers have been on full time all week, but the rest of the hands have only had four days and the markets are as gloomy as ever . . .

December

4th There is very little news of any kind lately that I have made no note of it. Lincoln has been re-elected President of America and there has been nothing but skirmishing since, and it is likely that there will not be much

---

* They did – 2,216,076 for Lincoln and 1,808,725 for M'Clellan.

done until spring. At home we have nothing but stormy weather and bad work, and a poor prospect for Christmas.

[And on that dismal note the Diary ends, half-way down the last page of the book.]

William Luby
*sweet-boiler**

William Luby was born in Hulme, near Manchester, in 1883. His early life as an assistant to a sweet-boiler and a worker in a fustian factory was recorded on 5 June 1963 in an interview with John Berger for Granada Television, when he was eighty. The extract is taken directly from the tape-recording, with some cuts, and the addition of punctuation for clarity; it is reproduced by courtesy of Granada Television, who hold the copyright.

Berger: Can you tell me when and where you were born?
Luby: Eh . . . now then. I was born in Hulme off Claridon Street in 1883 – 16th April, that's correct. Yes.
Question: Tell me a bit about your family then.
Answer: Well of course naturally – my family to start with. My father was an absolute drunkard. He was from an Irish family. You see there was a lot of Irish emigrants in those days. They came over somewhere about 1840 onwards. Well they settled mainly on the West coast, Preston, Liverpool, then they gradually worked in . . .
Question: How many generations back had his family come?
Answer: I'm only going back to . . . eh . . . my grandfather.
Question: Your grandfather came over from Ireland?
Answer: He came over from Ireland. Then he had . . . he married a Liverpool woman and he came to Manchester and he had oh, six children. Three girls . . . oh seven . . . three girls and four boys. That's right. Well he naturally, he being an old Irishman – you see in Ireland they always have a kind of clannish – they all live together, put it that way – they all live on one farm. Well they brought that idea to England but they lived in houses not on farms so it made my grandfather, you see . . . he kept, he tried to keep a hold on his children. I should think I've seen six or I've seen seven of his family taking the money for drink, what they should have taken home to their parents . . . to their wives and families.
Question: Taking the money to him?

* From 'Before my Time', Granada Television interview, 1963.

Answer: To him. Yes.

Question: And then what would they do? I mean what would he do with it?
Answer: Drink, for all of them. I don't think the Irish in those days were
great people for going to the pubs; they mainly used to drink in their
houses. You see, now he used to drink in his house, you know. And they'd
all get together. You see, for instance, I know that I had a job carrying
beer at one period. I was only about eight or nine. And my job was to fill
a bucket in the centre of a table and besides filling the bucket with beer,
I had to keep four or five men or perhaps more, in drink – go like . . . go
twice. You see, if you went for a quart in those days, you got one long
pull, you follow, so naturally, you went twice, two pints and you got two
long pulls . . . Now that would be from half past twelve on Sunday until
half past two. Then at half past two, when the public houses closed, they'd
all start feeding. In those days well, eh . . . my grandfather . . . we used
to have cow's head, dumpling, carrots, turnips . . .

Question: How was that cooked?
Answer: . . . leeks. They were all in an egg-shaped pan, if you like. The
whole lot of it. The cow's head was thrown in with the tongue, all the lot
together. And potatoes boiled in their jackets. And a good saucer full of
salt. Then you'd all help yourselves.

Question: Would they be drunk by this time?
Answer: Well I don't know. You see, with always being amongst them,
I'd have a job to recognise. The only time I could see when a man was
drunk, was when he couldn't get up. Or a woman. I've seen women on
stretchers, being taken to the police station. Now I'd say she was drunk
. . . You see drink in those days and drink today, then again, it was drink
in those days, don't forget. You had half a dozen or a dozen pints. Well
you were knocked over.

Question: When you were with your grandfather fetching the beer, were
you also living in that house with him?
Answer: Now then. I used to live between my father and my mother.
You see my father . . .

Question: How do you mean . . . between?
Answer: Between. From house to house. When I got in trouble at my
mother's I went to my father's. I got in trouble at my father's, I went to
my mother. And I used to get in plenty of trouble, you see, because they
were separated and I was supposed to be kind of telling tales from one
house to the other . . . So . . . eh . . . I really did live between them both.
But I'll tell you this. I always got plenty to eat. I never was short of food.
If I couldn't find it one way, I should get it another.

Question: How's that? What's the other way?
Answer: Well, one way for instance, was the old man, well the old grandfather, who . . . he had a tick, a tick book. You see. All right, – I'd get his
tick book and I'd go and buy food. You see, you hand the book over the
counter, you ask for what you want and then they book it. And you come

away, and of course, naturally he'd think it was for the grandfather. Well of course, it was for me. I'd eat it. Of course, he used to carry on with the grocer, because his bills were sometimes higher than they ought to be.

Question: But he never suspected it?
Answer: Well I suppose he would . . .

Question: The family gathered together, not your mother, but your father and your grandfather and the other sons, they would gather together every week on Sunday?
Answer: Practically every week.

Question: On any other occasions?
Answer: Eh . . . funerals. Eh . . . in fact, funerals were good. This is true. The only times that we really did get good feeds. I remember one, it was a wake, an Irish wake – I remember it very well. Of course in a wake there was the usual long bench, there was three candles each side of the coffin – in the coffin of course was the body. Well on the Friday night – in those days, mainly, funerals were on Saturdays, couldn't afford time off during the week, you see, it wouldn't do . . . even to bury your dead . . . you see.

Question: Supposing he died on a Tuesday? Or Monday?
Answer: Well it didn't matter. It was Saturday, because it wouldn't do you see, the man'd be off work, you see, and a lot more people and don't forget you know, a funeral used to last. It wasn't just like they do today. They have a funeral today, and they all hop it somewhere. Leave it you know. Go off. Very much like weddings today. You see, youngsters get married and they're off for a fortnight, you see, well they wouldn't in our day. We had to go to work you see. But anyhow, this was a wake . . .

Question: Who was he?
Answer: An uncle . . .

Question: . . . yes . . .
Answer: An uncle of my father's. All right. Whilst they were drinking, we youngsters were eating, you see, anything that was lying about, no matter what it was – we'd eat it. You see because they were that busy supping beer, you see, and lamenting, as I say, and of course as far as we were concerned, well, we were concerned it didn't matter whether he'd lived or died. You see . . . By the way, they used to have church warden pipes, you know, the long-stemmed clay pipes, they used to have in those days, and they used to smoke them at the funerals. Of course . . .

Question: They were special for funerals?
Answer: Well I wouldn't say that, exactly, no I wouldn't say that, but it used to be rather . . . well it was thick twist – you've heard of it. It used to be – I think it was threepence an ounce. Well, you used to cut it up fine, you know, and grind it in the fingers and of course, I might tell you the atmosphere in that room – they were only small rooms you know, was shocking you know. But anyhow, they were very happy. But really, funerals, weddings and christenings we children done well. You know . . .

Question: When did you first begin earning some money?
Answer: Well . . . eh . . . first . . . shall I start at the beginning?

Question: Yes, the first time you earned any money.
Answer: Well, the first time I started – I led a blind man about – and I got sixpence a week.

Question: How did you find him? How did it begin?
Answer: He . . . the way that begun . . . I lived on one side of Chapel Street and he lived in a lodging house on the other side. And he asked me would I take him round. So what I done – when I used to go to school – I used to go at nine o'clock of a morning. Well, I'd take him to his stand on London Road Approach, leave him until half twelve. Call for him coming back from school, take him to his dinner, then when I was going back to school, call for him again and leave him there till half four or five, then I would bring him home.

Question: By this time you would be how old?
Answer: I'd be about nine or ten. I wouldn't be ten – I'd be about nine, then. But I got sixpence a week for that. But on top of that, I used to sell wax lights. Now we used to buy wax lights at a halfpenny a box and we sold them for a penny. I also used to sell newspapers . . . I used to buy the newspapers – fourpence a dozen or fourpence halfpenny a dozen – thirteen to the dozen, and of course, you got a halfpenny each for them, so that meant you got sixpence ha'penny, so you got tuppence profit . . .

Question: How long, per evening, would you spend selling papers?
Answer: Well, I should say I'd get home some nights somewhere about eight o'clock . . .

Question: And beginning immediately after school?
Answer: Oh yes. Well in between the blind man.

Question: So you were going around with the blind man and . . .
Answer: Yes . . . yes . . .

Question: and selling newspapers . . .
Answer: I'd take the blind man home and then I should run to Store Street – course, you may not know Store Street, but it juts on to London Road—there used to be . . . a cart used to come there from the news office – like a milk cart . . . Well, he used to sell us the papers there on that stand, and we'd run off and sell them. You see.

Question: And then you would be getting sixpence a week then from the blind man.
Answer: From the blind man.

Question: How much from the newspapers, about?
Answer: Well, it depended – the newspaper business you see did . . . there's such a thing as 'I haven't sold them'. You follow? Perhaps if I got a shilling at the outside.

Question: A shilling a week?
Answer: If I got that. Yes.

Question: What did you do with this money?
Answer: Oh well, of course, some went to my mother, and I had some for food.

Question: For food outside. . . ?
Answer: Oh yes . . .

Question: The home. . . ?
Answer: Oh yes . . . yes I always looked after food. It was rather strange. All my life, you know, I've always seemed to have got it from somewhere.

Question: Were you eating at home at all?
Answer: When I could. When I could get it.

Question: But often there wasn't any food?
Answer: No food of course. We used to. . . if we did get any, it'd be two rounds of bread for breakfast – that's all. When I was working all I got was a hap'orth of soup and chunks of bread and very often the soup was very thin because the man who was selling the soup was having a good day and he added water to it to make it thin—then we'd soak it up with bread. We used to do that . . . Whilst I was leading the blind man and selling newspapers I made a certain customer of mine, my last delivery, if you like, the last and he was a sugar-boiler.

Question: Mmm.
Answer: And I went away with this sugar-boiler.

Question: Tell me about him. Why did you make him the last?
Answer: Because the place was warm. You see. It was a nice fire and he had the heat of the sugar boiling and he used to give me a sweet and then some nights – some nights, I'd work all night and he'd give me sixpence. And I . . . the work I would be doing would be dipping egg-moulds – I don't know if you know what an egg-mould is – get an egg, push it half-way into something, do you follow, let the something set, then pour something else on top, do you follow me? Then pull it apart and you've got the makings of a . . . you've got a mould. Well we used to make moulds with . . . we'll say about half a dozen eggs. Well through pouring the molten sugar into the mould and pouring it out and then pulling the mould apart you had a shell – six shells. You've got that . . .

Question: Mmm.
Answer: You'd have six shells. Then that mould was warmed through the hot sugar. Well my job was to dip those moulds in a big tub of water to cool them. Well I was doing that all night.

Question: Whereabouts?
Answer: In Adair Street, in Ancoats, in his house.

Question: In a . . . what did he have. . . ?
Answer: A four-roomed house.

Question: A whole house?
Answer: Yes. Front part sweet shop. Living portion, boiler and fireplace to boil his sweets on and so on.

Question: And if you stayed there all night nobody bothered. I mean nobody . . . your mother didn't notice it. . . ?

Answer: Oh no. Not my mother. I'd go to school the next day and of course naturally I would be partly asleep. The teacher used to come behind me and knock me off the bench. In those days the school benches had no backs. Do you follow? You couldn't lean back. Well I used to get knocked off the bench. In fact the teacher thought it was fun by his appearance.

Question: What sort of man was this sugar-boiler?

Answer: Well, the poor chap was a drunkard. And a gambler. That was his trouble. In fact, the woman he was living with was somebody else's wife. He'd gambled there. You see. He brought her away from Newcastle on Tyne. And he was a man – he could start, in fact he could start with practically nothing. I've seen him pretty well down and out – he's had nothing but his coat and vest and he's given me his coat and vest and I've taken it to the pawnbrokers and I've got two and six on the coat and vest and I've bought sugar at a penny a pound and a ha'penny a pound, because those days you used to buy scrapings out of the windows – sugar that was destroyed by cats and dogs, do you follow? . . . Flyblow – all sorts. Then I'd take it to him. You follow? He would boil it – he'd make sweets of it, perhaps butterscotch – never mint rock, because mint rock was always clear. It had to be clean. It shows itself clear. And he'd make treacle toffee and all kinds and he'd send me out with it to sell it and I used to sell it for tuppence ha'penny a pound.

Question: On the streets or to shops?

Answer: On the streets – or to shop-keepers. And those shop-keepers would sell it for a penny a quarter. I've seen him make chocolate sticks . . . Have you ever seen what the kiddies used to have at one time . . . a dear little toffee stick? Well he . . . he used to make those about . . . about twelve inches long and perhaps half an inch diameter. Well we used to make chocolate sticks of those by the simple method of buying a pound or two pound of wax candles, extracting the wicks out of the wax and buying brown umber and mixing brown umber with the wax until such time as it came the colour of chocolate. And then he'd get the toffee sticks which were cold, and he'd dip them in this mixture, and with their being cold naturally a certain quantity of the wax or if you like, what he said was chocolate, you see, stuck to it. And they were sold as chocolate sticks, at a farthing each, ha'penny each, to the children round about.

Question: What did they taste like?

Answer: As far as I was concerned, they were all right. You see at that period we . . . eh . . . we were not like things are today. You see. We were thankful to get them.

Question: How did he treat you? This man?

Answer: Well he didn't treat me too well, really. He did treat me pretty well when I was calling on him with the newspaper but you see, I left home with him.

Question: Tell me about that.

Answer: Well, he got in debt. He got in debt with local grocers. He was buying sugar and various things on the I.O.U., mints, essences, and coconut, various things which you need for sweets. Well, he got in debt. So of course, in those days one way of getting out of debt was to remove. Naturally. If you got a removal well then you were all right. Well, he decided to remove from where he was and he took me – oh, he asked me would I go with him. Well, of course, to me what did it matter? He sheltered me. The place was warm. When I went home I got in trouble, when I went to father's I got in trouble – all right, I went with him.

Question: How old would you be now?

Answer: I'd be about ten, then. Well, I went off with him and we went to Preston first. He packed his oddments up, you know, and we went to Preston and when he got to Preston we got there before the furniture – took an empty house, you see. In those days you could get an empty house as you know . . . well you may not know – but you could. Any amount of empty houses. And he'd take a couple of doors . . .

Question: You mean he'd rent this house?

Answer: Well yes, or he just . . . or he'd just promise to pay for it, put it that way, you see. He'd get a couple of doors, or first he would get a couple of orange-boxes, put them in the room and put a couple of the doors out of the rooms on to the boxes. Him and his wife would sleep on there.

Question: On the doors?

Answer: On the doors. I slept on the floor. I suppose I must have been extra hard, you see. But anyhow, I slept on the floor.

Question: What did you have to keep you warm?

Answer: Nothing practically. Cause we'd brought nothing, you see.

Question: What sort of clothes would you have taken with you?

Answer: Ah . . . well my clothes. Might have a coat, ragged, might have an old shirt, an old pair of trousers, barefooted . . .

Question: Were you always barefooted?

Answer: Always. I was barefooted up till about twelve, I should say.

Question: Summer and winter?

Answer: All the time . . . But anyhow, after the furniture came along he re-addressed it to Blackpool. That's right. Re-addressed it to Blackpool from Preston. Then we went to Blackpool. The same procedure – a house, and so on. Then when the furniture came to Blackpool he addressed it to Newcastle on Tyne. Never come in any of the houses and away it went to Newcastle on Tyne. But Newcastle on Tyne was his home town. He was bred and born there and his people were very respectable. He must have been an outcast as far as I could see . . . Well anyhow, when we got to Newcastle . . . we got a house there, and then we done the usual. We got a tea chest, tin tea chest built inside it brickwork, made a fire and he made an opening from the fire into the fire in the house, do you follow me? Then we started our sugar-boiling. And I'd go out with a little box on two basinette wheels and I'd sell his sweets, you see, for twopence ha'penny a pound. Sometimes when he was pretty what to say . . . a . . . a bit on the respectable side, he'd get a handcart. And he'd load it and we'd walk from Newcastle to Tynemouth. And sell it on the way, to shops. You see.

Question: And he and the woman with him and you were all living off this?
Answer: All living off this, yes. And by the way I slept in the same room, and in the same bed as them. They were kind, you see, or perhaps they didn't want to spend too much on bedding, you see, but that's how I slept.

Question: Did this worry you?
Answer: And then . . .

Question: Did this worry you at all?
Answer: No, not in the least. You see I hadn't been . . . I hadn't been used to much all my life, much like a dog or any animal, do you follow? . . . I hadn't learned my rights as a human, you see . . . [*Returns to Manchester.*] But anyhow, I got home. Now then, the same trouble at home, the same trouble started as I had before. My mother, she'd got four of us, four she couldn't keep, so I had to start the best way I could.

Question: Were you never going to school at all at this time?
Answer: For that two years I never went to school. And I . . . when I was with the sugar-boiler I went very little, because when they used to beat me for not going, follow, when they used to beat me for not going I decided it's as well to be beaten for not going. So I stopped away. You see. When they gave me the sixpence for the nights and I went next morning and I got knocked off the form, I naturally weighed it up – it'd been sensible from my point of view. I said 'No'. I didn't go to school. And I never went to school when I was at Newcastle on Tyne . . .

Question: When you were . . . when you were in the streets like this selling newspapers with the blind man, later with the sugar-boiler, did yourself do any begging?
Answer: Yes, I used to beg, of course, outside the workshops. Of an evening, at half past five.

Question: Tell me about that.
Answer: Well, eh . . . the workshops at that period, the men were going to the work and especially Mondays after a good week-end in the pubs, they used to carry their dinners out, which was generally a penn'orth of corned beef or pig's cheek between a couple of rounds of bread – well, through the drink they didn't want it. And at night-time they used to give it to us youngsters at the workshop gates. And we . . . that's how we used to go on. And we'd get pretty often at nights, but Monday was the best night. We had all this cut and dried, you know, it was a business . . .

Question: Was there much fighting amongst you?
Answer: Fighting?

Question: Yes, amongst the kids.

Answer: Well, fighting was that common that you . . .

Question: Do you remember your first fight?

Answer: . . . My first fight was for a pair of trousers. I remember it very well. I'd be about six or perhaps five. My father bought two pairs of trousers for sixpence. He gave me one pair – I had one pair on and then . . . by the way, it was the first pair as ever I had. And I went out with these trousers on – and I seen another boy with the other pair of trousers on – and I wanted to know where he got them from. Of course that was the beginning. Then he told me. My father had sold a pair of trousers to his mother for threepence. You see, I thought I had two pairs of trousers and I only had one. That was the very first . . . You always settled your arguments with a fight. You see it was the only expression you had. They wouldn't listen to you arguing, you know what I mean. He'd be looking while he's arguing with you . . . he'd be looking for an opening to let you have one. You see. Oh no. It was very common. In fact the workshops, the public houses at the time of Sullivan or Corbett, the men were always fighting. In fact, behind my grandfather's house there was a canal and a croft. Any quarrels which my grandfather and any of his sons had with anybody would be settled by one son on the Sunday morning on this croft.

Question: How do you mean . . . how do you mean by one son?

Answer: Because one son was kept for that purpose, fighting.

Question: He was a fighter for the family?

Answer: He was a fighter for the family. Bare fists . . . And very often his opponent was knocked out. They'd throw him in the canal and then bring him out when he'd recovered. 'Course, often as not, a ducking would be enough. Then was the times I used to go for the beer. You follow. And they'd all enjoy themselves very much . . .

Question: Were you often forced to stealing directly?

Answer: Well, when I was a youngster, very young, I remember stealing a hen at one time and it gave me away. It made a noise in the coal-hole. I remember that very well . . .

Question: How in the coal-hole?

Answer: Well, you see in the four-roomed houses under the stairs is generally the coal place. So a neighbour of ours kept hens. Well, for some reason, I couldn't tell you why, I went and I stole one of the hens. And I put it in . . . our . . . coal-hole. Do you follow? I didn't know what to do with it, more than you would at that period . . . 'course, there's a great noise from the neighbour. Somebody had stole his . . . they found it. I suppose they'd have an idea it was me. I suppose I'd be marked. Do you follow? At that period. Although mind you, there were plenty of young-sters like me. Oh yes, I wasn't alone . . . Now then I was about twelve and a half one way and another and I had to live and my brother was fourteen. Now you couldn't get work those days until you were fourteen. So I took my brother's papers – birth papers, and I went and I started at a place called – Crabtree's in Canal Street at the age of fourteen on the

4

papers. Do you follow? In my brother's name. Well, that went on. It wasn't too bad for about three months . . .

Question: What was Crabtree's?
Answer: Crabtree's was a velvet, fustian, cords and all that kind of business. They used to stiffen cloth, cords and velveteens. I don't know as to how you would know but when they stiffen that kind of stuff, they . . . there used to be a barrel of something – I don't know whether it was worms or what it was – but when we opened the barrel there was all insects of all kinds. We used to boil them, do you follow, in a big vat. In the bottom of the vat there was a tube used to run to a trough. In that trough was a roller revolving and over the roller used to come the cloth. Face side up. Have you got me? All right. I used to . . . as the cloth came over the roller I used to what they call fold it and when a certain quantity of cloth had come across I used to lift it and put it on to what they call a set of drying tins. Tins to dry the gum or whatever the mixture was to dry it in. Well that was . . . that was what . . . they called fustians you see. And then sometimes they'd take the damp cloth and stretch it – do you follow – to go in the machine perhaps . . . eh . . . eighteen inches. It'd come out perhaps twenty or nineteen. You see it was a machine used to gradually open out and whilst the cloth was damp you could stretch it . . .

Question: How long did you stay there?
Answer: Well I should think I stayed there about twelve month. I should say so. . . .

Question: What would your wages be from that one?
Answer: Six shilling a week.

Question: How much of that would you keep for yourself?
Answer: Threepence. Oh, my mother knew how much I got.

Question: And you were still living . . .
Answer: I lived at mother's then.

Question: When did you first go away?
Answer: Well, eh . . .

Question: I mean for any length of time?
Answer: Well, when you say, when did I first go away.

Question: I don't mean with the sugar-boiler but . . .
Answer: Well, about that . . . oh when did I leave home finally?

Question: Mmm.
Answer: Oh well, I left home finally when I was about sixteen. Like finally. I got an offer of a job in North Staffordshire and I took that . . .

Question: All this time, these early years living under the kind of conditions you were, you survived somehow.
Answer: I did, yes.

Question: How do you think that was?
Answer: Well, because I had plenty to eat. Plenty to eat and I was healthy. That's a great thing you see. And then again, I may have lived

under dirty conditions, but I suppose I must have kept myself clean else I would have got disease. You see. That's how I account for that. Plenty to eat and mind you this, there was one thing, I'm not praising anybody, but the Roman Catholic church puts the fear of God in you, you're frightened of doing wrong, don't forget that. Not because you love God or anything of that type, but they put it in you you see and I kept pretty decent – in fact I was up to the day I was married . . . Of course I was decent then. But I was all right.

Question: Do you ever think of the people who didn't survive the same kind of conditions?

Answer: Eh . . . not then. No, because it was the survival of the fittest – if I left a man behind, well, that's his fault. It wasn't mine. You see . . . and I . . .

Question: If you could choose the choice of being young again then or now which would you choose?

Answer: Well, you're asking . . . you're asking . . . you see, I've not been young now, do you see, so you can't really say . . . You see, your child that's young today is brought up to those standards which he's living in today, like I was only I was on a lower standard. You see, your child today is from the very cradle he's petted and he never does wrong and you can't do wrong, do you see . . . When you ask me to compare – well I couldn't. In fact, I'm a bit sorry for the child of today – personally. He tries to live or he tries to live up to something which he can't . . . I feel sorry for the child. It's always wanting and it's always been used to having. But now that it's got to get it itself, you see, it hasn't got the mother and father, you see. Things are different, Oh no, I won't . . . I can't . . . I can't compare . . .

Thomas Jordan
*coal-miner**

Thomas Jordan was born at Birtley in Durham in 1892. He was educated at St Joseph's Roman Catholic School, Washington, and followed his father down the pit in 1906. Rebelling against life below ground, he enlisted in the army in 1912, and saw service in the First World War in France, the Balkans, Egypt and Palestine. He returned to mining as a coal-hewer in 1919, but was forced to give up in 1928 due to the effects of malaria, dysentery and gas poisoning. For a few years he worked as a labourer or was unemployed, but in 1936 he recovered his health due, he believes, to the practice

---

* Unpublished autobiography.

of Christian Science. For the next twenty-seven years, until 1963, he led an active life in many different jobs, with scarcely a day's absence. Now, at eighty, he is Chairman of the Senior Citizens' Fellowship at Newton Aycliffe and an active Christian Scientist.

In his brief autobiography he writes lovingly and sensitively of the village, the countryside and the people, though he always hated work in the pit.

There was a strike in the Durham coalfield in January 1892 when I was born. My parents lived in a colliery house at Birtley, Co. Durham, not far from the pit where my father worked. The harsh noises of the colliery broke into the home but my parents were very healthy people who seldom complained about anything, as I learned in after years.

My father, an old soldier, had served eleven years in India in the Royal Regiment of Horse Artillery. He was a noted figure, tall, smart with a perfect soldierly bearing. A coal-miner before he went into the army in 1876, a coal-miner he became again when he left the army in 1889.

My boyhood days were therefore coloured by army stories early in my memory. I knew of Peshawar, Bangalore, Poona, Calcutta, etc., as soon as I learned to read and write.

Leaving Birtley when I was very young we moved to Usworth Colliery where my father became a deputy overman. He was never known to be absent from his work, either through sickness or otherwise. Consequently the family of six never knew the hardship which seemed to be common at that period. We were always well-clad and booted with strong boots for school but finer ones for Sundays.

Mother was a gentle little woman who believed that God would always see us through. She was thrifty and knew how to sew, knit, and could easily operate a Singer sewing-machine. Although there was no gas or electric light in our home she would pedal that machine under the light of an oil lamp. We, therefore, were assured of warm underclothing in the winter, made up from material bought at cost price from shop sales.

I commenced school when I was three years old. I was in a dress the same as the girls, a petticoat. Every morning my older sister and I had to walk a mile and a half to school in Washington village. There were no buses, cars or lorries on the road in those days, only a horse and cart now and again we would see. Hence the walk was safe and very beautiful. Our parents were free from fear when each morning they set us out for school.

There were no particular places to have a mid-day meal. In the summer-time we sat on the village green and had the food given to us by mother. We would get a can full of cold milk for twopence at the farm nearby to wash down our food. In the winter the school mistress allowed us to warm our can of tea on the school fire and we could sit at our school bench and have it there.

Washington village is a lovely village with a long history. Soon we became aware of this, and our imaginations were aroused with its tales of long ago. George Washington, the ancient church and the underground tunnels underneath the old Hall gave romance to this imagination.

The green grass, the very green trees and especially the large sycamore tree in the grounds of the ancient church enhanced the supreme loveliness of the scene. It was serene, so quiet, that the birds could be heard at all times, no pollution, no noise except the daily clang of the village blacksmith's hammer. Strange as it may seem this clanging on his anvil was a very pleasant sound in the otherwise silent village green. We welcomed this sound upon the peace and quiet of the day.

They were very happy years and all my boyhood friends and relatives exuded this happiness. We could sing, play games, swim in the unpolluted River Wear and watch the rowing boats rowing slowly up to Lambton Castle, with the music of the new-found phonograph, or the sweet strains of the melodeon, or concertina wafting their sound to us sitting on the river bank. The banks of the river were made beautiful by the masses of deep red poppies growing upon them.

The school I attended was a Church School. The school marm was a very capable lady. Whilst she gave copious doses of religious doctrine, she also gave you a great deal of learning. She insisted that you learned to read and write or she could be very angry with you. Her teaching of singing and dancing was very high. The school concerts and pantomimes she organized drew people from all sections of the village to see them. All my praise for her devotion to her calling.

In 1897 was the Diamond Jubilee of Queen Victoria and the villages of Usworth and Washington celebrated it in grand style. We, from the various schools, assembled on the village green. I can still remember how nicely dressed all were on that warm summer day. Each of us was presented with a cup with the regal image of the Queen stamped upon it. Our teachers led us into a large field where we sat down and were given a large paper bag packed with food and fruit. They filled our mugs with tea and we ate to the sound of the colliery bands playing nearby. It was wonderful to me.

Many prizes were given for the best runners, jumpers, dancers or footballers or cricketers. Big bonfires lit the skies and fireworks spread their display everywhere.

In those early years of 1900 I knew that someday I would be a soldier because faraway places fired my imagination. *Robinson Crusoe* was my favourite book which added fuel to this fire, in the year 1903, as I sat one warm March day and read it through. I also loved Bible stories taught at school.

Usworth Colliery was situated amidst very beautiful surroundings. Cornfields edged their way around it and reduced the grimness of the colliery and its huge slag heaps. Its satanic structure never bothered me, in fact I was impressed by its boldness and very towering presence. The loveliness of the countryside was always there to compensate against any ugliness of the pit.

We lived in a house with a huge kitchen, and above it a huge bedroom.

Six of us slept in the upstairs bedroom. My father and mother slept in the kitchen and although the colliery was only a stone's-throw away, my Dad, coming off night shift, could sleep soundly. My mother had to pull him hard to waken him. The blacksmith's hammer constantly clanging did not disturb him, nor did all the other noises associated with the colliery – the railway engine dragging the wagons laden with coal – he slept peacefully on with never a murmur. A grumble from my mother could be heard when the northern winds blew muck from the high chimneys on to her washing hanging in the garden.

There were three streets of houses with the colliery at the top forming a square, and in this square was a very ample green grass playing-field. Football, cricket and quoits were played on it. Lads got their first introduction to football there, which led some of them to first-class football. They came out of the mine after ten hours down there and then played a hard game of football without flinching. A tough breed that knew no fear or weakness, yet law-abiding, and always ready to give assistance to anyone in need of help.

When I was ten years old I got a job with Mr Scott, the village newsagent. The papers I delivered took me into many a home in Usworth, and into the homes of a little hamlet called Waterloo. Waterloo was reputed to be a very drunken spot. Relays of beer-carrying men carried their large pails of beer from the 'long pull' at New Washington. I entered these homes with my newspapers during these drunken sprees and was never molested. In this hamlet there were one or two chapel people and I soon noticed that their homes were nicer than my drunken customers. One of them had a large ornamental oil lamp hanging over his table. He and his brother used to bring me in and I would listen to him playing the piano, inspired with the brightness of the home and his music which were mainly hymns. Despite the vice of drink the other inhabitants of Waterloo made me very welcome and showed kindness to me. It was a dark and bleak spot with no outside lights. I used to walk alone down a very dark road to it and was admired by the lads of the hamlet for doing so.

In 1906 my school days terminated. I had not been a very clever scholar. I could read and write; my spelling was very poor, history and geography I liked but after simple arithmetic I could not learn the higher mathematics so I was doomed for the pits.

My father when I was twelve took me one Sunday night into the pit, as he did often after that. He was a deputy overman and I was company for him as he went to the coal-face, only himself in the district. Going down in the pit cage, in the deep hole was a huge cavern on the side of the pit-shaft; my father told me that his father fired the furnace in there for ventilators and took him (my father) when he was seven for company. He said he slept for twelve hours on canvas while his father stoked the furnace; mechanical ventilators were unknown then.

These excursions into the pit, along these grim galleries, awed me no end. The coal-seam was about five feet high. There were railroads leading into places where men hewed and filled the tubs coming along these rails.

Young men brought these tubs sitting on the limbers which a pit pony was yoked into. My father had to go into each of these places to test for gas and for safety of the roof. With only the two of us in the district, and nearly three miles from the shaft bottom, I did not feel very good. Loud rumbles could be heard here and there in the roof. It seemed as if the stone and coal strata were about to break loose upon us. The flicker of our tiny oil lamps would cast its minute glow on a mouse scuttling across our path. The entire area was eerie but it did not unruffle that deep calm of my dad.

The coal-hewers came in at 4 A.M. They assembled at the 'kist' and he directed them to their work, after testing their safety lamps. He then wrote his report the best way he could because he only faintly could read and write. Afterwards we travelled back to the shaft bottom. It was a long haul up a very steep gradient but the electric lights – a novelty there – were a welcome sight as we approached. Only the colliery boasted electric dynamos; the village was in black darkness at night time.

When we got out of the pit cage and directed our steps the short distance toward home, he always asked me how I liked the experience. Always I answered that I liked going into the mine, which I did several times until I was fourteen years old. He was a fearless man and I did not wish to let him know that I was nervous or else he might have thought I was 'queer'.

January 1906 ushered in my parting way with schooling. Mr Scott the newsagent wished me to stay with him and he offered me 5s. a week, he promised to teach me the business. I came to my parents and told them of this but my dad was adamant that I go to the pit because I will earn 6s. 6d. a week there!

Dressed up as a little miner in a blue flannel shirt, short breeches and strong shoes, my bait a white cotton bag tied round my arm, on a cold winter night, I descended the mine to earn my living. It was 9 P.M. and I might ascend that shaft at 8 A.M. if my relief came in early. I was a 'trapper-boy' pulling open and shutting a door to allow the 'putters' to come through with their ponies and coal-tubs. I must stay in this position until relieved or the ponies would crash the door and I was for it by the overman.

The workaday activity of the coal-mine was totally different from what I experienced with my father with the monk-cell silence, which was only broken by the noises of moving strata. Here now was pandemonium let loose. The empty tubs in sets of sixty hurtling their way down the steep incline and the full ones pushing their way to the shaft bottoms; one had to jump quickly into holes to avoid being crushed to death by them!

There seemed to be wild excitement everywhere. Overmen shouting, cursing and hurrying everyone into greater effort so that the precious coal could get to the surface and meet the demand of its buyers. All was hustle and bustle, nowhere peace and quiet. The quest for the black diamond overruled sanity, order and grace. Yet men and boys did not go insane but rose above the terrible scene and became a peculiar breed of humans.

Down the pit appearing to be demoniac, up above other qualities came out of them. The churches and chapels were full, the organs giving forth delightful music that encouraged the many choirs to give forth their best. With an odd exception violence was not rife, only perhaps if there was contest between them and the management.

The mine, to me, was an ugly place, a hell condemned to just as the village green was a heaven where we often wandered when out of it and the beautiful River Wear crowning us with its joy as we felt its waters swathing over and around our naked bodies. I got on very well with my workmates; of those that are still around, I love to meet one who is now much above eighty. I still remember him running to me stark naked in the pit demanding I get more tubs to him because he had just been married, and needed furniture for his new home!

They gave me a pony named Sharper when I finished the trapping job, and promoted me to be a driver. He was a beautiful animal slick and shiny but unmanageable. I could not couple him to the tub as he refused to stand still, and kicked furiously at me. Hence the stark naked chap always at me for empty coal tubs. Afterward they gave me a pony named Donald but he was docile and slow, so the naked man was not much better off. The roof of the pit where I hung the tubs on was in a deplorable condition with huge shives of stone ready to slither down upon you. When Sharper turned his limbers he usually caught the side props making me run out of danger. Donald was a taller pony than Sharper and his horse collar got entangled in the broken baulks which gave me the jitters, fearing that the whole load of stone was about to fall on me.

With the passing of the years I became indifferent to the many dangers in the mine. When someone was killed I might become apprehensive for a day or two, then the incident was completely forgotten. This training was valuable to me during the First World War when men were yielding their lives on a far larger scale.

The year 1910 ushered in a shorter working day for lads in the mine. The eight-hour shift became law instead of ten hours, donating to us time for other pursuits under the blue skies. Football, cricket, quoits, whippet-racing, etc. were livened up and young pit lads found their way into professional sporting avenues. My dad took me into all the things he was interested in. He played the violin and we both used these instruments in the village string band, entertaining people in an age starved of any culture for a long time but now emerging fast to the surface. Some of the musicians in that band got opportunities in the silent cinema era.

My father umpired cricket matches and it was a delight to me to be at the marking board while he umpired the game. Alongside the cricket field was a rifle range he was interested in, and which introduced me to small arms and target practice.

Gay and lighthearted was the mood of many of my wide circle of friends, earning up to £2 per week, sometimes more if you were a crack putter lad. My mother gave me half a gold sovereign for my pocket and she bought me good-style suits and shoes. The weekends found us in the city of Newcastle where we found entertainment in its theatres and music halls.

Martin Harvey in *The Tale of Two Cities* was our favourite along with *The Christian, Sign of the Cross, Face at the Window* etc. entertained us. Harry Lauder, Wilkie Bard, Gerty Gitana, Marie Lloyd brought us into the music hall, Charlie Chaplin was just being heard of.

Usworth Colliery was a booming place. It had the best conditions in all the Durham minefield and its workpeople were earning good wages. Cinemas and a theatre appeared in New Washington and they were filled to capacity. Thrifty men built their own homes. Others spent a lot of money in the new workmen's club. Usworth railway station, at the week-ends, was full of people waiting for the train to Newcastle. It was always a merry scene seeing the droves of men and women walking a mile or two to the railway station dressed in their best. The 11.30 P.M. return was a sight to remember. Some had been to the match – Newcastle United – others to the pubs there, then open all day, and the rest mainly at the Empire Variety Theatre; all of them good-humoured and telling of their experiences of the day.

The year 1911 was a memorable year to me because events in it decided that my work in the pit was ending. I joined the 9th Battalion of the Durham Light Infantry territorials and commenced army training. Working down the pit for eight hours, Billy Bottoms, Paddy Fraser and me would ascend the pit, wash ourselves, don our khaki uniforms and walk over three miles to the Drill Hall. There Colour Sergeant Ernie Crouch would work upon us to teach us the rudiments of soldiering.

We went to camp in August in Strensall near York. It was a red-hot month. We marched, had make-believe battles, dug trenches and fired rifle rounds. We had to fight to get our share of the food dished out but we felt very fit and tanned with the heat of the sun. Our white pit-made faces now showed a very healthy glow. It was a hectic fortnight; Colour Sergeant Crouch did not spare us, drilling us, marching us sometimes at the double, in the terrific heat of those August days of long ago.

Returning to my work in the pit, going along those long galleries leading my pony in, I thought that the wide open spaces of Strensall Common, or any other common, were preferable to this. Stooping, crouching, taking care of oneself and of the pony on a road so narrow and low made me decide there and then to enlist in the Army.

I told my mother of this and she pleaded with me not to. My earnings were helping her to run the home. Daughters in those days earned little or nothing unless they went out as servants to better-placed people. They were not keen on going for about 5s. per week, so therefore they remained at home to be kept by the male members of the family. I promised mother I would stay with her for a little longer but my intentions were for the Army.

During 1911 there were stoppages of the colliery, putters refusing to go down the pit on the slightest pretext thereby holding to ransom the colliery production and reducing my earnings. This dragged on more or less the whole year. Several young men left to join the Army, two of them enlisted in the 5th Dragoon Guards stationed on the Curragh, Ireland. In March 1912 there was a national coal strike, the first full stoppage in the coalfield for twenty years. The pit ponies were brought to the surface and allowed to roam and jump freely around the large fields. It was a wonderful sight to watch them enjoying themselves, and enjoy themselves they did, as soon as they were let loose upon the luscious green grass.

The strike gave us opportunity for a variety of activities, walking, swimming, plenty of sport and also enabled my territorial mates and I to get along more often to the Drill Hall. Colour Sergeant Crouch was a Boer War veteran and we loved to hear him relate his experiences in that war.

He was looking forward to the day when he finished his Army career and hoped nothing, no mishaps, would come in his way to interfere with his pension rights. He, however, became a Colonel in the war just two years ahead.

The pulley wheels began to go round again in the middle of April. It was sad to see the ponies lowered again into the mine but they had had six weeks of glorious freedom which I wondered whether they remembered, in the many years again before they saw the light of day. In the ensuing years some of them became blind and, therefore it would still be a dark world to them the next time they emerged from the black pit into those green fields.

The afternoon shift was ready to restart work, I among them; after six weeks' idleness I knew there would be no sporadic strike by the putter lads. Quietly we waited to get into the cage after the coal-hewers descended. I looked around them all. They were a sturdily built body of lads well equipped for their arduous task below, wrestling with ten-hundredweight iron tubs, and often a refractory pony which only their massive strength would bring into subjection.

Among these lads I was light and frail, unfitted to compete with them in the field of heavy work. Any kind of mining in those days was a terrific job. Clever machinery was rarely seen like that seen and used today. Brute strength was needed and I had little of it. The goodness of my parents in bringing me up in the finer things was hardly the training needed for the rough and tumble of pit life.

We descended that sunny afternoon into the mine and went to our work in different sections of the mine. The six-weeks stoppage had made me very tender and soft. Crawling along the narrow roads gave one the feeling of stiffness in every joint of the body. Pulling the pony through the low places was a job. He would whinney, cry, and stand fast whenever he came to a ragged patch. I had to bend my body to get through but Defty – my pony – refused to bend his knees and had to be manhandled to get him to go.

Finally we got to where we commenced the operation of putting empty tubs to the coal-hewers and getting their full ones in return, a process that was repeated many times, and before the shift was completed I would be bleeding and torn with the awkward and heavy iron tubs. I made my mind up that evening when the morrow came I would go along to see Colour Sergeant Crouch.

The wide stretches of Strensall Common, or the like, beckoned me away from the restricted confinement of a coal-mine. Troopers Richardson and Gillespie in the Dragoon Guards came to my thought. I left my village early the next morning not telling my parents my errand, and was duly enlisted in the Army on April 15th 1912, little thinking that future meetings with my Usworth putter friends would be on the battlefields of France, the Balkans, Egypt and Palestine.

B. L. Coombes
*coal-miner**

The author was born about 1894 in Herefordshire, where his father earned a very poor living as a smallholder. By the age of eighteen, in 1912, he had determined that he must get away in order to earn a decent living, and left to work in the South Wales coalfield (he does not identify the precise area). Within a year he was earning 36 shillings a week and, subsequently, up to £3 or £4 a week when the coal was working easily. He was the first local miner to operate a mechanical coal-cutter in 1914, and in later years became a specialist at this work. *These Poor Hands* covers his experiences up to and during the First World War; two subsequent books, *Those Clouded Hills* (1944) and *Miner's Day*, cover the inter-war depression, strikes and unemployment.

Two excerpts are given: the first describes the complicated system of wage-payment in operation before 1914, the second the introduction and effects of the first mechanical coal-cutter in that part of South Wales.

By the end of the first week most of my stiffness had gone, but a deal of the soreness remained in my hands and knees. There have been very few weeks since that I have not been glad of the Sunday rest to give some cuts or bruises a chance to heal. It seems part of the job, that getting battered about.

I had a week's pay in the office after that week's work, but had none to draw because of the custom of keeping a week's pay 'in hand'. This is necessary owing to the need for counting up the coal accounts and other

* From *These Poor Hands. The Autobiography of a Miner working in South Wales*, Gollancz, 1939.

bookings, but it is a severe handicap to a man who has been away from work for a while or a stranger to the place who has no way of paying for his keep for the first week. One has to wait for a fortnight before getting the first pay; then there are two weeks' lodging and living to be paid. It is a safeguard that a man cannot leave his work without notice unless he is prepared to leave a week's pay behind. The sole advantage I found with this system was at strike time, when we had a full week's money to draw several days after we had finished work.

During the second week I worked by day. This was more pleasant, as I was home and washed by half-past four, and could go out in the evening content that work was over for that day and that I would have a night's sleep before I worked again.

The men in the headings were the only colliers that worked by night. The stall-men worked only by day. The repairers, timber-men, rippers and labourers were working by night so that they should not delay the output of coal.

Coal was the only thing that mattered by day. A 'turn' was kept so that each collier had his tram in rotation and with regard to the conditions under which he was working. A collier with a helper could claim a tram in every turn if he had the last one full. A collier who worked alone could only claim a tram on the odd turn – first–third–fifth. This turn lasted all the week, and each collier had to mark the number of trams he had full as well as his marking number. All the others could see this mark, so no 'dodging the turn' was allowed.

I have met people who imagine it is possible to do any amount of work-dodging in the darkness of the mine. Some may be done, but the work is so measured, allotted and weighted that a man must show some work before he can claim any pay. The men are good guardians against scheming, also, for what one man dodges another must do, often in addition to his own. Men who do not do their share are treated with contempt and are given nicknames, such as 'Shonny one tram', by their fellow workmen, who are usually too ready to pour out their sweat and their blood.

During the last five years I have known three men who have died after no apparent signs of illness, and the doctor has stated that they died because their work drew all the moisture from their bodies in the form of sweat and it was not replaced.

Thursday night is 'jib night' at the collieries. This term is supposed to refer to the men's faces when they get the docket which shows how much pay they should draw on the morrow. Some of the men looked at the paper for a few seconds, then pushed it into their pocket and walked away. Either they had received somewhere about what they expected or they were too disheartened to make any fuss. Others would jerk upright and stare at the paper with their mouths open and their eyes bulging before they made the usual comment of: 'Well, I'll be damned! Just look what the blasted old sod have put in for me!'

I had expected to find men with a prayer on their lips when at work underground, but I soon discovered that there was a lot of swearing and very little praying there. Some of the men were convinced that the sledge would not hit so hard or the horse pull so well if a little swearing were not done, just to help. 'Erny' was by no means an isolated example. When he hit his head against the top he swore, when he pinched his fingers with a stone, or hit his shoulder against the side, or knocked his lamp in the dark he swore, and as one or other of these things was happening to him all his working day, it became second nature for him to swear at anybody or anything. One night he swore in the railway waiting-room and was summoned. He vowed it was unjust – 'because I wasn't swearing proper, like'.

'What did you say, then, Erny?' I asked him.

'The train was late, see mun?' he explained, 'and I only asked the porter, "When the h— is that b— train coming to this b— station?" Just like a chap would ask the b— haulier about the b— tram, like. An' I got to pay two b— quid for that. B— shame, I calls it.'

Yet I do not believe he would willingly have hurt a fly, and I have known him give his last sixpence to a tramp.

On Friday of that week I saw the 'measurers' for the first time and learned a little about the method of paying for colliery work. In small seams such as this one it was necessary to rip the top down, so that height would be made to allow of the passage of horses and trams. This ripping was paid for by the inch of thickness per yard forward. About six feet wide would have to be ripped. Twopence an inch was the price here, so that if we ripped one yard forward and it was two feet thick, we got four shillings. In this price was included the time for boring holes, the cost of powder, the use of your own machine, and the time taken for breaking the stones small enough to get them into the waste behind and making a wall of them so that they would support the roof. The posts that support the sides of the roadway – none others – are paid for at sixpence each. Then there would be the price for filling the larger coal. Any coal that falls through the smaller screens is not paid for. I believe the price at this colliery was two and fivepence a ton. This price varies at almost every colliery according to the thickness of the seam or the difficulty in working it. The big seams of nine to eighteen feet are lower in price than the small seams that range from a yard down to eighteen inches or even a foot in thickness, or thinness.

Each colliery has its own price-list which is supposed to govern payments. The price on these lists is constant, but after the items have been totalled up there is a percentage added, which varies according to the agreement in operation at that time. Thus, when the percentage rate ruling the coalfield is twenty-five %, five shillings would be added to each pound earned on the price list.

On that Friday morning I had noticed that my mate was continually adding little items to a list he had chalked on our curling-box. These curling-boxes are like very wide and large sugar-scoops, and are used for carrying the smaller lumps of coal. John had written several queer figures and words on this tin box, and seemed quite satisfied with his markings, then he went on cutting coal.

Then some lights showed higher up the heading, and John said, 'Here they comes. The measurers', in a tone that gave no hint of welcome.

When the new arrivals got near to us they made a deal of noise. One shouted, 'Where's your ripping mark, John?' at the same time as another bawled. 'How many posts here, John?' There were five of them, and all seemed anxious to talk at once. But John was not perturbed. He was wise to that game, and rose from his knees slowly while he waved his hand to the side and stated, 'Six posts.'

Three of the newcomers started to speak in English and the other two in Welsh. John pushed past them, and did not say a word in reply. Then he knelt down before his chalked list and called out each item singly. He refused to mention the next until he was sure the last one had been booked. One man measured the rippings and shouted his findings to the under-manager. That did not suit John. He insisted on another measuring, and held his lamp to the tape so that he proved himself to be right. During this argument the fireman who was scratching the posts to show they had been paid for had been shouting that he could only find five: 'What d'you mean by this game, eh? There's only five new posts here.' John walked across and counted the six to him very deliberately.

Another fireman was bothering John about the football team, while one of the others tried to get him to argue about the Cymanfa Canu – or singing festival – that had been held on the previous Saturday. I do not know what the other said in Welsh, but he talked with scarcely a pause. They were wasting their breath, for John closed his mind to them until they had finished his items.

When they saw John had finished his list, they paused, and my mate – seeing the under-manager's book still open – suddenly remembered another thing.

'Aye,' he said, 'the coal's sticking to the top pretty bad here, aye it is. There's allowance on the list for that, ain't there? What about some for me this week?'

The under-manager frowned, then asked sharply: 'How many trams have you got full?'

John gave the number – we had less than the previous week.

'You're down,' said the under-manager. 'We daren't give any allowances unless you've got enough coal to cover it.'

'And last week,' John answered very slowly, 'you told me as you couldn't give me nothing for it because I had a lot of coal full.'

The under-manager snapped the book closed, rose from his sitting, and walked away, with the fireman hurrying behind him. About one minute later we could hear another argument starting in the next working-place.

John told me afterwards about their methods. He was a Welshman, and had to choose his English words carefully. He considered them bullies who were intent on avoiding payment for work done. Their intention was, so he explained, to badger the workman in every way, to talk about his interests, or frighten or fluster him – anything to make him forget some

item in the measuring. After they had once passed it would be very difficult to get paid for it. It would be claimed that the work had been
measured and that ample witnesses were at hand to show the man had
had a chance to book it, but had not done so.

I noticed on that first Friday – as I have done ever since – that there are
plenty who solicit help from the miner. Beggars were outside the pay-
office, holding out laces, moth balls, or lavender packets – anything for an
excuse – and almost every pay-day some organization had an appeal or
flag day.

There was a large group waiting to see the manager to get their money
made up to the minimum wage. They had to go into his office and
answer questions as to why they had not filled more coal, and so on.
There was nothing courteous about the questions or the way they were
put, but the answers had to be given very humbly. Even humility did not
always succeed, for I know that many men had to go home short of the
wage that the law is supposed to enforce.

The method was to promise to give it next week, then the week after,
and on in that way until they would argue that it was so long ago that they
could not recall the exact happenings. Some men went without what was
due to them because they feared victimization. Another man who was
afraid to ask for what were his dues kept count of the amount he was
short, and seemed to get some satisfaction by telling us, confidentially,
that the company already owed him about forty pounds.

I do believe that they tried to avoid letting any man go short of his pay
if they judged him likely to make a fuss over it, but occasionally a man
would refuse to let them avoid payment, and the committee would be
compelled to take action. This would take time, and after a series of
delays and evasions the case might be taken to court. The usual method
then was to pay on this case before it was judged and leave the others still
unsettled.

The man who forced a payment in this manner was wise if he tried to
find a new job, and it would be very probable that he would have to go
some distance, for he would be marked in that area. . . .

After the double shift was going properly, rumours started that they were
going to try coal-cutting machines in that colliery. These machines were
rare in South Wales then, and there were none working in our valley or
anywhere quite near. Tommy and I were set to open a cutting-face for
this machine. It had to be about one hundred and fifty yards long, and as
straight as possible. There was a commotion over that machine-face;
several times a day we had to put our lamps in a row so that the officials
could survey which was behind and which in front. There was no question of working only eight hours at our place then; one man who wanted
to go away and would not work on was sacked.

If Tommy would not get to work in time in the morning, he made up
for it at finishing time. He was never anxious to go out from work. He
always had something he would do after all the others had gone, and it

mostly took an hour or more to complete. Then, as we tramped over the mountain together he would tell me of his ambitions.

Tommy did not intend being a miner for long, and he wanted to make as much money from it as he could in a short time. He was trying to save quickly, for there was a little cottage at Blackpill that he wanted very badly, because it was handy for watching the fishing-nets, and he was thinking of getting married.

He succeeded in the marrying part of this programme. She was a girl from that village. I remember that we worked the Friday together, and so late into the Friday afternoon that we only had time to tramp home, get more food, see that our money had been paid properly, and return to work. There was not even time to bath, for we had to be back across the mountain by eleven that night and ready for the night-shift.

We had twenty-four hours of hard slogging straight off, and Tommy was getting married on the Saturday morning. That was no way to treat the marriage ceremony, nor a young bride. I was too tired to go to the house to see him off, so I got a chair by our front door and waited to wave when he went by. I was sound asleep sitting up when they passed, and never saw them, but it did not matter, for Tommy himself was fast asleep in the car, and they told me that they could not keep him awake long enough to have their photographs taken.

While we had been preparing the long coal-face, things had been coming into the colliery yard: thick electric cables and bigger switch-boxes, as well as other parts of machines that we had never seen the like of before. We examined them well on Sunday afternoons, and made vague but hopeful attempts to explain their construction and use.

Then the expert arrived. He was a very energetic fellow, with a suit of overalls and a Yankee accent. He knew how to fit those complicated parts together, for he was the staff man from the coal-cutter works, and had only recently come across from America; but he did not know how to carry a lamp, so someone had to walk alongside him and show him light. The next day he arrived near where I was at work, and the parts of the machine were there before him. After a lot of loud shouting and heavy lifting, we got it fitted together. Then a long, rubber, snake-like thing was trailed down the coal-face and we were warned: 'Say, you fellows. If you're wise you'll keep away from that thar cable. Thar's enough electric juice in thar to shrivel the hides off on yuh.'

Having no wish to shrivel just then, we obeyed. The majority obeyed to the extreme, and kept as far away as possible, but the hum of an engine has always been music to my ears, and this powerful machine interested me very much. I watched his every move, and asked a lot of questions. His bluster was only the veneer over a decent instinct, and he showed me very willingly all he could.

It was a powerful machine, and seemed immense in comparison to the limited space it had to work in. It was over ten feet long to the extent of the jib, eighteen inches high, and over two feet wide. It weighed three and a half tons, and was so heavily steel plated that no falls of roof would damage it. It had a hundred yards of electric cable; thick cable this and flexible; always called the running-cable, but I never saw it run much—in fact, it was very hard work dragging it along the coal-face.

The chain had thirty-eight detachable picks screwed into it, and revolved at about three hundred revolutions a minute around the four-feet-nine-long jib. It undercut the coal to the depth of the jib – four feet nine – and travelled forward at about a yard a minute, being drawn by a steel rope fitted to a sloping post and moving along on a steel slide. It made a terrific noise when cutting, and the dust was enough to choke anyone very close by. It was a waste of effort to speak when near it – the only way to explain was to wave your lamp and make signs.

What a collier could do by working hard all day, this machine would accomplish in two minutes. The holing had been such hard and monotonous work that I considered this machine a boon, for it did the very hard slogging for us. The drawback was in the added danger, because we could not hear the roof cracking, and with such a large undercut there was the likelihood of it falling any second. Timber could not be set so close, either, because space had to be left for the passage of the machine.

Some of the men took a long time to learn that they had to keep their working-place straight and clear of posts. They seemed to imagine that this powerful machine was made of elastic, and could be turned at any angle.

If a post or stone gob was left in the way, the machine would shift it all right, but there might be hundreds of tons above that was steadied by the gob or post, and that would come down in the shifting.

A man who had worked with machines in the North of England had been persuaded to come there to work the machine. He had been offered more money than he was earning elsewhere, but was soon regretting the change. It was a type of machine that he had never seen before, and the seam was strange; he could not become accustomed to it.

The coal-cutter seemed to dislike him too, for it would stop working on almost every occasion that he was trying to handle it. I remember watching him on the sly one day when the machine was stuck and he thought no one was about. He took some stones from the gob and slammed them at the steel sides of the machine. As each stone hit it he growled: 'Now go, you Yankee b—, you.'

It made no difference; his luck was out, and he was disheartened. He went back twice with the excuse that the noise made him ill, then got drunk a few times and was ill in reality. He begged to be taken off the job, and the demonstrator wanted to go back to the firm, but had to get the machine going properly before he did so.

He suggested to the manager that he try to persuade 'that young feller that was with me the first day. He's the likeliest coon for the job that I've set me eyes on in this area so far.'

I refused at first, for the work was reputed to be very dangerous, even among men who had spent a lifetime in danger, but the throb of the machine was in the pulse of my blood, and I agreed at last – after I had been guaranteed a day wage above the minimum rate and a lot of overtime. The American gave me a booklet, explained the workings of the machine and the electric circuit, then I had a trial run, during which he stated that I handled it almost as well as he did himself.

'Born for the job,' was his comment, 'and we've bin wasting time with that other goosoon.'

The manager warned me to be careful how I handled it, because it was worth well over a thousand pounds, yet the minute after he told me he wanted that machine pushed for all I was worth, because the output would very soon all depend on it, for they were abandoning hand-cutting.

I was given a blue paper vesting authority for the handling of machinery and electricity, and found myself a coal-cutter operator with the sincere, if profane, good wishes of the departing American.

I was given the chance to pick my mates for the work, and although Tommy did not like the new job, he preferred doing it to parting with me, so he came. His job was posting behind the machine, and he was helped by another young chap whose name was shortened to Hutch for our convenience, and who was never called anything else. He was a good worker, and not afraid of anything under the ground.

The fourth member of the working gang was George Bennett. He came from the borders of Herefordshire, and was a year older than myself. We were all in the early twenties, and were but little concerned with the risks we were running. Every hour of the day I was learning things about that machine, and in spare hours I used to study the diagrams in the booklet. I had to find out from experience, and that was often painful. I learned to respect electricity – but only after I had been knocked down by it twice and had days when my wrists and ankles were made useless by the shocks.

Stones fell from the roof and sliced through the outer casing of that thick cable; then there came a flash of flame and the switches blew out. I had my waistcoat partly burnt while on my back on one occasion, and Hutch's trousers were singed by the current that was leaking along the rope. Picks wedged in the chain, and we had to cut out sections to replace them; to splice the rope that drew the machine; to adjust the sprocket springs on the haulage gear; to replace blownout switches, and to see that the score of holes for the oil and grease were working as they should. On one occasion we were on stop, and thought the electric fingers that touched the controller were to blame. We opened the machine and rubbed the faulty finger with a rough stone, then with the striking side of a matchbox, because we had no sand-paper. When the chain started to fly round again and the roar assured us that we had repaired the fault, we shook hands with one another very gravely to show our appreciation of our own skill and ingenuity.

The mechanic and the electrician were only there on the day-shift. It would have taken more than two hours to get them there after that, so we had to manage, and they knew little more about this strange machine than we did; but we were using it for quite sixteen hours of each day, so we were learning faster than they were, and we were accustomed to being underground, while they dreaded and detested coming there at all.

Very soon the management started to pit the machine against the men. There was a speeding up in all the jobs. When the demonstrator had started this machine, the manager had been delighted with a cut of a hundred yards long in the eight hours. Cutting is only part of the work – oiling and greasing must be done constantly, picks have to be changed, timber has to be kept tight up, and the machine has to be guided and stayered to keep alongside the coal. We learned how to do these things quickly, and we were a gang that worked to answer one another very well, so that in little more than a month we managed to cut a hundred and sixty yards in a shift. The officials made a fuss about this new record, and professed to be proud of us, but they were very sarcastic if we cut any less in a shift afterwards.

It was necessary to wear leather knee-pads because we wore through thick trousers in one shift, and our knees were stiff even after a rest at the week-end. About this period the week-end break lasted from two o'clock on the Saturday until six o'clock on Sunday morning. We never knew when we would finish work. Every day was an emergency. The officials would be behind the colliers all day hurrying them to clear the coal, else they would delay the machine, then they would hurry back to warn us to hurry up, or the colliers would be clear and waiting for coal. That was the way of it every day – rush us up to the colliers, and rush them so that they should not delay us.

Soon the cutting-face was extended to almost five hundred yards, and we always had a stretch waiting for us. For months we worked a double shift each day, crawling on our knees under low height for sixteen busy hours. Several times I went to work on the Sunday morning and returned home late on the Monday afternoon. One week I was in bed only eight hours in all. We had to start for work at various hours, whenever it suited the management. We went to call for Tommy one evening, and his wife said that she had failed to wake him, so she asked us to try. We took off our working boots and went upstairs. We shook him roughly, but he only grunted; we lifted him up and punched him, but he did not mind. Then we carried him from the bed on to the oilcloth so that we could pummel him easier; but it made no impression, he still snored away, and so we had to put him back into bed and leave him to that glorious sleep – with very sincere regrets on our side.

Winifred Griffiths
*shop assistant**

Winifred Griffiths was born in 1895 at Overton, near Basingstoke, Hampshire. Her father worked at a local paper-mill for 30s. a week,

* From *One Woman's Story*, unpublished autobiography.

was a Methodist lay preacher and brought up his family in a strong puritanical tradition. Winifred left the local church elementary school at fourteen, having been top of her class; the High School at Basingstoke was considered, but rejected on grounds of cost. Her first work was at Burberry's gaberdine factory as an apprentice at 3s. a week, plus 2s. 6d. for rail-travel, which she left for work with a ready-made tailoring firm (6½d. for all the stitching in a lined suit jacket). From here, she went into domestic service as a house-maid at East Oakley House for four happy years and, after the outbreak of the First World War, became a grocery assistant in a Co-operative Stores in order to release men for military service. During the war she met and married Jim Griffiths, then a Welsh miner, who was to have a spectacular career in the Labour Party as Party Agent for Llanelly (1922), President of the South Wales Miners Federation (1934), M.P. for Llanelly (1936), Minister of National Insurance (1945), Colonial Secretary (1950) and Secretary of State for Wales (1964). During these later years Winifred Griffiths was herself active in local politics and in social work.

The following extract from her unpublished autobiography describes her experiences in shop-work during the first war.

I become a socialist

In May 1914 I had my nineteenth birthday. I had spent three years at East Oakley House and life still went on in a fairly pleasant way. One day I was glancing through a magazine which had been left around the house when I chanced to read a short article by an economist which I shall always remember. It caused a profound change in my thinking about life. I had never met a socialist and yet this short article was to make a socialist of me. The article gave as the author's opinion that the world should and could be organized so that every able-bodied person did a fair share of useful work and that everybody – children, the aged and the disabled included – should have a fair share of the necessities of life and of the results of human labour. In other words the rule should be 'From each according to his ability, and to each according to his need.' The writer also gave as his opinion that a great many people worked very hard at tasks that were unnecessary and did not contribute to the common good, instancing those who worked to provide luxuries for the rich, while the poor were in dire need.

The impact on me of this article was something akin to a religious conversion. It changed my thinking about life so completely that I no longer felt the urge of personal ambition. Henceforth I had a guiding light which gave life a new meaning. I imagined a society in which men and women worked together gladly to provide all that was needed to banish poverty and distress, and equally gladly went without luxuries and services they had been used to, in order to further the common good. It seemed very important to me that I should bring my own life as far as possible into line with this ideal. I suddenly saw my present occupation as a useless one – doing things for people that they could quite well do for themselves and helping them to sustain a standard of life completely unjustified while so much poverty existed. For the moment I could see no way out, but the way out was to come more quickly than I expected and that through the terrible calamity of world war.

The outbreak of war

Increasingly as the days of that summer of 1914 wore on I noticed a certain unease in the bearing of my employers. Dr Scott especially showed signs of anxiety and sometimes of agitation. Nellie the cook heard from a relative in the Army of a rumour that was going the rounds that there might be a war. I recollected something I had read about the Germans building a Navy more powerful than ours. Then came the news that members of a distant royal family had been shot somewhere in Europe, and talk about the Triple Alliance and treaties and Russia. Early in August suddenly the tension snapped – we were at war with Germany.

In those far-off days of 1914 – long before the coming of radio – our only means of getting news was through the papers and by word of mouth. Even in our large house there was no telephone and Dr Scott began to make it a practice to visit the post office at least once a day to get the news from London. When the papers were delivered at the house in the morning we all made a bee-line for them in order to scan the headlines before Dr Scott came down and carried them off to his study. During these first months I had no doubt that our country was in the right. We heard of the invasion of Belgium followed by atrocity stories and soon our picture of the enemy was of people less than human. We heard of the call-up of Reservists, and some middle-aged, rather untidy soldiers appeared in the locality – whose duty was to 'guard the bridges' over the railway. At first I could not understand who they were supposed to guard them against, but soon I realized that there was widespread suspicion that there might be spies and saboteurs in our midst . . .

In the meantime the war was changing people's lives. There was a great deal of talk about 'jobs of national importance' for women as well as men. Surely soon *my* chance would come. One day Mrs Scott spoke to me, letting me know that she knew how I was feeling. She told me that the manager of the Co-operative Stores in Basingstoke was on the look-out for young women to train to take the places of grocery assistants who were joining the Forces. She was prepared to give me a very good reference if I would like to apply. I accepted her offer with alacrity and in due course was taken on in the grocery department of the Co-operative Stores.

Thus I left my job at East Oakley House which I had held for four pleasant years. In the end I felt sorrow at leaving both the family and the staff and especially did I regret leaving my little room in the tower. I went into lodgings in town where I shared a room and bed with another girl, paying 12s. 6d. a week for board and lodging. My mother did my washing, for which I gave her 1s. per week. My wage was £1 so I was left with 6s. 6d. to cover everything else including running my bicycle. The landlady was kindly and the food adequate though, of course, not at all like we had at East Oakley House.

I found on my arrival at the Co-op that I was not expected to serve in the shop right away but was to have some time to get used to the variety of goods and the prices. During this period I worked in what was called 'Dispatch'. This was a room behind the shop in which orders were put up. In charge of this room was a little man with a fair moustache. He was not at all formidable as a 'boss', but was quiet and firm and slightly humorous and organized the work very well. The first job I was put to do was weighing sugar. Sacks of sugar were stored in a loft over Dispatch. This sugar was tipped down a shute to a bench below. It was my job to stand all day by this bench opening bags, filling sugar into them with a scoop and weighing them in one, two, three and four pounds. As a variation I sometimes switched over to lump sugar and when sufficient sugar had been done soda was sent down the shute. Soda was a commodity bought by most housewives before the advent of soap powders. After a few days at this rather monotonous task I was allowed to help with putting up orders. A very large number of these orders were from country customers. These were collected in late afternoon by the carriers who plied between villages and town.

Friday evening was a busy time in the shop, as many members came then to collect groceries and to pay bills. As bad luck would have it I was sent down for the first time to help on the grocery counter on a Friday evening. I was so bewildered that I am afraid I made a fine mess of things. I had to take payment of bills and the method of receipting had not been explained to me. When trying to serve customers I did not know where things were kept, nor yet had I memorized all the prices. I had not acquired the knack of making tidy packets for goods like dried fruit, rice and tapioca, and numerous others which were kept loose in drawers and had to be weighed as needed. To crown all, most customers expected their goods to be done up in a large paper parcel.

It seems now at this time, when all goods are packeted, and self-service is the order of the day, almost incredible the amount of work involved in serving just one cusomer under the old conditions. We sold some goods for which there was no room in the shop, such things as potatoes, corn for chickens, barley meal, bran and other animal feeding-stuffs which had to be measured in pint, quart or gallon measures and packed in paper bags. Another article was common salt, which came to the shop in long thick bars, from which we had to cut a thick slice to be sold for 1½d. Yet another commodity was a long bar of household soap which might be bought whole or in halves or quarters and, for a change from solids, there was draught vinegar, to be drawn off into a measure and transferred to customer's own bottle or jug. All these goods and others too were stored in rooms behind the shop and had to be fetched and weighed or measured as needed. The shop assistant's job was not a light one in those days, neither was it a clean one. So many things to weigh and so much to fetch and carry played havoc with our hands and with our overalls. We had a little retreat where we could wash our hands, in cold water, but too many trips to 'Scarborough', as it came to be called, were apt to be frowned upon. So we just wiped our hands on our overalls – and that was that! I soon learned to be wary of 'Committee men' who sometimes appeared without warning, and were suspected by the employees of 'snooping'. At the back of the grocery premises was a baker's where not only bread but confectionery was made. One of our shop windows was given over to a display of cakes which could be bought at the provision counter. In course of time I was given the job of dressing this window and I found it a pleasant interlude.

Just after I was taken on at the Co-op two other women also made a start. Both had come long distances, one from Somerset and the other from Yorkshire. Jennie, the Yorkshire lass, was soon the life and soul of the place. In no time she became, without doubt, the most popular member of staff. She was good-looking, vivacious, cheerful and kind. Obviously life was a great adventure: exciting things were always happening. Life's little incidents took on a magical quality when Jennie recounted them. No one could be cross or gloomy when she was around. I was thrilled when she asked me to come out with her to an evening class, or to the cinema on our half-day, or to church or a walk on Sunday. The Co-op had found 'digs' for her but the food was in short supply and soon she was looking for another place to stay. An elderly woman, who lived just opposite the shop, offered her a room. She found on going to visit Mrs Diddums that there was really place for two, and that two sharing would pay less. Jennie asked me if I would like to join her. We would share a room and have all our meals provided for 10s. a week each, on condition that we gave a hand with the housework. So we clinched the deal and moved in . . .

At the shop we were always busy for there never seemed to be a complete staff. Men left to join up and as yet the management could not imagine they could get along with women only. In years prior to the war recruits to the grocery and provision trade had been required to serve several years' apprenticeship and afterwards a long period as ordinary assistants before they could become 'first hand', that is to be in charge of either the grocery or provision counter. Hence the Co-op tried whenever possible to replace the men who left for the army by other men. One day there appeared a young Welshman, who obviously knew his job very well, although this was the first post he had ever taken outside his native Wales. He was a pleasant bright-eyed little fellow in his early twenties who soon became popular with the staff. I discovered in conversation with him that he had his serious side and he had thought quite deeply about life and that he was a socialist. I was quite thrilled to meet a real live socialist, for I had known, in a sense, that I was one ever since I read the economist's article that had so affected me when I was at East Oakley. Now I was to be persuaded of wider implications of socialist thought. Up until now I had been a loyal supporter of the war effort, only wishing I could play a more useful part in helping the country. But now under the influence of this young Welshman, I was to revise my ideas. He contended that the ghastly war was the outcome of the capitalist system and that socialists ought to resist it. Of course it took time for me to be wholly convinced, but Edgar lent me books and pamphlets to read, and gradually I came round to thinking he was right.

Edgar soon joined the crowd of us from the shop who went together to the cinema on Thursday evenings and sometimes on other little outings. The Women's Co-operative Guild was very good to the staff in arranging little farewell parties for the boys who left to join the Army. Daisy, the girl from Somerset, was in digs with a girl called Dolly, who worked in a rather high-class grocery store in town. She would bring Dolly along with her to our outings. In this way Edgar met Dolly and they became very friendly and soon they were as good as engaged.

Looking back it seems as if we were all there together for a long time, but in reality it was only a very short period. Change was in the air, first one left, then another. Conscription was now in force and all the youngsters had to go in turn. Edgar had his calling-up papers and had to go back to Wales. He had at first some thoughts of resistance as a so-called C.O. but it did not come off. I think Dolly had not developed any understanding of that point of view, and her attitude was probably the deciding factor. Anyhow he joined the Army. Meanwhile in the shop still more changes. Suddenly we heard the manager was leaving, not for the Army or anything like that, but to take on a business of his own in a little town some few miles away. Worse was to come. He persuaded Jennie and Daisy to leave and to take jobs with him at his new shop. This to me was a great shock. To lose Jennie was to lose the last bit of sunshine from our little circle. I really felt quite dejected. Now some of Mrs Diddums's family were coming home and she needed my room, so I decided to approach Dolly and see if I might join her in place of Daisy. Soon this was fixed up and Dolly and I became room-mates and pals. Then one day I was surprised to receive a letter and a parcel of books from Wales, from a young man who it appeared was a close friend of Edgar. This young man was a miner and an active socialist and he signed himself 'Yours in the cause, J. Griffiths'. Thus through the pages of a letter and the loan of some books I met the man who was to be my husband. From then onward we corresponded regularly, expressing in our letters our ideas and ideals about the world and its problems. It seemed that we had a good deal in common. Later in the year Dolly had an invitation to come down to Wales when Edgar had leave from the Army, and I received an invitation from J. Griffiths to come down with her and meet the socialist group to which both he and Edgar belonged.

All my life had been spent in Hampshire in rural and semi-rural surroundings. I knew nothing of the scars that mining and heavy industry could make on nature's fair face. So from that point of view this first visit to Wales was quite an experience. I shall never forget the impression of desolation I had when passing through Landore, the district outside Swansea which had been blasted and scarred by industry and left denuded of trees and green things – an area which nature seemed to have abandoned and where even weeds would not grow. Then on to the mining valley which was our destination. Here was a little town in a valley which was pleasant and green in spite of several collieries and accompanying slag heaps. Here we were to experience our first contacts with the Welsh way of life. We learned about the hard work and the danger of the pits, of the dirt that was brought back to the homes, where miners' wives and daughters waged an incessant war on coal dust and grime, keeping tremendous fires burning to boil hot water for baths, to dry pit clothes and to cook meals. At that time there were few homes with baths, the tub in front of the fire was the usual thing. Then there were the chapels, still well attended in those days, when a good preacher was a great man in the community, and the singing in the chapels and the eisteddfods connected with them formed an important part of the social life.

We paid a visit to the socialist club – The White House – and met the comrades there. I was thrilled and thought I was getting near to the heart of things that mattered. Near the end of our visit, after Edgar had returned to the Army, Jim and I came to an understanding as to how we felt towards each other. From then on we considered it an engagement, though it was not formalized with a ring – as we did not believe in such conventional arrangements!

I become a 'first hand' on provisions but give it up to go to live in Wales

And so, for Dolly and me, an end to our holiday adventure in Wales, and a return to work. For me there was no longer much joy in work. Almost all the staff from the manager down had changed, and I came to the conclusion I also would seek a change. There was a grocery and provision business in town called Walkers Stores which was advertising for a girl to learn the work of the provision counter. I applied and got the job. There were two men, the first and second provision hands, on the counter and I was to assist them and learn the job so that I could take the place of the second hand when he would be leaving to join up. I had to keep the shelves filled up with stock of tinned and bottled goods; I had to weigh up lard and margarine in pounds and half pounds, I learned the knack of patting up butter on a stone slab with pats kept in a bucket of cold water, and of cutting up fifty-six-pound cheeses into sections easy to handle; and I had to acquire the skill to cut up sides of bacon into different parts to be sold at differing prices. Soon the second hand left and I officially took his place. By now my immediate boss, the first hand, was the only male left in the stores, except the manager and the warehouseman. Before long I learned to my consternation that he also was due to join up. When he eventually left, the manager took it for granted that I should step into his place. So after only two or three months of training, as against several years that the old-time apprentice would have had, I found myself in charge of the provision side in a very busy stores, where we sold thirty sides of bacon a week when we could get them and as many cooked hams, as well as the whole range of other provisions. To help me I had as second hand a cheerful hard-working girl who had had some experience in other stores. The shop opened every morning at 9 o'clock and closed at 7 P.M. on the first three days of the week, at one o'clock on Thursdays, 8 P.M. on Fridays and 9 P.M. on Saturdays. We had an hour for lunch and twenty minutes for tea but often worked for some time after the shop closed. We had a till on our counter and took the cash ourselves. It was of course before the time of automatic reckoning-machines so we had to enter each amount as it was paid in. When we had finished taking money the roll had to be removed and the items totted up. If they did not correspond with the contents of the till we had to try and try again to get the total right. I remember an occasion when there was a great deal of fuss and some veiled accusations, not on our counter, but on the grocery, where five girls were serving. It was found that they were 10s. short. Each went over the roll in turn to try to find where the error was, but without success. It threw everyone who used the till under suspicion . . .

With wounded Canadian soldiers around, with train-loads of wounded passing through the railway station, and with films of the war, with its mud and slaughter, being shown in the cinema, the terrible nature of this conflict was brought home to us. It had a very depressing effect and hung all the time, like a cloud, in the background of one's mind. By now I was convinced that it had come about as a result of the 'capitalist system' under which we lived, and now to have something on which to pin the blame seemed to ease the burden a little. Jim wrote to me regularly and I answered every letter. We poured out our protests about the war, and the condition of the world around us and about the way people were oppressed. We professed our firm belief in socialism as the shining light which would guide mankind to peace and happiness – 'When the war drums throb no longer and the battle flags are furled, in the Parliament of man the Federation of the World.' Such was our faith in socialism and our belief in the essential goodness of human nature that we were convinced that after the war people must turn to socialism, and then 'all would be better than well'.

As for our own plans we had thought in terms of a two-year engagement. However it was quite a strain living so far from each other and the life I led was very limiting. I began to think of the possibility of getting a job in Wales so that Jim and I could at least see each other more often. My parents naturally enough did not care for this idea, although Jim had been up to Hampshire on a visit and they had been won over to accepting him as a desirable son-in-law. The snag was of course that to them, at that point of time, south-west Wales was a great distance away. I had always lived near home, had visited them often and been on call if my mother had fallen ill. However I was determined, and in the event went off to Wales and found myself a job in the Co-op in Llanelly, a town not many miles from the mining village where Jim lived.

I found digs with a youngish married couple who lived in a substantial house in a road which consisted of about a hundred terraced houses, all as like as postage stamps. There was no front garden, one stepped out of the front door straight on to the pavement. I had fondly hoped that there might be a bathroom, but alas the only water tap was on a standpipe in the scullery, and the water-closet was at the end of the tiny garden. However I was kindly treated and made to feel one of the family. I had a comfortable bed and there was always a good fire in the living room. The house was very well furnished according to the ideas of the period. The kitchen fireplace was surrounded by quantities of brass which looked wonderful when shining brightly but needed to be cleaned at least once a week, while the Welsh dresser of the open type was covered in china, which being exposed to the dust from the fireplace, had to be washed frequently. There was a small middle room, furnished with table, chairs and a small organ, and this was often used to sit in. The front parlour was very grand with a wonderful suite of furniture, which looked very comfortable but was never used.

The branch of the Co-op at which I worked was in the Station Road, a gloomy and depressing road with small shabby shops, and at the bottom before one reached the railway station were two tin-works, one on either side of the road. Dust and grime from these works spread all over the immediate neighbourhood. This general environment of dust, grime and shabbiness seemed to have had a bad effect on those responsible for running the Co-operative Stores in the town and more especially this particular branch.

When I first started at the shop I really thought I must be dreaming. I could hardly believe it was possible to carry on a business in such a slipshod and slovenly fashion. The people I had to work with were pleasant and friendly, but my liking for them could not obscure the fact that they just had no idea how to run a shop, let alone how to handle food with the most elementary care for hygiene. There was no organization of the work. Fittings were only filled with goods if someone felt like doing the job. Otherwise, when serving, we must fetch all we needed from the warehouse behind the shop. The window dressings were never changed and the only concession to a provision counter was a marble slab, hidden behind a mound of tins and equipped with just a knife for cutting up either bacon or fats. I wondered how I could ever manage to work in such a place. However I got used to it in time, and tried to make the best of a bad job . . .

A great many of the Co-op members were the wives of steel- and tin-plate-workers. When I heard stories of the large earnings many were receiving, albeit for very hard work, I did feel that as good trade unionists and co-operators they should have seen that we were paid more than a pittance for the long hours we put in at the shop. And a pittance I certainly thought it was. Twenty-seven shillings per week was not much to live on when prices were rising. I paid 7s. per week for my lodgings and bought my own food, and I must perforce save some money if only to get home for a holiday. I also must save to get married some time in the future. I therefore cut my eating down to three simple meals a day, cutting out supper entirely. It took a bit of doing as I was young and working hard and often felt hungry. One of the worst things was not being able to afford fruit. I soon came to realize that very few other shop girls in the town had to live on the small money they earned. Most lived at home and their earnings were mainly for clothes and pocket money. However the monotony of my rather impecunious life was relieved once a fortnight when I was able to visit Ammanford. Jim had been active in politics since he was a lad in his teens. He had become the first secretary of the newly formed Trades and Labour Council for the Ammanford district. This entailed frequent visits to Llanelly. Meetings he attended were held there on Saturdays. Afterwards he would meet me at 9 o'clock when I finished work at the shop. We then had just time to catch the last train up the valley. Owing to wartime restrictions this train only went as far as Pontardulais leaving the last five miles of our journey to be made on foot, except when we could 'cadge' a lift in the guard's van of a goods train. In Ammanford I always stayed with our good friend Mrs Jenkins who lived in the same road as Jim and his family. Sometimes on Sunday morning we would attend the English church. In the afternoon we would roam the mountains or the countryside, and in the evening there was the Workers Forum, the socialist debating society, which Jim and others had got going in 'The White House'. In Ammanford I made acquaintance with Jim's relatives who were always very kind to me, though I now realize that they were probably concerned as to what kind of wife I might make for Jim with my different background and, perhaps, rather unconventional ideas.

I enjoyed these visits, but I found my life in Llanelly and especially my job, increasingly frustrating. Jim and I began to discuss the possibility of getting married in the autumn – we should by then have completed the two years 'engagement'. Our difficulty was money. It was not easy to save and I must at least have a new suit to be married in and there would be fares to travel home for the wedding, and a few other expenses, however simple the ceremony. Jim had no savings to speak of, although like me he was now trying to put something by. Before meeting me he had never felt any great interest in money matters. Like a good Welsh son, at that time, he handed over his pay to his mother. She not only kept him, but bought all his clothes, and he received back from her just pocket money. Most of this went on books and socialism! However we came to the conclusion that we could just about get together enough money to marry in October – and so we did . . .

Rosina Whyatt
*munitions-factory worker**

Rosina Whyatt was born in Somerset in 1888, the daughter of a farm worker who brought up a family of six on a wage of 16s. a week (raised to £1 in 1916). After working for some years as a domestic servant, she went into munitions work at Luton in 1915 and quickly disclosed unsuspected abilities as an organizer and administrator. She became a deeply committed trade unionist, and in 1918 became a full-time officer of the Workers' Union (later the Transport and General Workers' Union) until her retirement in 1951. She died in 1971.

Although written in the third person, Miss Whyatt's account is strictly autobiographical. She speaks, simply and naïvely, for the thousands of women for whom the First World War brought a new involvement in society, greatly increased earnings and a measure of independence and emancipation.

Miss Whyatt's manuscript was kindly brought to my attention by Dr Richard Hyman, School of Industrial Studies, University of Warwick.

Jenny had to clock-in at the factory at eight o'clock in the morning. This was new to her, and it was a comforting thought that she would not have to get up at five or six o'clock as she had done during her domestic-service days. She would start work at 8 A.M. and finish at 8 P.M. What would she find in this great new venture? She had already a feeling of a new freedom, and of time to think. While Jenny had been in domestic service she had always felt a driving force of something unexplainable; in actual fact she had been told many times that she ought to be doing something better than domestic service. The only book that she had ever read had been a gift at Christmas from one of the families with whom she had lived; it was called *The Wide, Wide World*, by Ethel Wetherall – a story of the hardships and troubles of a girl called Ellen. She had won her battles, and Jenny could win hers. She would have time now to read, and to learn something of the world she was stepping into.

She arrived at the factory quite early. It was called Chaul End, a very large one-storey building just outside the town of Luton – for safety reasons, she learnt later. She had to find out where to clock-in; having done this she was taken to the dressing room, where she was given a

* Unpublished autobiographical extract.

fireproof overall and cap that must cover the head, together with rubber shoes. Not a hair of the head must be loose; no pins, brooches or rings must be worn, in fact metal of any kind was strictly prohibited. Jenny was then taken down long corridors to the room where she was to work. She was given boxes of small brass parts for fuses to be gauged and checked for rejects. She was an apt pupil and soon learned what she had to do and how to do it. Her first impression was one of wonder; she had never seen so many people in her life. There seemed to be hundreds of girls and women doing the same thing, others buzzing about hither and thither doing Jenny knew not what; but she soon realized that this was war work, and every available person was wanted on munitions. Notices were posted everywhere telling the workers where to go in the event of a raid by Zeppelins or other aircraft . . .

Looking around, Jenny was puzzled to see so many girls with their fingers bandaged, but she very soon discovered the reason. The brass parts had sharp edges which cut the fingers, and she herself soon had her own fingers bandaged. In cases of septic poisoning the girls had to attend surgery to have their fingers dressed each day.

The dinner hour having arrived Jenny went with the girls to the canteen, where a meal of meat and vegetables, together with pudding, was served for the price of 9d. A cup of tea or coffee, one penny extra. An hour was allowed for dinner, but she had to remember to clock-in at 2 P.M. because wages were paid according to the hours clocked-in.

Jenny had heard that girls were earning big wages on munitions, but she soon found out that the basic wage was 4d. per hour plus a bonus earned by a number of girls in a team; a pool was divided between them, and averaged about 5s. a week. Her weekly wage, for the first month, was about 30s. for seventy-two hours.

She was not on munitions long before she realized what war meant. Every day there was news of fathers, husbands, brothers or other relatives having been killed, wounded or reported missing; or there were groups of young men going to the war. Sometimes the lights in the factory would suddenly dim and everyone would march to the shelters, which were mainly surface shelters or stoke-holes large enough to take a number of girls. If they went out it meant imminent danger . . .

Jenny's thoughts naturally turned to her home. She wondered what was happening there with her family. By this time her two brothers were at work; the elder had left farm work and gone on the railway as a shunter in Salisbury, the younger had become a farm labourer, her sister Elisabeth had gone into domestic service in Leeds, and another into service in Wroxall; her sister Florence had left the farm; some of her uncles and cousins were Territorials and she assumed that they would be called up, although many of them were coal-miners or agricultural workers. She had had no news of any of their movements, but a recruiting drive was on, and her brothers might have to go. Jenny herself, being on munitions work, worried her family more than anything else. From now on she must write every week as her mother was of a very nervous disposition, and the war upset her very much. Jenny's sister Edith was in service, and she wrote to say that she wanted to leave and go on munitions, and would like to come to Luton; and so it was that Jenny got her a job and lodgings. This was the first time for years that Jenny was able to talk to a near relative, except when at home on holiday. Edith soon settled down in her new job and environment, enjoying a freedom that she had not known for a long time, having been like her sister in domestic service.

After a few months in the factory Jenny was asked to go on night work. This still meant a twelve-hour shift, but time-and-a-quarter pay was given, with time-and-a-half on the Sunday night shift which started at ten o'clock instead of eight; the shifts changed over fortnightly. She accepted, but it took some time to get used to the changing over, and sleeping by day, which was not always easy. She was told that this new operation was very important and needed care and attention, but she was thought capable of doing it by the management . . .

It so happened that the secretary of a trade union, the Workers' Union, was working in the department. Jenny was given an application form and asked to join the union, at an entrance fee of 6d. and 2½d. a week subscription. This was something new to her; she had a vague idea that there were trade unions, but did not know the first thing about them. She explained that she knew nothing about it; what was it for? She was given an invitation to attend a special meeting called for women workers in the town that week, at which an organizer from London would be speaking. This, thought Jenny, might be very interesting, and she decided to join up. Little did she realize then that this was going to be the means of a further and wider venture for her in a not-too-distant future. She attended the meeting and found there many girls and women, not only from her own factory, but from other factories: the Diamond Foundry Works, the Skefko Ballbearings, the Commercial Cars, the Vauxhall Motors, and other engineering firms in the town. Jenny learned a lot that night about the principles for which trade unionism stood: protection of workers in industry, dealing with problems of wages, hours of work and conditions, factory acts (concerning ventilation, lighting and heating). She came to the conclusion very soon that here was something interesting and exciting. She attended branch meetings and found herself taking part in discussions. It was an outlet for her pent-up impressions and emotions, held within herself for some time. She attended lectures, bought books and studied the problems of economics, and social life and welfare. Yes, Jenny was learning fast and furiously. It was not long before she became the chairman of her own branch of women workers.

The time came when she was moved to another job, this time to a machine-shop where she was to use a press for pressing detonators, a job where special care and attention was needed because any careless move might cause an explosion. Only two machines were in each room, for safety reasons. The detonators were placed inside a metal cup, which was put into the machine, and a lever was pulled to press. Jenny did have one mishap through a slightly faulty detonator. Fortunately she always took

the precaution of closing her box of twelve whilst one was being pressed;
this saved what might have been a serious accident. If they had gone up,
Jenny would have gone up with them; as it was, the only damage was that
the press jammed and two fingers on Jenny's right hand were cut. An
examination was made after the mishap, and she was exonerated from
blame: she could not have avoided it, and she was commended for taking
the precaution of keeping her box of uncut detonators closed. Her cut
fingers did not prevent her from carrying on at the press for some
time.

The next move was to the spinning room, for an operation to test the
springs of the fuses – a very exacting job, requiring good eyesight and
constant vigilance to ensure the accuracy of the spring. Without this the
fuse would be useless. This operation caused dust and chemicals to fly
about the room, making the skin and clothes yellow. Jenny had often
noticed this among the girls, and had wondered how they became yellow;
they were in fact called 'Chaul End Canaries'. Even the bed-linen became
yellow. Jenny found that she had to pay her landlady more money for
laundry, especially for the feather-bed, and felt a little incensed about
this; after all, she was helping the war effort, to help the lads at the front.
Her landlady continually grumbled about this, until Jenny changed her
lodgings to a more understanding family, who made allowances for any
inconvenience caused by discoloration of clothes. Not only did Jenny
become yellow; she found after a time that the powder was affecting her
skin. Her face, neck and legs began to swell, so much so that she could not
see and had to be led home. She was ordered to stay home for ten days on
half pay. For three days she could not see anything. On being examined
by the works doctor, T.N.T. poisoning was diagnosed. This was something Jenny had not bargained for. She had to be bandaged, as the skin
had now broken and the fluid was escaping; she looked something like a
member of the Ku Klux Klan or an Egyptian mummy for some time. But
it was a good thing that the fluid did escape; had it gone into the body she
would not have lived to tell the story. The swelling having gone down,
Jenny returned to the factory. She was not allowed to do any more spinning, and was given another job away from any dust or powder, this time
in charge of a small inspecting shop with twenty girls. It was weeks before
she could dispense with the bandages on her neck and hands, in fact the
effects of the poisoning lasted for months – despite the fact that she had
two pints of milk every day to drink. Some of the girls who had contracted this condition obtained permission to leave munitions and return
home; it was only girls and women whose skins were not as sensitive as
Jenny's who could stand the spinning-shed. The management themselves
were very worried about this and did everything they could to deal with
it. Masks and rubber gloves were provided, but the girls could not stand
them; goggles affected their eyes even more, and did not prevent the
swelling. Finally it was decided that the girls should have only a short
time at the job, which meant that several shifts were arranged with girls
working only a week or two at a time. Jenny was not the only one by any

means who suffered from T.N.T. poisoning; and it was not only painful, but an irritation set in that was almost unbearable at times. After some months Jenny thought that she was going to be disfigured for life, but by good fortune and perseverance with the rations provided, the skin cleared and became normal . . .

Meanwhile she had continued her study of the trade union movement, and was appointed a union representative at her factory. This gave her an opportunity of coming into contact with the management, and she was able to discuss with them improvements of conditions, particularly in personal welfare and lavatory accommodation for the girls. She never obtained all she wanted, but she was always well received and she gained quite a lot of small but important concessions, including extra milk for girls on powder work. In the early part of 1917 Jenny was still in the throes of T.N.T. poisoning, and an order was given by the works doctor that she must leave Chaul End factory, if she was ever to recover. It so happened that the firm had another and much larger works at Biscot Road, Luton, where shells and other war essentials were produced. She was transferred to this factory with a recommendation of her capability of doing important work. Here the girls were called 'Biscot Road Blackbirds', as this kind of work made them black instead of yellow. She was made an assistant forewoman, and was given a biscuit-coloured overall with red collar, cuffs and waistband; also a triangular badge bearing the words 'War Work'. She was now in charge of some fifty girl inspectors in a large machine-shop. Whenever the work was too high or low she had to stop the machine and have it put right by the setters (male). Many gauges had to be understood, but Jenny had learnt all this at Chaul End, and it presented no difficulty to her. This was a very large factory, employing some thousands of men, women and girls. The canteen, although large, could only accommodate some 1,500 at one sitting, but another was under construction. Jenny would still have to do a twelve-hour shift, alternate fortnights, but by now her pay had increased to £3 a week plus an allowance for assistant forewoman's duties. Her work was now intensely interesting, and she came into contact not only with her own girls but with the governors of the factory, which gave her an opportunity from time to time to do a lot for the girls and deal with their problems, regarding time sheets, wages and welfare – especially as she had been made a union representative and held an authorization card for this purpose. She was never refused a reasonable request, and was always well received by the management. It was not long before her advice was being sought by all and sundry . . .

After ten days' leave, Jenny returned to her job in the factory, refreshed and ready for anything. Indeed, the girls were anxious to tell her of all that had happened since she had been away, especially of two bad accidents. In one, a man had got two fingers cut off by an automatic machine; in the other a girl, whilst bending down to pick up some work she had dropped, had got her cap and hair caught up in the flywheel of her machine and was scalped. For the rest of her life she would have to wear a wig, and she was

5

only twenty-two years of age . . . As time went on, Jenny noticed that the long hours and exacting work were telling on the girls, especially on the night shifts in the early hours of the morning, when energy was at its lowest ebb. She wondered what she could do to help them. The new canteen was now in operation, and she thought of a plan to arrange a half-hour or an hour's music, and if the girls liked, dancing at the midnight meal hour. The girls were very excited at the prospect of such a break, and Jenny lost no time in approaching the management for permission, which was readily granted; but she had to be responsible for seeing that the timetable was kept to. The plan proved very successful, and the girls who could play the piano were only too willing to take turns in playing; so after their meals they would enjoy the half-hour's recreation. This made all the difference to their work for the rest of the night. Jenny also arranged parties for the chargehands and forewomen in the town each Saturday night, which also proved successful.

By now Jenny had been recognized as something of an organizer. She had been chairman of her trade union branch for some time. The official of the Workers' Union had been to Luton from London, and had arranged a recruiting campaign in the factories in Luton; and she was asked to take charge of the women's side of the movement. She had learnt a great deal about the union and its activities by attending meetings, lectures and economic discussions, and talks on methods of recruitment. She had learnt all about the subscriptions and benefits of the union, and was quite capable of enrolling members. She was responsible for a large number of women and girls coming into the union. She had also learnt a great deal of the political side, and of the fight of the suffragettes for women's fran-chise. In her service days she had heard something about these women, and on one occasion a stone had been thrown through the window of a downstairs room with a label attached which said 'Votes for Women'. She was unaware at the time what that meant, but now she began to under-stand the movement.

After some weeks, Jenny was called upon very suddenly one day to give her services as a union representative. The girls and women em-ployed by a large factory just outside the town had asked for an improve-ment in wages and working conditions; they had been patient for some time with no result forthcoming, and then struck work and made their way to the centre of the town – some 200 of them – and sent for Jenny to deal with their problems. She consulted her colleagues, and asked per-mission of the management to leave her job for a couple of hours in order to try and get the girls to return to work. Jenny was rather reluctantly given permission; she must get them back, and return as soon as possible. In a very short time she found herself standing on a beer-barrel outside a pub, holding forth; she had never given a speech in her life indoors, let alone in the open air. She explained that she was not authorized to negoti-ate; if they would go back to work, especially as they were on government contracts, she would get the London officers to come down as soon as possible. She collected all the details, and wired to London for officers.

She got them back to work, and went back to her own work, but the news had reached her firm before she could get back. This gave Jenny another line of thought: how careful one must be in what one says and does, even in times of emergency, and how quickly news travels. The excitement was so quick that Jenny really wondered what had happened; but this incident was only the beginning of her activities which, although she did not know it, were at that very moment brewing for her.

One morning, when Jenny got to work, she was told that an accident had happened at Chaul End factory; a number of girls had been hurt and several killed by an explosion in the very department where she had worked; had she still been working there, she would have been a casualty herself. There had been several minor accidents before, but this one was really bad. Jenny wondered what she could do to help, and soon decided that something ought to be done to help the girls and their families in this critical time. She asked the management for permission to organize a collection throughout the factory to help them financially; normally this would not be encouraged, but this tragedy was something different, and the management agreed to her proposal. She set to work first of all to get an announcement written and placed in each department, stating that a collection would be made by permission of the firm; she then arranged for several of her colleagues to collect in some departments, while she herself did others. She stayed in the factory for twenty-four hours, in order to get the two shifts, and a goodly sum was collected and distributed among the families, proving a very valuable help. Much gratitude was shown for what was termed a kindly action by the firm, in practical help in time of trouble . . .

On returning to the factory, Jenny discovered that following the strike a number of shop stewards' committees had been set up to cover the factories, meeting from time to time to deal with any problems that might arise in any department. There was also a joint committee including the management, when the need required it. Jenny was one of the representatives covering both Chaul End and Biscot Road factories, and so she had the opportunity of seeing some of her old colleagues again, from where she had learnt so much, and suffered T.N.T. poisoning for a long time. Meantime she was called upon to take over another important job for a few weeks, testing a new process with new metals, which was very secret. It proved successful and speeded up production considerably.

After Christmas 1917, when she arrived at work on the night shift, she was handed a very important-looking envelope addressed to her; it contained a printed card which read:

George Kent Limited – The Directors have great pleasure in notifying you that they have recommended you for the Medal of the Order of the British Empire, in recognition of your great service during the war. While it is improbable that medals will be awarded to all those recommended, the Directors none the less wish to record their opinion that you wholly deserve the honour, and express their appreciation of your splendid efforts. December 31st, 1917, (Signed) George Kent Ltd.

Jenny was naturally excited about this, and was congratulated from all sides. It was something she had not even dreamed of, and it came as a delightful surprise; it was something she would value for the rest of her life. That night in the canteen, during the sing-song (which was still going strong, and thoroughly enjoyed) she was treated to a meal, and songs were sung in her honour. It so happened that only two medals were given – to the Works Manager and the Welfare Superintendent; these people were very worthy recipients, because their responsibility was great. To Jenny the recommendation she received compensated her to the full, and the knowledge that her services were appreciated sufficed . . .

Early in 1918 Jenny was faced with another problem: an important decision to make. She had by now become well known for her trade union work and her ability to organize and deal with questions in connection with trade union principles, and in no small measure with negotiations. In London, organization among women was increasing, and more trade union organizers were needed. The London woman organizer, a Miss Saward, had been in Luton quite a lot, and in fact had taken Jenny under her wing and left her in charge of the women's membership in Luton – except for the legal problems in settlements for accident and workmen's compensation. One day, to her astonishment, she received a letter from the President of the Union, a Mr Jack Beard, asking her to go to London to see him. This she did, and he told her of the reports he had received of her work in Luton; the Executive Committee had considered asking her to become an organizer, and to work from London under the direction of the London Divisional Organizer, a Mr George Dallas . . .

Jenny returned to Luton, thinking about the proposition and wondering what she should do. Would the job last, or would she find herself out of work when the war was over? Would the organization of women's membership continue after the war? The salary would be less than she was getting in the factory: 30 shillings plus £1 bonus; would she be able to keep herself in London? All these thoughts came trooping into her mind in some confusion. Would she be allowed to leave her job before the war was over? Would she be doing the right thing in leaving? The uppermost thought in her mind was that if she refused this offer, she might have to go back to domestic service when the war ended, as she would not be wanted in the factory . . .

One day the decision had to be made; a telegram called her to London again to discuss the question. After being assured that the prospects were good, she decided to accept the offer and take up the post in two weeks' time. And so it was that in April 1918 Jenny found herself in London, installed as a full-time officer of the Workers' Union.

Domestic Servants

PART TWO

Domestic Systems

INTRODUCTION

1. Throughout the nineteenth century and until the First World War domestic service constituted the largest single employment for English women, and the second-largest employment for all English people, male and female. Yet it is a largely unknown occupation. No Royal Commission investigated it or suggested legislative protection of the worker; no outburst of trade union activity called attention to the lot of servants, as it did to that of the building workers, the cotton-spinners and the dock labourers; no Joseph Arch or Tom Mann arose as spokesman of their cause to draw forth the pity of the Victorian middle classes. Immured in their basements and attic bedrooms, shut away from private gaze and public conscience, the domestic servants remained mute and forgotten until, in the end, only their growing scarcity aroused interest in 'the servant problem'.

The nineteenth century was a period of transition for employment in Britain, the principal feature of which was the decline of traditional occupations like agriculture and cottage industries and the expansion of new ones associated with an industrial economy – manufacturing, commercial and service industries. Women were profoundly affected by these developments, which brought major changes in the division of labour between the sexes, and in the role and status of women in society. Ultimately, women gained immeasurably from these changes, and the growth of new occupations, the removal of work from the home and the receipt of an independent wage may be seen as the necessary foundations on which the emancipation of women in the twentieth century was built. But in the mid-nineteenth century, before the development of mass-production methods had created a major opportunity for the employment of women in factories, and the invention of the typewriter and telephone had revolutionized clerical work, there was little that an unskilled girl who was under the unfortunate necessity of having to earn her own living could do except to clean, cook and generally minister to others' wants.

In this sense, the growth of domestic service paralleled the growth of the middle classes who were its chief employers. Large domestic staffs had, of course, characterized the great houses of the nobility for centuries past; what was new in the nineteenth century was the burgeoning of those 'of moderate incomes' – the manufacturers and merchants, the bankers, brokers, lawyers, doctors and other professionals whose incomes depended, directly or indirectly, on industrialization and the rapid growth of towns that accompanied it. The large family, the large and over-furnished house, the entertainment of guests at lavish dinner-parties, and the economic ability to keep one's wife in genteel idleness, all of which were essential attributes of the institution of the Victorian middle-class family, required the employment of domestic servants on a vast scale. By their number, dress and function they proclaimed in an outward and visible way the degree of success in life that their employer had attained and, by implication, conferred upon him membership of the class. At the end of the century Seebohm Rowntree, in his study of poverty in York, drew the upper limit of the working classes at 'the servant-keeping class', because to keep one 'skivvy' in the kitchen as surely announced middle-class membership as the possession of a cottage piano indicated the 'respectability' of a working man. In very wealthy households where twenty or more servants might be kept an extreme differentiation of duties was observed. The symbolic and decorative function became more important than the useful; status required an establishment of a certain size, whether it could be justified in practical terms or not. Thus, the growth of domestic service mirrors and reflects the growth of the middle-class, mid-Victorian family pattern. Similarly, when that pattern began to change in the late nineteenth century, when parents began to limit the size of their families, when 'women's rights' came to be discussed and exercised, and when the pressures of an increasingly competitive economy began to demand a more expensive education for middle-class children, domestic service entered upon a long-term decline which was accelerated by the social upheaval of the First World War and its aftermath.

The Census of 1851 gave a total female population for England, Wales and Scotland of 10·7 million, of whom 8·1 million were over ten years of age and, therefore, by the standards of the day, potentially employable. Excluding wives, who, except in certain well-defined industries and geographical areas, did not usually continue in full-time employment after marriage, widows, girls at school, female paupers in institutions and women of 'rank and property', there were 3·4 million at work, or slightly over two-fifths of those of employable age. For the great majority of these women, manual and menial occupations were the sole outlet, and domestic service was easily the most important. In 1851 this accounted for 905,000 women and 134,000 men, making it the second-largest occupational group after agriculture; the other main employments for women were, in order, milliners, dress-makers and seamstresses (340,000), cotton-workers (272,000), agricultural workers (227,000), washer-women (145,000), woollen-workers (113,000), silk-workers (80,000), and linen- and lace-workers (each 56,000).[1] The figures imply that one in every nine of all females over ten years of age, and one in every four of all females in employment worked in full-time domes-tic service throughout Britain as a whole. Their distribution was not, of course, regular. The main pool of servants was country girls, attracted to the towns and cities by the hope of experience, gaiety and a possible match. London was always the strongest magnet, and as railways cheapened travel and newspapers diffused advertise-ments over the countryside, its field of influence ever widened: already in 1851 domestic servants comprised 39,000 of the 115,000 London women of all classes aged between fifteen and twenty.[2]

It is hardly surprising that domestic service exercised such a compulsive influence on the female labour-force. It would accept entrants at an early age – typically at twelve or thirteen in the mid-nineteenth century – without previous experience or training; it offered them the opportunity of learning those skills associated with home-making which, hopefully, they would be able to employ in later married life; it provided board and lodging as well as a cash wage, in a sheltered environment where a young girl or boy would be subject to the control and moral care of older servants and em-ployers. In this sense, employment in a good household was akin to membership of an extended family group. It was a secure and regu-lar occupation for which there was a steady demand both in town and country, and for the ambitious it provided a clearly defined route to respected and responsible positions. Above all, it reduced the strain on a poor family's budget and living accommodation by removing daughters from overcrowded households as soon as they were old enough to be of use to another.

With expansion in both the size and the prosperity of the middle classes, the total number of domestic servants continued to grow throughout the second half of the century. The statistics cannot be entirely precise,[3] though there can be no doubt about the order and direction of change. A comparison of the 1851 and 1871 Censuses for England and Wales only, during which time the categorization did not change, indicates the following growth as shown on page 138.

In this period the number of domestic servants increased twice as rapidly as the population as a whole (26·7 per cent), clearly re-flecting the years of most rapid advance of the middle classes. It is

5*

Table 1 Domestic Servants (England and Wales)

	1851	1871	Increase %
Females			
General servants	575,162	780,040	35·6
Housekeepers	46,648	140,836	201·9
Cooks	44,009	93,067	115·5
House-maids	49,885	110,505	121·5
Nurse-maids	35,937	75,491	110·1
Laundry-maids	n.a.	4,538	n.a.
Total	*751,641*	*1,204,477*	*56·6*
Males			
Indoor general servants	74,323	68,369	−8·0
Grooms	15,257	21,202	+39·0
Coachmen	7,030	16,174	+130·1
Total	*96,610*	*105,745*	*+9·5*
Total (male and female)	*848,251*	*1,310,222*	*+54·5*[4]

also evident that domestic service was becoming increasing differentiated, and that the largest increases were among the more skilled and specialized staff like housekeepers and cooks, nurse-maids and coachmen. These were the necessary accompaniments of a life-style which included an average family size of six children (in 1871 177 families in every 1,000 had ten or more children), a weekly dinner-party and 'carriage exercise' for the ladies in the afternoon. In other respects the middle-class housewife was increasingly functionless, the 1871 Census remarking that 'wives and daughters at home do now less domestic work than their predecessors; hence the excessive demand for female servants and the consequent rise of wages'. The expansion of male servants was markedly less rapid, mainly because the growth of industry and commerce was now offering attractive alternative employment free from the constraints of life in service. Compared with the increase in the number of separate households (36 per cent) there was a relative fall, though significantly the numbers of coachmen grew three times more quickly than the rate of household formation.

From 1871 onwards, however, the pattern began to change.

Although total numbers continued to rise, the rate of growth was noticeably slower than in the previous decades, and fell considerably behind the growth of population. Domestic servants increased by 0·41 per cent per annum between 1881 and 1901, compared with an increase of 1·26 per cent per annum for the population as a whole, and by only 0·21 per cent per annum from 1901 to 1911 compared with 1·09 per cent.[5] Equally significant, recruitment to service was clearly being avoided by young girls, and the occupation was increasingly made up of older women: between 1881 and 1901 the number of girls under fifteen in domestic service fell by 34 per cent and those aged fifteen to nineteen by 7·3 per cent, while women between twenty-five and forty-four rose by 33·1 per cent and those over forty-five by 20 per cent. In part, this falling-off was due to the advent of compulsory elementary education in 1876 but, more importantly, it was due to the development of new and more attractive forms of employment for girls. For the better-educated nursing, school-teaching and clerical work grew rapidly in the closing decades of the century; for the rest, shop work and factory work offered higher wages, shorter and more regular hours and freedom from the incessant demands of an employer's bell-push, all of which served to give a girl a sense of independent identity in the 'real world' rather than of anonymity 'below stairs'.

Complaints at the difficulty of obtaining good servants were perennial, though the first half of the nineteenth century seems to have been unusually quiet on the subject. They reappeared in an article in the *Westminster Review* in 1862[6] which drew attention to the problem of obtaining and retaining good servants when industry offered better wages and more personal freedom. Later censuses noted the 'increasing disinclination' of girls for domestic work, and commented that 'young women were preferring other employments'. By the end of the century servants were becoming noticeably older, scarcer and more expensive, and at the same time more selective about the household and the locality they would work in. The 'servant problem' was especially difficult in the old centres of towns and cities, where dirt, smoke and many-storeyed houses provided an unattractive environment, easier in the suburbs where the more manageably-sized villas offered a lighter work-load. The proportion of servants to families was lowest in manufacturing and mining areas, and highest in residential counties: thus, in 1881 Burnley had only forty-five servants per 1,000 families, Lancashire as a whole ninety-seven, Surrey 353, Bournemouth 415 and Kensington 700.

It appears that the chief source of new recruits was drying up. In the middle of the century it is likely that two-thirds or more of all

servants came from the countryside, but as the numbers of agricultural labourers steadily diminished by migration and emigration
(from 965,000 in England and Wales in 1851 to 643,000 in 1911)
there were fewer daughters to be recruited. Once settled in a town
and educated at a town elementary school they were much more
likely to look to factory or shop work than to what was increasingly
considered a low-status occupation, fit only for country bumpkins
and orphan girls from the Poor Law institutions.

Again, the statistics at the end of the century are difficult to inter-
pret because the basis of classification continued to change. It is
clear that there was no overall decline in numbers, for between 1881
and 1901, the census category 'domestic service, etc.' rose from
1,519,000 to 1,691,000 (female) and from 88,000 to 141,000 (male).[7]
The difficulty is that the classification included many service occupations that were not strictly in the home – for men, work in hotels,
restaurants, clubs and colleges, hospitals and institutions of many
kinds, and for women, work as laundresses, charwomen and washer-
women. As middle-class family size declined, and the cost of maintaining 'living-in' servants continued to rise, more domestic work
came to be put out to daily cleaners and steam laundries, and more
entertaining was done outside the home in the palatial hotels built
towards the end of the century. Labour-saving devices like gas and
electricity, the vacuum-cleaner, the gas cooker and piped hot water
to bathrooms were, in part, a response to the same pressures, and
the advent of the telephone tended to make the footman even more
superfluous than before. The developments of 'federalized' apart-
ments and service flats, especially in London, and the spread of the
smaller, two-storeyed house in the suburbs undoubtedly helped to
reduce demand for residential staff. Of the 141,000 men described
as domestic servants in 1901, only 47,000 worked in private homes,
and this almost certainly represented a substantial decrease since
1851.[8]

Up to 1914, then, the total number of domestic servants was still
growing, though at a slackening rate compared with the later decades
of the nineteenth century. In 1901 it still accounted for 40 per cent
of all employed women, compared with 44 per cent twenty years
earlier. It was the First World War, and particularly the advent of
conscription in 1916, that caused the first major inroad into the
predominant position of domestic service, and brought fundamental
changes to the occupational opportunities of women generally.
Patriotic and personal interests combined to bring thousands of
kitchen-maids, cooks and parlour-maids into munition factories, the
public services and the subsidiary armed forces, where not only did

they enjoy greater personal freedom and a sense of involvement in the war effort, but substantial improvements in earnings and status. During the four years of war women munition workers rose from 212,000 to over 900,000, while women domestic servants fell from 1,658,000 to 1,258,000.[9] Of the 2,500 women tram- and bus-conductresses of 1917 some half, it was said, were former domestic servants; many more found their way into other forms of transport, into nursing, catering and agricultural work. Clearly, domestic service was far from being wiped out by the war, and after the Armistice many had to return to it; but the permanent legacy of the war was to widen the boundaries of women's employment, and to lower still further the status of domestic service. Servant-keeping was never again easily available to the middle classes as a whole, and in the post-war world it increasingly became a privilege of upper income-levels. In the commuter areas of London the number of servants per 100 families fell from 24·1 in 1911 to 12·4 in 1921, while in the West End it declined only from 57·3 to 41·3.[10]

By the 1920s and 1930s domestic service was no longer the natural outlet for women's employment that it had been in Victorian times. Girls could now go into shop work, into the new light factory trades and into the booming area of clerical work, which already by 1931 was taking one in every five of employed women; for those with higher education teaching, nursing and the minor professions were all developing. Domestic service was increasingly the refuge for the poor and ill-educated, for the over-large families where every additional child was an extra mouth to be fed, and for the daughters of normally comfortable working-class parents hit by depression and unemployment. The more remote areas of the North of England, Wales, Scotland and Ireland, where the new technologies had had little impact, provided the main pools of such labour, still willing to migrate to London and the other great cities for the escape and the opportunities they seemed to offer.

By 1923 middle-class anxiety about the growing scarcity of servants resulted in the appointment of a Ministry of Labour Committee under the chairmanship of Mrs E. M. Wood. The daily press had been full of complaints that able-bodied women were preferring to draw unemployment benefit rather than enter service, and that when Labour Exchanges did offer candidates they were almost always totally unfitted for the work. The Committee identified five main causes, in order, for the scarcity – the lack of facilities for training, the question of status, 'psychological aspects', the hours and conditions of employment and the defects of the present system of recruitment.[11]

The War [it said] accentuated the problem and precipitated the crisis by widening the scope of women's activities while, in addition to this, many of those who had been previously employed in domestic work found the comradeship, definite hours and routine of factory, office or shop life very much to their liking, and had no desire to return to their former occupation.

While conditions of industrial employment had improved radically in the last half-century, domestic work had remained unchanged, and 'we are informed that house-maids' "mats" and "boxes" and other common objects of our homes would, in the Overseas Dominions, be regarded as mysterious articles of incomprehensible purport, and would probably be placed in a museum'. Attitudes of employers, and of the popular press in which domestic servants were constantly held up to ridicule, would have to change, it was felt. A parlour-maid witness reported, 'I do not believe any girl minds the work. They do mind being ridiculed. I have suffered untold misery by the name "only a servant". Invitations out state "Be sure and do not let it be known you are a domestic. We should not like our friends to mix with servants." It is the snobbery of our own class.' An employer commented:

> The domestic servant must only take a respectful interest in the doings of those for whom she works. She must minister but not participate. One real way to establish status is to offer such conditions as will attract girls to whom you are prepared to extend the same quality of respect as is expected from the worker, and give them such opportunities of personal life as would be possible to an office clerk or factory hand.[12]

The Committee recommended that training in domestic service should form part of the education of all girls in elementary schools between the ages of twelve and fourteen, that unemployment benefit should be extended to cover all domestic servants, that all registry offices should be brought under the control of local authorities, that servants should become entitled to the parliamentary vote on the same residence-qualifications as men, and that local committees of employers and employees should be formed 'to endeavour to agree upon conditions [of employment] in their area'.[13] There is no evidence that these recommendations had any effect on the flight of women and girls from what had now been publicly recognized as a 'problem' occupation. The Second World War completed what the first had begun, and of the 1,330,000 women indoor domestic servants of 1931 only 724,000 remained in 1951.[14] In the same period a spectacular rise of 122 per cent had occurred in the category of clerks and typists who, at 1,271,000, for the first time in 1951 constituted the largest occupation for women.

2. The duties of domestic servants depended primarily on the size and wealth of the household they served and on the number of staff kept. In small households many roles had to be combined – the extreme instance of this being the 'maid-of-all-work'; in large establishments roles were strictly and minutely subdivided within a rigid hierarchical structure which gave little opportunity for demarcation disputes. The general historical movement was towards ever-greater differentiation of functions, reaching its greatest development in the closing decades of the century when the numbers of domestic servants were at their height: thereafter, as numbers contracted and the size of households declined duties again tended to be amalgamated into the category of 'general' servants.

Household offices in their modern form had been developing from the seventeenth century onwards. Changes in architecture, in domestic habits and in ceremonial had profound effects on the medieval pattern of management on great estates, while price-inflation and the burdens of the Civil War forced economies on the extravagant household organization of the Middle Ages.[15] Although the steward continued to act as the general manager of the household, the clerk of the kitchen was now giving way to the housekeeper, the gentleman-usher to the butler, and the yeomen of the hall and chamber to footmen and house-maids. By the eighteenth century, the structure of the Tudor household had become radically changed: women, who seem to have played a rather small part in the earlier period, had become much more extensively employed, while male servants were now being drawn from a distinctly lower social class than formerly. 'Even the upper servants,' writes Dr Dorothy Marshall, 'were in the majority of cases the sons of labourers, artisans or small farmers rather than recruits from the ranks of reduced gentlemen.'[16]

In middle-class households the domestic staff had always been smaller and more predominantly female, no doubt because female servants were cheaper and easier for a woman to control. Here, too, the origins of the Victorian pattern can be traced from seventeenth-century changes, when a household of moderate means had typically employed a cook, a chamber-maid or house-maid, a waiting-woman, a manservant and an odd boy. Under somewhat different names, and with the addition of more specialized staff such as laundry-maid, nurse-maid and coachman as circumstances allowed, this is the pattern that developed in the eighteenth century[17] and persisted throughout the nineteenth. The main change was that whereas in the eighteenth century one or two male staff were common even in quite modest households like that of Parson Woodforde, by the nineteenth the possession of even one manservant was a mark of distinctly higher social status, serving to separate the middle from the lower middle classes. By early Victorian times few men servants were to be found in households employing less than six servants,[18] which placed the household income at something approaching £1,000 a year. In J. H. Walsh's *Manual of Domestic Economy*, first published in 1857, it was calculated that an income of £500 a year would provide three domestic servants – a cook, a house-maid and either a parlour-maid or a general manservant, though it seems that the former was more common; £1,000 a year permitted six, of whom two would be male, a butler and a coachman or groom. But by the second edition of the same book in 1873 the incomes had been raised to £750 and £1,500 a year respectively, and it seems certain that menservants were increasingly regarded as status symbols confined to clearly 'successful' business and professional men. A manservant was now almost invariably associated with ownership of a coach and horses, and 'carriage folk' constituted a clearly-defined stratum of the middle or upper middle classes.

Domestic help was necessary to the Victorian middle and upper classes, partly because wives and daughters had become virtually functionless and partly because the accumulated paraphernalia of gentility had become so demanding of attention. It is also fair to say that the household supplied many more of its own material needs and services than its modern counterpart, and lacked many basic amenities of domestic comfort. Houses were inconvenient and often on four or five floors, crowded with furniture, ornaments and hangings, and with all principal rooms carpeted; it was the age of cut-glass chandeliers, carved, gilt-framed mirrors and pictures, silver and silver-plated articles for the dinner and tea-tables, antimacassars and dust-collecting bric-à-brac of all kinds. By contrast, the basements and attics, used as sleeping-quarters by male and female servants respectively, were usually cramped and airless, furnished in the sparsest way, and sometimes having no external windows. Work had to be carried on with almost no labour-saving devices. Water was seldom laid on upstairs, and bathrooms were a rarity until late in the century; although gas cookers had been patented in the 1850s, most kitchens were still encumbered with a roaring open range, the lighting and tending of which could be almost a full-time occupation. Most houses were still lit by oil-lamps (twenty or more in a large house) requiring trimming, re-filling and cleaning daily, while the washing of china, glass and pans and the cleaning of floors, furniture and silver were still unaided by mechanical appliances or proprietary polishes.[19] The American vacuum cleaner was introduced early in the twentieth century, though early models were so cumbersome that they had little immediate success. Again, it has to be remembered that bread was still baked in brick ovens in many houses, that washing was done largely at home, and a great deal of clothing, including men's shirts and underwear, was made by servants who were expected to spend their spare time in sewing.

Victorian households built up their staffs of domestic servants in accordance with a well-understood pattern: this was based on a natural and logical progression from general functions to more specialized ones, heavily reinforced by an outpouring of literature and advice on domestic economy and household management.[20] Domestic help began with a daily girl or charwoman. The first living-in servant would be a 'general' maid-of-all-work, almost always a young girl often of only thirteen or fourteen: the next addition a house-maid or a nurse-maid, depending on the more urgent needs at the time. The third servant would be the cook, and these three – either cook, parlour-maid and house-maid, or cook, house-maid and nurse-maid – then formed a group which could minimally minister to all the requirements of gentility. At this point, the first manservant would usually appear, whose duties would combine indoor work such as waiting and valeting with care of the horse or pony and carriage; J. H. Walsh placed the income level necessary for this at £500 a year in 1857.[21] Beyond this, the progression was not so predictable. The fifth servant might be a lady's maid or a kitchen-maid to act as assistant to the cook, or a nurse-maid if there was not one already. The sixth would almost certainly be another man, acting as butler and releasing the other as a whole-time coachman or groom, which would be necessary with ownership of a four-wheeled carriage and an income of £1,000 a year. Beyond six servants, increases would follow as a result of increasing specialization – on the male side footmen, valets, a chef and a house-steward, and on the female a housekeeper, a governess, more lady's-maids, upper and lower parlour-maids, a laundry-maid and additional kitchen- and scullery-maids. On landed estates, there would, of course, also be outside staff such as gardeners and game-keepers, as well as many more men and boys working about the stables.

Thus, in a very wealthy town house there might be up to about twenty servants, and on a country estate up to thirty or forty. Great establishments like this could still form in the nineteenth century very much the same kind of total communities they had in the Middle Ages, highly structured, authoritarian and inward-looking, largely self-sufficient and independent of the rest of society, local and national. Writing of these in 1908, W. T. Layton remarked:

The premises constituted a settlement as large as a small village; carrying coals, making up fires and attending to the vast number of candles and lamps required in such houses necessitated the employment of several footmen. Every department was under the general supervision, as regards the men, of the house-steward, and of the women, the housekeeper.

So much was largely unchanged from earlier times. What was new in the nineteenth century was that the middle-class suburban villa with its three reception rooms, six or seven bedrooms and two or three domestic servants aimed at being a microcosm of the great estate, performing many of the same functions and sharing many of the same attitudes, assumptions and beliefs.

Turning to the actual duties of domestic servants, the great household, as previously explained, was still presided over by a house-steward, who, according to Samuel and Sarah Adams's *The Complete Servant* (1825), was appointed only at an income level of above £4,000 a year, and when the total staff amounted to eleven females and thirteen men.[22] He was the nearest thing, among servants, to a 'gentleman': probably recruited from the farming class, of some education and greater dignity. His duties included the hiring and regulating of all staff (except, usually, lady's-maids), ordering, marketing and checking of supplies, keeping the accounts, paying bills and undertaking confidential assignments for his master. He had his own room, separate from the servants' hall, where he could entertain visiting senior servants in considerable state, evening dress being the rule. Though the numbers of stewards must always have been small, and probably declined through the century, they survived into Edwardian and later times, mainly in noble households and in those of ambassadors and public officials where much ceremonial entertaining was done.[23]

In order of precedence, the male chef probably ranked next, at least equal to the butler. Traditionally French, extravagant and acutely conscious of their creative art, some had found employment with the English aristocracy after fleeing from the French Revolution,[24] and conferred enormous prestige on the dinner-tables of their patrons. Although much criticism continued to be made of Continental cooking by passionate anglophiles throughout the century, French practice and nomenclature gradually overcame all opposition, and there was intense competition among the wealthy to secure the services of a French chef or, at least, of a 'professed cook' who had worked under a Frenchman. Dr Kitchiner's belief that 'an English girl properly instructed can equal the best foreign gentlemen in everything except impudence and extravagance, and send up a delicious dinner with half the usual expense and trouble'[25] was evidently not persuasive in royal circles, where French chefs and Italian confectioners were the rule throughout the reigns of Victoria and Edward VII. The chef had complete authority and control within his own domain, the kitchen. Normally, under-cooks would prepare breakfast and the simpler parts of luncheon and dinner, leaving him to concentrate on the difficult and spectacular dishes, the sauces and dressings. All preparation and cleaning was done by kitchen-maids and scullery-maids: the chef merely demanded the ingredients and utensils he required, and left his kitchen in disarray to be cleaned up by underlings. His hours were shorter and his freedom greater than that of any other servant, and his high earnings amply justified by the compliments of his employers' guests at a dinner-party.

Mrs Beeton's *Book of Household Management* (1861), aimed primarily at a middle-class readership, devoted sixty-four pages to the duties of servants, but did not contemplate a male chef. The highest-ranking male servant here was the butler – the servant 'out of livery' who wore the gentleman's clothes of the period distinguished by a deliberate solecism such as the wrong tie or the wrong trousers. In earlier times responsible only for the wine and the cellar, the butler's functions developed into management and supervision of everything concerned with the service of meals and, more widely still, responsibility for the performance of all household duties; in this sense, therefore, he performed very much the same function as a house-steward. Mrs Beeton requires him to bring in and serve breakfast, luncheon and dinner, assisted by the footman and other servants: he is to make sure that fires and lamps are in perfect order in the dining- and drawing-rooms, and at bed-time he is to supply candles, to make sure that the plate is locked away and that doors and windows are secure. He is to supervise the other staff, pay bills and do some valeting as necessary, and he should be an expert in the selection, storing and preservation of wines, qualified to 'fine' and bottle them and also to brew, rack and bottle malt liquors. 'The office of butler is thus one of very great trust in a household. Here, as elsewhere, honesty is the best policy . . . Nothing spreads more rapidly in society than the reputation of a good wine-cellar, and all that is required is wines well-chosen and well cared for . . .'[26] The butler was addressed by his surname by the family, and as 'Mr' by the lower servants, over whom he had the right of dismissal: he was supposed to be unmarried, presumably because a wife and children ('encumbrances' as they were usually termed) might be thought to detract from his dignity. When not in the dining-room he usually inhabited his pantry, where he polished the silver and warmed and ironed any dampness out of the newspapers; from there he answered the door, showed in visitors or turned away unwelcome callers. His duties gave good opportunities for the receipt of tips and also for commission on the tradesmen's bills he paid, and a successful butler expected to substantially increase his wages in these ways. Retirement was usually to a public house or boarding-house, not all of which became so famous as that established by an ex-butler and ex-housekeeper, Mr and Mrs Claridge.

According to the Adams's scale, a valet was appointed only at the income level of £2,000–3,000 a year, and with a total household staff of sixteen. His function was to perform for the male head of the family what lady's-maids did for the ladies: his duties would include maintaining his master's wardrobe and putting out the right clothes for the occasion, helping him to dress, shave and arrange his hair, to clean his boots, shoes, hats and generally to be responsible for his appearance and comfort. At table he stood behind his master's chair, both at home and when visiting: he accompanied him on foreign travel and in his sports, and was expected to have some command of foreign languages, at least at the tourist level. Like the butler, he was an upper servant 'out of livery', and could expect to be well-dressed from his employer's cast-offs. One of the principal determinants of servants' status was nearness to the employers, and in this respect valets naturally ranked high: they were, wrote Mrs Beeton, 'the confidants and agents of their most unguarded moments, of their most secret habits . . . they themselves being subject to erring judgment, aggravated by an imperfect education'.[27]

The most ceremonial function of all was that performed by the footman, who was employed chiefly on account of his appearance in the dining-room and behind the carriage. Footmen were, of course, liveried servants, wearing an adaptation of eighteenth-century dress with elaborate braided and buttoned coat, knee-breeches, buckled shoes, powdered hair and tricorn or top hats: when two or four were kept, they had to be carefully matched for size, and Charles Booth at the end of the century quoted rates of pay which depended solely on height – five feet six inches, £20–£22 a year, up to six feet, £32–£40 a year;[28] besides height, the appearance of the calves, encased in silk stockings, was also important. Footmen were addressed by formalized Christian names – usually Charles, James, John and John Thomas in order, presumably so that employers would not have to remember changes of personnel. In earlier times they had acted as guards and escorts, accompanying the ladies when shopping in order to defend them if insulted, clearing the way in front of the sedan-chair, and so on, but when streets became safer and transport easier in Victorian times the footman's place became very much a sinecure and he degenerated into an ornamental parasite. His duties now included laying the table and waiting at it, 'carriage duty' which involved standing behind the carriage to deter illicit urchin-passengers, lowering the steps, helping his mistress in and out, and knocking at the doors of the houses she visited, and accompanying his mistress on foot when she was shopping or attending church. His duties were far different, however, in a small household which employed only one man. Here, he had to combine the duties of footman, butler and valet, and would do everything from cleaning boots and shoes and sweeping the hall to caring for the silver and glass, waiting at table, announcing guests, taking messages and so on. This 'man-of-all-work', though still called a footman, received six closely-written pages of duties from the pen of Mrs Beeton.

The coachman, assisted by one or more grooms in large establishments, began his day by cleaning the stables and preparing a pair of horses, then spending a couple of hours on cleaning and polishing the coach and harness. By eleven the carriage would be at the door and ready for orders for the day. The master or mistress was expected to specify the speed to be taken – four, six or eight miles an hour – Mrs Beeton preferring the higher speeds since 'less speed is injurious to the horses, getting them into lazy and sluggish habits . . . the whip is, of course, useful and even necessary, but should be rarely used, except to encourage and excite the horses'.[29] Her *Book of Household Management* envisaged a coachman, a groom and a stable-boy as sufficient for a coach, four horses and possibly a pony, but wealthy households, especially in the country, might have several coaches, a dozen or more horses and a considerable staff of under-coachmen and stable-hands. Even a one-horse coach such as a gig or tilbury added very considerably to domestic expenses, the author of *A New System of Practical Domestic Economy* putting the cost of maintenance at £54 a year.[30] Manuals of the period usually assumed that 10 per cent of income would go on horses and carriage, in addition to staff wages, so that the minimum on which one could keep one's own carriage would be £500–£600 a year and £750 would be a safer allowance. A four-wheeled carriage and pair of horses was estimated in 1873 to require £207 a year including wages,[31] implying an income of £1,500–£2,000. Nevertheless, the number of coachmen increased three times as rapidly as the number of households in the period 1851–71, clearly indicating the importance of the coach as a status symbol for which considerable sacrifices were justifiable. It is remarkable that numbers should have risen so rapidly at precisely the time when personal mobility was being greatly expanded by the new railways.

Among female staff, the highest place was that of the housekeeper, who, according to the Adams's scale, was appointed at an income level over £3,000 a year and when the total staff was twenty; she therefore performed very much the same duties as a house steward in an even larger establishment. Like him, she was 'out of livery', her badge of office being her great bunch of keys; she was addressed as 'Mrs' (like the cook) to denote maturity and respectability, and had her own comfortable room (the 'Pugs' Parlour') where she entertained the upper servants to breakfast, tea and supper, and was waited on by the still-room maid. At dinner in the servants' hall the housekeeper took the head of the table opposite the butler; on her right sat the cook and on her left the lady's-maid, while the under-butler sat to the right of the butler and the coachman to his left; lower servants sat in appointed places in the middle. The usual practice was for the upper servants to stay only for the meat course, adjourning to the housekeeper's room for pudding, cheese and conversation. The hierarchy of the servants' hall was, of course, an exact copy of the order of precedence 'above stairs'; an unwritten code, it presumably originated in aristocratic households and spread by example to become the accepted pattern in Victorian times, doubtless approved by employers as inculcating a proper respect for rank and authority. The housekeeper had the appointment and dismissal of all female staff except the cook and personal maids, she controlled the still-room, the store-rooms and linen-cupboards, was responsible for marketing, giving orders to tradesmen, issuing all supplies and presenting a weekly account to her mistress. More duties included making the drawing-room tea, pickling and bottling, making home-made wines, cordials and medicines, and, sometimes, making the more delicate articles of pastry and confectionery. She might also be required to dispense local charity on behalf of her mistress.

Next in seniority were the cook and the lady's-maid. The latter was required to perform all manner of personal services for her mistress, to be able to dress her and her hair expertly, to repair and make many of her garments, to accompany her on visits, read to her, administer to her whims and minor ailments, to wake her in the morning and see her to bed at night. The skills she needed most were hairdressing and needlework, besides a great deal of tact and good temper. The most sought-after lady's maids were French on account of their supposed expertise in coiffure and fashion, though most families had to be content with an English girl who had probably come from dress-making rather than risen from the ranks of the house-maids. Like the housekeeper, she had her own room and privileges, and the anonymous author of *The Lady's Maid* in Houlston's Industrial Library saw serious temptations in her life on the fringes of luxury:

As long as the rich pay for what they desire to have, they have every right to please themselves. But it is far from being true that they live in luxury for the sake of pleasure . . . they have business to do, too, as much as the working man, and very serious business indeed. The chief purpose of the many comforts and conveniences that rich people have about them is to set their time and their thoughts free for their serious occupations . . . A rich lady has a great many servants not because there is any pleasure in ordering a number of people about, but because she wants to save her own time and thoughts . . . for her children, her friends, her books and all the serious things she has to think of. She has many things to think of and to do that you know nothing about.[32]

The lady's-maid could expect to be well-dressed from her mistress's cast-offs, and to receive commissions from the drapers and haberdashers with whom she dealt. The greatest disadvantage of her office was its insecurity, for a lady's-maid was preferably young and there was no certain promotion to housekeeper for someone who had little or no knowledge of cooking and ordering food. Houlston's manual therefore advised that 'your heart should still be where your station is – among the poor, so that if you have to return to your old ways of living . . . you may not feel hurt or degraded but as if you were returning home'.

To a very large extent the Victorian middle-class household revolved round the kitchen. Substantial cooked breakfasts, four-course luncheons and dinners and a weekly or monthly dinner-party of eight or ten courses required the skill of a cook, preferably assisted by at least one kitchen-maid for preparation and a scullery maid for washing and cleaning. Cooks probably had more opportunities of augmenting their wages than any other servants, since their official perquisites included the sale of dripping and spent tea-leaves (used both for cleaning carpets and for adulterating pure tea) and their unofficial ones many more. In the absence of a housekeeper or butler, they were responsible for ordering and for paying bills, which gave many opportunities for commission. But a cook who was capable of serving one of Mrs Beeton's dinner-party menus (such as that for November which contained thirty-five dishes including turbot and lobster sauce, soles *à la Normandie*, pike and cream sauce, *filets de bœuf à la Jardinière*, oyster patties, lobster rissoles, partridges *aux fines herbes* and croquettes of game *aux champignons*), was a 'treasure' whose minor failings could be overlooked. Her skill was born of a long apprenticeship as scullery-maid and kitchen-maid, and she was unlikely to be appointed before her thirties; a good cook was eminently marriageable, but if she remained single she became an obvious choice for house-keeper.

Two further departments of domestic work require brief mention – house-cleaning and the care of children. The generic term for a cleaner was 'house-maid' and in a small establishment the whole house was her responsibility; with a larger staff her duties were sub-divided between parlour-maids and chamber-maids, or between upper and lower house-maids. The work to be done remained the same, beginning soon after five o'clock with lighting the kitchen fire, cleaning out the grates in the principal rooms, dusting and polishing, sweeping the hall and stairs, washing the front door steps and polishing the brass door-furniture, then lighting fires in dressing-rooms and carrying up hot water to the bedrooms. After breakfast, bedrooms were to be cleaned and aired and beds made, mattresses being turned daily; other downstairs rooms such as the study could then be tackled, and fires lighted where necessary. This would occupy the morning until luncheon, when the house-maid might or might not be required to wait at table, depending on the size of the staff. The afternoon was supposedly the quiet time, when a maid could change her working dress for a black gown and cap and sit down to mend and darn the family linen, between answering calls. Then she would prepare the dining-room for dinner, light bedroom fires, wait at table as necessary, bring tea to the drawing-room later in the evening and, in the absence of a lady's-maid, lay out her mistress's night-clothes and prepare her toilette. In addition to these daily tasks the weekly washing and ironing had to be fitted in, the cleaning of carpets, windows and wallpaper, the washing-down of paintwork and, of course, an annual spring-clean. Mrs Beeton, re-marking that the duties of the house-maid were 'very numerous', devoted twelve pages to their description, as well as several more to 'useful recipes' such as 'To brighten Gilt Frames', 'to Clean Marble' and 'to clean Decanters'.

Finally, the Victorian family would almost certainly require assistance with the rearing of its numerous children. The average family size of six children in 1871 and the still high incidence of miscarriage and still-birth meant that some fifteen years were typically spent in child-birth and recovery from it. Assistance to the expectant mother usually began with a 'monthly nurse', and immediately after birth the services of a 'wet-nurse' might be necessary. Thereafter, a full-time nurse would take over, assisted in large and wealthier families by one or two under-nurses or nurse-maids. Their duties were to clean, dress, feed, occupy and generally care for their charges through day and night except for that one hour, usually between five and six in the evening, when children would be presented to their parents. Beyond necessary discipline and elementary moral guidance, the nurse was not expected to teach her children; boys might go to a preparatory school at the age of eight or nine, or might stay at home to be taught with the girls by a governess until entering public school. The governess usually occupied an unhappy and ambivalent position in the Victorian household. Officially, she was an 'upper servant', equal in status to a housekeeper; she had her own room, but might be treated as a member of the family to the extent of sharing the drawing-room, meeting guests and eating at the family table. Their numbers grew in the middle years of the century, reaching 21,000 in 1851, before reputable girls' schools were established in later decades. They were supposed to be 'of gentle birth', a contributor to the *Quarterly Review* stating that 'the real definition of a governess, in the English sense, is a being who is our equal in birth, manners and education, but our inferior in worldly wealth';[33] this meant that they were generally recruited from the daughters of 'failed' gentlemen, or clergy, who saw in governessing the only way of preserving a position in the middle ranks of society. The outstanding difficulty was that although she might be required to teach English, mathematics, geography, drawing, music, elementary French, Italian and even Latin, besides some 'ornamental' accomplishments, there was no recognized qualification for the post until the establishment of Queen's College in 1847 and Bedford College in 1848; long after this, most governesses were still uncertificated and spent their lives in socially isolated drudgery with little hope of escape and none of promotion, oppressed equally by their employers, the children and the other servants. That some women of intelligence and imagination entered the occupation is evident from the considerable number of governess–authoresses which the nineteenth century produced. Some were respected, admired and happy in their work, but many more seem to have been like Charlotte Brontë, who abhorred her 'governess drudgery' and would gladly have exchanged it for 'work in a mill'.[34]

3. The pattern of servant-building was regulated by a well-understood system, dictated primarily by income, and by a strict hierarchy and differentiation of function within the servant community. Numerous publications on household management and domestic economy throughout the period attempted to place a monetary value on these services, and to determine the exact proportion of income to be devoted to them, and although there can be no certainty that actual households deployed their incomes precisely in the recommended ways, these estimates are important as indicating the priorities thought to be necessary in the middle-class budget.

Such estimates date from at least the 1820s, and therefore well before the accession of Victoria to the throne. One of the earliest was *A New System of Practical Domestic Economy* (1824), which made class-distinction rest entirely upon income, and after discussing budgets for the poor in Part I, commenced the budgets of 'gentlemen' in Part II with an income of £150 a year. At £250 a year a man was fairly and squarely in the middle class and his wife had been promoted to a 'lady'; they were now employers of labour, with a maid-of-all-work at £16 a year. At £400 a year a household would need two maids as well as a horse and a groom, at £1,000 a year three maids, a four-wheeled carriage, two horses, a coachman and footman, and at £5,000 a year nine female and thirteen male staff. In the £1,000-a-year budget the coachman receives £24 a year, the footman £22, the cook £16, the house-maid £14 14s. and the nursery-maid £10 10s., while the pair of horses cost between them £65 17s. a year. For the income range £1,000 to £5,000 a year 'servants and equipage' are presumed to take 22 per cent of income (i.e. for horses and carriage 10 per cent, for male servants 8 per cent and for female servants 4 per cent) compared with 36 per cent for food and household provisions, 12 per cent for clothes, 12 per cent for rent, taxes and repairs, 8 per cent for education and private expenses and 10 per cent for savings.[35]

The high degree of correspondence between the scales proposed by different authors suggests that they followed a widely accepted practice. Other budgets of the period[36] also indicate that a full-time servant 'living-in', as opposed to daily or occasional help, only became possible at an income of between £200 and £250 a year, where there was a family to be maintained, though a single lady or widow might afford a servant at a considerably lower income. The scales also closely agree in suggesting about 12 per cent of income to be devoted to domestic service, and another 10 per cent where horses and a carriage were kept. In Samuel and Sarah Adams's *The*

Complete Servant (1825) 25 per cent is suggested for servants and equipage – £250 at £1,000 a year income and £2,500 at £10,000 a year. It seems clear that the horse and carriage was the critical item in the budget, and that in their absence domestic service took a substantially smaller proportion of income. Thus, the costs of service tended to rise as a proportion of income with increased wealth, an estimate of 1845 suggesting that at an income level of £100 a year domestic service took only 4 per cent, at £250 6 per cent, but at £500 (when a horse and some sort of carriage appeared) 15 per cent.[37]

The Adams's 'Number and Description of Servants Usually Employed' is among the most detailed of such tabulations, and worth quoting in full:

£100 a year	a widow or other unmarried lady may keep a young maid at a low salary, say, from five to ten guineas a year;
£150–£180	a gentleman and lady without children may afford to keep a better servant maid at about ten or twelve guineas;
£200	*ditto,* a professed servant maid of all work at from twelve to fourteen guineas;
£300	*ditto,* with one, two or three children, two maidservants;
£400	*ditto, ditto,* three female servants, or two and a boy; viz. a cook, housemaid and nursery maid, or else, instead of the latter, a boy; with gardener occasionally;
£500	*ditto, ditto,* three females and a boy; viz. a cook, housemaid and nursery maid, with a boy as groom and to assist in the house and garden. A gardener occasionally.
£500–£600	a gentleman and lady with children: three females and one man; viz. a cook, housemaid and a nursery maid or other female servant; with a livery servant as groom and footman. A gardener occasionally.
£600–£750	*ditto, ditto,* three females and two men; viz. a cook, housemaid and another female servant; a footman and a groom who may assist in garden; and a gardener occasionally.
£1,000–£1,500	*ditto, ditto,* four females and three men; viz. a cook, two housemaids, a nursery maid or other female servant; a coachman, footman and a man to assist in the stable and garden;
£1,500–£2,000	*ditto, ditto,* six females and five men; viz. a cook, housekeeper, two housemaids, kitchen maid and nursery maid or other female servant; with a coachman, groom, footman, gardener and an assistant in the garden and stable;

£2,000–£3,000	*ditto, ditto,* eight females and eight men; viz. a cook, lady's maid, two housemaids, nurse, nursery-maid, kitchen maid and laundry maid; with a butler, valet, coachman, two grooms, a footman and two gardeners;
£3,000–£4,000	*ditto, ditto,* nine females and eleven men; viz. a housekeeper, cook, lady's maid, nurse, two housemaids, laundry maid, kitchen maid and nursery maid; with a butler, coachman, two grooms, valet, two footmen, two gardeners and a labourer;
£4,000–£5,000	*ditto, ditto,* eleven females and thirteen men; viz. a housekeeper, cook, lady's maid, nurse, two housemaids, laundry maid, still-room maid, nursery maid, kitchen maid and scullion; with a butler, valet, house steward, coachman, two grooms, one assistant groom, two footmen, three gardeners and a labourer.

The same source also quotes a budget for the 'Household establishment of a respectable country gentleman with a young family, net income £16,000 to £18,000, and whose expenses do not exceed £7,000'; this is also useful for giving suggested wages for the twenty-seven servants, as follows:

Housekeeper	24 guineas
Female teacher	30
Lady's maid	20
Head nurse	20
Second nurse	10
Nursery maid	7
Upper housemaid	15
Under housemaid	14
Kitchen maid	14
Upper laundry maid	14
Under laundry maid	10
Dairy maid	8
Second dairy maid	7
Still-room maid	9
Scullion	9
French man-cook	80
Butler	50
Coachman	28
Footman	24
Under footman	20
Groom	liveries and gratuity
Lady's groom	12
Nursery room boy	clothes and gratuity
Head gamekeeper	70 guineas a year, and 13s. a week board wages; a cottage and firing;

Under gamekeeper	one guinea a week
Gardener	40 guineas a year and 13s. a week board wages; a house and firing;
Assistant gardener	12s. a week.

In 1857 J. H. Walsh's book recommended 5 per cent at £100 a year, 7 per cent at £250, and 12 per cent at £500 and above,[38] though in the following year a correspondent to *The Times* disclosed that he employed a maidservant and a nursery-girl for only £12 6s. a year out of his income of £300 (4 per cent) while spending £25 a year on rent and £22 on meat. There had been a heated correspondence as to whether it was possible for a 'gentleman' to marry on £300 a year, arising out of the publication of William Acton's book *On Prostitution* in which the author had alleged that the vast extent of the immoral trade was due to the enforced delay of marriage by a society which prescribed that a man must first adequately establish his financial position. A later edition of J. H. Walsh's book, published in 1873, indicates that an income of £750 a year would permit a general manservant, a parlour-maid, a second house-maid and a cook, whose total wages would be £95, or 13 per cent of income, but a horse, or a pony and gig, would require another £75, or 10 per cent of income, making 23 per cent in all.[39] Recommended budgets from the late Victorian and Edwardian periods suggest that the fraction remained similar, and that ownership of a horse and carriage, and the consequent necessity of employing increasingly expensive male servants, imposed a growing strain on family budgets.

Although, then, there is a general consistency about the advice given to households on the numbers of servants to be kept and the proportion of income to be devoted to them, there is considerable difficulty in discovering the actual wages paid. For one thing, there was a wide margin allowed in the recommended scales to cover varying degrees of skill, age and experience, Mrs Beeton suggesting, for example, that a butler might be paid between £25 and £50 a year, a footman between £20 and £40, a lady's-maid between £12 and £25, and so on.[40] The evidence from autobiographies suggests that professional domestic servants were well aware of these variations, and that they were prepared to move up from, say, third footman to second footman to first and then to under-butler and butler even though this involved frequent changes of employer. Upper servants, and especially upper menservants, seem to have been highly mobile, moving easily from one part of the country to another, between England, Scotland and Ireland, and even to Europe and North America. The new railway systems, the practice, common by mid-century, of advertising vacancies in the daily press, and the fact that employers normally paid travelling expenses all contributed to this mobility of men and women who had special skills to offer and could often be tempted to move by the offer of a few more pounds a year. A second variable is that wages were almost always larger in large establishments, and lowest in lower-middle-class households where only a single maid-of-all-work was kept. The hierarchy of the servants' hall implied wage differentials as well as the division of functions, and the difference in status between, say, a kitchen-maid and a scullery-maid was necessarily reflected in the salaries paid. In this sense, the large establishment formed its own economic system, protected in some degree from the market forces which determined wages in a single-maid household. Again, in domestic service as in other occupations, London rates were higher than provincial, and town rates higher than those in the country.

There is even greater difficulty in estimating the real, as opposed to the money, earnings of domestic servants. One of the major attractions of the occupation was that it normally offered board and lodging and, for men servants, livery where required, so that the wage was clear of outgoings and available for spending, saving or other uses. Additionally, it was common to give allowances for beer, tea and sugar, or to make an addition to the wage where these were not taken; thus, on Mrs Beeton's wage-scales a housekeeper received £20 to £45 a year without such allowances, or £18 to £40 with them. As late as 1927 Jean Rennie was being paid £28 a year as a scullery-maid, plus 2s. 6d. a week beer-money and 2s. 6d. a week washing-money. The difficulty is to put a monetary value on this board and lodging, the quality of which obviously varied widely. Generally speaking, it may be said that servants were housed and fed at no lower level than that of most of the working classes in the period: if they shared a bedroom, and sometimes a bed, with one or two others, this was normal in overcrowded working-class houses, and if their food was plain and unappetizing, usually cooked by one of the lower kitchen servants, it compared closely with what they would have eaten at home. Almost certainly, there was more of it, and the accounts suggest that considerably more meat and beer were consumed, especially by men servants, than among the working classes generally. A single maid-of-all-work probably did far less well than this, existing on scraps left over from upstairs with a great deal of bread, and inhabiting a tiny, ill-ventilated attic bedroom, but on the other hand servants in large and wealthy households sometimes enjoyed very good daily fare, augmented by occasional delicacies left over from dinner-parties. Unlimited table beer and a quart of ale a day would also have added to the nutritional content of the diet. It seems that 'allowances' became increasingly normal as the century progressed: tea and sugar were rarely included in the early decades, but by the 1860s were being given as a definite weekly allowance, and similarly holidays and 'evenings out', which were often specifically forbidden in advertisements of the 1850s, became increasingly common towards the end of the century.[41] Though difficult to quantify, such considerations entered importantly into the servant's standard of living.

Some idea of the value that employers, at least, placed on the cost of food and drink of servants may be gathered from the practice of paying 'board wages' in large establishments. This was originally done only when the family moved from one to another of its houses, or from its country house to a town house for the season, leaving behind some staff for cleaning and maintenance. A weekly sum was then paid for board, which servants might spend as they wished or might 'pool' together to be catered for by one of the other servants. Similarly, an employer might choose to pay board wages when living in town, on the assumption that servants could then buy food more easily and male servants could eat in public houses and restaurants. The scale seems generally to have been about 12s. a week for men and 10s. for women in mid-century, and this accords well with estimates by domestic economists that the real cost of maintaining a female servant was between £25 and £30 a year.[42] It is noticeable, however, that in the first edition of his book in 1857 J. H. Walsh estimated the cost of maintaining a male servant at £30 a year, but in the second edition of 1873 commented that 'a man-servant in the house is an expensive luxury, adding, according to my experience, at least £50 or £60 to the kitchen expenses, and leading to various kinds of annoyance in addition'.[43] The increasing cost of providing an acceptable standard of maintenance, especially for male servants, was doubtless one of the main reasons why the practice of paying board wages spread in the closing years of the century: in 1896 Charles Booth noted that 'the plan of paying board wages throughout the year instead of providing food is increasing, and is usually at the rate of 16s. per week for upper menservants, 14s. for footmen, and 12s. to 14s. for women servants'.[44]

Wage-rates from the Adams's *The Complete Servant* (1825) have previously been quoted. In the Carlyle's household in the 1830s a succession of maids-of-all-work slaved for £8 a year, sleeping in the basement kitchen, and working very long hours under constant supervision and criticism,[45] and in 1837 the footman–butler William Tayler was earning 40 guineas a year, plus another £10–£15 in tips and commission from tradesmen.[46] No great change is noticeable in the scales proposed by Mrs Beeton in 1861. Here, the house-keeper is to have from £18 to £40 a year, the cook £12 to £26, the upper house-maid £10 to £17 and the maid-of-all-work £7 10s. to £11, with tea, sugar and beer in each case: menservants' wages included the butler £25 to £50, the coachman £20 to £35, the footman £20 to £40 and the stable-boy £6 to £13.[47]

The usual contemporary opinion was that, when the cost of board and lodging was added, these wages were not unreasonably low, and compared not unfavourably with working-class earnings generally. If, for example, the coachman in Mrs Beeton's scale was earning £30 a year, the value of his board would double this and an annual livery add a few more pounds; he was as well off as, and more securely employed than, it was claimed, many factory workers and almost all unskilled labourers. The economist Leone Levi, in his survey of wages in 1867, did not consider domestic servants badly off, drawing attention to the fact that some 258,000 held bank or savings accounts with an average deposit of £27 per head. One difficulty in such calculations was that although a board allowance of £30 a year might feed a male servant more than adequately, it in no way helped his wife or children at home; the fact that only half, or less than half, of the real wage was disposable income was a major disadvantage of domestic service. An even greater difficulty in the economists' arguments was that they were so often based on the earnings of upper servants, who were always a minority of the occupation. This point was well made by a contributor to the *Edinburgh Review* in 1862, who wrote:

We must carefully remember that the class concerned does not consist of butlers at £50 a year, or cooks or lady's-maids with about the same pay in money or gifts. We must include a million and more of general servants, housemaids, middle-class cooks and nurserymaids, whose wages lie between £18 and £8 a year . . . Of the 400,000 maids-of-all-work few have more than £10 a year, and many have no more than £8. It is absurd to talk of their laying by money . . . How much can the housemaid lay by of her £10, £12 or £15 a year, or the middle-class cook out of her £12, £15 or £18? Some persons who lecture them on improvidence assume that out of £15 they might lay by £10, and so on; but any sensible housewife will say at once that this is absurd. The plainest and most economical style of dress, respectable enough for a middle-class kitchen, cannot, we are assured, be provided for less than £6 in the country and £7 in town. Then, is the maidservant never to do a kind thing to her own family or anybody else – never to pay postage – never to buy a book or anything that is not wearable? . . .

'The number of old servants who are paupers in workhouses is immense . . .' we learn from Prince Albert's address to the Servants'

Provident Society on 16 May 1849. 'How can the position of the domestic servant ever be elevated if the career ends in the work-house?...'[48]

Wage-levels increased somewhat during the 1870s, 1880s and 1890s, mainly in response to increasing competition from alternative employments. The growth of new, light factory employments and of shop work was particularly important as offering much greater freedom to working-class women and girls at wages comparable with and often higher than the real earnings of domestic servants, and for many the prospect of work in a shop at £30 to £40 a year with meals provided was an attractive alternative to endless confinement in a kitchen or scullery. In 1885 Leone Levi noted some rises in servants' money wages – general maids £16 to £30, footmen £16 to £36, valets £40 to £70 and butlers £50 to £80,[49] the increases for male servants being particularly evident. Later editions of Mrs Beeton's famous work suggest the same improvements. By 1888 the general servant was receiving £10 to £16 a year, plus allowances, a cook from £16 upwards and a valet from £35 upwards (compared with £7 10s. to £11, £12 and £25 respectively in the 1861 edition); by the end of the century £18 had become usual for a maid-of-all-work, and £20 the minimum for a cook. In 1896 Charles Booth and Jesse Argyle gave the average wage of all female servants as £18 12s.; they again noted the differences in wage-levels between single-servant households and large establishments, citing the example of cooks in two-servant households whose wages averaged £18 16s. compared with £30 where more than four servants were kept. Similar conclusions were reached in 1899 by the only government inquiry to be made in the nineteenth century into the wages of domestic servants: this gave £17 16s. a year as the average wage of female servants in London, and £15 10s. in England and Wales outside the capital.[50] The report was also valuable in showing the relationship between the wage and the age of the recipient, average wages in London increasing from £7 9s. a year for servants under sixteen to £20 6s. over twenty-five, £23 2s. over thirty and £27 8s. over forty.

The impressionistic judgement to be derived from these random surveys is that domestic wages showed a continuous improvement over the Victorian period and that they rose particularly during the closing decades of the century. These tentative conclusions can be substantiated from the collections of wage-rates made by the statistician, W. T. Layton, in 1908. Four main sources of data were used – the wage-books recording the wages paid in the household of Lady Bateman's family from 1822 onwards, advertisements in *The Times*

Table 2 Annual wages of domestic servants in the upper and upper middle classes

From Sir A. E. Bateman's Record

Year	Cooks	Housemaids	Nurse-maids	Man-servants	Parlour-maids
	£ s. d.	£ s. d.	£ s. d.	£ s. d.	£ s. d.
1820–22	12 10 0	n.a.	n.a.	n.a.	n.a.
1823–7	12 10 0	7 14 0	,,	,,	,,
1828–32	12 5 0	9 8 0	,,	,,	,,
1833–7	13 10 0	10 0 0	,,	17 0 0	,,
1838–42	14 0 0	11 2 0	,,	20 0 0	,,
1843–7	15 10 0	12 2 0	,,	20 0 0	,,
1848–52	16 6 0	11 13 0	12 0 0	11 10 0*	,,
1853–7	14 12 0	12 0 0	12 0 0	14 6 8*	,,
1858–62	15 14 0	12 4 0	12 0 0	16 8 0	,,
1863–7	18 4 0	12 0 0	12 6 0	18 0 0	,,
1868–72	18 14 0	14 0 0	14 0 0	18 10 0	,,
1873–7	20 6 0	15 12 0	16 0 0	19 12 0	,,
1878–82	20 16 0	16 10 0	18 16 0	18 10 0	,,
1883–7	19 12 0	18 14 0	20 16 0	n.a.	19 8 0
1888–92	22 10 0	18 19 0	21 8 0	,,	19 8 0
1893–7	24 0 0	18 16 0	22 0 0	,,	19 10 0

From Times *advertisements*

Year	Cooks	Housemaids	Nurse-maids	Parlour-maids	Generals, etc.
	£ s. d.	£ s. d.	£ s. d.	£ s. d.	£ s. d.
1848–52	15 0 0	11 0 0	11 0 0	n.a.	11 0 0
1858–62	16 0 0	12 13 4	12 10 0	14 0 0	11 5 0
1868–72	19 6 8	14 2 6	17 2 6	17 7 6	14 0 0
1878–82	23 10 0	16 17 0	21 0 0	19 5 0	18 8 0
1888–92	26 13 4	19 16 0	20 0 0	23 14 0	17 13 4
1907	25 0 0	20 13 4	23 5 0	26 8 0	19 10 0

* During these years a lad was employed as footman.

from 1848 onwards, when this became a commonly-used form of employment bureau for middle- and upper-class servants, advertisements in the *Christian World*, a weekly journal used mainly by lower-middle-class readers, and finally, statistics supplied by the longest-standing registry office, the Metropolitan Association for Befriending Young Servants. Tables 2 and 3 summarize the information from the first two sources, which give the longest series of years.[51]

Finally, Layton combined the four scales into an index number of servants' wages, and placed this alongside the index numbers of industrial wages for women workers and for all workers, previously constructed by G. H. Wood:

Table 3   Comparative changes in wages in domestic service and other industries

	Domestic service			Industrial occupations	
	Private	*Institution*		*Women only*	*All workers*
1823–7	42	n.a.	1824	60	65
1828–32	46	,,	1833	58	60
1833–7	50	,,	1840	59	58½
1838–42	54	61	1845	61	57
1843–7	59	67½	1850	62	60
1848–52	59	68½	1855	65	68
1853–7	58	69	1860	72	68
1858–62	60	68½	1863	73	71½
1863–7	63	74½	1866	78	77
1868–72	69	75	1870	84	77
1873–7	77	80	1874	95	94
1878–82	84	78	1877	98	n.a.
1883–7	88	86	1880	97	84
1888–92	92	92	1883	98	88
1893–7	96	n.a.	1886	91	85
1898–1902	100	100	1891	96	95
1903–7	103	112	1895	98	93
			1900	100	100

Although the statistical evidence is still only partial and selective it would suggest that the rise in domestic servants' wages was greater than in other occupations, doubling between the 1830s and the end of the century and being particularly rapid from the 1870s onwards.

They show a greater rise than those of women in industrial occupations, mainly, of course, because they started from a lower base and had more leeway to catch up. The effect of competing occupations in the late nineteenth century seems to be well borne out.

Domestic servants' wages shared in the war-time rise and post-war fall of all earnings, though, as a 'sheltered' employment, they tended to be less responsive to violent fluctuations. Although the decline in total numbers was accelerated by the war, and the change from private domestic service to institutional work fostered by structual changes in the inter-war years, the long-continued depression ensured a steady flow of recruits into what was now the lowest-status occupation for women. Jean Rennie, a High School-educated girl from Greenock, was forced to take a third house-maid's job in 1924 at £18 a year,[52] while Winifred Foley's job as a maid-of-all-work at fourteen was paid only 5s. a week.[53] In 1930, when a *New Survey of London Life and Labour* was undertaken, a cook's wages were given as £54 to £63 a year, a general servant's from £40 to £52, a working housekeeper's £45 to £52, a house-maid's £40 to £50 and a parlour-maid's £45 to £52.[54] These were London rates, where the competition for trained staff was now intense, and much higher than provincial and country wages. A government scheme to train unemployed boys from the Welsh valleys as house-boys and kitchen assistants offered a weekly wage of 10s. to 15s., and many girls in the 1920s still took their first job at 5s. to 7s. 6d. a week.

4. All the evidence suggests that the status of domestic service suffered a progressive decline throughout the nineteenth century to reach its lowest point in the years between the wars. That menial work had never been a high-status occupation is obvious, but it seems that in centuries before the nineteenth work in another's home had not been regarded with that opprobrium and dislike which it acquired in Victorian times, especially if the home had been that of a nobleman or person of public importance. The status of the employer reflected on to the servant, and even in the nineteenth century employment in a 'great house' with a dozen or more other servants was viewed much more favourably than work as a single maid in a suburban villa. The hierarchy of a large establishment carried its own kind of status within its own closed system, and domestic work seems to have been chiefly resented in proportion to its degree of social isolation and anonymity.

Although the Victorian house, its furnishings and equipment, may have been even more difficult to care for than its predecessors, and although standards and expectations of comfort and cleanliness had undoubtedly risen, the work of domestic servants had always been much the same. What had changed was the position and function of the female employer. In earlier times, and throughout the eighteenth century, she had worked with and personally supervised her domestic staff, at least in all but noble households; servants were assistants, who helped the housewife to bake and brew, wash and mend linen, cook and clean. But Britain's industrialization had produced, by complex processes, the stereotype of the middle-class family pattern and the wife who was functionless except for a long period of child-bearing. A 'lady' did not work, and the husband's success in life became measured by the extent to which he could keep his wife and daughters in genteel idleness. The Victorian housewife no longer worked alongside her servants any more than her husband assisted his factory-hands: at worst, she 'approved' the daily menu and left all detailed arrangements to her housekeeper or other principal servant, at best, she acted as a domestic entrepreneur, regulating and supervising, sometimes with tyrannical authority, the daily tasks of which she had become a non-participant observer.

This social segregation was epitomized by the perpetuation of the terms 'servant' and 'master' to describe the relationship between employer and employee. Before the nineteenth century 'servant' was not a term of disrespect and had been widely applied to apprentices, wage-earning journeymen, agricultural workers ('servants in husbandry') and others; the law continued to refer to 'master' and 'servant' long after 'men' or 'hands' or 'workpeople' or 'employees' had come into general use in industry. By the early nineteenth century 'servant' had generally come to mean domestic servant, and had sunk in connotation as being associated with lack of independence, subservience and servility; if not quite the status of slavery, it was not very far removed from it, and the fact that in the seventeenth and eighteenth centuries negro slaves had been bought and sold openly as domestic servants cannot have helped its public image. Subsequently the spread of popular education through agencies like the Charity Schools, the Methodist revival and the movement for the reformation of public manners and morals all played a part in reinforcing the orders of society on which the nineteenth century class system was built, and while democratic Americans preferred to call their slaves, euphemistically, 'servants', English employers had little compunction in referring to their servants as 'slaveys'. Already in 1788 Philip Thicknesse was recording in his *Memoirs* that the 'veriest slaves' he had seen in two hemispheres were the all-work maid-servants of London.

Legally, of course, the servant was far from rightless, though as Dr Marshall has pointed out[55] the scale was weighted in the master's favour and servants were never in a position to demand legislation favourable to their interests. Their whole time was at the disposal of their employer, all of whose legal commands must be obeyed, and in Tudor times disobedient servants could be committed to the House of Correction with little difficulty. Under the Statute of Artificers (1563) hirings were supposed to be for a year and wages to be assessed annually in relation to skill, but these regulations early proved unenforceable in the case of servants. By the eighteenth century a month's notice of termination, or a month's wages in lieu of notice, had become conventional, though the employer also had the right of summary dismissal for what were supposed to be serious offences. Since domestic service normally provided board and lodging as well as a wage, the ease of dismissal by paying wages in lieu could obviously work very hardly on a servant who was suddenly required to find living accommodation. Again, it seems that the payment of wages, which was in theory required to be quarterly, was frequently in arrears, and that it was difficult for an aggrieved servant to set the legal machinery in notion for their recovery. Normally, however, employers were not permitted to deduct the cost of articles broken or damaged from the wage, and by Victoria's reign wages could not be attached to satisfy a judgement against a servant.

A major disability of domestic servants was that they were regarded as part of the household and properly subject to the discipline of the employer. Where the servant was a thirteen-year-old girl and the discipline humanely exercised, the rule might well be beneficial, but it also treated adult servants as though they were children and, in earlier centuries at least, correction included physical punishment. Corporal punishment certainly continued during the eighteenth, and probably during the nineteenth centuries, though legal opinion became less favourable to it and in 1819 a Captain O'Brien was ordered to pay £200 damages for having knocked senseless his dismissed servant when he asked for his clothes and wages; the servant had sustained a fractured jaw and concussion of the brain. In the previous year an employer of Hinckley was imprisoned for twelve months for administering laudanum to his daughters' governess 'with the view of rendering her subservient to his passions'.[56] Generally, however, Victorian employers contented themselves with laying down minute instructions as to the duties and hours to be observed, especially with regard to 'free time', sometimes locking the servants in the house when they were out, allegedly for their protection. The threat of dismissal without reference, which the employer had no duty to provide, was usually sufficient to ensure obedience.

A second main reason for the low social status of domestic service was that it was recruited almost exclusively from semi-skilled and unskilled occupations, and predominantly from the children of agricultural labourers. Here, too, it seems that the nineteenth century was less fortunate than earlier times, when the daughters of tradesmen and small farmers had not scorned service, and when the close relationship between employer and employee had often demanded a degree of skill and even culture on the part of the servant. But, with the exception of the governess and, possibly, the housekeeper and house-steward, 'low' birth and lack of education became the characteristics of most Victorian servants, their humble origins concealed by a 'respectable' livery or dress and their ignorance by a thin veil of polite manners enjoined by their employers. Many entrants to the occupation in the eighteenth and early nineteenth centuries were orphan or pauper children, the inmates of workhouses which found a convenient economy in binding out such children to housewifery. Some workhouses undertook to train orphans for domestic service, others 'apprenticed' them to families for a nominal premium; in either case the main object was to dispose of an unwanted burden rather than to educate for a career.

So long as country girls continued to come forward in their thousands, employers found no great difficulty in recruitment. But already by mid-century the growth of manufacturing industry in many parts of the country was beginning to offer attractive alternatives. As an article in the *Edinburgh Review* pointed out in 1862:

When we obtain the details of the Census Returns, we shall find how far above a million the number of domestic servants in England and Wales has now risen . . . Of these nearly two-thirds come out of the rural labourer's cottage . . . and in the labourer's cottage, therefore, we shall find the source of the public opinion about domestic service which we now want to ascertain. What is the view of kitchen life which we shall find in the village alehouse, and among the gossips of the hamlet, and in the cottage itself?

When the labourer's daughter becomes a sensible burden, from her fine growing appetite and her wear and tear of clothes, something must be found for her to do, some means to support herself. The boys can get work in the field or the stockyard, and few of them, therefore, think of domestic service; but there is scarcely any other recourse for the girl. If there were, she would not be a servant . . .

The reason is, that the training is one of great hardship, when it begins, as is usual, in the kitchen of the small farmer. We are told that a great number of young girls are worn out by such service before they have completed their growth. They are up early, and often late; their work is severe, their treatment coarse, and their earnings £3 a year. As soon as the girl can get away from such a place, she does; and as she is then supposed to be more or less trained, she is hired at the village shop, or as help where there are so many children that another pair of hands must be called in for the rough work . . . Always on the watch for something better, she escapes, sooner or later, into the kitchen of the curate or the half-pay officer, or the widow or single lady who can afford only a cheap servant . . .

In every village there is somebody who knows somebody else in a town, and most probably in a town where there is a staple industry . . . Wherever a manufacture flourishes within a hundred miles, there will be an eager pressing into it from almost every other occupation, and especially on the part of young girls . . . Mistresses of households in and near every manufacturing town can bear witness to the difficulty of obtaining good and self-respecting female servants . . .[57]

In the closing years of the century the increasing scarcity of recruits revived interest in pauper children as a source of labour. 'In the future, we will draw our servants from the Union,' declared Mrs Eliot James in *Our Servants: Their Duties to Us and Ours to Them* (1883). The idea met a good deal of opposition, not least from the Girls' Friendly Society who thought that workhouse children were 'too often the offspring of sin'; that they laboured under 'the sad heritage of an inherited disposition to vice', and that their upbringing unfitted them for work in a gentleman's home. Some control over ex-workhouse girls was kept in London by the Metropolitan Association for Befriending Young Servants, which stipulated that their minimum wage should be £5 a year, that they should be allowed time off on Sundays and that they should be visited regularly by officers of the Association.

One of the main reasons for the low social status of domestic service was, then, that it had to draw increasingly on the casualties of society – the unintelligent and uneducated, the paupers and orphans, the feeble-minded and physically handicapped – while expanding opportunities in industry, commerce and clerical work continually creamed off the more able. The occupation never succeeded in attracting better-educated, middle-class women, despite a serious attempt in the 1890s to interest them as 'ladies' helps', the American euphemism which it was hoped might raise the status of life below stairs. Some 'ladies' helps' operated a body known as the Household Auxiliary Association, which proposed that its members should eat apart from other servants and should do no scrubbing or carrying of heavy objects upstairs; some took a training course sponsored by the Guild of Aids and the Guild of Household Dames. It appears from a pamphlet of 1906, *Lady Servants, For and Against*, that few found themselves accepted, or a career in domestic service acceptable, and this brief entry of a few middle-class women into the occupation did nothing to arrest its social decline.

Again, unlike most major occupations in the nineteenth century, domestic service was almost untouched by the growth of trade unionism which might have ameliorated the conditions of employment, improved wages and ultimately raised the status of the occupation. Effective unions would, in any case, have been difficult to organize among workers who were so scattered and widespread, and in this respect domestic servants suffered from the same disadvantage as agricultural labourers. Working normally only with one or two other employees, under the employer's own roof and constant supervision, with no regular free time, and with a work-force predominantly female, the conditions of effective association were all lacking for the domestic servant. Moreover, in an occupation so rigidly authoritarian and hierarchical there was little sense of common purpose or even common injustice: between the lordly butler and the lowly kitchen-maid, the haughty housekeeper and the urchin stable-boy, no bond existed which could have drawn them into alliance against the employer. In small households the maid-of-all-work was isolated and impotent, while in large establishments, where the toast of 'The Master and Mistress' was drunk nightly in the servants' hall and the employer–employee relationship was still essentially feudal, a 'peasants' revolt' was unthinkable. Attempts in 1872 to form unions of domestic servants in Dundee and Leamington came to nothing. In 1890 a more concerted plan to establish a national association resulted in the formation of the London and Provincial Domestic Servants' Union, with an office in Oxford Street, and in 1894 a mass meeting at Kensington Town Hall was addressed by Archbishop Farrar on the disabilities of domestic servants. But plans to establish a well-regulated registry office and a home for old and unemployed servants came to nothing, and after a few years of ineffective existence interest in the union died. The main, almost the only, weapon of the dissatisfied servant was to withdraw his labour and try to find a more congenial place, and the accounts suggest that there was a very high labour turn-over, especially in single-maid and small households; they also indicate that among upper servants at least 'bad' employers were marked down and an informal 'blacklist' operated. The difficulty with frequent changes was that no reference could be expected, and a 'short-charactered' servant might well find it difficult to get employment elsewhere. In her 1861 edition Mrs Beeton recommended personal inquiry among friends and tradespeople as the best means of

6*

recruiting servants, though by 1888 she suggests advertisement in the national press. The alternative, for servants as well as employers, was to use one of the many registry offices, some of which had an evil reputation in mid-century as 'covers' for procuring prostitutes; in any case, they exacted substantial commission, and had an interest in a high turn-over. Later in the century, semi-philanthropic bodies like the Metropolitan Association for Befriending Young Servants, the Girls' Friendly Society and the Ladies' Society for Aiding Friendless Girls provided a better-controlled service than the commercial registry offices, and in London between 1905 and 1910 the LCC laid down rules for the operation of all employment agencies.[58]

The fundamental reason for the low social status of domestic servants must, however, have been the degrading, and sometimes inhuman, conditions under which many of them worked. Although, as the nineteenth century progressed, the legal position of servants probably improved, the right to free time and holidays became better established and accommodation became slightly more comfortable, these in no way compensated for the sense of social inferiority which separated domestic servants from independent workers. It may well be that long-standing servants became inured to this and accepted their lot ungrudgingly. Charles Booth observed in 1896,

> It is, in fact, almost necessary to have an inherited aptness for the relationship involved – a relationship very similar in some respects to that subsisting between Sovereign and subject. From both servant and subject there is demanded an all-pervading attitude of watchful respect, accompanied by a readiness to respond at once to any gracious advance that may be made without ever presuming or for a moment 'forgetting ourselves'. It is a fine line not to be over-stepped ... but those who are gifted with the tact or the experience to tread safely are not only able to keep with perfect comfort within the line, but even acquire an exceptional dignity of their own which is very far removed from servility.[59]

The combination of drudgery and isolation was the worst feature of the job of a maid-of-all-work. Again, Charles Booth recognized this clearly when he wrote, 'The dullness which is the complaint universally urged against single-handed places of all kinds is felt very keenly by children of fifteen or so; they have always been accustomed to living in a crowd, and are frightened by the loneliness of the long evenings in which they have to sit in the kitchen by themselves, or perhaps to be left entirely alone in the house.' In this respect, domestic service compared very unfavourably with the camaraderie of factory life, as the *Edinburgh Review* pointed out in 1862. Servants missed

the annual or half-yearly festival – the picnic in summer and the ball in
winter – which is a conspicuous event in factory life . . . Servant-girls and
foot-boys see the vans go by in the summer morning, and hear the fiddles
and the dancing in the winter evening, and feel they are 'in bondage' and
'get no pleasure'. They cannot dress as the factory lads and lasses may –
buying and wearing whatever they take a fancy to. Worse still, they have
not the daily stimulus and amusement of society of their own order . . .
The maidservant must have 'no followers', while the factory-worker can
flirt to any extent. Servant-girls rarely marry, while factory-girls probably always may, whether they do or not . . . Public opinion among the
class is in favour of the independence of factory and other day-work . . .
In one word, it is *independence* against *dependence*.[60]

Added to these disadvantages, the hours worked in domestic
service, unregulated by any legislation, were undoubtedly longer
than in factory work. It was calculated in 1873 that a house-maid's
day extended from 6 A.M. until 10 P.M., during which she had two-
and-a-half hours for meals and an hour-and-a-half in the afternoon
for needlework, a total of four hours' 'rest'. This meant twelve hours
of actual work, longer by two hours than a factory woman's day.
On Saturday, when the factory hand worked two hours less than
usual, the servant worked longer, and on Sunday, when the factory
worker could rest completely, the servant was still required to work
almost a normal day.[61] Eighty hours of actual work a week, against
fifty-six for the factory worker, may well be a fair estimate for the
late nineteenth century, and must have been exceeded in many
single-handed households.

The outward and visible sign of servility was, of course, the
uniform, and in this respect, too, the nineteenth century was a
period of deterioration for women servants. Menservants had always
worn livery or an adapted form of the ordinary dress of the period,
but women servants in the eighteenth century had dressed as they
pleased and were not uncommonly mistaken for friends of their
employer. Early in the nineteenth century it seems to have become
usual for a maid to keep a simple stuff gown for her indoor duties,
and by the 1830s the now cheap cotton print dress was being widely
used. As yet, however, there was no prescription about dress provided it was neat and simple. A magazine article of 1843 noted that
'many ladies object to a servant fastening her collar with a brooch,
but it is surely more tidy than a pin, and if the brooch be not tawdry
we do not think it need be objected to. We have always encouraged
our servants to ask our advice on the subject of dress, and have
occasionally made their purchases for them.' By the 1860s custom
had hardened into law, and there was now a recognized uniform for

female servants – a cotton print dress for the morning, with black dresses, white aprons and caps for the afternoon. 'Crinolines are decidedly inconvenient for parlourmaids' and housemaids' work', it was commented in 1877; 'She has no room to pass behind the chairs at table, and she sweeps the ornaments from the tables and what-nots.' A few concessions to vanity were made later in the century – aprons trimmed with lace or frills, and ribbons to the cap – though basically the servants' uniform remained unchanged up to the Second World War.

A number of factors, therefore – economic, legal and social – contributed to the low and declining status of domestic service in the nineteenth century. Material disadvantages were no doubt im-portant – the limited opportunities for promotion, the large degree of mechanical repetition in the work, the length and irregularity of working hours, the lack of free time and the ineffectiveness of labour organizations. Yet it was the social disabilities which ultimately weighed more heavily: the isolation of the servant, both from his employer and from the community outside, the virtual absence of a private life, the degree of control exercised by the employer, the use of the term 'servant' and the enforced uniform which went with it. In great households the upper servants, at least, might be able to identify with the employer, basking in a reflected glory of which they could feel a part. In their autobiographical accounts such ser-vants rarely voice resentment or discontent; on the contrary, they stress the responsibility of their positions, their satisfaction from work well done and the enjoyment to be derived from the commu-nity of the servants' hall. In the conflict between social aristocracy and political democracy they were unquestionably on the side of the former. 'There is no class less open to democratic ideas than a contented servant class,' wrote William Clarke. 'Compared with them, their titled and wealthy employers are revolutionists. They cannot bear change, their minds are saturated with the idea of social grades and distinctions, they will not even live with one another on terms of social equality.'[62] But as the century progressed the num-bers of such 'contented' servants, and the prevalence of such atti-tudes, declined. Single servants, always a majority of the occupation, found it hard to identify with a shopkeeper–employer, and became increasingly alienated and discontented when more interesting opportunities began to open up. By the closing decades of the century, social imitation was no longer restricted to the middle classes, and as early as 1862 the *Edinburgh Review* had indicated the real root of 'the servant problem':

If popular education has improved in quality, as well as improved in extent, one consequence must be the diversion of a large number of young persons from domestic service. Of the female pupil–teachers, the greater number would have been domestics; and when there is one of these in a family, the other members assume that the whole household has risen in rank. When once a pupil–teacher has become a certificated school-mistress, her sisters consider it beneath them to be in service. When one girl becomes Miss A. or B. the others desire to leave off their caps and to take rank among the educated class. If that fortunate individual has dined at the house of a school manager, and has had a footman stand behind her chair, the rest cannot be contented with the kitchen . . . they look about for the chance of obtaining some post as a teacher of something – of be-coming, in some way, however humble, connected with a school; and if that be out of reach, they will follow any employment which exempts them from 'bondage' to authority, and enables them to call themselves 'Miss', at whatever risk of precarious subsistence, poverty, or even want.[63]

Fundamentally, the low social status of servants derived from the inferiority with which they were regarded by society generally and by employers in particular. Although successful middle-class family and household maintenance depended upon their skill, hard work and probity, servants were in no real sense members of the institu-tions they served; they were 'dependants', for whom employers had a Christian responsibility, but were not expected or required to have thoughts or opinions, identities or personalities beyond those necessary for the discharge of their duties. An exact analogy is not easy to draw, but in the Victorian attitude to servants there was much in common with the attitude towards children, dumb animals and the feeble-minded; as God's creatures, all deserved kindness and consideration, but above all, they required firm authority, discipline and the direction of their natural superiors.

Such attitudes found expression in some curious practices. One writer on etiquette thought that

It is better in addressing [servants] to use a higher key of voice, and not to suffer it to fall at the end of a sentence. The best-bred gentleman we ever had the pleasure of meeting always employed in addressing servants . . . a gentle tone but very elevated key. The perfection of manners in this particular is to indicate by your language that the performance is a favour, and by your tone that it is a matter of course.[64]

Again, it was a convention that housework should be done silently, even secretly, that maids should not be seen about the rooms and passages when the employer or his guests were likely to be about; the maintenance of the house was to be a clockwork function and the separation of master and servant complete. It was mainly out of concern for the possible embarrassment of lady and gentleman

travellers on the railways that the middle- or second-class carriage
was introduced, and at some refreshment-rooms signs read 'For
Second-Class Passengers and Servants'.

In holding such attitudes, employers could always take refuge
in the sanction of the Church. It was not difficult to find Biblical
authority for the obedience owed by servants to their masters, even
if it involved transposing the social relationships of Old Testament
times to the nineteenth century. A tract containing 'Advice to
Young Women on Going to Service', issued by the Society for
Promoting Christian Knowledge in 1835, put the matter thus: 'Had
God seen that it would have been better for your eternal good that
you should be great and rich, He would have made you so; but he
gives to all the places and duties best fitted for them.' The Christian
duty of servants was, therefore, to accept their lot willingly, to thank
God daily for providing them with work, food and shelter and,
above all, to honour and obey those divinely set in authority over
them. The most-quoted text, not uncommonly framed over the
servant's bed, was from Ephesians vi, 5–6, 'Servants, be obedient
to them that are your masters according to the flesh, with fear and
trembling, in singleness of your heart, as unto Christ; not with eye-
service, as men-pleasers; but as the servants of Christ, doing the
will of God, from the heart.' A spate of pamphlets and tracts cautioned the maidservant against moral dangers and warned her not
to lust after the finery of her mistress ('While you are in service,
don't copy ladies. Wait until you have the same income and a home
of your own'); compilations of prayers included one for the lady's-
maid which ran, 'Give me patience under rebuke and set a watch,
O Lord, before the door of my lips . . . Preserve me from idleness
and from wasting the time which is another's.' Restless servants
were advised by the *Servants' Magazine* in 1867, 'Never change
your place unless the Lord clearly shows you it will be for your
soul's good.' Yet in many churches and chapels, especially in those
where pew-rents were charged, servants were strictly segregated
from their employers, often being relegated to distant galleries, or
placed behind screens. The relationship between master and servant
depended upon the acceptance of a social 'apartheid' sanctioned by
the law of God, and on an economic system which justified sweated
labour on the argument of providing work for those otherwise un-
employable. When other, more satisfying, forms of work became
available to women, when religious belief waned and when the
'natural' obedience of one class to another came to be widely dis-
puted, this kind of relationship no longer carried either public
approval or private acceptance.

William Tayler
*footman**

William Tayler was born at Grafton in Oxfordshire in 1807, one of a large family of a yeoman farmer. Like many more in his day, William joined in the migration from the countryside, taking up 'gentlemen's service' first locally, then in London. In 1837, when the journal was written, he was in the employ of a wealthy widow, Mrs Prinsep, of 6 Great Cumberland Street, whose husband, John Prinsep, had been M.P. for Queensborough and an Alderman of the City of London after making a fortune with the East India Company. William married in 1834 when he was twenty-six and his wife eighteen; she and their children were lodged comfortably nearby, and William maintains the convention of bachelordom by referring to her always as 'a certain person' or 'a particular friend', visited only on Sundays. Clearly, he was literate, intelligent and perceptive; he was also fond of drawing and painting, and was a competent artist. In Mrs Prinsep's service he was paid generously, at 40 guineas a year, and tips added another £10–£15 a year. In later life he became a butler, and on retirement was able to rent a whole house in Paddington. He died in 1892.

The journal covers one year, 1837, and was undertaken 'to improve my handwriting'. The following extracts are from the months of January, May, July, August and December. The original spelling has been retained.

January 1st 1837 As I am a wretched bad writer, many of my friends have advised me to practise more, to do which I have made many atempts but allways forgot or got tired so that it was never atended to. I am now about to write a sort of journal, to note down some of the chief things that come under my observation each day. This, I hope, will induce me to make use of my pen every day a little. My account of each subject will be very short – a sort of multo in parvo – as my book is very small and my time not very large.

I will begin by giveing a short account of the people I live with. I am the only manservant kept here as the coachman is only a sort of jobber.†

* From *Diary of William Tayler, Footman, 1837*, edited by Dorothy Wise, with notes by Ann Cox-Johnson, St Marylebone Society Publications Group. 1962. William Tayler's Diary is the property of Mr Richard Willoughby Bartlett, and the editor, Dorothy Wise, acknowledges his permission to reproduce.

† A job-master was one who kept and hired out horses.

Here are three maidservants, very quiet good sort of bodys, and we live very comfortable together. Here is only a mistress and her daughter, the first a widow and the latter an old maid. She is at least forty years of age, therefore I think she deserves that title. They are also very quiet good sort of people but very gay and sees a great deal of company. They made their money in the East Indies but since then has lost it in bad speculations. Five of the sons are in the East Indies now, makeing their fortunes if they can. The father is dead and so are two of the sons; their widows are very often visiting here as well as some of the other sons' children – much oftner than we want them. The latter are here at present during the holidays.

The first of January is ushered in with very cold frost and snow. This being Sunday, nothing has transpired of consequence. I got up at half past seven, cleaned the boys' clothes and knives [and] lamps, got the parlour breakfast, lit my pantry fire, cleared breakfast and washed it away, dressed myself, went to church, came back, got parlour lunch, had my own dinner, sit by the fire and red the Penny Magazine and opned the door when any visitors came. At 4 o'clock had my tea, took the lamps and candles up into the drawing room, shut the shutters, took glass, knives, plate and settera into the dining room, layed the cloth for dinner, took the dinner up at six o'clock, waited at dinner, brought the things down again at seven, washed them up, brought down the desert, got ready the tea, took it up at eight o'clock, brought it down at half past, washed up, had my supper at nine, took down the lamps and candles at half past ten and went to bed at eleven. All these things I have to do every day, therefore I have mentioned the whole that I mite not have to mention them every day.

2nd Done the usual business of the morning by eleven o'clock; took a walk, called on a friend and had a glass to drink to the new year. Got home again at half past twelve, got lunch, had dinner, went out with the carriage, went round Hyde Park, saw some thousands of people sliding and skaiting on the Serpentine. Several got a ducking from the ice breaking but all got out safe. Got home by 4, had tea, got parlour dinner and tea, spent the evening in writing and reading until twelve o'clock and then went to bed.

3rd Done the usual work of the morning. Took a walk, came back, found my tailor waiting for me, paid his bill, drank a few glasses of wine with him, spent the afternoon in drawing and the evening in reading and finished my screens which I have been makeing to be raffled for. Went to bed at eleven.

4th Got up at seven o'clock. This is a very buisy day, nothing but work all day – company to dinner in the parlour and a children's party in the evening, play acting and dancing and a grand supper. It's not fashionable for jentlefolk to have supper, only on such occasions as this. Did not get to bed until one o'clock and very tired.

5th Got up at half past seven. Has a great deal of work to do this morning with cleaning lamps, knives and plate. All our people dine out. They go to the old lady's marreyd daughter who lives in Belgrave Square. Went at five o'clock and stayed until eleven. I went to see my friends; allso got home at ten, found company in the kitchen, drank elder wine until eleven, went with the carriage and fetched home the gentry, got to bed by twelve.

6th Rose by eight; not much to do today as they dined out yesterday. Spent the afternoon in drawing and have just been and had my supper of rost turkey and mincepies and critens.* Intend to go to bed before eleven o'clock.

7th Rose at half past seven; done my work at eleven. Went out and took a walk; back to dinner. Went out with the carriage at two, went about paying visets, called at ten houses. At six of them the people were all ill so that they could not see visitors and at two more the ladies were just confined. Came home again and had my tea, got parlour dinner over and spent evening in making scrap book; went to bed at eleven.

9th Up at eight. It's realy very little use getting up sooner as the mornings are so dark and I detest working by candlelight and, more than all, I am very fond of my Bed this cold weather. I spent this morning in work and fiddleing about the afternoon. I done a little drawing until between three and four when, to my great surprise, my Aunt Puzey called to see me. I found her looking exceedingly well and I think gets younger instead of older. She stayed to tea and left about six o'clock this evening. I took a short walk, got home to supper, went to bed at eleven o'clock.

10th All the people in the house are ill with the influenza. The old Lady and two of the boys and one of the maids are ill in bed now, therefore we that are well have plenty to do to wait on the others. I cannot hardly leave the house in consequence, obliged to remain at home all this day, amused myself with drawing and reading. This evening the old lady thought herself worse; went for the doctor. He was gone to the play; came back – the patient is better and I am just going to bed.

11th Got up at half past seven. All the sick people in bed; very buisy; obliged to be in attendance. John Tayler, the shoemaker from Turnham Green, has called to see me this morning, haves lunch, sits gosiping till dinner time and then sits gosiping until tea time and now he is gone home. So much sitting indoors do not suit him all though my pantry is a very comfortable room. I did intend to have gon out but here are two more people has just called on me. I wish them farther but I sopose I must be satisfied with it. It's half past ten and I am just going to bed.

12th Up at half past seven; done the usual business of the morning which is not much as all the people are ill. They cannot make use of many things belonging to me. Went out for an houre or two. Miss P. took one of the boys to Clapham and left him there; I am not sorry for that. The old Lady's daughter that's married and her husband called this afternoon. He gave me a sovering for a Christmas box for which I was greatly obliged to him

---

* Scraps of meat left after lard-making when the pure lard had been strained off. Mixed with currants and peel, they make an excellent pie.

for, but it's no more than he ought to do as they very frequently dine here. Spent the evening in makeing a scrap book. Got to bed at eleven.

13th Up as usual. Some of the sick people getting better. Took a walk this afternoon; called on a tradesman. He gave me five shillings for a Christmas box for which I was not sorry. Spent the evening in drawing; got to bed at eleven . . .

15th This being Sunday of course I went to church – or rather, I took a little walk elsewhere. The old Lady, I am sory to say, gets worse; I am afraid we shall soon lose her. The cook is very ill too; she keeps her bed. A gentleman called, a nephew of the old Lady's, expecting to get a dinner but I told him everbody was ill in the house but me, which news very soon started him of, to my satisfaction.

16th Got up at half past seven; done my usual work. The old Lady and the cook both very ill in bed. the housemaid gone home to bury her Mother, the Ladys maid very ill but obliged to keep about – myself and Miss P. are the only two that has not had it. We expect to be caught hold of very soon. The Influenza was never known to be so bad as it is now. Seven hundred policemen and upwards of four thousand soldiers are ill with it about London, and many large shops and manufactorys are put to great inconveniences on account of it. I am obliged to stay within to help the sick. This is what I don't like as I like to get a run everyday when I can . . .

I took a short walk today, saw a new machine for scrapeing the roads and streets. It's a very long kind of a how [hoe], very much like an ell rake. One man draws it from one side of the street to the other, taking a whole sweep of mud with him at once, cleaning a piece a yeard and a half at a time. There are two wheels, so, by pressing on the handles, he can wheel the thing back everytime he goes across the street for a hoefull. It's considered to do as much as seven men. It's eleven o'clock and I am of to bed. It was so dark today at one o'clock that one could not see two yards before one; people were obliged to burne lights. . . .

19th Went for a walk, came home, had my dinner, done a little to drawing. Went out to pay some bills. Man put three and sixpence in my hand – I pocketed the afront. Spent the evening in writing and the best way I could.

20th Up at eight. The sick people are getting better, all but the old Lady; she is very poorly and I don't know which way she intend to take yet. I have five shillings gave me today for a Christmas box; I did not give it back again. It's just gone two o'clock and it's so dark that I am obliged to burn a candle to write this by. All the shops have lights and every body elce or they could not see.

22nd This being Sunday of course I went to church. I think I will give an account of our liveing during the next week. They breakfast at eight in the kitchen on bread and butter and toast – or anything of the kind if they like to be at the trouble of making it – and tea. All most all servants are obliged to find their own tea and sugar. For my own part I care but very little about breakfast at all, therefore I jenerally wait until the breakfast comes down from the parlour at ten o'clock when my apatite has come and I can then git a cup of coco, which I am very fond of, and a rowl or something of the kind. Anyone that like to have lunch, there it is for them but, as I have breakfast so late, I want no lunch. This day we had for dinner a piece of surloin of beef, roasted brocoli and potatos and preserved damson pie. We all have tea together at four o'clock with bread and butter and sometimes a cake. At nine o'clock we have supper; this evening it's cold beef and damson pie. We keep plenty of very good table ale in the house and every one can have as much as they like. This has been a miserable wet day and I have spent most of it in reading the news paper . . .

25th Been to Hamstead with the carriage. It's about six or seven miles out of London. It's where a great many Cockneys goes to gipseying and to ride on the jackasses. It's a very plesent place. Had for dinner today a rost leg of mutton, potatos and suety pudding: supper, cold meat and rosted potatos and rabbit.

26th A very wet day. All the patients quite well except the old Lady who continues very poorly. Amused myself with makeing scrap book which I am going to send into Oxfordshire when it's finished. Had Irish stew and rice pudding for dinner. I went out to supper where I had some mince pie that came from Grafton.

27th This afternoon I have imagined a picture, drawn it and coloured it and all in a little more than one houre and a half. The subject is servants helping themselves in the dining room. Finished the scrap book and sent it to George Castle for him to look over before I send it off. For dinner had a roast shoulder of mutton and savois and potatos.

Miss P. and two young Gents. going to the play [at] Drury Lane. The old Lady treated me to see it. The first part was *Sinderella*. I saw her in the kitchen among the sinders and saw the old wich turne her into a lady and made a carriage out of a pumpkin, four horses out of white mice, a coachman out of a rat, two footmen out of grasshopers. This was done by the stage opening and the real things being pushed up by people below and the rat, mice and pumpkins and things being pulled below at the same time. Saw Sinderella go to the ball and lose her slipper and in the end was married to a Prince. The second part was a pantomime, where the clowns and harlaquins made a great deal of funn by turning one thing into another, such as an old woman into a young one and turning a bublick house into a watermill. In this part I saw the Devil in hell. The place looked very firey and hot – not anything at all tempting. There were more things to numerous to mention. Got to bed by one o'clock.

28th A cold day, some snow. There is a great deal of illness about London. There were to of been fifty persons buried at St John's Wood bureying ground in one day this week, but they could only bury thirty of them as the days are so short. I continues quite well therefore I hope the complaint has missed me quite. Had hash and vegitables for dinner, cold mutton and rice pudding for supper. We have more change in our liveing in sommer and we can get veal sometimes beside what I have mentioned. We get many little nice things that come down from the parlour. In the course of a fiew weeks, I will give a little account of their liveing in the parlour. I have just had a good blow out of egg hot* and am now going to bed.

29th This is Sunday and I have *realy* been to Church. We have had a great deal of snow today. This day for dinner had a part of a round of beef with potatos, cabbage and carrots, scimmerlads† and bread pudding. For supper roast beef, pickle cabbage &c. &c. Had a Lady to dinner here to-day. The Lady's maid is taken very sick today; I sopose she has been eating to much or something of the kind. But she is very subject to sickness. Last summer, when we were coming home from Canterbury, she actually spewed all the way, a distance of sixty miles and not less time than eight hours. The people stared as we passed through the towns and villages as she couldent stop even then. It amused me very much to see how the country people stood stareing with their mouths half open and half shut to see her pumping over the side of the carriage and me sitting by, quite unconserned, gnawing a piece of cake or some sandwiches or something or other, as her sickness did not spoil my apatite. It was very bad for her but I couldent do her any good as it was the motion of the carriage that caused her illness. I gave her something to drink every time we changed horses but no sooner than it was down than it came up again, and so the road from Canterbury to London was pretty well perfumed with Brandy, Rum, Shrub, wine and such stuff. She very soon recovered after she got home and was all the better for it after. It's eleven o'clock. My fire is out and I am off to bed . . .

31st This is a very much finer day than we have had latly. I have been to Richmond today to take the young gentlemen to school and I am very glad to get rid of them. When I was there, I went into a publick house to have something to drink. There was an old woman in there who gets her liveing as well as many more, by drawing soft water into Richmond with donkeys and there sells it so much a pail. This old woman can frequently earn five or six shillings a day by selling water and I beleve the most of it goes for gin . . .

May 10th Have been out. Saw G. Castle. He tells me his father and his cousen Pike are in great hopes of makeing something of their dog. They have taken a room at St James Theater to show it to people that like to go and see at so much a head

It's surpriseing to see the number of servants that are walking about the streets out of place. I have taken an account of the number of servants that have advertised for places in one newspaper during the last week; the

---

* A hot drink made of beer, eggs, sugar and nutmeg.
† A dumpling cooked with the vegetables and skimmed off with a skimmer.

number is three hundred and eighty. This was the *Times* paper. There is considered to be as many advertisements in that as there is in all the rest of the papers put together, therefore I mite sopose there to be 380 advertisements in the rest. I am sertain half the servants in London do not advertise at all. Now, soposing seven hundred and sixty to of advertised and the same number not to of advertised, there must be at least one thousand, five hundred and twenty servants out of place at one time in London, and if I had reckoned servants of all work – that is, tradespeoples' servants – it would of amounted to many hundreds more. I am sertain I have underrated this number. Servants are so plentifull that gentlefolk will only have those that are tall, upright, respectable-looking young people and must bare the very best character, and mechanics are so very numerous that most tradespeople sends their sons and daughters out to servise rather than put them to a trade. By that reason, London and every other tound is over run with servants . . .

14th This is Sunday, a very dark, foggy morning and very wet and a great deal of thunder with very heavy hail.

I said some time agoe I would give an account of the way the people live in the parlour. Now I think I will begin just to give you some idea of it, but as the old Lady and her daughter are quite allone at present, there is not so much cooking for the parlour as there is in general. For the parlour breakfast, they have hot rolls, dry toast, a loaf of fancy bread and a loaf of common and a slice of butter. They have the hot water come up in a hurn that has a place in the middle for a red hot iron which keep the water boiling as long as the iron keep hot. With this, they make their tea themselves. They have chocalate which is something like coffee but of a greasey and much richer nature. This is all they have for breakfast and it's the same every morning. They have it as soon as they are up, which is nine o'clock. It take them about three-quarters of an houre to breakfast.

Lunch at one, the same time we dine in the kitchen. They generally have some cut from ours or have cold meat and some vegitables. Dinner at six which is considered very early. This day they had two soles fryed with saws, a leg of Mutton, a dish of ox, pullets, potatos, brocolo, rice and a rhubarb tart, a tabiaca pudding, cheese and butter. Has tea at eight o'clock with bread and butter and dry toast; never any supper – it's not fashionable.

Had one gentleman and a lady to dinner and two old maids viseting in the kitchen. They has been servants but, being unsuccessfull in getting places, they took a bublic house. They say, when in service, they allways heared servants very much run down and dispised but since they have been keeping a bublic house, they have had an opertunity of seeing the goings on amongst the tradespeople. They consider them a most drunken, disepated, swareing set of people. Servants, they say, are very much more respectable in every point and deserve to be thought better of than they are at present. Mechanics and tradespeople in general speak disrespectfully of servants. If they meet a servant in company, they will say one to the other, 'It's only a servant,' but everyone must think and must know that servants form one of the most respectable classes of persons that is in existance. In the first place, they must be healthy, clean, respectable, honest, sober set of people to be servants; their character must be unexceptionable in every respect. They are in the habit of being in the first of company and are constantly hearing the first of conversation. Being so much in the company of the gentry, from the private gentleman to the Highest Duke in the land allways traveling about with their masters, learning and seeing hundreds of things which mecanics or tradespeople never knew there was in the country, and of the two (trades and servants – I mean gentlemen's servants) I think servants are the most respectable in consequence of their characters and actions being so thoroughly investigated by their superiors.

18th This is a very buisy day as we are going to have a party this evening something larger than usual. We had four to dinner and about fifty or sixty in the evening. The plan of manageing these parties are thus: – there were two men besides myself, one opened the door and let the Company in, I shewed them into a parlour where there was three maidservants to make tea and give it to them and take off their cloaks and bonnets, and the other man shewed them up into the drawingroom and gave in their names as lowd as he can bawl in the drawingroom. There is very good singing and music in their way. After they have been here some time, we carrey them up some refreshments on trays and hand about amongst them. This is all kinds of sweet cakes and biscuits, lemonade, ashet, negos,* orangade and many other pleasent drinks but the best is the different kind of ices. This is stuf made of ice pounded, mixed with cream, and juce of strawberrey, some of apricot and oranges – in short, there are many different kinds. It's quite as cold as eating ice alone. It's eat out of glass sawsers with a spoon. It's from ten to sixteen shillings a quart, it depends on what fruit it's made of. The company comes jeneraly about ten or eleven o'clock and stays until one or two in the morning. Sweet hearting matches are very often made up at these parties. It's quite disgusting to a modist eye to see the way the young ladies dress to atract the notice of the gentlemen. They are nearly naked to the waist, only just a little bit of dress hanging on the shoulder, the breasts are quite exposed except a little bit comeing up to hide the nipples. Plenty of false haire and teeth and paint. If a person wish to see the ways of the world, they must be a gentleman's servant, then they mite see it to perfection.

19th Got up with a headache and feel stupid all day. Been out with the carriage this afternoon with Miss P. She kept me out longer than I thought she aught to of done, therefore I gave her a little row for it. I hope it will do her good. I served the old lady the same way the other day and it did her a deal of good, and I have no doubt that it will act the same in this case. Breakfast as usual, lunch seago and cold duck, dinner veal and minced mutton, soop and vegitables, pudding . . .

* I have been unable to trace a drink called ashet. In Scotland this is the word for a large tray or dish. Perhaps the diary should read 'ashets of negus'. Negus – port, sherry or some other wine, sweetened with spices, lemon and hot water.

At Brighton

July 7th We have been very buisy preparing to go to Brighton tomorrow. Plenty of packing up and running about.

8th Got up very early and of course very buisy loading the carriage and one thing and the other. We started at half past ten with post horses, traveled on very pleasently through Surry. The whole road is a complete mass of hills, which make the road very plesent for us but very bad for the poor horses. The road is very pleasent and butifull views from the hills. We stopt about two o'clock at one of the places where we change horses and had some dinner of cold roas beef and pickles and goosberreys tart. I made no small hole in it and the other servant did the same.

I should think this part of the country produces the worst sheep in England. Sussex is worse than Surry. Some of the half starved creatures apears to be hardly able to stand. We arrived at Brighton at six o'clock, tired enough as the sun was enough to scorch us as we set outsid the carriage. Brighton is a very pleasent place something like London but not so big. We have a butifull view of the sea which comes allmost up to the houses. We have a very nice house and very pleasently situated.

9th This is Sunday. Had a very bad night's rest last night. I slept downstairs in a little room but, when I came to lay down, I found the bed covered with bugs. I began to kill them, but they were so numerous that I found it imposible to kill all. Therefore I shook the bedding and layed it on the floor. There a great many of them found me, so that I could get but little rest. Took a walk this morning along the beach to view the sea. This being Sunday, I shall be under the necessity of passing this night as I did the last.

10th Had a walk before breakfast. The sea air gives me an exolent apatite. The house have been thronged all day with tradespeople wanting to serve us with different things. I am going to sleep in one of the upper rooms which is much more airey and more healthey. Our family consists of Mrs & Miss P., and Mrs T. P. and Master W.P., three maid servants and myself.

11th Have been this morning and had a bathe in the sea for the first time in my life. I like it very much. Have been walking about townd to make discoverys.

12th I got to the sea side two or three times a day and amuses myself by seeing the pleasure boats or seeing the fishermen come in with their vessils of fish, or sometimes I stand and watch the large waves jump over the small ones.

13th Been walking about seeing all I could. Here are many things to be seen here. Brighton is a very pleasent place. The tound lays two miles along by the sea side and the shore is verey smothe and gravely and lays full south which causes this place to be very warm in the summer. The back or north part of the tound is sorounded by a rang of hills called the

Brighton downs or South Downs, where the South Down sheep come from.

14th This day I have been seeing some of the most grandist sights that can be seen. That is some large ships going past here in full sail going out to India.

15th Have been looking about Brighton Market today. A very exalent market, well suplied with fruit, vegitables, meat, &c. &c. A very fine building.

16th Went to church but it was so full that I could not get inside the door, therefore I took a walk and called at a Methadist Chapple. There I stayed but a very short time. From there, I went to another Chapple but on looking at a board on the door, I found I must pay a shilling if I went in and that would not do.

18th Went on the pier. This is a kind of bridge brojecting into the sea a quarter of a mile. It's a great curiosity as it's hung on chains. People can get from that into the boats without going into the water at low water.

19th I get up every morning at half past six and goes out on the beach looking at the boys catching crabs and eels and looking at the people batheing. There are numbers of old wimen have little wooden houses on wheeles, and into these houses people goe that want to bathe, and then the house is pushed into the water and when the person has undressed, they get into the water and bathe, and then get into the woden house again and dress themselves, then the house is drawn on shore again . . .

December 25th This is Christmas Day, which is, I am sorry to say, almost forgot in London except by the drunkards. We had here roast beef, plum pudding, turkey, and a bottle of Brandy to make punch, which we all enjoyed very much. In many gentlemen's famleys, there is a great deal of egg hot and toast and ale at these times and great sereymoney in puting up the miseltoe bow in the servant hall or the kitchen, but our famly is to small for any thing of the kind.

26th This is what is called about here Boxing Day. It's the day the people goe from house to house gathering their Christmas boxes. We have had numbers here today – sweeps, beadles, lamplighters, waterman, dustmen, scavengers (that is the men who clean the mud out of the streets), news-paper boy, general postmen, twopenny postmen* and waits. These are a set of men that goe about the streets playing musick in the night after people are in bed and a sleepe. Some people are very fond of hearing them, but for my own part, I don't admire being roused from a sound sleep by a whole band of musick and perhaps not get to sleep again for an houre or two. All these people expect to have a shilling or half a crown each. Went out this morning, saw plenty of people rowling about the streets in the hight of their glorey . . . Miss P. gave me half a sovering for a Christmas box, one of the trades people gave me half a crown, another gave

* The Twopenny Post, serving the London area, was distinct from the General Post. The two services overlapped badly and were combined in 1854.

me a shilling. I mite get fuddled two or three times a day if I had a mind, as all the trades people that serve this house are very pressing with their glass of something to drink their health this Christmas time . . .

30th Have been very buisy and at home all day. The life of a gentleman's servant is something like that of a bird shut up in a cage. The bird is well housed and well fed but is deprived of liberty, and liberty is the dearest and sweetes object of all Englishmen. Therefore I would rather be like the sparrow or lark, have less houseing and feeding and rather more liberty. A servant is shut up like a bird in a cage, deprived of the benefit of the air to the very great inguery of the constitution. In London, men servants has to sleep down stairs underground, which is jeneraly very damp. Many men loose their lives by it or otherwise eat up with the rhumatics. One mite see fine blooming young men come from the country to take services, but after they have been in London one year, all the bloom is lost and a pale yellow sickley complexion in its stead. There is money to be made in service, but the person must be luckey enough to get in good places and begin service when very young. I was very much to old when I began service, therefore I never shall be worth a jot.

If a person wish to see life. I would advise them to be a gentleman's servant. They will see high life and low life, above stairs as well as life below. They will see and know more than any other class of people in the world.

31st This is the last day in the year. We all ought to do what I fear but very fiew do, that is to thank God for bringing us through this year and pray to him to take us through the next in health and happiness. I have at last finished the task which I have been heartily sick of long agoe and I think it will be a long time before I begin another of the kind. Now all the readers of this Book mite give an idea of what service is.

William Lanceley
*house-steward**

Born in 1854, William Lanceley was one of nine children of a small farmer who died early, leaving his widow in debt. William began work as hall-boy to the local squire at the age of sixteen, and spent the next forty-three years in service, moving up through the ranks of footman and butler to become house-steward to Lord Roberts at the Curragh. His last appointment was in royal service as steward to the Duke of Connaught, a post requiring considerable organizational ability.

* From *From Hall-Boy to House-Steward*, Edward Arnold & Co., 1925.

Untaught save by experience, Lanceley has all the prejudices of the 'successful' servant, reflected from the attitudes of his employers. The extracts illustrate the progress of his career and his views on the occupation.

In the year 1870, the writer of these random lines left home with a carpet bag, containing an extra pair of trousers, a change of underclothing and five apples. With fivepence in his pocket he walked five miles to begin his career as a foot-boy in the local squire's beautiful home. This was situated in the middle of a well-stocked deer park, containing a good-sized lake. There was an island at the end of the lake, a pretty summer cottage on the island, together with a boathouse and a suspension bridge to the mainland. The surroundings were a picture and the envy of a neighbouring millionaire Duke, who on more than one occasion remarked that it was the only place on earth he coveted.

The squire's family had been settled there since the days of the Conquest, and on the ceiling of the ancient entrance hall was carved on oak shields the family pedigree from the year 1700 back to the Conqueror's shield of 1066 . . .

The house viewed from a distance made a charming picture, nor did it lack anything on closer view, with its black-and-white walls, its gables and leaded windows giving ample light in the interior. Carved upon the heavy oak beams running across the front of the house was Noah's Ark with the animals approaching it in pairs – an object of great interest to the antiquarian.

Such was the scene of my first venture from home. On arrival I was met at the door by the footman, who, in turn, took me to the butler's room, where a most awe-inspiring individual about six feet high, portly and dignified, told me what my duties were to be, adding that the footman would coach me and would see how I got on. My wages were to be £8 per year, with plenty of good food besides; clothes found except underclothing and boots, which I had to provide for from my wages. I was then told in a confidential way that if I looked well after the visiting ladies'-maids, cleaned their boots nicely and got the luggage up quickly (which was my job with the aid of the odd man) I should pick up a nice little bit in tips, which proved correct. Even the small sum of £8 I saved during the first year and took it home (it was paid yearly and not in advance), handing it over with pride to my mother. She had been left a widow with nine children, the eldest eighteen years of age, and to make matters worse my father had died in debt. I can still see her face when she took it and then, giving me £2 back, said, 'I cannot take it all, lad.'

'But, Mother,' I pleaded, 'you must want it and I can get plenty in tips to keep me.'

On leaving I put the £2 quietly on the cottage table where I knew she would find it. Next year my wages were raised to £12, and I felt myself a millionaire and saved the whole of it, again disposing of it in the same way.

My duties, which started at six o'clock A.M., were as follows: first light
the servants' hall fire, clean the young ladies' boots, the butler's, housekeeper's, cook's, and ladies'-maids', often twenty pairs altogether, trim
the lamps (I had thirty-five to look after, there being no gas or electric
light in the district in those days), and all this had to be got through by
7.30; then lay up the hall breakfast, get it in, and clear up afterwards. Tea
was provided at breakfast for the women servants and beer for the men.
I was not rated as a man, but was allowed tea with the women servants,
and was duly railed at by the other men. The coachman was the head of
the servants' hall and the grooms in livery had their food in the house
and slept over the stables. The food generally consisted of a large dish of
stew served on a flat pewter dish; a big joint of cold beef with bread and
cheese completed the menu. The beer was drawn from seventy-gallon
casks into a leathern jack and drunk from pewter and ordinary beer horns.
A fine of a penny was enforced if a man drank from a glass.

My day's work followed on with cleaning knives, house-keeper's room,
silver, windows, and mirrors; lay up the servants' hall dinner; get it in
and out and wash up the things, except dishes and plates; help to carry up
luncheon; wash up in the pantry; carry up the dinner to the dining-room
and, when extra people dined, wait at table; lay up the servants' hall
supper; clear it out and wash up. This brought bedtime after a day's
work of sixteen hours; yet I seldom felt tired as the work was so varied and
the food of the best, and we generally got a little leisure in the afternoons ...

Another old servant was the head house-maid, who had been in the
family for thirty years. She was always proud to relate that for twenty-five
years she had been in charge of the best dinner service and nothing had
been broken or chipped. She would allow nobody to handle the plates and
dishes, but washed and wiped them herself and she alone would carry
them to the dining-room door and wait there to bring them back to the
house-maid's pantry where they were washed. She was quite sure that
each plate had cost £5. This no doubt was an exaggeration, though probably they were not bought under £2 apiece, as they were old Worcester
ware with the coat-of-arms painted in the centre of the plates. The care
bestowed on this dinner service shows what can be done by servants who
take a keen interest in their work and are as devoted as our head house-
maid was to her employers.

After two years I was promoted to footman, the squire telling me he
had never engaged a footman eighteen years of age before. I was quite
rich now on £25 per year. My place was taken by another boy whom I
had to coach . . .

After four years' service I was offered a holiday as the family were paying a round of visits lasting six weeks and those servants who cared to
take a holiday did so. Very few did in those days and no servant would
dream of asking for one unless the family were away from home. The
butler and housekeeper arranged the allotted time for each. My first holiday
was three days, quite enough at that time. Our cottage homes and food
were no comparison to what we had left behind. I spent my holiday at

home and took my mother by surprise by getting there on a Wednesday. The only two butcher's shops in the village were open only from Friday till Monday so no meat could be procured. Unknown to me my mother in desperation killed a fowl, which was boiled, and I undertook to carve it. I sharpened the knife and tried many times to cut the wing off, but failed.

'Mother,' I said, 'this chicken is very tough.'

'Chicken!' replied my mother. 'That's no chicken – it's old Jim. Surely you remember old Jim.'

It was the old rooster that had met his fate and I could well remember him as a fine bird for the previous eight years.

'I thought he would make us a pot of broth,' continued my mother, and I chaffed her for killing the fatted calf on the return of the prodigal.

I was now twenty-one, and a longing to go to London seized me. I determined to get a situation in a family that spent the season in Town. I had to give in my notice to leave to the squire, who flew into a great rage and asked why I wanted to leave his house and go to London to learn drunkenness and dam' rascality. London had no attraction for him.

However, the time came for me to bid adieu to the servants, the squire and the rest of the family shaking hands with me and wishing me success in my new venture. I felt the parting and well remember taking a long look at the beautiful old place, fully intending when I came home on holiday to revisit it. That was not to be, for it was later burnt to the ground, which was a great loss to the family, and perhaps a greater loss to the country, as they do not seem able to build the like of these houses nowadays . . .

My next venture was footman in the family of a gentleman and grandson of a peer, one of the premier peers of England. He rented a very old house in the Midlands, the seat of a celebrated General in Cromwell's time. There seemed nothing ancient or modern about it, being just an ordinary Manor House with a few old family portraits on the walls and old oak furniture in the principal rooms. However, it suited my master, who revelled in hunting six days a week and would have hunted seven had there been a Meet, a sentiment he often expressed. This made it very hard for me, as I had hunting kit as well as footman's duty to do. The clock in the village church steeple struck twelve most nights before I left the brushing-room; but still I liked the place.

My duties in London were light, and two or three times a week I was given 2s. 6d. to go to the theatre, the next morning having to give a description of the plays seen, which generally amused the lady, who was an habitual theatre-goer . . .

My next move was to the service of another Baronet, and strange to say another Sir H—, but totally different in every way to the one I had just left. He, too, came of a long line of ancestors who had played their part in Scottish history and in the union of Scotland with England. He was proud as only a Scots gentleman of the old school could be, quiet, reserved, firm of purpose, a man of very few words, and matter-of-fact in his ways.

I well remember my interview with him when he engaged me. The butler had to write down my duties and read them out to me before Sir H—, who then asked me in slow measured tones if there was anything read out to which I objected.

'No, Sir H—,' I replied.

'Very well then, so long as you do these duties satisfactorily you will not hear from me. If you don't, you will soon hear. Good morning.'

I then took my departure and in less than a week commenced my duties. I was six months in his service before he spoke to me, so I felt assured I was going on all right. Neither Sir H— nor Her Ladyship rang a bell unless something urgent was required, and when this occurred it aroused about half a dozen servants, all eager to know what was the matter. The servants had been there the greater part of their lives, and the under house-maid, scullery-maid, steward's-room boy and myself were the only young servants in the house. My fellow footman was over sixty and too old for carriage work, so it all fell to my lot. This suited me, for I was always fond of carriage work, and as Her Ladyship was popular in society and entertained a good deal, and had a town house and two large country seats, one in England and the other in Scotland, we had plenty of changes.

The butler, coachman and lady's-maid had been in the family before the railway was built from London to Scotland. The butler was at his best over his nightcap when nearing bedtime, relating stories of the old coaching days, the maid helping him with additions as to the experiences *she* had gone through. With a sigh he would say, 'They were good old days after all – no horrid rush as there is today.'

The coachman who drove was old and tottering, and his chief duty was looking on in the stables. He kept the old family coaches in good order, though they were not now in use, and filled up his time trout-fishing, at which he was still an expert. He made his own rods and dressed his flies and there was nothing amateur about them – they were finished off in a very neat manner. He was too old for London, so a town coachman was kept who knew London perfectly, having been coachman to a leading London doctor for several years. The under-butler was an oddity, and had been so many years in the family that he almost took it for granted that the plate was his to display, according to his own ideas. During the house-parties he would unearth a different table decoration for each night, and if Her Ladyship wanted some piece of plate in place of what he had prepared, it would upset him sadly, and that night he would sulk and imbibe the old ale freely but apart from this he could match things to a nicety – in fact, his whole heart and soul were in his work. His only hobby was an attempt in astronomy; and after a few glasses of old ale he would give us a lecture on the aurora borealis, or to put it into the steward's-room boy's words – 'Order, ladies and gentlemen. Old George will now oblige with his fascinating lecture on the hairy-hory borealis.' The scorn and contempt which would gather on the old man's face were very real and the boy had to keep at a respectful distance during the evening.

The under-butler sat at the head of the table in the servants' hall when in Scotland, while the coachman did this when the family was in residence at their country seat in England. The food was of the best and no stint. Wine and whisky were provided for the upper servants in the steward's room – beer and old ale for the servants in the hall. The healths of Sir H— and my Lady were drunk every night, in both rooms, the butler proposing it in the steward's room, and the under-butler proposing it in the servants' hall. A rap on the table, then in a reverential tone came the toast—'Sir H— and my Lady.'

'With all my heart,' was the response.

The second toast given in old families is the 'Young Family', but as there was no young family's health to propose, it was substituted by another, 'Our noble selves.' It was the custom to fill a half-pint horn and drain it off for each toast. The ale was strong – it was not brewed in the house, but was supplied by a noted Edinburgh firm, and two horns were as much as could be taken in safety, which put some of the drinkers in a merry mood for the rest of the evening.

The servants' hall was a very large room and made a capital ballroom. A servants' and tenants' ball was given annually, opened by Sir H— and Her Ladyship, Sir H— leading off with the housekeeper, and my Lady with the butler, in the old country dance 'Hands across and down the middle'. This gave them a chance to dance with all that stood up in this jolly old country dance. They would stay with the rest of the house-party until supper time, then wishing all good-night and hoping everybody would enjoy themselves, they took their departure amid the rousing cheers that were so heartily given by the guests for their host and hostess . . .

The house was a very large one, and the fire-places in the principal rooms were built to burn logs, which were between two and three feet in length, having been cut from a tree-trunk and then split into four parts. They were conveyed round the rooms in a wheelbarrow specially designed by Sir H—, with a solid rubber tyre on the wheel and the crest painted on the side of the wheelbarrow. It was just the thing for the purpose and was more or less a sensation for staying guests. I never in my long service came across a second one. Another invention of Sir H—'s was a dumb-waiter for the breakfast table, which was simply a second table-top above the round breakfast table; this revolving top just cleared the plates laid on the table proper. The breakfast was laid out on the dumb-waiter, except the hot and cold dishes which were at a side table, and no servant waited at breakfast. The guests just turned the dumb-waiter for what they wanted, which saved passing things to each other. Special linen was provided for it with tapes to draw it tight on the surface so that nothing would slip or capsize . . .

After four happy years and seeing no chance of promotion, I reluctantly left this comfortable home and took service in the household of a Viscountess.

Here I would like to be allowed to say something about servants, as I found them, and the same about employers, and service in general. For thirty-one years I was responsible for servants under my care, sometimes with a housekeeper, sometimes without. The establishments were large and I had the engaging of the servants, with the exception of the house-keeper, cook, lady's-maid and valet. I never had any trouble over them, with the exception of two menservants, to whom I will refer later. The women servants never gave me a moment's anxiety. Fortunately for me, I had the help and advice of an old house-steward at the start, and being only thirty-one at the time, his help was needed and appreciated. He had always been most careful in selecting a servant, and was convinced that the best servant in the making is a servant's son or daughter, or, second best, the child of a small farmer. Both from the cradle are early risers and have a very good idea of the life they are about to enter. A good early riser is a boon to any home. If an early start is made things will be done properly, and complaints will be rare from the employer. Great care and tact should be exercised when engaging a servant. If their appearance is what you know your employers will like, put them at their ease before you question them. Some are nervous when coming for an interview, especially those who do not like changing situations, but these generally turn out the most suitable. The one to be avoided is the short-charactered man or woman who, when asked why they left their last situation, generally say, they thought they would like a change, and at the same time, they will assure you that they hate changing. Some servants have to leave through a death in the family, or a break-up of the establishment. They have a short reference, and it is only fair to consider their application. The next thing to do is to explain as fully as possible the duties they are expected to under-take, and don't add, 'Of course, you may be called upon for some other little things.' Most servants will take that as something you don't care to speak about.

Dress is another bogy. Some years ago, men had to go to church in livery and the women in little hood-shaped bonnets. This is all very well where the church is attached to the house, but if not, the sooner it is dropped the better, though it is still carried on at some large houses. The best way to reconcile maids and menservants to this rule is to engage them in your own neighbourhood. Those from a London agency would most likely refuse the situation. If a servant is told that she is expected to dress neatly and in a becoming way, she will give very little to complain about as regards dress. Servants in a small establishment are, as a rule, more prone to indulge in the fashion of the day. Their employers are mostly successful businessmen, and do not trouble themselves in this direction. Employers should keep pace with the times. Most servants have sisters and brothers in business houses, especially those whose homes are in London, and they like to meet their own kin on something like the same footing. A lady by whom I was employed was dead against dress, and would not engage a servant unless they attended church regularly, and dressed in simple attire; but this did not prevent them from buying smart clothes, and on Sunday, when one was leaving the house, some of the other servants would help her to slip out and would let her in on her return. This only added expense to the girl's outfit, and although it was a

most comfortable place, two years was about the longest servants stayed
in it. They left for no other reason than the restriction in dress, and Her
Ladyship, not being told this, could not imagine why they left.

Promoting servants seems at first sight a fair and just thing to do. It
has its drawbacks, however, and often leads to jealousy, sometimes to
what nearly amounts to trickery. As a young man I had to leave one situation to obtain promotion, as no servant was promoted there unless
through a death or a marriage. In this establishment there was a feeling
of security among the old servants, some of whom had been from twenty
to forty years in the family. Where promotion is the rule, you cannot well
deny it to one you feel will not fill the position as it should be filled. If you
don't promote the individual, the chances are you will have two places to
fill instead of one . . .

There is a quotation among old servants on the good breeding of the
old aristocracy, where they have not impaired their lineage, which runs:

> You may break, you may shatter the vase as you will,
> But the scent of the roses will cling to it still.

And there is another on our new society, which is the reverse:

> You may rub up and polish and dress as you will,
> But the style of the plebeian clings to him still.

I remember a guest arriving late at a house-party (he was one of the
newly rich), and apologized for doing so, through what he called a d—n
row with his chef, but was at once politely stopped by this remark from
His Lordship: 'My dear fellow, leave your domestic troubles at home; you
have only just time to get unpacked and dressed for dinner.'

Ladies who are constantly finding fault with their servants, and pouring
out their woes over five-o'clock tea, would not feel flattered if they heard
the remarks passed on them by the very people who so sympathized with
them when relating the same. If overheard by servants, they, in their turn,
will not fail to put the establishment on the black list and warn others not
to go after a vacant situation there. We often hear the cry that good servants are so scarce. Well, I never found it so. If an establishment has a
good name amongst servants, there is seldom a lack of applicants when a
vacancy occurs. Several times after settling with an applicant others have
called, and I have known houses where a servant was wanted, and when
telling the caller of the vacancy, received in reply, 'Thank you, but I don't
think I should care to go there.' It was not for me to ask why, but being a
servant myself, I quite understood there was something not quite right,
or the house had undeservedly got a black mark against it in the eyes of
servants.

I remember in my young days there were two very large establishments
which were always shunned by servants, and both were continually
changing, because in one case, to use a servant's expression, 'the lady
was too hot', the same being said about the steward in the other. I pre-
sume this sort of thing will go on so long as there is employer and employed, but when continual changing is taking place, there must be a cause.

When once unrest gets into a house, it takes a long time to settle down.

Sometimes the best of places get spoilt by a general break-up. With a new staff the old comfort seldom returns. If you are fortunate to get a nice lot of servants, never pat them on the back, or let others see you favour one more than another. You are bound to have a preference for some, but don't show it before the others – it is bad for the servant since jealousy is sure to arise. A kind word and a pleasant look will tell your appreciation of man or woman far more significantly . . . Servants, undoubtedly, are an anxiety at times in most houses, and a steady discipline is necessary to keep things in order. In the very large houses this is left to the steward and housekeeper, and when the two work together, things will not go very far wrong.

The Great War undoubtedly upset service and this is not to be wondered at by those who know the servant question. The war called for hands to help, and many servants responded to the call. The work they were asked to do was a novelty to them, the pay was big and they had short hours, hundreds being spoilt for future service through it. It made those who returned to service unsettled. They had money to spend and time to spend it when on war work, and to come back to one or two evenings a week was to them a hardship. Time only can remedy this, and employers, I fear, will have to put up with the inconvenience for a few years longer. It will right itself. As the young girls enter service from school, they will fall into the old groove, and it is up to employers to be as liberal and considerate as they possibly can be to the young servants. Parliamentary commissions of inquiry I fear will help very little, and schools for training servants will not settle the matter. I never knew a servant from an orphanage or institution shine in my time, and they were more often given the cold shoulder by the others. Besides, no two houses are alike, and the training received in an institution may not be in keeping with what the employer expects. It is to be hoped that the country, with its crushing taxation, will not go to a big expense over servant training. It is doomed to failure. Teach the girls in the schools to be clean and tidy in their habits and appearance. The head house-maid or kitchen-maid will soon put them wise to their duties . . .

Gabriel Tschumi
chef *

Gabriel Tschumi was born at Moudon, near Lausanne, Switzerland, in 1882, the son of a professor of languages who died three days

* From *Royal Chef. Recollections of Life in Royal Households from Queen Victoria to Queun Mary*, as told to Joan Powe, William Kimber, 1954 and 1974.
7

after he was born. Through the influence of his cousin, Louise Tschumi, who was one of Queen Victoria's dressers, he was appointed in 1898 at the age of sixteen as apprentice to the Royal Chef, M. Menager, at Buckingham Palace, and after being taken onto the permanent staff remained in royal service through the reigns of Edward VII and George V. Pensioned off in 1932 as part of the economy cuts in the Royal Household, he became chef to the Duke of Portland at Welbeck Abbey from 1933 to 1943; his last appointment was as Royal Chef to Queen Mary at Marlborough House. He retired in 1952.

The extracts describe his work as an apprentice in the royal kitchens at Windsor Castle and Buckingham Palace towards the end of Victoria's reign.

Buckingham Palace in the spring of 1898 was different in many respects from the way it is today. It was a time of gas-lighting and hansom cabs, and through the great wrought-iron gates came a constant procession of coaches and carriages bringing guests who were invited to luncheons, dinners, or the Drawing Rooms of the time, now known as Courts. Frequently there would be several hundred people entertained at a time; and as the footman who met me on my arrival mentioned one or two of the functions which Queen Victoria had held before she left for Windsor, a sudden thought struck me. There were only thirty or forty servants at the dinner in the servants' hall on my first night at Buckingham Palace. How could they possibly manage to run things satisfactorily?

I mentioned this doubt during the course of the meal, a quiet affair at which the atmosphere was rather subdued. My neighbour, a young house-maid, laughed.

'Wait until you get to Windsor Castle tomorrow. Most of the staff are up there. We're just a handful left behind, and things are very dull until the Queen comes back to London.'

I realized what she meant the following day, when . . . I made my first entry into the servants' quarters at Windsor Castle. I felt I had never seen such a vast collection of people, and when it was explained to me that they were all indoor staff of various kinds serving in the Royal Household my question of the day before sounded very stupid indeed. No wonder things were dull in London when most of the footmen, valets, butlers, dressers, house-maids, parlour-maids and Indian servants, not to mention almost the entire kitchen staff, had preceded the Queen to Windsor and had been in residence some weeks.

It took me a long time to discover what the duties of many of these servants were, and in some cases I did not ever find out, for on Queen Victoria's death in January 1901 there was a complete reorganization of the Royal Household and a great many of them were found redundant and pensioned off. At the time I joined, however, there was an indoor staff of

more than three hundred, and a permanent kitchen staff of forty-five . . .
Naturally with a Household staff of three hundred there was little opportunity for supervision, and a good deal of laziness resulted. Queen Victoria's four pages were rarely called on, and the Scottish servants who
rode on the box of her carriage in full regalia did not seem to have too
difficult a time of it. Nor did the Indian servants, whose sole duty was to
prepare the curry that was served each day at luncheon whether the
guests partook of it or not. But if I thought the same rather easy attitude
would prevail in the royal kitchens also, I was soon disillusioned. For
this was the centre round which the whole life of the Royal Household
revolved.

In these kitchens were prepared every day the meals for all the lower
servants, as well as the breakfasts and ten- or twelve-course luncheons and
dinners served to the Queen, the Royal Family, their guests, and the
lords and ladies-in-waiting who were in residence. Each day the Master
of the Household sent down instructions about the numbers of guests
expected at these meals the following day, and menus were worked out
by the Royal Chef, M. Menager, and sent up for approval. Everything
was in a constant state of bustle and activity, and during my first day at
Windsor Castle it took a little time to distinguish amongst the many
figures working in the kitchens which were the skilled cooks and which
the subordinates.

I had expected to see one chef in white overall and magnificent chef's
toque, but there were eighteen of these men besides M. Menager, the
Royal Chef, eight of them with their own tables in various parts of the
kitchen. These, I found out, were the master cooks, some of whom one
day might rise to the position of chef, with large staffs of their own. In the
meantime they worked under M. Menager's supervision, preparing the
most elaborate and difficult dishes on the day's menu. They were assisted
by the heads of various other sections, the two pastry cooks, two roast
cooks, bakers, confectioners' chefs and two larder cooks. Then, in dimin-
ishing order of importance, came two assistant chefs, eight kitchen-
maids, six scullery-maids, six scourers and, finally, the four apprentices. . .

By 1899 I had already become interested in the vast subject of royal
cuisine, and after my mother's death and the breaking up of my family in
Lausanne I devoted myself to its study in earnest. Regularly during the
year Queen Victoria made trips to Windsor, Sandringham, Osborne and
Balmoral, and when I did not accompany the Royal Household I spent
my free periods in London working for a week or two in the kitchens at
one of the big London hotels to get as much experience as possible. All
the chefs at these hotels were Europeans, and there was a great deal to be
learnt from their methods.

Then I tried to compare conditions in these London hotels with those
at Buckingham Palace.

The kitchens at the royal establishments, particularly those at Windsor
Castle, were vastly superior in every way, and each senior member of the
kitchen staff had his own set of kitchen utensils which no one else used

and which were kept clean and in good order by the kitchen-maids. Consequently when the Royal Household moved to Balmoral, Sandringham or Osborne everything functioned just as smoothly as it had at Buckingham Palace. There was no delay, things rarely got lost, and should a hair-sieve or a pastry-brush need renewing an order was given to the royal kitchen clerk and it was replaced from a stock cupboard which was always kept up to date. All the kitchen equipment was of the finest order, and I remember on my first day at Windsor thinking how much the kitchen reminded me of a chapel with its high domed ceiling, its feeling of airiness and light, and the gleam of copper, well worn and burnished, at each end of the room. The copper glint came from the stewpans which were ranged on hooks in a vast half circle above each of the two coal fires. Each was numbered, and the moment it was no longer in use it was the scullery-maid's job to clean and polish it and return it to its place in case it were needed again by one of the chefs. Close by the tables at which each master cook worked were the large steam hot plates which could keep food for sixty or seventy people at the right temperature until it was due to be served.

Around the huge centre table, where each morning the royal kitchen clerk weighed up the food that was delivered by tradespeople, were marble-topped pastry-tables, the L-shaped corner tables of the master cooks, and rows and rows of shelves neatly stacked with stewpans in smaller sizes, omelette pans and every conceivable item of kitchen equipment.

Two things made a particular impression on me in those early days. One was that, in contrast to the easy-going routine of other sections of the Household service, the kitchens had some of the discipline of the barrack room. There was hardly any conversation apart from the giving of orders connected with the dishes on which each master cook was working, and I never saw anyone lounging round or sitting down during a spell from work.

While I was at the stage of observing the senior staff at work, and occasionally fetching and carrying, I found the silence in which everyone worked a little unnerving. It must be a rule, I decided, that talking was not allowed. Later, when I was allowed to carry out the preparations of certain stages of a dish myself, I realized the standard of cuisine insisted on by M. Menager demanded intense concentration, and that each man was in his way an artist with food.

The slightest carelessness or error in judgement could ruin a dish for thirty or forty people, and far more important than any question of waste was the fact that the full menu had to be ready for Queen Victoria and her guests promptly at meal-times.

The role of the Royal Chef of those days was an interesting one. Despite the large staff working under him, he both supervised and tackled difficult dishes himself. He was the only member of the kitchen staff who was in contact with the monarch, and it was his responsibility to see that all royal requests about meals were carried out. If there was praise for any particular dish, he received it. If there were complaints he took the blame. But as no Royal Chef could last long when there were complaints about the food served guests, it was M. Menager's task to see that each of the ten courses served daily at luncheon and dinner reached the standard of perfection at which he aimed.

Consequently, rather like schoolboys before their professor, the master cooks and chefs brought their dishes to him at various states of preparation to be passed before they could go on to the next stage.

Usually if there was the slightest fault they would have detected it themselves and begun the dish again, but there were times when M. Menager was not satisfied. He was a tall Frenchman with a bushy grey moustache; and though in all my dealings with him I found him extremely easy to work with, he would not tolerate any of the tricks or effects which so many cuisine experts use to disguise faulty workmanship. When a big banquet was being prepared it was the custom to bring to Buckingham Palace a number of chefs from Paris to assist the regular staff, and M. Menager was particularly watchful with the fellow-countrymen who worked under his supervision.

There had been twenty-four extra French chefs brought in for Queen Victoria's Diamond Jubilee banquet in 1897; and as a great many foreign guests were entertained, the Queen's chef felt that *rosettes de saumon au rubis*, a salmon dish served cold with claret jelly, should be the highlight of the banquet, which ran to fourteen separate courses, each of them elaborate and requiring several days' preparation.

Had there been time he might have insisted on making the whole dish himself, but with so many people in the kitchens, some of whom were unfamiliar with its normal working, he was needed in half a dozen different places at once and he left the preparation of the *rosettes* to several of the Paris chefs.

The secret of this dish is that it must be a rich clear pink, and if the salmon is overcooked to the slightest degree it loses its colour and cannot be used. At the first attempt M. Menager refused to pass the salmon. At the second everything went smoothly until the *rosettes* in their rich pink claret jelly came up for the final inspection before being passed for the banquet.

One of the Paris chefs, I learnt, was considered an expert in his field but was a man who was fond of a drink when he was off duty. Though his training had been excellent at various continental establishments, he was not such a stickler for perfection as M. Menager and he was not above using one or two effects if he thought they were necessary. The claret jelly was of the deepest shade of pink, made earlier from fish bones and gelatine, but it had not cleared sufficiently. He had disguised this fault, as he thought satisfactorily, by skilful blending in of the claret.

But he had not disguised it sufficiently to escape M. Menager's notice.

His comments on this occasion were remembered for years afterwards. 'A good jelly,' announced M. Menager in thunderous tones, 'should be like a drop of whisky, quite clear, without the slightest cloud in it. Whisky.

You know what that is, eh? Then *make* the claret jelly as clear as whisky.'

There was very little talking during the rest of the preparations for this banquet, and work went on late into the night. But the results M. Menager wanted were achieved. The *rosettes de saumon au rubis* were excellent, I believe, and the jelly as clear as a drop of whisky.

His post as Royal Chef brought M. Menager a salary of £400 a year, and a living-out allowance of an extra £100 a year. In the 1890s, when apprentices were paid £15 a year, this was considered a magnificent salary, and he was able to live extremely well. He had a London house, and because of his position he did not live in the servants' quarters but came to Buckingham Palace each day by hansom from home, arriving soon after 8 A.M. All Queen Victoria's upper servants wore formal dress on such occasions, and M. Menager's immaculate top hat and well-cut frock coat were badges of the high office he held.

As *chef de cuisine* at a big London hotel he might have earned even more, but it lacked the prestige of the post of Royal Chef, as well as the many privileges.

The chief privilege of working in the Royal Household was the opportunity it gave for travelling with the monarch and the royal party, and M. Menager accompanied Queen Victoria everywhere. As the last apprentice to be taken on, I was fortunate in being allowed to go on some of these trips before the Queen's death; and later, when I rose to master cook, I made a great many of them. They were always looked forward to by the kitchen staff, for the work was no heavier, and there was more spare time in which we could go on sightseeing tours in the countryside round Windsor, Balmoral or Sandringham.

Spare time was not always spent in this pleasant way, however. During my first day or two in the Royal Household I had wondered why I never saw anyone in the kitchens sitting down. The reason was that it was thought, in the days of an earlier chef, to encourage inefficiency, and on his instructions all chairs and stools had been removed from the kitchens. They had not been restored under M. Menager, with the result that during any pauses in the preparation of a meal the chefs and master cooks had to stand by their tables until the break after luncheon at one-thirty gave them an hour or so free time. There was a billiard-room for the servants at Buckingham Palace in Queen Victoria's reign, but few of the kitchen staff used it. They preferred to use the free hour for resting in their rooms. I found that standing on the stone flooring used in those days was very tiring, and discovered that most of the kitchen staff who had fifteen or twenty years' royal service invariably suffered from fallen arches.

The second fact which struck me during my early impressions of Royal Household service was the immense quantity of food that arrived each day at the Buckingham Palace kitchens. I had mentioned in my informal meeting with Princess Beatrice in the corridor my surprise at finding there was meat three times a day for the apprentices and chicken as often as we felt like eating it. But that was only a small part of my astonishment at finding myself in a world where there were greater stocks of food available for cuisine than I had ever dreamed existed. The vans which rattled into the courtyard at Buckingham Palace would regularly unload two hundred necks of mutton or two hundred and fifty shoulders of lamb at a time. There would be pheasants, partridges, quail, plovers, woodcock and snipe from the various royal estates, and it amazed me to find that the chefs thought nothing of using two hundred pheasants for one meal. Besides huge quantities of fruit and vegetables, there were delicacies like prawns, oysters, Italian truffles, and the enormous hot-house grapes grown by the gardeners at Windsor Castle brought to the kitchens solely for use as garnishing.

Queen Victoria's guests regularly partook of a dish of quail each stuffed with *foie gras*, and each garnished superbly with oysters, truffles, prawns, mushrooms, tomatoes and croquettes.

We ate a great deal of deer and venison, as well as lamb, which was always sent to Buckingham Palace from Wales. Queen Victoria considered it to be the tenderest and would have no other lamb served in the Royal Household . . .

I had spent a good deal of my time watching how things were done, working for a fortnight at a time with the various departmental chefs. As meat was eaten in enormous quantities, my spell with the two roast chefs was a good preparation for a fuller study of cuisine. I worked with them before the huge coal ranges which roared away at either end of the Buckingham Palace kitchens, learning the finer points of basting and roasting on a spit. There were six in front of each range, sufficient to take thirty-five plump chickens at a time, and often up to 350 pounds of meat would be roasted a day. The 140-pound barons of beef served at banquets or during Christmas were always roasted in front of these open coal ranges, and so was all the food served at breakfast each day for the Royal Family and the Household.

I remember my surprise on coming down to the kitchens on the first day of my duties at Windsor Castle to find that breakfast was as big a meal as the main meal of the day in Switzerland.

I had risen about 7 A.M., washed and dressed, and come to the kitchens expecting that, as lunch and dinner were meals of about eight or ten courses, breakfast would be a very light meal indeed. I found, instead, that the coal ranges were red-hot and the spits packed with chops, cutlets, steaks, bloaters, sausages, chickens and woodcock. The roast chefs were deftly removing them and piling them onto huge platters. In other parts of the kitchens cooks were trimming rashers of streaky bacon, a quarter of an inch thick for grilling, and preparing egg dishes . . .

After a fortnight learning the elements of roasting I spent a certain amount of time studying the methods of the Palace bakers, confectioners and pastry-cooks. They, too, were craftsmen, but because of the shortage of materials many of their arts have died out today. The confectioners often used hundreds of pounds of sugar for the elaborate decorations and *petits-fours* cases they made, and some of the finest work I have ever seen was on the sugar baskets for a dessert called Miramare. It is a strawberry dish with a base of vanilla cream and jelly; and the confectioners used to make baskets of sugar paste to hold the dessert, measuring six inches by four inches. The handle and lid of each basket was in perfect proportion to the base, and the sugar paste was coloured to give a grained effect like dark oak. Each basket held sufficient for ten people at a dinner, and I have seen Victorian and Edwardian confectioners spend three days working on them. The *petits-fours* cases were decorated with sugar flowers, and each petal on the roses, pansies or carnations that bloomed in sugar at a royal dinner represented a great deal of work. They excelled themselves at wedding and birthday cakes. When Queen Alexandra was at Buckingham Palace, before sugar had become scarce, the four- and five-tier birthday cakes made for her every year in the kitchens were magnificent.

All the bread eaten in the Royal Household was made daily by the bakers, and so were the various rolls, buns and cakes. The pastry-cooks made the steak, venison, deer and game pies served at shooting-parties and at race-meeting luncheons in Victorian and Edwardian days. Whenever the German Emperor William I, who died in 1888, visited Queen Victoria his favourite raised pie was served, a dish which could only be made in a time when food was cheap and plentiful. It consisted of a turkey stuffed with a chicken, inside the chicken a pheasant, and inside the pheasant a woodcock, made into a pie and usually served cold. On the other hand, the mutton pies made from a recipe popular with Queen Victoria are still served on occasions today at Buckingham Palace.

It was some years before I attempted elaborate dishes at the Palace, and in the early stages, while I was learning, I spoiled a good deal of food. If it was eatable it was given to the staff or to one of the charitable organizations who called regularly collecting food for the poor. After any big function at Buckingham Palace there would be queues of people with baskets to collect the broken food from dinners and banquets, and a few of the staff always saw that wasted food went to the needy.

If a dish were hopelessly ruined, however, it was thrown away. Sometimes dozens of pheasants or soufflés in which four or five dozen eggs had been used found their way to the garbage pails. So did quantities of salmon, sturgeon, trout or *foie gras*, which had been spoilt at some stage of their preparation. No one can learn cuisine without making a good many mistakes in the process, and it is essential that those learning have the best materials at their disposal . . .

A great many of the subtle flavours obtained by chefs preparing Victorian meals came from the use of wines. There was a wine cellar adjoining the kitchens at most of the royal establishments, and each cook drew what he needed, usually about six bottles at a time. As these were finished they would be replaced from the store.

By present-day standards some of the menus used at Buckingham Palace would be considered very extravagant indeed. We used twenty-four bottles of brandy in the preparation of the mincemeat made each

Christmas for the Royal Family, and one hundred and fifty eggs in the plum puddings for the Household. These plum puddings, made every Christmas from a very old Buckingham Palace menu, were a great success and contained four gallons of strong ale, a bottle of rum and a bottle of brandy. The ale gave them a particular richness which you do not find in plum puddings these days, and we had our own method of cooking them.

They were never put in a pudding basin, but were boiled in a cloth. Each year we made one hundred and fifty of these puddings, each one weighing about two pounds.

Rum and brandy were also used in the making of Queen Alexandra's birthday cake, a rich fruit cake mixture containing forty eggs. Most of the soup and fish dishes were cooked with wine.

Turtle soup and game soup were flavoured with sherry, while Dutch brandy was used in the making of crayfish and lobster soup. We used claret in many salmon dishes, and chablis for sole or trout. *Sole bonne femme* and *truites au bleu*, frequently served to Queen Victoria, were simmered in chablis. Others were cooked in champagne.

Queen Victoria always looked forward to receiving the first food in season, and we went to immense trouble in the kitchens to prepare really elaborate dishes for the first grouse of the season or the first partridge.

During the summer months we could be sure of receiving plentiful supplies of plovers' eggs, oysters, salmon, asparagus and fresh peas. Grouse came to table on August 12, from September 1 there were partridges and venison, and from October a good stock of pheasants, Roe deer, teal, woodcock and snipe were regularly on the menu.

It took many years of training to learn how to prepare such dishes as they should be done – lavishly and without any thought of the time it might be necessary to spend on them.

There was one apprentice, I remember, who was always in a hurry to get things done, and once or twice he was rebuked for not taking enough trouble in the smallest matters.

'A chef is an artist,' M. Menager often said. 'And like an artist he strives constantly for perfection. But he has as difficult a task as any man who creates beauty from wood or stone, and there are no memorials to his art. His triumph is a momentary one, between the serving of a dish and the minute when the last few mouthfuls are taken. To achieve that short triumph he must expend all his skill and experience.'

Of course, in those Victorian kitchens it was no use being in a hurry, for everything had to be done by hand and labour-saving devices were unheard of. You could not whip eggs in an electric machine or find gadgets to cut down the drudgery of vegetable-peeling and grating. The cakes and puddings were all stirred by hand, and it became very tiring stirring a 300-pound Christmas pudding mixture that was to make 150 small puddings . . .

We did not begin making curry and rice in the kitchens until Edward VII's reign, for while Queen Victoria was alive this was the special province of her Indian cooks and servants. For religious reasons they could not use the meat which came to the kitchens in the ordinary way, and so they killed all their own sheep and poultry for the curries. Nor would they use the curry-powder in stock in the kitchens, though it was of the best imported kind, so a part of the Household had to be given to them for their special use and there they worked Indian-style, grinding their own curry powder between two large round stones and preparing all their own flavouring and spices. Later an Egyptian coffee-maker was taken on the Household staff to make and serve the coffee for royal guests after dinner ...

The following Christmas at Sandringham I was amongst the staff who were given a small gift by the Queen. These Christmases were vastly different from the pleasant informality which has existed in the Royal Household since the late King George VI came to the throne, marked particularly by the staff Christmas dance held at Buckingham Palace before the Royal Family leaves for Sandringham. We would have never believed it possible in Queen Victoria's reign that the staff would be entertained in the circular State Ballroom and given the opportunity to waltz with members of the Royal Family. But the last fifty years has seen a great change in almost every aspect of royalty and royal life.

There was no trade union for servants in Victorian days. But during the last three years of King George VI's reign every royal servant had joined the Civil Service Trade Union, and union meetings are held in the servants' quarters. Queen Victoria had no difficulty in finding staff, for there were waiting lists of those wanting to join the Household. Now the staff problem is a great one at Buckingham Palace, and people are sent for jobs at the Palace from their local Labour Exchange. When I was chef to Queen Mary at Marlborough House from 1948 I had the greatest difficulty in finding kitchen-maids who also had the necessary cooking experience, and in obtaining staff generally ...

John Robinson
*butler**

Articles on 'the servant problem' appeared frequently in the daily and periodical press from the 1840s onwards, and became legion by the end of the century. Almost always written by employers, earlier comments were generally critical of servants' inefficiencies, ignorance, dishonesty and excessive wage-demands, but as the scarcity, especially of menservants, became acute, more constructive policies

* 'A Butler's View of Man-Service', *The Nineteenth Century: a Monthly Review, January–June 1892*, Vol. XXXI, 1892.

aimed at rationalizing the burdens of service and raising the intellectual and moral level of servant life came to be advocated. The subject was well reviewed in a symposium on 'The Domestic Servant Difficulty' in the *Lady's Realm*, June 1897.

The following article is unusual in being written by a butler of fourteen years' experience, who was clearly an intelligent and well-informed man. Though fully admitting the shortcomings of his colleagues, he places the blame squarely on the attitude and irresponsibility of their employers.

To judge from the number of magazine articles which have of late appeared, touching more or less upon the subject, an unwonted interest is being taken in the domestic servant. To judge from the subject-matter of some of these articles the fact that this unwonted interest exists is not surprising.

In the February number of the *National Review* Lady Violet Greville narrates the result of her observations upon certain characteristics of the English manservant. Lady Violet manages to put quite a kindly complexion on the manservant's foibles, but unfortunately, if the glamour thrown by her ladyship's clever pen be taken away, he is found to appear in a much less amiable light. But, before proceeding to read between the lines, it may be pointed out that it is through such distorted media as are afforded by Lady Violet's article that employers (when they have thought of them apart from their work at all) have been wont to regard their servants. These are low, mean and degraded, but if there be maintained towards them a repressive attitude of haughty disdain, society will be preserved from contamination. Their faults must be borne with, for are they not indispensable 'to that delicate art of living'? This, it may be remarked, looks like the Belgravian version of an important tenet of the social polity of the ancients in which flunkydom bears the same relation to the denizens of Vanity Fair that slavery did to the élite of Athens or Rome.

Signs, however, are not wanting that this superficial attitude is not universal, but that some regard servants with a more human and appreciative eye. In the March number of this *Review* Lady Aberdeen records an attempt to do something towards raising the moral and intellectual standard of servant life. For her efforts in this direction Lady Aberdeen deserves the sincerest thanks of all intelligent servants. It appears to me, however, that her ladyship has not, in her experiment struck at the root of the upas-tree. She seeks to apply the remedy before she has ascertained the nature and extent of the wound. The real state of affairs is much more forcibly implied in Lady Violet Greville's episodes of servant life than expressed in Lady Aberdeen's more explicit statement. These episodes, which are by no means caricatures, reveal an amazing amount of ignorance and meanness on the part of the domestic servant. This reputation for meanness and general depravity is abundantly supported from other sources. Plaints are continually being made in the daily papers about the difficulty of getting good servants. The registry offices tell how few names there are without some blemish; and employers are fain to accept the inevitable and be content with a very humble mediocrity of character and attainments in their servants. Finally, the contempt with which the servant is regarded by his employer and by the world at large affords a fairly adequate criterion of his real worth.

It has seemed to me that this inferiority of the modern servant is not, as Lady Aberdeen suggests, due merely to the deterrent conditions which tend to eliminate the better class of men and women, but that certain enervating conditions exist which have a debasing effect on those who actually choose service as a calling. I also believe the latter set of conditions to be much more operative than the former. To indicate some of these conditions and their effects with special reference to the manservant will be the object of this paper.

I will begin by accepting the general verdict, and at once admitting that the average manservant is a very poor creature indeed. Aim he has none beyond that of gaining a sordid livelihood. His daily life is a mean and shallow affair. *Carpe diem* is his motto. In his spare time he will play for hours at a childish game of push-penny. 'Ha'penny nap' ranks with him as an accomplishment, whist means too much mental effort. His wages gravitate to a convenient 'pub' in the shape of drinks and bets on the current big race. He rarely makes any individual effort at self-improvement, consequently he never combines for that end. His ambition never soars beyond the proprietorship of an inn or lodging-house.

Yet this phenomenon finds its place about the vanguard of nineteenth-century civilization! How infinitely superior was the manly and self-respecting lacquey or major-domo of one hundred years ago to the servile and obsequious servant of modern days! This wretched creature may be seen touching his hat or forelock with every word he utters, conscious of his inferiority to a master morally low. Spectacles like this (and they are frequent) mark a degree of degeneracy alike in master and man; for the love of such homage, from such a source, is certainly incompatible with that magnanimity which in theory at least is one of the prime characteristics of a gentleman.

The scene just described is, moreover, typical of the relationship which subsists between the servant, as a class, and society, in the fashionable sense of the word. The employer has hitherto been accustomed to look on the servant and his peccadilloes as something quite outside of himself. He will be surprised to hear that there is an organic connection between the life the servant leads and that led by himself. To one behind the scenes the terms of this relationship are not difficult to make out. Thus when a man enters service he sacrifices all freedom. Any preconceived notions he may have of living his life in a particular way must be thrown to the winds. He becomes the creature of his surroundings, which are determined by the people with whom he lives.

Accordingly, what a splendid training in gluttony and peculation is usually afforded the young servant when first he enters service! Probably he is heavily handicapped from the first, since he not seldom enters service on the same principle as that on which his employer's boys enter the Church, namely, as being fit for nothing better; consequently he starts with some moral or intellectual shortcoming. Thus inadequately equipped he passes at once from comparative privation to the midst of luxury. If there be, as often is the case, any morbid cravings begotten of the penury of his early life, here is his opportunity. Without any restraint other than that which an embryo conscience affords, he finds himself amongst dainties that would tickle the fancy of a sybarite. Questions as to *meum* and *tuum*, qualms as to the manliness of such indulgence are set aside as squeamish fancies, and the youth is soon well on the way towards making a confirmed thief and sensualist. Many I know will smile incredulously at this picture and declare it to be overdrawn; it describes, nevertheless, what personal observation leads me to believe takes place in the case of a large percentage of young servants. There is a great lack of efficient supervision. Those in charge are often too indolent, frequently they are gourmands themselves, and so encourage rather than repress this guilty indulgence.

There is another circumstance which greatly tends to encourage enervating practices of this kind. It is commonly supposed that at their legitimate table servants live better than those on a similar plane of well-being out of service. This is in a sense true, but in the case of most households more false than true. The condition of the servant – that section at least which lives in the servants' hall – may often be described as a condition of starvation in the midst of plenty. Food there is usually enough and to spare, but is it a suitable kind of food, and how is it prepared? In bygone days, the large joint of beef, no doubt, formed the fitting fare for the burly retainers, whose duties kept them for the most part in the open air. The bumper of strong ale wrought but little harm on the man who rode to hunt or fray. The conditions of the servant's life have long since altered, but not so the manner of living, that is, so far as his food is concerned. Physiological considerations and dietetic principles have both in substance and preparation completely revolutionized the table of the master, while the servant's fare remains unchanged. The work of many menservants is lighter than that of shopmen, and yet they are fed like navvies. What the effects of this system are, the statistics of the London hospitals will show.

The *preparation* of the food sent to the servants' hall is often grossly inadequate. The energies of the head of the kitchen department are usually absorbed by the upstairs dinner, or if not, by below-stairs social obligations. It is a principle with most cooks that they are not engaged to cook for servants; consequently the servants' hall is left to the tender mercies of the kitchen-maid, who usually does most of the cooking of the house while the responsible person receives visitors in the 'room'. The result of all this is that a huge badly cooked joint is sent to the servants' table. This appears cold again and again at a succession of suppers and dinners, till someone, nauseated at its continual reappearance, chops it up and assigns the greater part to the swill-tub. This is followed by another joint, which goes the same round and shares the same fate. Any variety beyond that of a very occasional sweet is out of the question. The physiological effects of such a dietary on those capable of assimilating it I need not point out. That those whose digestive powers are not equal to this coarse abundance must either starve or make rogues of themselves is equally obvious.

But if the coarse fare of the Middle Ages is out of place in our present-day life, there yet remains an institution still more fraught with danger. I allude to the household beer. How this pernicious practice is perpetuated passes my comprehension. The effects of ill feeding are not at first sight obvious, the effects of alcohol are clamant. One would think the shrewd employer feared the servant should emerge to true manhood, and sought to enervate and keep him malleable by this means. Hundreds of men get their first start in a drunkard's career from this hateful practice. If the youth escapes falling a victim to his gastronomic propensities he is often caught here. The claims of good fellowship, the anxiety to be thought a man, the stimulus he finds drink gives him when called upon to make a spurt, all combine to foster the habit. He is soon fit to join the ranks of the 'swill-tubs', who measure their daily consumption by the gallon. And this class we know to form no inconsiderable number of English menservants.

Suppose, however, that a servant escapes the snares which beset him at the outset of his career. Suppose strength of character or quality of temperament enables him to steer clear of the debilitating traps laid for him, what are his chances of developing a strong and intelligent manhood? His opportunities for self-improvement are usually very small. The hours he may call his own are fitful and rare. His duties may be light, but if he wishes to prove himself a good servant he must always be on the alert. Under such circumstances fruitful application is out of the question. If he persists he must take time from his sleep, which he can often ill afford. If, again, he seeks for some society in which he may find help towards better things, he finds himself, as we have seen, surrounded by sensualists in a more or less advanced stage of degradation. If he looks abroad he finds himself shunned. He is a servant, and as the kindly world measures the individual by the type, it will have none of him. Help he has none, and he passes through life cursing the circumstances that placed him in domestic service. The higher qualities in a servant are decidedly at a discount. To methodically perform certain stereotyped duties in a stereotyped manner is in service the highest virtue. Whether the agent is drunk or is sober, has a soul or has not, is seldom taken into account. Any departure from certain conventional rules is sternly repressed, and yet, if an emergency finds him unprepared to take the initiative, he is sworn at for his incapacity . . .

Duties which in the nature of things he would, and which he could very efficiently perform, are passed over him as beyond his abilities or as affording a test his integrity cannot stand. If in any difficulty he ventures to make a suggestion, he at once evokes a more or less direct reminder of his position. A careful conning of his weekly book and a critical surveillance of the monthly bills convince him that he is not trusted. If he is a butler he has the wine put out for him in driblets, and in every way his unfitness for any real responsibility is emphasized. This, of course, is not felt by the average servant who recognizes it as his due, and, like the dog for his thrashing, he is obsequiously grateful. It is, however, extremely galling to a good man to find his master refuse him the confidence which he readily accords to his clerk. Treatment of the kind described unfortunately does not end with outraged feeling. There is nothing more readily makes a rogue of a man than systematic distrust. If a butler is given out six bottles of wine, he can by careful manipulation have one for himself. If his stores are measured out to him in handfuls, he can easily represent that he uses more than he does. If the man does not at once sink to these practices under such a régime, it is generally only a matter of time. The treatment he experiences saps his self-respect, and by-and-by he comes to think of himself as his master thinks. He argues that he is not trusted, therefore there can be no breach of confidence in taking all he can get. He does not care a straw for the wine or the stores, but he learns to take a pleasure in showing that his would-be clever master can be 'done'.

I think it will be seen that the conditions of life in domestic service are such as would tend to produce the very results we find. And yet the complaints we hear about servants are based on the assumption that the servants themselves are entirely responsible for their shortcomings. Employers see their servants surrounded with temptations and debasing influences to an extent unknown in other walks of life, and expect them to be free from vice. They require them to perform certain duties which involve the loss of freedom and opportunity for moral and intellectual improvement, and then complain of inefficiency and stupidity. They treat their servants as immoral, they unnecessarily limit their exercise of responsibility, they frown on any spontaneous action which does not fall in with their own caprice, and then look for the development of high moral character.

If employers really wish for improvement amongst their servants, it lies for the most part with themselves to effect the change. They must first of all put a stop to that wasteful and noxious license which I have the best reason to believe goes on in at least six houses out of every ten. At the same time they must see that their servants are provided with well-prepared food, adapted to the work they have to perform. As matters stand, the servant must either gorge himself with half-cooked meat, or steal what he can from the upstairs table, or starve. This kind of thing ought not to be. Those who keep servants ought to see that the conditions of life are healthful, both physically and morally. The practice of giving beer, too, ought to be abolished in every house in the kingdom. If employers once realized the amount of disgusting animalism this habit perpetuated they would stop it at once. They cannot, however, of themselves readily find out the real state of affairs, and many who do find out do not trouble. The domestic servants' duties make so little demand upon the faculties that when once a mechanical habit has been formed they are as well done by a man in a besotted condition as when sober.

No doubt changes like those proposed would involve trouble, but why should not trouble be taken? The *laissez faire* policy is far too prevalent in dealings with servants when the discharge of duties is not in question. Society is too much taken up with its balls and millinery, its dinners and matchmaking, ever to think of its duties towards dependants. The care of servants is too often relegated to a butler or housekeeper more debauched than those over whom they have charge. They possess neither the strength of character nor the tact required to rule others, for they have never learned to rule themselves. They manage by such extraneous aids as assuming the title of 'Mr' and 'Mrs' and retiring to the sacred precincts of the 'room' to procure a little show of respect, which most often veils the heartfelt contempt of their subordinates. Responsibilities so serious should be attended to first hand, or, if they must be discharged vicariously, it should be seen that really competent persons were set to such a task . . .

It will, however, be little use to remove the obstacles which lie in the way of the servant's material well-being unless there be given him at the same time some opportunity for mental improvement. The servant is, as a rule, far less well-informed than any class in the same plane of life. His inability to talk on any subject, unless perhaps horse-racing or the latest music-hall attraction, is well known. This is primarily due to the low kind of life he is forced to lead, and in a less degree to the want of opportunity for self-improvement and social intercourse. The paralysing influence of the servants' environment has prevented his calling very loudly for more freedom. It does not, however, follow that because he does not ask for it it should not be given him. Employers of labour believe that the stimulus and friendly rivalry afforded by clubs and social meetings tend to increase the efficiency of the hands, and accordingly they voluntarily promote, and even support, such institutions. Something of the kind, on the lines indicated by Lady Aberdeen, ought to be encouraged. If, moreover, a little more liberty and opportunity for profitable social intercourse were to be granted, one of the drawbacks which prevent a better class from going to service would be taken away. Thus agencies would be set to work by which, both from within and without the standard of character and efficiency would be raised; a result which could not fail to be welcome to the employer . . .

No doubt the enervation of the servant by the causes mentioned in the earlier parts of this paper has done much to expose him to harsh treatment. It is, however, unjustifiable, and it has been shown to be disastrous to the servant of better character. It is the distrust, the nagging and worry of domestic service, which perhaps more than anything else drives men to get away from it as soon as they can. And it is indeed hard that, after giving up the best years of his life to service, he should be driven to invest his savings in some business for which he has had absolutely no training, and in which in 50 per cent of cases he is doomed to failure. Surely domestic service might be made so that a man could end his days in it with some approach to comfort! Intrinsically there is nothing in service of which a man need be ashamed. There is nothing derogatory to a man's dignity or self-respect in the discharge of its humblest duties. But the thorn lies in the fact that a man, for peace sake, is reduced to a kind of degrading sycophancy; or, to use a phrase common among servants, 'he cannot call his soul his own'.

Let the conditions of domestic service be improved, and with improved conditions let the standard for the performance of duties be raised. Put service more on a level with a trade; let better service be required; but let the servant be treated as a man. In this way the existing corruption would be abolished, and the abuses servants now complain of be a thing of the past. The place of so many ciphers would be taken by men, a state of things which would inevitably revert to the well-being of society at large.

Edward Humphries
page-boy[*]

Edward Humphries was born in Totnes, Devon, in 1889; his father was an NCO in the Royal Marines, his mother had been a cook. Educated at National Schools in Exeter and Plymouth, he started work part-time at the age of nine on a milk-round, and full-time at the age of eleven, as page-boy in a series of clubs and hotels. In 1906 he enlisted in the Royal Scots Regiment, serving in India and in France and Mesopotamia during the First World War. He retired in 1934, but rejoined the Army in 1939 with the Intelligence Corps as a Security Officer under M.I.5; he was awarded the MC, DCM and the Russian Medal of St George.

So early in 1903 (I think), when aged thirteen and a half, I found myself living in a large bed-sitter with my mother in a terrace house in Teddington, not far from Bushey Park.

I found a job straight away as an errand-boy to a fishmonger in Teddington's main shopping centre. This was a cold, cheerless fishy business in which an abundance of ice and cold water quickly damped my enthusiasm.

---

[*] The extract, which describes his life as a page-boy at the Almacks Bridge Club, London, in 1904, is from *A Ranker's Ramblings*, the unpublished memoirs of Major E. S. Humphries (Retd.).

An errand-boy's joy of freedom when on a delivery round was greatly marred for me by the heavy tricycle provided.

The type of vehicle imposed on errand-boys in London at the beginning of this century deserves a brief description: it was simply a large wooden box on two big wheels with solid rubber tyres plus a small wheel fixed to the back of the box. The unfortunate errand-boy was seated in front of the box facing the traffic and from this vantage point he could certainly see where he was going. All that was then necessary was the strength to turn the pedals and the skill to control his direction by manipulating the stirrup-shaped handles fixed on either side of his body, which in turn moved the back wheel in the required direction.

This wonderful contraption must have weighed over sixty pounds. It was just possible for a young lad to propel this vehicle on level ground at six or seven miles per hour, or, by vast exertion even greater speed might be obtained. It was, however, absolute murder to propel the darned thing up the slightest incline. Another snag was the fact that the back wheel seemed specially designed to become lodged in the tram-lines and on more than one occasion I incurred the wrath of a tram-driver and sundry road travellers for holding up the traffic in the heart of Teddington. Imagine a small boy being required to trundle around sixty pounds of ironmongery in order to deliver a few pounds of fish – no wonder this treadmill is no longer seen on our roads.

Thank goodness I was able to quit this fishy job inside a month. A Baker Street domestic agency advertised for a page-boy for a club in the centre of London. I applied, went to Baker Street for an interview and got the job as page at the Almacks Club, Hay Street.

My mother was very pleased with my success as it was a big step upward from fishmongering for her son, and also because it meant my living away from home. She had recently been disturbed by hints she had heard that it was not right or proper for her to share a room with such a big boy!

The Almacks Bridge Club was located at the corner of Hay Street and Berkeley Street in the heart of the West End. The Club occupied the first floor and basement. The building still stands today, unchanged since 1904, and although no longer a club, its entrance hall and wide main staircase are as I remember them when dashing up and down the thick-pile-carpeted stairs as a page-boy sixty years ago.

There is no doubt that my job at Almacks was the highlight of my life in London, prior to joining the Army.

Here was I, a raw Devonshire dumpling suddenly brought into contact, however remote, with the aristocracy of Britain. Smartly dressed for the part, too, as the first instruction I received was to report to a West End tailor in Brook Street, to be measured for my page's uniform, plus box calf leather boots, black raincoat and a silk top-hat with a cockade.

The page's uniform was made of fine black Melton cloth with yellow facings and three rows of black silk-covered buttons; indeed, when we two pages (for there were two of us) were on duty we felt that we were the smartest pages in Town and held our own with the elegant appearance of the adult staff, dressed in their knee-breeches, black tail-coats with gold facings, yellow waistcoats and silk stockings.

My fellow page, a year or two older, but slightly shorter than me, was a genuine Cockney lad who had previously been employed as an apprentice stable lad with the famous Bob Sivier, who was I believe either the owner or trainer of the even more famous racehorse Pretty Polly – at least that is what my colleague told me; in any case, he was a smart lad who lost no opportunity of putting a country bumpkin in the picture, regarding the tricks of a page-boy's trade.

The Almacks Club was, I believe, the first mixed Auction Bridge Club in London. It was managed by the Secretary, Colonel Hugh Stewart, who was assisted by Mrs Caldwell; I imagine that the smart decor of the Club and our uniforms were probably due to the artistic good taste of this lady. Mrs Caldwell was undoubtedly the driving force in the establishment as she was an energetic hostess and did everything necessary to keep the all-male staff on its toes. Maybe she had a pecuniary interest in its success: in this she was not greatly assisted by her husband, a very elderly gentleman who came tottering around from time to time, nor by her daughter, a ravishing indolent young lady for whom I quickly felt a silent, ever-increasing, adolescent admiration.

One of the jobs I particularly liked was that of meeting electric Broughams and hansom cabs as they arrived and whistling for them for members when they left the Club.

In those days electric Broughams were much in vogue. A large number of our members arrived at the Club in these elegant, silent vehicles. I think it a great loss to London and other large towns that this form of transport has been allowed to lapse, due, I understand, to the difficulty found in producing a light 'long-life' battery capable of running say, two hundred miles without recharging. When so much technical knowledge is devoted to atom bombs and space travel, it is strange that no one has found time or sufficient technical enterprise to produce an electric vehicle which would revolutionize transport in our cities and in so doing reduce the noise and noxious smell.

Hansom cabs were the taxis of the early 1900s; right smart they were too, from the fast-trotting, well-groomed horse in the shafts to the top-hatted cabby in the dickie seat behind the cab. Quite a few of these fine old cabbies came from the West Country and more than once when I had finished telling a cabby the address to take his passenger, the cabby would lean out of his seat, offer me his hand with the query—'An' where be from, lad?'

On wet days our job of safely delivering members to or from taxis required a special technique. Armed with a huge umbrella and a half-hoop-shaped wicker-work contraption for fixing on the wheel. it was our duty to deliver our passenger dry and free from mud on trouser leg or flowing skirts, into or out of the taxi. This task was simpler when the member wore trousers but such was the voluminous nature of ladies' skirts and petticoats that a sleight of hand was necessary to protect the ladies' garments from being covered with wet mud.

It was a red-letter rainy day for me whenever I had the pleasure of performing this task for Miss Caldwell. I can still recall the thrill I experienced when I felt the soft firmness of her leg against my forearm as I protected the flounces of her dress from the wheel of the hansom cab.

Her kindly smile and nod of thanks together with the delightful aroma of her person was indeed a reward to remember these sixty odd years. Such is the strength of impressions formed in one's youth.

My nominal working hours were from 9 A.M. to 9 P.M., but such were the attractions of the Club staff-room, the interests of my job and the pleasure I felt in the company of my workmates that after the first few weeks I usually trudged back to my tiny bedroom in a Knightsbridge mews any time between 10 P.M. and 1 A.M. Often I was accompanied by Mr Newey, a Club waiter, a fine-looking man who admirably suited the Club's footman's uniform. Mr Newey lived somewhere my way which was fortunate for me as he took a kindly interest in my welfare and being a man of the world gave me much helpful advice in the course of conversation, which, without delivering any lectures, put me on my guard against the many pitfalls which might otherwise have engulfed me.

My route to my digs each night or early morning was along Berkeley Street to Piccadilly (the Ritz Hotel opposite Berkeley Street was being built about that time), down Piccadilly, then known as the prostitutes' mile, past Hyde Park Corner and the mobile coffee-stall outside its gates, and thence to Knightsbridge where I crossed to the south side, then first left and right to my dingy, tiny bedroom in the mews. I invariably stopped at the coffee-stall and chatted to its voluble Cockney boss and whilst drinking a penny cup of hot 'Camp' coffee, passed the time of day to all and sundry, including policemen, street washers, street-walkers and the occasional gent in tails and opera hat.

Hyde Park Corner to my eyes seemed huge and the centre of the universe; its vastness was enhanced from midnight onwards by the paucity of movement, the occasional hansom cab, a watering cart with its crew of street-washers armed with huge bass brooms, a beat-thumping policeman, a tiddly reveller or two in evening dress or an occasional forlorn prostitute prowling along on her way to her bed-sitter after an abortive night. All were facets of interest to tired eyes and gave us regulars something to talk about as we drank the steaming coffee. The stall-keeper's stock in trade was as simple as his paraffin-lamp lighting; hard-boiled eggs, bread-and-butter doorsteps, penny buns, coffee and cigarettes, all about a penny each. One could stoke up with a cup of coffee, two hard-boiled eggs, two slices bread and butter, a bun and a packet of five Woodbines for eight-pence.

There is still, I believe, a coffee-stall at night at Hyde Park Corner, but now stocked with a much wider variety of goods at a much higher tariff.

We had a 'ticker' tape machine at the Club and a street bookmaker who operated nearby. My fellow page and I devised a scheme for defrauding the bookie by placing a small bet on the winner of a race within seconds of the horse's name appearing on the tape machine. The scheme worked only on a few occasions and then probably with the connivance of the bookie who accepted the bet and paid out only when it suited his book. I guess that bookies then, as now, are not so easily defrauded. The servants' staff-room was a centre of attraction for me after 9 P.M. when my duties as page were finished for the day. The tables in the Green and Red rooms upstairs were by now fully occupied by members silently playing auction bridge in a haze of smoke from Turkish and Egyptian cigarettes. At that time practically all members of the Club smoked either Egyptian or Turkish cigarettes. These have a distinctive flavour and aroma. They were much more expensive than the Virginia cigarettes smoked by the general public. This class distinction in smoking habits was partly erased by the close contacts between all walks of life during the First World War.

From then onwards, until the last member departed, the 'waiting' staff would be summoned only occasionally to serve drinks and light refreshments. We had many trays full of once-used playing cards in the staff room so it was inevitable that the staff should emulate the members by also playing bridge for small stakes – I was allowed to watch and quickly assimilated the rudiments of the game and a 'card sense' which, however deplorable, has helped me to judge comparative values in other fields.

I enjoyed these nightly sessions so much that my hours of watching increased until it became a habit for me to hang on until after midnight; this stupidity brought about my downfall.

My first job each morning at the Club, after a 9 A.M. breakfast, was to tidy and dust the Secretary's office. The Secretary, Colonel Hugh Stewart, was a fine-looking soldier and in my eyes a 'Colonel' and a complete Sahib. He rarely spoke to me but when he did he was terse yet kind and usually sent me on my way with a smiling nod of approval. I, rightly I think, placed him on a pedestal and vowed to myself to do all I could to please him.

One day Mrs Caldwell arrived at the Club early to inform the staff that the 'Colonel' was now a Baronet, and in future the staff must always address him as 'Sir Hugh' instead of 'Sir'. I remember the self-conscious feeling I had on the few occasions I complied with this instruction.

The late nights began to take their toll. I arrived for work later and later, furthermore I fear I became too cocky and big for my boots. My lateness eventually extended to after 10 A.M. but I received no reprimand as I managed to scamper through my work. Then for three days running I failed to arrive before 11 A.M. and on each occasion Sir Hugh had arrived to find his office untidy and undusted.

Sir Hugh sacked me in no uncertain manner because of my slackness and unpunctuality. He was, he said, disappointed in me as I had started well but had steadily developed into a lazy layabout.

It was all too true, and now too late to recapture my desire to serve my pedestalled 'Colonel' well; indeed, my continuous late nights had undermined my will to work.

Fortunately for me, the Head Waiter did not take a serious view of my backsliding and promised to give me a good reference if I needed one to get another job.

So at the end of the week, with a few shillings in my pocket and a small parcel of my belongings under my arm, I joined the army of down-and-outs in a Rowton doss-house, near Waterloo Bridge, where for a shilling I got a bed for the night.

The next day I spruced myself up, rubbed my cheeks hard to induce the appearance of good health and wended my way to Hunts Domestic Registry Office in Baker Street.

Fate was kind to me as I was immediately lucky in obtaining a job as a still-room boy at the Union Club in Trafalgar Square.

I had visited my mother, who was still living at Teddington, on a few Sundays whilst working at the Almacks Club. My visits were not memorable in any way. I had a feeling of not belonging any more and it was several weeks since I had last been home. Consequently, without any planned intention to break with my mother I drifted away on my own. I felt no urge to return to her even when I spent a night or two at Rowton House, in a dormitory with tramps and other misfits; indeed, I can recall no feeling of apprehension about my future. After all, I still possessed a few shillings and I had no doubt of my ability to get a job quickly . . .

Lilian Westall
*house-maid**

Lilian Westall was born at Mortlake in 1893, one of nine children. Her father was a craftsman, a cricket-bat-maker, most of whose wages went on drink; her mother had been in domestic service before her marriage. Lilian went to elementary school until fourteen, leaving in 1907 to work at the Kings Cross Laundry; after nine months she went into domestic service at Palmers Green and elsewhere until the outbreak of war in 1914 when she went to work in a munitions factory. After marriage in 1918 she continued to work as a maid at the Langham Hotel and in private service until 1939, when she returned to munitions work. Subsequently she acted as an escort to deaf children for twelve years, finally retiring in 1964 at the age of seventy-one.

The other day I went back to the Kings Cross area in London. I walked along the Pentonville Road and looked at some of the pubs that had been there sixty years ago, and I was back in my childhood. I saw the same

* From *The Good Old Days*, unpublished autobiography.

swing doors that I had pushed open and remembered the noise that had gushed out; remembered running from pub to pub, long skirts flapping, a skinny, breathless, frightened thirteen-year-old, looking for my father, trying to get him to come home before he spent all his pay.

Usually I failed. There were many times when most of his money had gone by Saturday night, and on the Monday the bedclothes, the blankets, my mother's wedding ring would all go in pawn to give us enough money to get through the week.

In 1905 we lived in a terraced house in Kings Cross with eight children under the age of fourteen in the family. There were three rooms, the main bedroom, another just big enough to take a double bed, and the front room which was bedroom, living room, kitchen. It held a bed, sofa, table, half a dozen chairs, a wash stand, an open grate on which my mother cooked all the meals, on fuel of wood-shavings, cinders and a little coal. Two other families lived in the same house; water had to be fetched from the wash-house in the yard; we shared the same outside lavatory

Six of us slept in one bed, three at the top, three at the bottom. My mother always seemed to have a child at her breast, and, as the second eldest, I would often keep her company, sitting on the edge of the bed with her until late at night, as she nursed the baby and waited for my father to come home.

Every morning I had to be down at the butcher's by seven o'clock. As a child I never had a coat, and I used to dread the winds of winter as I waited in the queue with other youngsters, all of us anxious in case the 'pieces' went before our turn came. 'Threepenn'orth of pieces', the odds and ends from trimmed meat, about two pounds altogether, made into a stew with a pennyworth of pot herbs was a dinner for all of us.

At times there wasn't enough food for all the family in the morning, and some of us would go down to the Salvation Army hostel in Pentonville Road and get breakfast for a farthing, a cup of tea and a large slice of bread and jam. At home, our tea was usually three slices of bread and margarine each. Some of the younger ones would gobble their ration and say they'd only had two, but they never wangled another slice, for poverty had made my mother sharp as well as careful, and she never allowed their claims for more. Occasionally we would have a ha'p'orth of syrup between us, or twopennyworth of speckled fruit, half-rotten apples and soggy oranges.

There were times at school when one of the 'rich' girls would bring threepence for the other children. The teacher would ask those who were in need to raise their hands, and she would hand out six halfpennies to be used in the soup kitchen. I rarely raised my hand because pride held me back from admitting poverty, although it must have been plain enough to anyone, as I clumped about in my mother's cast-off lace-up boots, a skirt and blouse from the second-hand-clothes stall, and a boy's peaked cap on my head.

When I was fourteen I went out to look for a job and found one at a laundry in Kings Cross; 8 A.M. to 8 P.M. for 2s. 6d. a week. I was given a big basket and told to collect the washing from different addresses in

North London, often walking as far as Highbury and staggering back with a full basket. Then they put me on the machine that curled the stiff white collars of the men. The collars, coming along on some sort of belt, arrived too quickly for me to keep pace, and they began to fall on the floor, stiff and straight as rulers. The manageress decided I wasn't a laundry worker and in a short time I was looking for another job.

I found it at Palmers Green, nurse–house-maid, looking after three children, a baby girl and two boys, for 2s. a week. In the morning I did the housework; in the afternoon I took the children out; in the evening I looked after them and put them to bed.

My employers didn't seem to have much money themselves; he was a clerk of some sort, but they liked the idea of having a 'nurse-maid' and made me buy a cap, collar, cuffs and apron. Then the mistress took me to have a photograph taken with the children grouped around me. Perhaps someone still has that photo of themselves when children, showing the nanny with her charges. I remember that the father shocked me once by asking me to buy a paper on Sunday. I thought this was wrong, and I came back without it, saying the shop was shut. I thought it was better to lie than offend the Sabbath by buying papers. I stayed at this place until I was nearly seventeen, then I left – 'to better myself, mum'.

I went to Chiswick to work for a dentist and his wife. They were very respectable people and much better off than my last employers. I was to live in, and the wages were 5s. a week; it sounded good when the mistress told me.

I was the only servant. I had to be up at six in the morning, and there were so many jobs lined up for me that I worked till eleven o'clock at night. The mistress explained that she was very particular; the house had to be spotless always. After all, they were professional people and used to very high standards. I had to clean all the house, starting at the top and working down, sweeping and scrubbing right through. Hearthstoning the steps from the front door to the pavement took me an hour alone. I was most conscientious.

The meals I remember well. For breakfast I had bread and dripping. There were often mice dirts on the dripping to be scraped off first. Dinner was herring, every day; tea was bread and marge. I didn't have a bath during the month I was there, I wasn't given the opportunity; in fact there was no time to comb my hair properly, which was long – down to my waist; it grew so matted my mother had to cut a lot of it off when I finally came home again.

My room was in the attic. There was a little iron bed in the corner, a wooden chair and a washstand. It was a cold, bare, utterly cheerless room. At night I used to climb the dark stairs to the gloomy top of the house, go over to my bed, put the candle on the chair, fall on my knees, say my prayers, and crawl into bed too tired to wash. Once, quite exhausted, I fell asleep whilst praying and woke in the early hours of the morning, stiff and cold, still kneeling, with the candle burnt right down, and the wax running over the chair.

I gave in my notice in the first week, but a servant was obliged to stay at least one month in those days, and wasn't paid, of course, until the end of that time. I found out that a succession of girls before me had stayed only one month, but there were enough youngsters looking for work to ensure that a regular supply was maintained.

My employers must have accepted religious need, for they let me have Sunday off, and I was able to go to church. I had no shoes good enough to wear, however, and I remember having to make the hard decision of spending 1s. 11d. on a pair of shoes, only to find that they pinched my feet terribly, and I hobbled painfully to and from church.

My next post was at a house in Cheyne Walk, Chelsea. The mistress was a very grand person. I can see her now in a velvet dress, with a lot of jewellery draped around her. 'Open your mouth,' she said to me. 'Let's see your teeth.' I was used to obedience, and I wanted the job. I opened my mouth. She peered in. Whatever she saw, it seemed to satisfy her, for I got the job. But I didn't last long. There were a number of servants in the place, and besides preparing vegetables and washing-up, I had to wait on the other servants in the servants' hall. The cook sacked me, no doubt rightly, for I was not very experienced in waiting at table, and servants could be as demanding as employers at times.

After this I moved up into high society. I became a kitchen-maid at a castle at Blechingley in Surrey. I was just seventeen. There were a lot of servants here, five to look after the house during the week (and so many gardeners and grooms I never managed to count them all) and another five who arrived with the owners at the weekends. Guests came too, up to a dozen at times. I did *all* the washing-up on my own; it took me hours. I remember doing endless slices of toast. We had strict instructions never to touch a plate with our fingers, always they had to be held by serviettes. The plates were examined keenly for finger-marks and they came back at once if one was found.

The food was good here, but the work very hard. All the cooking was done on a huge range; I had to clean this range with black-lead, and the great copper preserving-pans I burnished inside and out so that they gleamed golden. The great kitchen had to be scrubbed daily, and it had to be spotless. I had one evening off a week, and one day off a month. I didn't dislike it here, but this sort of work needed the stamina of an ox, and years of semi-starvation meant I hadn't this sort of strength. I left after about three months.

After this I came nearer home again, to some mansions in Baker Street. The people here were very careless with money, they had a habit of leaving golden sovereigns all over the place. Perhaps it was their way of testing my honesty, but I found it was a great temptation as my own mother was so poor, and she was expecting another child. I was even more worried by the nineteen-year-old son of the mistress, who thought me fair game and kept trying to corner me in the bedroom. I grew very nervous, and once caused a terrible fuss by dropping a leg of lamb into a man's lap when I was waiting at table. At the end of a year I handed in my notice.

I wanted a change from being in service and I went to work at a piano factory in Islington, banging the keys while the man sorted things out at the back. Later I took a job making sugar sacks, but a few months after this I was back in service at a big house in Highbury. This was a good situation, house- and parlour-maid, 6s. a week and every other Sunday off, which seemed generous. Six months later the war broke out, so I went to work in a munitions factory. I was twenty-one; I seemed to have packed a lot into those first twenty-one years.

In the early part of 1917 my father was invalided out of the Army. He came home to join my mother, seven girls and two boys in our small flat. We were too big to use the three-up-three-down method in bed. Now four girls slept in the bed and three slept on chairs. The flock mattress didn't reach all the way across the bed and the iron edge of the bed frame was cold and hard; the girls on the outside edges didn't have much sleep. There was nowhere for any of us to keep our personal things, and clothes became common property. Last one out of bed had to make do with the leftovers! Things became so difficult for everyone I went back into service.

I applied for a post in a block of flats in the Baker Street area. At that time I had a bad cold; I was sniffing and snuffling as I waited in the hall. The mistress came out to interview me; she was aghast.

'Good heavens!' she said. 'You could be *most* infectious.'

She went hurriedly back into the room, closed the door, and addressed me in a muffled voice from the other side.

'Have you ever had measles?'

'No, mum,' I said, thickly.

'Have you ever had chicken-pox or mumps?'

'No, mum. Not as far as I know.'

There was a pause. 'Well,' said the voice, 'perhaps you'll be all right. Now this is what you must do. Go to bed and I'll tell cook to take you up a glass of lemon water.' I did as I was told. Cook came up as instructed, I sipped my drink and settled down comfortably, thinking that this was a very pleasant start to a new job. Ten minutes later cook was up again. She wanted help with the dinner, she told me to jump out of bed at once and start giving a hand. Anyway, I'd enjoyed the lemon water.

The mistress was a difficult person to work for. She was forever feeling the chair legs or under the table for signs of dust. Now and again she would find some, and I would be scolded harshly for neglect. At the end of the month, after I'd had my wages of £1, I put my few things in the little basket I took everywhere, leaned out of the window and dropped it down into the courtyard below. I'd had enough; working hard was one thing, continual scolding was another. I made my way down the stairs. At the bottom I ran into the yard, picked up my basket and was away.

For the next few weeks I worked as a house-maid at an officers' residential club near Piccadilly. I liked it here. Then one of the members asked me if I would go and work for his wife as a cook-general. I went, not wanting to refuse him. His wife was very young, and knew no more of cooking than she did of black magic. She embarrassed me with the most impossible requests. I'd been there about a fortnight when she placed about half a pound of cod on the kitchen table next to a big pie dish.

'I want fish pie for dinner today, cook,' she said.

The dinner was to be for her, the nurse-maid, myself and the two children. I was a cook, not a miracle-worker, but I hadn't the nerve to tell her. I didn't wait for my money; I packed my little basket and quietly left. I had forgotten one thing, it was war-time and my employer held my sugar-ration card. I haven't taken sugar since that day. Although I thought it mean of her at the time, I should be grateful, she helped to keep me slim all my life.

After this I was offered the job of house-maid at 7s. 6d. a week at residential flats in Manchester Street. I had to do housework and wait on the head nurse and the under nurse. One night after meeting my young man (later my husband) I got back about 11 o'clock. I should have been in by 10. To get to my room it was necessary to creep by the head steward's room. I was afraid to do this in case he woke up; I went to the under-house-maid's room and slept with her. But the head steward was up early and found that my bed hadn't been slept in. That was enough for him. He sent for me.

'Go at once,' he said, sternly. 'We don't want your sort here!' I made no protest; after all, I was in the wrong. I should have been in by 10. I packed my little basket once more.

By 1918 my father was a changed man, he no longer drank heavily, and in January of that year he bought me a wedding present, a 2s 11d. blouse. I think it was the first present he'd ever bought me. Looking quite fashionable in my blouse and an ankle-length skirt I caught a bus to the registry office and got married.

The following day my husband went back into the Navy, and I got a new job. It was in an upholsterer's. The money was good, 25s. a week, the hours were long, 8 A.M. to 7 P.M., but I was happy here, it was the best job I'd ever had. I left to have my first child, a boy, in November 1919. As soon as I could get someone to look after the baby I went back to work, this time at a hotel in Langham Place. My hours were from six in the morning till four in the afternoon; 15s 6d. a week. It was hard work; sweeping, washing paintwork in the long corridors, cleaning, making beds, turning out bedrooms. It's hard to imagine working without vacuum cleaners. We had stiff long-handled brushes for large carpets, small-handled ones for use when crawling under the beds; the beds of those days were heavy and couldn't be moved.

Well below pavement-level in the bowels of the hotel were the kitchens, floors of grey stone, ugly gratings and big zinc tubs for washing-up. One part of the lower basement held long wooden tables and forms, where chamber-maids and cleaners had their meals. Sweating cooks milled round the ovens, waiters scampered up and down the stairs; but two flights up was a different world. A world of carpets, soft lights, well-dressed people, all the signs of gracious, unhurried living. After a time I was offered an easier job, serving in the lounge, but by then I was expecting another child, a boy, born in September 1921.

In March 1922 I was back at work, this time at a store dealing in antique fireplaces in Fitzroy Square. I worked from nine till twelve each morning for 1s. an hour, general cleaning. Then a partner in the firm asked me to work from twelve noon onwards at his home. I did this three times a week, working quite often till nine at night. I was paid 10s. a week for this; meanwhile I paid a woman 5s. a week to look after the children for me.

These people had frequent guests and held dinner-parties. I was the only servant, and as the dining-room and the kitchen in their flat were on different floors I used to cook a three-course meal, then run up and downstairs to do the serving. My own children were underfed during this time, and my eldest boy, when he was four, suffered from malnutrition. A hospital arranged for him to be sent away to a place in Buckinghamshire, and within a few weeks good regular meals had changed him so that I hardly recognized him.

When I next changed jobs it was to be a house-maid for a widow in her late thirties. She had a flat opposite Kensington Gardens; it was beautifully furnished, and there were two other servants. My mistress was obviously a very wealthy woman, but the poor soul was a drug-addict and I witnessed such distressing scenes that I left after six weeks . . .

In mansions near Portland Place I went to work for another widow; another wealthy but unhappy woman who had grown dependent on servants and was incapable of looking after herself. I was sorry for her, and stayed with her for some time, but she plagued me with telegrams when I was at home asking me to drop everything and go up to the flat to help out at unexpected dinner-parties. She disrupted my life to such an extent, that I finally gave in my notice.

When I was fifty-two I felt I wanted to do something quite different. I became an escort, taking deaf children to a special school. I was happy to do this for twelve years, until I was sixty-four. For a time after this I looked after two old ladies, and did other work locally, but at seventy-one I went into retirement. To tell you the truth I was beginning to feel tired. I felt I'd had enough.

Lavinia Swainbank
*house-maid**

Lavinia Swainbank (*née* Morrison) was born in Newcastle-upon-Tyne in 1906, the daughter of a blacksmith-striker employed by Sir

* *Unpublished autobiographical extract.*

Charles Parsons and Company. She attended local elementary schools, passing the entrance examination to secondary school, but was unable to take up the place for financial reasons. Leaving school at fourteen, she helped her invalid mother at home for two years but in 1922 during the depression went into service 'so there would be one less mouth to feed'. After work in a hotel in Windermere, she became under house-maid in a private family and, in 1925, third house-maid in a 'stately home' at £3 a month. From here she moved to a doctor's house 'to complete my training to be a good house-wife'; she married in 1929.

The extract illustrates the limited employment opportunities for an intelligent girl from a depressed area in the 1920s, and the un-changing nature of domestic service at this time.

The year 1922 was not an easy time to be starting out on one's career. For those were the days of depression on the Tyne, when the shipyards were idle and pits closed down and every day the queue of sad-eyed men signing on for dole grew longer and hope of finding work grew more remote.

Passing the eleven-plus exam was just a matter of pride of achievement. One realized there was no money to spend on books or uniform. One could enter and pass the exams that meant a chance in one of the more exalted jobs, but here again one met with frustration time and time again, when it was pointed out (usually when one had succeeded in passing) that one needed to have graduated from a secondary school at least. The English teacher, too, who tried so hard, without success, to open the way to a career in journalism for a promising pupil must have realized from the start that he was fighting a losing battle, for where could the parents of that pupil find the necessary £50 premium?

Money alone was the key to success.

Thus at sixteen, I entered into a career of drudgery where long hours, low wages and very often inadequate food were accepted standards of a life that was thrust on one out of sheer necessity. The next six years of my life were to be spent in graduating from 'tweeny' in a Lakeland hotel, to second house-maid in gentlemen's service (strange term for a household comprising of mother and two spinster daughters). Ultimately I reached my peak as third house-maid in one of the stately homes of England. I took great pride in my work, and however menial domestic work was considered to be even at that time, I vowed to do it well and to the best of my ability.

I started out that day with high hopes and a sense of adventure which petered out within hours of my arrival at the small private hotel in Windermere. I certainly had not imagined that anyone expected a sixteen-year-old girl to carry luggage, clean shoes, work for cook and work for house-maids from 6.30 A.M. till 10 P.M. I expected to share a room, but

to have to share a bed with a kitchen-maid as bedfellow, whose preparation for bed meant the removal of dress and shoes only! I performed incredible acrobatics that night, clinging to the edge of the bed to avoid
physical contact. The most distasteful duties I had to perform during my
short sojourn in this post were to empty slops and wash the spittoon,
used by the husband who had literally come home from the sanatorium
to die one week later . . . As the youngest maid I was given the duty of
cleaning the invalid's room, and the coughing up of blood was a distressing sight. Even at that age I was somewhat shocked to see the room let
within two days of the poor gentleman's burial, just cleaned and a change
of bedding, but not a change of mattress as one would expect.

It was hardly surprising to find that my own health broke down within
a few months of taking the job. Lack of fresh air, long hours and indifferent food took their toll, and it took me several months at home to recover from the anaemia which the doctor diagnosed.

My second venture was a definite improvement, as under-house-maid
of two in a private house. The family consisted of mother and two spinster
daughters. I was to receive 30s. per month and my keep. I had a room to
myself here. The type of room I discovered through trial that one always
expected in 'gentlemen's service' has an iron bedstead with lumpy
mattress, specially manufactured for the use of maids, I suspect, a painted
chest of drawers, with spotty mirror, lino-covered floor and a strip of
matting at the bedside. Oh yes! The alarm clock. Here I was to familiarize
myself with The Timetable. I had never before seen one of these and on
first sight I could not see how one could possibly perform these duties in
one day. This proved a splendid basic training, turning an ordinary
human being into something resembling a well-oiled machine whose
rhythm and motion ran smoothly like a clock. To this day I have not lost
the clockwork precision instilled into me by a succession of head house-
maids and timetables forty-eight years ago. There were no vacuums, so
carpets were brushed with a small hard brush with either tea-leaves or
salt to settle the dust. In a kneeling position of course. There were awful
open grates, with steel fire-irons thicker than my skinny arms, to be
emery-papered each morning, the glass screen over the open grate to be
washed with wash-leather, and finally the basin of whitening powder,
with cloth for washing hearths. All this paraphernalia to be carried round
from room to room. The rooms were always fitted out with syphons of
soda water, which proved a boon to one overworked house-maid. Easier
to squirt the hearth than make those endless trips back and forth for water
to moisten the whitening.

The Timetable
6.30 A.M. Rise
Clean grate and lay fire in Dining Room. Sweep carpet and dust.
Clean grate and lay fire in Library. Sweep and dust.
Clean grate and lay fire in Billiard Room. Sweep and dust.

Polish Staircase.

Clean grate and lay fire in Drawing Room. Polish floor.

Clean grate and lay fire in Morning Room.

Sweep and dust vestibule.

Sweep and dust Blue Staircase.

8 A.M. Breakfast in Servants' Hall.

9 A.M. Start Bedrooms. Help with bed-making and slops and fill ewers and carafes.

Clean grates and lay fires. Fill up coal boxes and wood baskets.

Sweep and dust bedrooms.

Clean bathrooms.

Change into afternoon uniform.

1 P.M. Lunch in Servants' Hall.

Afternoons, clean silver, brass, water cans, trim lamps.

4 P.M. Tea in Servants' Hall.

5 P.M. Light fires in bedrooms.

6 P.M. Cans of hot water to bedrooms.

7.30 P.M. Turn down beds, make up fires, and empty slops. Fill up coal and wood containers.

Leave morning trays set in housemaid's pantry.

Time passed pleasantly enough here. The other servants were kind, the food was excellent, and I now possessed a second-hand bike to get into town on my days off. This had meant a four-mile walk unless one were lucky enough to be offered a lift. Cars were rare so this offer did not often come my way. One day I actually caught up with a hearse on my walk into town and when the very ancient driver offered me a lift I accepted and spent a very happy hour listening to this very humorous character; considering the nature of my transport, I fear my laughter was unseemly under the circumstances. When he asked if I remembered my 'Boss' who, he informed me, had been dead sixteen years, I naturally answered in the negative. He told me he himself had been a groom at the house and the master used to pass a clean silk handkerchief over the horse to see if it had been thoroughly groomed, and woe betide if there was a sign of grime on the handkerchief – he got a taste of the whip as likely as not. I could believe it too. His daughter used to whip her horse in her tantrums. In this house there were three bathrooms. Was it not strange that the maids were not permitted the use of one, but had to trundle a saucer or hip bath to the privacy of their room to perform their ablutions. Personally I was fastidious enough to prefer to use these when I discovered that the dogs were actually bathed in the family bath.

On Sunday mornings we attended the village church with the family, feeling distinctly important in our private family pew.

Family prayers were said in the drawing-room on Sunday nights at eight P.M. and all were expected to attend.

The butler was wont to summon us by the ringing of a small bell. Our reverence was simulated rather than genuine on many occasions, as he, unseen standing by the door, used to make funny faces at us as we took up our accustomed positions.

Early mornings, three times a week, I opened the massive front door to admit the head and under-gardener who used to arrive with masses of fresh blooms and proceed to make exquisite floral arrangements in the hall and public rooms. Later they brought the fresh vegetables to the cook. Her Ladyship's first chore was to summon the cook to her chamber to give orders for the menu for the day. The chauffeur made his daily visit too, standing cap in hand to receive his orders for the day, and so another day began.

Here I served twelve months. The anaemia that was to bug my life had made me so weak that awful giddiness overtook me, causing me one morning to fall down stairs carrying the early-morning tea-set to the kitchen. I was unfortunate enough to break the cup, saucer and teapot. My mistress called in her own doctor to make sure I had not got into 'trouble'. Anyhow, I was obliged to return to my home once more to recuperate, and found, to my dismay, that 7s. 6d. had been deducted from my wage for breakages.

When after six months I was able to apply for another post and required a reference, I had the most charming letter from this lady, inviting me to take up the position I had vacated. The offer was turned down. Nevertheless she furnished an excellent reference.

My next position was to be in the stately home of a titled lady and gentleman, and here for the first time I really learned the meaning of 'gentlemen's service'. For the first time I was treated as a human being by people with heart and consideration for all their staff. We were even granted the, then unknown, privilege of two hours free in the afternoons, either to rest or sit in the lovely gardens and grounds surrounding the hall . . . I took full advantage of this, usually finding myself a secluded spot near the river. I was a voracious reader and enjoyed most of all the history of the old house, from the many books in the library. Its ancestors became real characters to me. The hall was reputed to be haunted and on one occasion at least I thought I had at last come face-to-face with the supernatural and actually was more fascinated than frightened. It happened on the first night I had arrived at the hall. I was shown to a very pleasant bedroom, midway up a spiral staircase. It was rather splendidly furnished, but I thought this was only to be expected in a home of this type. Had I listened to the explanation given me by the upper housemaid as she showed me there I might have saved myself the acute disappointment of next morning.

I was very weary as I made to my bed. Travelling all day, then starting duties immediately made me so tired that I fell asleep almost as soon as my head had touched the pillow.

I was suddenly wide awake with startling suddenness to find my room flooded in moonlight showing what looked like an apparition which appeared to be suspended somewhere above the door. My heart pounded and I clutched at the bedclothes in terror. I just lay there trembling.

Suddenly I summoned every bit of courage I could muster, literally leapt from my bed to the door clutching at the 'thing'. At least it was substance and my fears somewhat abated; I lit my candle. The 'thing' was a man's dress shirt hanging on the door. Funny I had not noticed it when I came upstairs. On investigating I found the wardrobe, chest of drawers, all filled with gentlemen's clothes, but whose? Oh, that problem could be solved tomorrow, and I promptly fell asleep.

I had a rude awakening on the morrow when I was told to bring my things along to my own room. I might have known. This was just another maids' room like all the other maids' rooms I'd ever known. The same old iron bed, lumpy mattress, and so on.

The Servants' Ball was the highlight of the year. It was held shortly before the family left for the London season. The tables groaned under a load of delectable food, turkey, venison, beef, pork, duck and chicken, trifles, jellies and sweets and fruit, as well as a selection of drinks to suit every taste, including champagne – a feast to remember. On this occasion the staff were waited on by the family and afterwards, the Gentleman led the cook in the first dance, with the sons and daughters dancing with maids and footmen.

When the family and most of the staff left for the London season, three maids were left behind to spring-clean the hall. I was, by choice, one of the three. Our holidays were fitted in after this task was accomplished, supposedly one at a time leaving two in the house. Due to unforeseen circumstances two of the maids left on the same day and I was left in sole possession. I continued with my normal duties even without an overseer, like the conscientious worker my training had made me. I had no fear of the loneliness or the Grey Lady, the ghost. I used to think if she was going to walk, here was her opportunity, but nothing caused me any loss of sleep during my two weeks in solitary state . . . At length the family returned and it was once more the gay house with all the young family and their gay friends, 'the bright young things' they were dubbed. House-parties were frequent and though this meant more work, to me it was exciting to witness how the other half lived and there was no bitterness in this. I used to love to watch over the banisters the young people in their wonderful dresses dancing to the strains of the gramophone in the brilliantly lit main hall with the huge fire burning in the open grate. It was at one of these sessions, I remember, that I witnessed a demonstration of the Charleston. The current pop song was 'Valencia'. Nor was all the gaiety confined to the main hall, as the Servants' Hall too could boast of a gramophone and stacks of up-to-date records, where the gardeners, grooms and under-chauffeur joined the indoor staff of maids and footmen for dances after the day's duties had ended. We had dartboards, cards, and the ever-popular Ludo and snakes-and-ladders, in fact everything to make a contented staff . . .

This was a Roman Catholic household and I used to think it a little unfair to see most of the staff leaving each Sunday morning for mass in the fleet of very smart cars, while we, a very small band of C. of E., had

8

to cope with all the household chores. Perhaps it was only envy of the drive, but I think this was the only occasion I 'niggled'.

I found here that class distinction began and ended in the Servants' Hall. A certain amount of jealousy between the upper staff and an attitude of bootlicking to curry favour in high places was evident even to the most naïve of us, and I have no doubt our employers despised this exhibition as much as we, the pawns in the game did. To be kept up till after 11 P.M. to make sure that bedroom fires were burning brightly for late-night revellers helped the head house-maid to score a point over her rival, Cook. For some obscure reason one never attempted to speak directly to her Ladyship but always by the offices of the head house-maid, and I suspect it was a rule instituted by the house-maid herself. Now at the hall, as in most of the larger establishments of that time, the cook had her perks from the various tradesmen, and ours was no exception. There was undoubtedly some questionable dealing going on in this quarter that was brought to light when a dish of very tainted bacon was served up for breakfast in the Servants' Hall. No one was able to eat it and just made do with bread and jam. However, when it was served up a second morning this was just too much, and we were in a distinctly explosive mood. There was some discussion of what steps should be taken. The one I suggested was decided, if I was willing to be spokeswoman. This was the plan—that a deputation should take the bacon for her Ladyship's inspection. Through the head house-maid we were granted an audience with the august body. With shaking voice and knees I passed the dish of rancid bacon under her nose.

She was as indignant as we were, and said that for some time she had doubted the authenticity of her household accounts as they were enormous, but feeling that the staff were being well catered for had done nothing about it . . . Now she was aware that her suspicions were well founded. Two hours later an ex-Cook left by taxi with a mound of luggage and a set of golf clubs! By now I felt like a deflated balloon and felt guilty at being the instrument of another's downfall. I gave in my notice, and though her Ladyship cajoled and offered an increase in wages I left at the end of the month.

Winifred Foley
*general maid**

Winifred Foley was born in 1914 at Brierley in the Forest of Dean; her father was a miner, her mother the daughter of a Welsh farm labourer. Winifred was educated at the village school at Slad from

* From *A Plebeian's Progress*, unpublished autobiography.

five to fourteen, and took her first post in domestic service in Islington in 1928: 'I was very homesick, and overwhelmed by London.
Hitherto I had taken my bearings from woodland paths, trees,
flowers, fauna and hedgerows: fifty paces and I was lost in the repe-
titious jungle of streets.' She left after three months (at 6s. 8d. a
week) to become a general maid to a nonagenarian lady in the
Cotswolds at 5s. a week: then a general maid to an impoverished
Cheltenham family where, after three months, her emaciated and
semi-starved condition was reported to her parents by a servant
acquaintance. In 1929–30 she worked as maid on a farm at
Abergavenny, in 1930–32 in London again as maid to a family in
Aldgate at 10s. a week. After further work in a London University
hostel and as a teashop waitress she married in 1938, and continued
charring and part-time domestic work in London while her family
of four grew up. In 1955 the family moved to an isolated cottage in
Gloucestershire, 'tied' to work in a saw-mill for her husband. Now,
in her 'pastoral heaven' she has written a play and several features
which have been published in the *Countryman*. The extract from her
unpublished autobiography describes her work in the Cotswolds in
1928.

Like the sword of Damocles my fourteenth birthday approached – to cut
me in half; my spirit to remain with everything familiar that I knew and
loved, and the reluctant rest of me to go into domestic service. This was
the common lot of every girl in our mining village, unless she were too
mentally or physically handicapped, and I had grown up with this knowledge. Now the time had come, I found it hard to bear.

At home I was 'our Poll' to my beloved little sister and brother; 'my
little wench' to father; 'a reg'lar little 'oman' sometimes, but often 'a
slommucky little hussy' to my sorely tried mother. To Miss Hale, the
principal teacher of our school that served several scattered villages, I
was 'Polly, our school captain'. To the ribald boys 'Polish it behind the
door'; and to my best friend Gladys – just 'Poll'. Gladys was an only
child, always clean and tidy, but she never turned her nose up at playing
with me, even when the school nurse found lice in my hair, and my neck
was covered in flea bites.

Now I was to be parted from my family, my friends, my home, the
school, the village – all that I loved most dearly. To them too I was a
person; but I knew from hearsay that once I had donned the maid's
cap and apron I would become a menial, a nobody, mindful of my place,
on the bottom shelf.

Now 100 per cent willing if not very able I started my job as general
maid to an old lady in the Cotswolds. I was fourteen years old and just

emerging from my first childhood – she was ninety-one years old and tottering into her second, so we got on pretty well together.

Her treatment of the long string of unfortunate girls who had preceded me had given her a local reputation for being a 'cantankerous old tartar'. In their eyes I was an object for pity.

Actually age had softened the old tyrant quite a bit. I was the first maid allowed to sleep in one of the bedrooms. The others had had to make do on an old palliasse on the floor of the attic. I found this out when she poked me awake with her walking stick in the small hours to tell me there was a burglar up there.

If there was I didn't intend to disturb him.

With lighted candle in hand I climbed up through the trap door. I cast eerie shadows among the old junk and broken furniture. I could see it wasn't a burglar that had been sleeping up there – candle stumps, old novelettes, a chamber pot, and the smell of the urinated mattress from their nightmare dreams gave the clues; this had been the maids' sleeping quarters. I banged about a bit near the trap door to give the illusion of inspection, clambered down and firmly announced 'Not a sign o' a skerrit of any sorts up there ma'am'.

Because of her rheumatics I had to act as 'kneel in' for the old lady's prayers. I thought she had a fat chance of getting to heaven with that attic on her conscience and two spare bedrooms in the house! But she was old and pitiful so just in case there was a God up there listening I put a plea in for her on the quiet.

She was a proper old termagant for waking me up in the night on one pretext or another. Eventually she asked me to sleep with her in her big four-poster bed.

I had to undress her at night. It was a long business – nature's whittling had left very little under the voluminous layers of clothes. Her false teeth came out first – then her false hair which was attached to a goffered white headpiece in the manner of Queen Victoria. After I had removed the layers of day clothes and helped her on to the night commode I had all the rigmarole of dressing her up for the night. Woollen vest, flannel chemise, nightgown, bed-jacket and bedsocks, lastly a white silk scarf over her poor little balding head tied under her chin in case she died in the night – she didn't want the indignity of being found with her mouth agape. After that it was gently heaving her up into the great four-poster bed.

Before I could get in, I had to go through the nightly ritual of making sure every door downstairs, even the one at the bottom of the stairs, was chained and padlocked. As the windows were lead-latticed I kept assuring her that Tom Thumb couldn't get in, let alone a burglar.

It was a bit disheartening after all that trouble to be poked awake a couple of hours later to do a bit of exorcising. She used to wake up saying she was having horrible visions and the only way to get rid of them was for me to walk slowly round the bed three times saying prayers.

She had a great dread of dying and confessed this to me one day.

'Don't you fret about that, ma'am,' I comforted her, lying like a trooper on the spur of the moment. 'My old great auntie come to me in a vision and told me it was like going to sleep in a coalhole and wakin' up in a palace.'

The times I had to tell her that fib, adding bits I 'remembered' to convince and further reassure her.

At first I had to eat my food in the kitchen but she had to ring her bell so often for me to mop up the messes she made from her knockings over, she sacrificed dignity for expediency and said I could eat in the dining-room with her. 'Don't go getting big ideas that you are a lady's equal,' she warned me. Such a remote possibility had never entered my head . . .

My old mistress had to live on a very small pittance allowed her by a nephew in London. She was childless herself and had been a widow for many years. Her sea captain husband had left his money invested in German railway stock. It had gone up in smoke in the First World War.

Every year the nephew came down to make sure she had not altered the will leaving the cottage and its contents to him. Her longevity was obviously getting on his nerves but he was still getting a bargain I reckon. An antique dealer today would drool at the mouth over the furniture and knick-knacks.

When I cleaned the silver she told me the snuff box was engraved with the name Samuel Johnson to whom it had belonged. I had never heard of him so it got no more of a rubbing than the rest.

The cottage was a gem of Cotswold stone with lattice windows set in a quarter-acre of walled garden. The water supply had to be hand-pumped over the kitchen sink from a spring somewhere under the house. The kitchen was separated from the dining-room by the parlour. The access door from the kitchen was kept locked to this middle room so I had to run across the yard with the food. In a downpour the gravy got watered down a bit . . .

Though the old lady ate very little herself it was still a struggle for her to pay my £1-a-month wages. 'Don't you fret, ma'am, a plate o' taters wi' a knob o' marge would suit me fine for dinner,' I often told her.

In those days when short working hours were uncommon the baker's man called every day. Twice a week she took a fresh batch loaf from him, sometimes still warm from the oven. To sit with her in that dining-room with the sun streaming through the lattice window, watching the japonica blossoms nod against the panes, eating crusty buttered newly-baked bread, and drinking tea made with fresh spring water from a silver teapot, feasting the eye on a standard tea-rose through the open door, made up for a lot of my life's drawbacks.

There were other pleasures, too. I never had any free time off, but once a month she sent me into Stroud to get a freshly-laundered headpiece from a little widow woman who did hand laundry. At the same time I could send a postal order home to mother and buy myself needed black stockings or a pair of shoes. To save her the 2d. fare I offered to walk and what a bonus I reaped for this thought. A three-mile walk each way that was sheer delight from start to finish.

A white rose growing over the remains of a tumble-down cottage had gone into ecstasies free from the pruner's knife. Its profusion of flowers were so beautiful I wanted to cry that so few passed by to give it homage.

In late spring, wallflowers, tawny velvet to brilliant flame, excited the senses, tumbling from crevices in dry-stone garden walls. Sometimes a lady in one of the gardens would bid me a pleasant 'good afternoon'. Of course they didn't know I was a mere skivvy. It was nice to be spoken to as an ordinary human being.

As well as the wonders before my eyes I had all the wonders of a dream future to ponder on. I never stinted myself in this field. I was the fêted queen of many a glamorous profession on those long walks, for I had no sense then to distinguish the glitter from the gold.

A dawdler by nature, I didn't have to worry about stepping it out, as a woman from a nearby cottage got my mistress's tea on these occasions. This same woman had obliged when there was a gap between the arrival of a new maid and the departure of the last one.

All the same I mostly got a tart scolding for my tardiness, but it was water on a duck's back.

In my early days there, on Sunday mornings I had to help her up the hill to the nearby church, leave her at the door and be there to collect her when the service was over. Later on she sent me in her stead, sitting in for her in her designated pew six rows from the front. There was too much to be done for me to attend morning service, I went in the evenings instead. Before I left all the inside doors had to be chained and bolted, she herself locking and bolting the front door behind me; evidently she thought the Almighty was too busy in church on Sundays to pay attention to what the devil was getting up to behind his back.

Regurgitated through the rector's monotonous sing-song I found the words of the Bible illogical and meaningless. 'Blessed are the meek for they shall inherit the earth.'

I wondered when? The snobby lot sitting in the front few rows looked as though they had got a good whack of it and there was nothing meek about *them*. They were too high and mighty to lower themselves to speak to me. I found no comfort for my spirit in the service, either, but I found an object for my romantic notions on the organ stool. He was young, incredibly handsome, with a profile like Ivor Novello, and so remotely inaccessible he was just right for my daydreams. As yet physically un-awakened, what I was short of from the neck down was more than made up for by a noddle overloaded with romantic notions . . .

After that I persuaded my mistress to let me give her a proxy sermon at home. She didn't really like being left alone so she agreed. Because she couldn't kneel down I had to kneel on a higher chair than the one she sat on to give the illusion of a pulpit. Imitating the intoning manner of the rector I crucified the words even better than he did – but she was well satisfied with this arrangement.

I love the courage of old age, turning a deaf ear to Gabriel's trumpet, illogically struggling on with the daily grinds of living when they are no longer important. What mattered a few cobwebs now to my old mistress? Yet she informed me that the cottage must be spring-cleaned, starting with the dining-room. I had never heard of this custom, but my ignorance was about to be rectified, and how!

First the polish had to be made. Under her supervision I boiled up a mixture of beeswax, vinegar and linseed oil. Polish is a misnomer for this product, it's the elbow grease necessary to rub off its dulling patina where the shine comes in.

The dining-room was not large but it was very crowded. Apart from ornaments, pictures and knick-knacks there were a good many items of furniture. One wall was almost taken up with a magnificent Chippendale bookcase filled with leather-bound volumes. She usually kept it locked. Now I had to take every volume outside, open it, bang it shut in case it had gathered dust, then rub the covers over with a special oil. It was a lengthy business. Every time I went outside the fresh beauties of the garden, the view of the gently undulating hills and valleys and the sun kissing my face made me slower than ever.

I had all the time in the world. My mistress was exacerbated because hers was running so short. She would ring her handbell angrily to summon me inside and threatened me with the walking-stick for my dallying. 'Cetch me first,' I thought under my breath.

She *did* one day. I had found a book in the attic during one of my burglar excursions, *Uncle Tom's Cabin*. She never gave me a minute's peace to read so I hid it on a shelf in the kitchen cupboard; all my chores in there were done slapdash quick so that I could poke my head in and have a read. The tap-tap of her stick across the yard warned me of her approach.

One day I got so engrossed in the part where Eliza braved the frozen river with her little son in her arms, I was indeed deaf to the world around me, the scalding tears falling on a pile of plates already inadequately wiped. I came smartly back to earth with a stinging swish from her walking-stick across my behind. She had had a lot of practice so was quite a markswoman despite her age. My uncontrollable fit of crying against the cupboard door, for I had not yet found out if Eliza had got safely across, took my old mistress by surprise. She was quite contrite. I didn't bother to enlighten her on the cause of my tears – she might find me with my head stuck in the cupboard again!

The dining table was unique in that it had no join in its large round surface. It had been fashioned from an exceptionally huge slice of mahogany from a tree in the equatorial jungle brought home in the ship of her captain husband for the purpose.

If that table is now in the possession of some lucky owner they can thank me for helping with its preservation. Drops of my sweat went into the polishing of that table. I have swept enough dust under the carpet in my time to fill a few window boxes, and concentrated my energies only on the parts of objects that showed – but there was no dodging this job –

it was too big to take outside – under the old lady's strict eye, perfection was the target.

The old man who did the gardening helped me to hang the faded carpet over the clothes-line. She sat on a chair by the door to make sure I whacked the hell out of it. Then it was laid on the flagstoned yard and sprinkled with a thick layer of salt and used tea-leaves saved for the purpose. It was left like this whilst we had our dinner. Then I had to brush off every tea-leaf with a small hard brush, then go over it with a cloth wrung out in a bucket of water laced with vinegar to restore the faded colours – on to the line again to dry.

I had to scrub the tiled floor underneath three times with hot soda water before I was allowed to polish the surrounds till the sunlight brought a sparkle to the tiles.

Every job took ages. Also I didn't make a very early start. I was supposed to get up at 6.30 A.M. Old people are poor sleepers at night though they like to doze the days away. She had me out of bed so often for one thing and another we were both tired out when it was time to get up. She could see the clock-face with her eye-glass but couldn't hear it tick.

'Get up, you lazy creature, it's gone 9 o'clock!' she would fume, digging me in the ribs for all she was worth.

'That clock must 'ave stopped last night, ma'am,' I lied, and turned the hands back on the clocks downstairs before I got her up. She often complained how quickly the evenings drew in.

My tortoise pace was hared up a bit on two occasions – once when the nephew brought his wife and two young daughters down to stay for a few days, and once when a distant lady relative came for a weekend.

My domestic deficiencies were not altogether wilful; ignorance from my primitive home conditions which had given me no clue to the household priorities was also to blame. I was quite willing to do as I was told providing I was told. For me a cobweb was a fascinatingly dainty flycatcher rather than something to ruthlessly brush away, dirt stains round cup handles didn't matter, it was the inside one drank from. What was the odds about thick layers of dust where they didn't show?

What escaped the rheumy eye of my old mistress was soon spotted by the nephew's wife. Every bit of household neglect 'quite shocked her' – she must have had quite a strong constitution. I had got some shocks for her all over the house. The end of her tongue must have got red raw with the tut-tutting she did.

I was up at 6.30 pronto and on at the double until nearly 11 o'clock every night whilst they were there. I was not helped by the two girls, Barbara and Beatrice. Barbarous and Beastliness I thought them, for torturing maids was their idea of fun.

They kicked me on the shins as I went across the yard laden with trays from kitchen to dining-room. It was high summer; through the open kitchen door I was the target for all the stones they could find to whizz through it; one caught me on the forehead and fetched blood. Worse than that was their toffee-nosed attitude of looking me slowly up and down as though I was dirt. I detested them then, but, poor kids, it was the way they had been brought up. Their mother was quite aware of most of their antics, but as it was only the maid she turned a blind eye. If they soiled the front of their dresses, that was a different matter.

After all, maids in those days were two a penny, yet to illustrate the covetousness of human nature, maid-pinching was a common practice. I don't mean what the masters did, a bit of your rounder parts between thumb and forefinger; I mean the wholesale enticing away of another woman's maid by the mistresses.

The day before they left to go back to London, the nephew's wife came into the kitchen all smarm and charm to tell me I'd be much happier up in London working for them. She gave me a stamped envelope addressed to her, for me to let her know when I would be coming. I was not to tell the old lady.

When she went out I stared into the little mirror in the kitchen to see if I looked as big a simpleton as she took me for.

The distant lady relative tried it on too. She was quite a charming maiden lady who had been left very well off at the death of her widowed father. She lived in a small select house somewhere in Sussex. I can't think why, but she reckoned I was just the sort of girl she had been looking for. If I went to her I would be more than a maid, a sort of lady's companion. She had a local woman to do the rough work. She also hinted that if I stopped with her it would eventually be much to my material advantage.

All this again was said behind my old mistress's back, which, as far as I was concerned, killed the notion from the start . . .

Though I had some loyalty to my mistress and some pity, if not quite affection for her, it didn't stop me giving her my month's notice when the six months was up. I should have to wait another six months before I had earned the annual two weeks' holiday she allowed – I knew I couldn't bear the separation from my family that long.

She automatically pooh-poohed the idea; I told her I meant it and she must start looking for another maid. She did nothing of the sort. She gave me a sort of bribe, a fine wooden needlework casket with a sampler in it which she had worked at the age of six. I felt I could not accept it and gave her my notice in writing. I had heard my aunties say this made it legal. She threw it on the fire. Two more weeks of longing to get home went by and it was my afternoon to walk into Stroud. I was upstairs getting ready when I heard footsteps in the yard, and got the surprise of my life to see my sister standing there.

'Where be the old varmint?' she asked.

I nodded towards the dining-room door.

'I be come to fetch thee wum.'

'I can't come,' I wailed, 'she's got nobody yet to take my place.'

'Not likely to, you saucy ha-porth, as long as you be muggins enough to stop 'ere. Where's your things?'

8*

'Up here,' I told her, 'but my box is in the washhouse through the kitchen there.'

'Chuck thee things out through the winda then. I'll put 'em in thee box and thee canst run away then.'

Now I can't say I needed a lot of persuading to do as she said. Her very presence – so strong a reminder of home and family, and the knowledge that they too were anxious to see me stilled the small voice of conscience.

I wrote a little note to say that I was running away to prop up by the tea caddy where the woman would be bound to see it when she made the tea.

The sight of the old lady nodding by the fire – her hands veined and thin as the claws of a plucked chicken – began to give me second thoughts, but she stirred and sharply ordered me to be back before dusk. I didn't answer – the fluttering feeling in my stomach was agitating my clipped wings back to movement. For a while, a little while, I could escape from servitude. I was going to see and touch again my little sisters and brother, my mum and dad, and the dear familiar sights of home . . .

Jean Rennie

*scullery-maid, kitchen-maid and cook–housekeeper**

Jean Rennie was born in 1906 in Greenock, Scotland, in a 'single-end' tenement, the daughter of a Clydeside rivetter. At thirteen she passed the qualifying examination for Greenock High School, leaving at seventeen with the Higher Leaving Certificate with Honours and a scholarship to Glasgow University which she was unable to take up owing to her father's unemployment during the depression. After a short spell as a parceller at a worsted-mill at 10s. a week, she went into service in 1924 as third house-maid in Argyllshire at £18 a year. From 1925 to 1927 she was a scullery-maid at Sawley Hall, Ripon, Yorkshire, and from 1927 to 1929 at Floors Castle, Kelso, where her cooking training began under M. Édouard Brunet, a former pupil of Escoffier. For the next ten years she worked in various posts as kitchen-maid and cook–housekeeper, latterly with Lady Constance Combe of Pierrepont, Farnham, Surrey. In 1942 she opened the American Red Cross Services Club in Greenock, first as cook and later as manageress. Jean Rennie married in 1950, and since 1965 has been cook to a firm of London solicitors.

Every Other Sunday is a revealing and fascinating account of

* From *Every Other Sunday*, Arthur Barker Ltd, 1955.

domestic service in the 1920s and 1930s, and of the attitudes of employers and employees towards it. The following extracts describe some early experiences of service life for an educated and sensitive girl who eventually found an outlet for her creative talent in cooking (and in writing).

Now the Depression was making itself felt all over. I didn't know anything about world economics, or politics. But it seemed that people weren't buying so much wool or knitted garments. It seemed silly, because maybe they needed them but they hadn't the money to buy them.

So it was February 1924 when I was 'suspended' – the polite word for 'sacked' – because of redundancy.

This time I did get unemployment benefit. Six shillings a week.

My father took a ship to Australia – he was three months going out – and I believe the voyage of that little ship made history.

He was four years in Australia and sent my mother £4 in all those four years. Sometimes he worked, sometimes he didn't. When he did, he drank; when he didn't, he starved (no new thing for him) and slept on the beach . . .

The spring of 1924 dragged on till May.

I kept writing to the pitifully few jobs advertised in the local paper, and went constantly to the library for more opportunities in the bigger papers. Then one day there was an advertisement for a third house-maid in the Highlands.

I hadn't any idea what a house-maid was. Vaguely, I thought she might do housework. And I never had done any housework – I was never strong enough.

Well, I wrote that I had had a good education (more of a handicap than an asset, as I found out), a good home training(!) and I was willing to learn. I enclosed a reference from my minister.

And, glory be, I got the job!

With minute instructions about what I must wear, when and how I must travel, and where I would be met.

And my wages would be £18 a year, all found.

I can only vaguely imagine what my mother must have felt. All that time, and all those books, and all my education – I know she was inarticulate – but I can see now the hurt in her eyes, that after all that, her daughter, her eldest, gawky, clever, talented daughter, was going 'into service', as she herself had done at the age of twelve – without education.

I felt it a little, and I tried to understand. I tried to tell her that it wouldn't be very long – that I'd get a better job after a while.

I didn't know then.

My greatest horror was the knowledge that *I* would now have to submit to the badge of servitude – a cap and apron.

So, on a clear May day, my mother, my aunt and I sailed on the little *Comet* to Tighnabruaich, where a groom in a dog-cart met me, and drove me twelve miles across to the shores of Loch Fyne.

My mother left me at the pier.

She said, 'Be a good lassie now, and dae whit's right.'

There were tears in her eyes, as I started on the long road that only ended in 1940 – a sixteen-years' sentence.

I came to a grandly beautiful Highland castle, with towers and battle-ments and all, standing high on the hill on the shores of Loch Fyne. I don't remember the exact moment of arrival at the back door, but I do remember walking along a seemingly endless red-tiled corridor. I heard the sound of scrubbing as I went along and I saw a young girl on her knees scrubbing energetically, and seemingly enjoying it. I caught a glimpse of what I afterwards found was the scullery. It was down two steps, and it had the same cheerful red-brick floor. Rounding a corner, I saw the kitchen – a wide, gleaming place, with a long spotless white table down its middle, big windows, barred with railings, like parks, spiked at the top. It looked so clear and clean and friendly. And there was no one in it. I was taken along the passage, right to the end, where I was put into a room with two single beds.

I was introduced to Jessie, the second house-maid, with whom I was to share the room. She was a nice-looking girl, slim and petite, fine-boned, and with smooth skin and silky brown hair. I thought she was lovely, and wished I were like her. She was slim, I was skinny; she was graceful, I was gawky. I found out later that she didn't wear corsets – she never needed them, so I threw away mine, with disastrous results.

Then it seemed that tea would be ready soon.

'You needn't change yet, Jenny. I've done the tea for today, but that is your job. You can change after tea.'

Jessie took me along to the 'hall' – the servants' hall – where we ate and sat in our leisure time, which was never very long at a stretch. She picked up a hand-bell and rang it furiously, then took me along to the lovely kitchen. She took me to the big kitchen range, all hot and glowing, with three great big kettles standing on it, boiling quietly and cheerfully.

She showed me how to make the tea in a great big teapot, and fill a large jug with hot water. She put them on a tray, and the whole contrap-tion looked as big as herself, as she led me back to the hall. This time the table, laid with a white cloth, was occupied.

Only, at this meal, the cook did not appear. She had a cup of tea taken to her in her room, and only appeared at 6.30, when she started getting the dinner ready.

At the cook's place there were a lot of cups and saucers, milk and sugar, and we each had a small plate and a knife. The table was loaded with cut bread, two large plates of butter, two dishes of jam, a plate of home-made scones, and a large fruit cake. The kind of cake that I had only ever seen at New Year, and we knew as 'bun'. I watched very closely what the others did, because we had always had 'something to our tea' at home, which meant a knife and fork. And I thought, privately, that this was a very poor show for a big house.

But I watched how they put a lump of butter on the side of their plates, then a great spoonful of jam, and they used their own knives to spread the butter thick on the bread, and then thick with jam. So I did the same . . . Then we started on the scones, with more butter and jam. And then – I saw it for the first time, but not for the last: butter – *and* jam, spread thick on the lovely fruit cake – and, to add to my horror, some of it was left on the plates, and, of course, put out to the pigs at the home farm. I nearly choked with anger at the wanton waste. I could remember so many hungry children – and here was good food being contemptuously pushed aside. And I must be allowed to say, here and now, that in all the sixteen years that were to follow, I never met a single domestic servant, male or female, who was at any time satisfied with the food served to them.

But I had to swallow my anger, and we went back to our bedroom to 'change'. Now I felt the real feel of a black frock, a little white apron, and a white muslin cap, with black stockings and shoes. My mother had turned me out well. I had three morning 'wrappers', but the humiliation of them was awful. They were old ones of my mother's, and the only concession she had been able to make to modernity was to shorten them a little. But they had mildly leg-of-mutton sleeves, and they were tucked here and there, and buttoned very much up to my neck, so that I had to wear a collar. I was laughed at quite a lot over those dresses. And I was horribly sensitive, and hated being laughed at.

When I had changed I went with Jessie to clear the tea and wash up, which I did in the scullery. I found Maggie there, peeling potatoes. It seemed to me a funny time of day to be peeling potatoes, but I didn't say anything.

That earned me the reputation of being 'stuck-up', I wasn't. I was frightened and shy, and not very sure what I should say to people.

Tea things washed up, we could go for a walk, or do some mending, or write letters, till dressing-time, at seven o'clock. As the letters wouldn't go out till next afternoon at three o'clock, I decided I'd write to my mother when I came back, so Jessie and the kitchen-maid and I went for a walk. We went through a deep wood, which had a downward path and brought us on to the pebbly shore of the loch . . .

The kitchen-maid had to be back by six, so we went with her. I was too new and too shy to say I'd like to stay and look.

So we went back.

Jessie and I went to our room and put on our caps and aprons again, and Jessie helped me put my few belongings away. Then I wrote a letter to my mother, and soon it was seven o'clock, the hour when I was to be initiated into the mysteries of being a house-maid.

I don't remember the exact way from our kitchen corridor into the house beyond. I can remember a narrow passage with a baize door at the end which led into the front hall, because it was on a shelf in that corridor where reposed the grog tray, from which the butler had taken the whisky he handed to me at six o'clock one morning to wake me up!

I don't remember how I got to the bedrooms, but here we were, and I followed Margaret meekly. We took a dustpan and brush with us, and a duster, into the bedroom belonging to the eldest daughter of the house. There was the laird and his lady, two daughters and a son, a lady house-keeper, and some visitors.

Margaret showed me how to pick up bits of ash and paper and things from the carpet, to draw the curtains and shut the windows. To shut the windows and draw the curtains on the glorious sunset over the purple hill seemed to me sacrilege, but it seemed that the 'gentry' didn't have time to look at sunsets.

We straightened the room and then Margaret moved to the massive wardrobe. She opened the doors wide, and there were hung dresses and coats and costumes, enough to take my breath away. She dug out a black lace dress and laid it across the bed. Then she looked at the other side of the wardrobe and chose from dozens of pairs of shoes a black satin pair, and put them on the floor beside the dress. She went to a drawer and took out a long black slip and some other black underclothes, and from another drawer full of stockings she selected a pair which she examined very care-fully before she laid them, with the foot tucked in, across the bed with the other clothes.

I was full of questions, and some I managed to ask, but mostly I just wanted to touch and look at the lovely dresses in the wardrobe.

Why did she put out that dress? Why not another one? Why couldn't Elspeth – well, Miss Elspeth, then – pick her own dress? Suppose she didn't want that one, suppose she wanted a different colour – she'd have to get out all her own things then?

'You ask too many questions, Jane – we've got to do it – it's our job.'

We lit the fire and made sure it would burn up, and that was that room done. We had several more to do, and we had to hurry apparently. It seemed the dressing-gong would go soon, and we must be out of the bed-rooms and be ready to go into the drawing-room and other rooms.

In each room we did the same things. Margaret did unbend sufficiently to tell me that you get used to what the ladies wear, especially when they're alone. When there were visitors, or very important visitors anyway, per-haps they preferred something different, in which case they usually told Margaret during the day. But usually it was the same old black frock . . .

Then I heard the deep reverberating tones of a gong just as we'd got back into the dining-room passage. Margaret and I stood with the butler, who was putting finishing touches to the dining-room table. He went through into the front hall, and after a few minutes he came back and nodded to Margaret.

'They've gone up,' he said.

Margaret gathered me up, dustpan and brush and duster and all, and we went into the drawing-room.

The same performance as the bedrooms – bits gathered up, papers and magazines straightened, cushions plumped up and put in their proper places. Firesides swept up and dusted, and fires made up. There were two fires in the great white drawing-room, both blazing high.

Then we went to the gun-room, but Margaret just looked in and said, 'No, that's all right. Come on, billiard-room.'

The billiard-room was just that, and nothing more. Two large billiard tables filled the whole length of the room, and stacked under the tables till they were almost pushing the tables up, were newspapers – I think every *Glasgow Herald* and every *Scotsman* that had ever been printed.

Here, too, there was a huge fireplace, with a blazing fire, and we had to tidy up here as well. The same in the front hall, curtains and windows to shut out the still loveliness of the evening.

We were still scuttling round when the gong rang through the house again, and we had to pick up our brushes and dusters and run quick.

Apparently we mustn't be seen. It was to be assumed, I suppose, that the fairies had been at the rooms.

However, it was now eight o'clock, and I was feeling hungry and tired. We went and put our dustpans away, then went to the servants' hall, where we got out a bag of linen and Margaret showed me how to darn tablecloths and patch sheets and things. I had learned how to patch at home, and I could darn socks and stockings, but I had never darned tablecloths before. But I enjoyed it . . .

Then when we'd been sitting about half an hour, Margaret said we'd have to go upstairs again.

'What for?' I asked.

'To put away the things,' was the answer.

'What things?'

But Margaret was too impatient to reply, so I had to follow her again. There seemed to be no end to it, I thought.

'No end to it?' said a whisper from the future. 'You wait, my girl, you've only begun . . .'

We toiled up the three flights of stairs again to the same bedrooms which we had tidied so nicely just over an hour before.

It didn't seem possible that one woman could make such a mess when all she had to do was step out of the clothes she was wearing, and scarcely needing to move, step into the other ones put ready for her.

It is true that one of the ladies of the house made no kind of a mess at all. You'd scarcely know she had been in the room. But the other one – she hadn't used any of the things we'd put out for her, and so they had been flung anyhow all over the bed.

Drawers were open, powder was spilt lavishly all over the place, stockings, shoes, underwear, all flung anywhere.

Margaret said nothing. I said plenty.

But what was the use – we were 'supposed' to do all this – we were paid for it, after all, 'They' were 'gentry'. I still couldn't see any real reason for this wanton destruction.

We tidied up, then we had to turn down the bed. We took the eiderdown off, and then the silk cover, which we folded very neatly. Under the silk cover was a white patterned cover-sheet. This we had to make sure was folded over the blankets, at the top, with the top sheet coming right over both blankets and cover, so as to prevent the least touch of blanket coming into contact with the fair lady's skin. Then, having put that straight across the bed, we turned down one corner, and very carefully turned in any smallest sight of blanket, so that it was a perfect triangle.

'Now we'll go and have supper,' said Margaret.

Oh! so we were to get supper! That was something new, and I was really hungry.

At nine o'clock, with the sound of the bell still ringing in my ears, we sat down to supper. In the same order as tea-time, but this time there were no teacups on the table. Instead there were tumblers, and jugs of water, and places set with knives and forks, and dessert-spoons, just like dinner-time.

I think we had cold meat and fried potatoes and some kind of pudding. Whatever it was, it was all very new to me, and I ate up every scrap.

It was now I saw that important person, the cook, for the first time. She sat opposite the butler, a vast mountain of a woman in spotless white. When I came to know her afterwards, she was a gem of goodness, honesty and generosity. But at first, at work, she was rather frightening.

Well, we had supper, and, when it was over, young Maggie, the scullery-maid, cleared away the things and carried heavy trays of dishes into the scullery. I would have liked to help her but I was told I mustn't.

Then, apparently, we had to go upstairs again. This time with bottles.

'Bottles? In this weather?'

'Yes. They never use them, but they never tell us to stop them, so we must put them in.'

That, I supposed, is one of the intelligent things which I was supposed to admire in 'Them'.

At ten o'clock we took bottles up and put them in the beds. Curtains drawn, windows shut, hot-water bottles.

God Almighty! The joys of being rich!

I was aching with weariness. But it seemed the evening wasn't over.

'Do you dance?' asked Margaret.

'Dance? Oh, yes!'

'Well, some nights we go over to the gardener's bothy and have a wee dance. Sometimes we just have a cup of tea and a sing-song. Would you like to come?'

'Oh, yes – when is it?'

'Now, As soon as you're ready.'

'Now? But we're supposed to . . .'

'Yes, we're supposed to be locked in by 9.30, but if we don't make our own fun here, we'd never get any.'

And I, who came from a big ship-building town, heartily agreed.

So we changed out of our caps and aprons quickly, and into an ordinary frock. Then we went along the passage and met Maggie and Ella, and wonder of wonders – the cook!

Yes, there she was, with a coat over a dark dress, all ready waiting.

We all trooped out of the back door, we three house-maids, the cook, kitchen-maid and scullery-maid, and James, the young red-headed foot-man. I think I fell madly in love with him, until I met Donald, the keeper, in his kilt, playing the pipes.

The butler saw us out and locked the door.

It seemed that the procedure was that he kept the door locked until his 'Lordship', the Colonel, had been on his rounds, and then unlocked it for us . . .

We got back uneventfully [at 2 A.M.] and were up at 6.30 next morning.

I had to 'do' the gun-room, the front-door steps, and the billiard-room. I liked doing the front-door steps, because the front door faced directly on to Loch Fyne, and it was so lovely. I could gaze at it to the full while I was polishing brasses. I didn't dislike the gun-room either. It was always very muddy, and the floor had to be polished every morning. I didn't mind that, because I could see results, and I used to polish until the wood felt shiny and soft to my cloth. And it looked so good and smelt so rich after it was done.

But the billiard-room! It was a long dreary room with nothing soft or lovely about it. The first morning I did it I naturally picked up the price-less rug at the fireplace, took it outside and swept it. I was surprised to see a half-crown lying on the floor beneath it. It was a heavy rug and the half-crown wasn't at the edge, it was right in the middle. I thought nothing of it, however, and put the half-crown up on the mantelpiece.

I learned more of the mysteries of being a house-maid during the day. The beds, the 'slops', the carpet-sweeping, the dusting. I gradually learned whose job was which, and that one must not do anyone else's job. Not even to help them. So nobody helped me.

But I must get back to the billiard-room and the rug. A few days later I found, when I lifted the rug, a pack of cards spread out face upwards, all over the floor.

I was extremely annoyed, because it takes time to pick up a pack of cards all spread out on the floor. I know I said something very rude, but my mind was, as yet, completely innocent of any double-dealing, or hypocrisy, or spying, and I still thought it had been carelessness. So I picked them up and put them on the mantelpiece.

During the day I mentioned it casually to Margaret. Her face set in angry lines.

'God! She's still at it, is she? The old – !'

I looked my surprised questioning.

'That's to make sure you lift the rug every morning,' Margaret said. 'And if you don't, *I'll* get the trouble.'

I told Margaret about the half-crown.

This time she called the old — something worse.

'That's to make sure you're honest.'

I burst into tears and I wanted to go home.

That anyone should question my honesty in such an underhand, sneaking manner was even worse than an insult, it was unthinkable.

But it seemed it was the kind of thing 'They' could do to us.

Well, I watched that rug and, sure enough, in a few days a pack of cards was spread out face upwards under it. I was early – I had rushed over my steps and gun-room to be sure of the billiard-room.

I looked at the cards, and at something else – a half-crown in the middle of the floor. She's doing it thoroughly this time, I thought.

I hurried along to the butler's pantry.

Yes – he had some glue.

I took the little bottle and, very carefully, I smeared some glue on the half-crown and pressed it on to the floor. I quickly turned each card over, with its back facing upwards, and left them. I managed to smear a few and left them stuck to the floor. Then I did the rest of the room and went on with my day's work, not without fear, for already I had been warned of the awful consequences of 'not getting a good reference', and I was a wee bit scared of what my mother would say, because she would never have dared to do a thing like that.

There was nothing said, at least not to me. But I know that that marked the beginning of my doom. But as long as I was there, there was never again anything under the rug.

Now I know I am not original in what I did. I know that kind of thing went on for years before I went to service, and that the glued money usually cured it, but branded the servant as a rebel, and that was a dangerous thing to be in 1924 . . .

At Sawley Hall, Ripon, Yorkshire, 1925

Swiftly the days drew in to preparations for Christmas. Again we were to have visitors . . .

On Christmas Eve there was to be a tree in the front hall, and her Ladyship would give us all our Christmas presents. She usually gave us a dress length. I thought that would be very nice.

So, after an early dinner on Christmas Eve, we all trooped into the front hall – Mrs Preston in white, Molly and I in our print dresses and cap and apron, black stockings and shoes. The house-maids in black and white, and lace caps; Miss Bentley in a nice dark dress; the butler in his evening suit; and George in his wasp waistcoat and his tail-coat with brightly-polished buttons.

We stood awkwardly huddled together in one corner; Sir James came forward and led Mrs Preston to the tree, which stood ten feet high, and glittering in the opposite corner.

We all thawed a little at Sir James's patronizing joviality as he shepherded his servants to partake of his Lady's bounty.

The youngest son, Master Edward, shyly handed each one of us a parcel with a murmured 'Merry Christmas'.

Sir James made a little speech, which we all acknowledged with sheepish giggles, in which he thanked us for our service during the past year, and spoke of the nobility of service in a gentleman's house, '. . . they also serve who only stand and wait' – with a sly look at Mr Carter and George, whose faces were stony – and now to the high spot of the frolics.

Snap-dragon.

Mrs Preston and Mr Carter left the hall, and in a moment came back, Mr Carter carrying a big oval silver dish, a big flat one, almost as big as a tray.

It was piled high with almonds and raisins, and it was placed in the centre of the table in the front hall, on a big square of green felt.

The fruit and nuts seemed wet and were glistening under the lights.

Sir James put a match to the dish and all the lights were turned out. The little blue flames leapt among the fruit as the brandy burned.

Somewhere among that pile was a sixpence, and we had to put our hands in and grab a handful of the fruit and nuts.

George got the sixpence.

Then the fun was over and we went back to our kitchen to open our presents.

I hugged my parcel tightly, dying to open it.

What would it be?

Black velvet? I did so long to be sophisticated in black velvet!

I opened the parcel.

There, in its hideous glory, was a length of that god-awful pink cotton – a length sufficient to make a morning dress – for work.

Not a piece of material for a dress for the very rare times I was off and could dress up. Not a dress to dance in – just the one thing that mattered to her Ladyship – work; the nobility and the privilege of working for her, dressed in the hideous pink, for about threepence an hour.

I never made it up and I never wore it.

I don't know what became of it.

Next morning Sir James asked George for the sixpence! George just looked at him in amazement, then fished in his trousers pocket and threw a sixpence on the floor of the dining-room and walked out.

He nearly got the sack, but good footmen who would live in the country were scarce . . .

In London, 1929

I should have stayed with Chef for another two years. It wouldn't have done me any harm if I'd stayed with Chef for another *ten* years, I would certainly have saved myself a lot of pain and sorrow.

But in a fit of childish temper one day, because of a silly quarrel with Barbara over the scrubbing of the kitchen floor, I gave my notice.

And I wasn't going back to the scullery either. I went to a well-known agency and they gave me about ten jobs to go and see. I wanted a kitchen-maid-with-scullery-maid job, and very soon I found one that I liked.

The cook was young and pleasant, and she was quite satisfied with the training I'd had. We would be going to Staffordshire, and we had a shooting lodge in Lincolnshire, and, of course, London in the season. I would get every Thursday afternoon and evening off, and, of course, Sundays alternately.

In the usual way I came by taxi and, by this time, I was growing nearly callous about taxis. I suppose it cost me about two and sixpence from the bottom of Regent Street to Grosvenor Crescent in those days, but I quite cheerfully made out my list of 'expenses', and put 'taxi five shillings'. It seemed to be the recognized thing to do.

I was taken up to my bedroom – still I had to share – and I was longing for the day when I would have my own bedroom and a bedside lamp.

Up the usual five flights of stairs to the top, but this house had a back staircase right to the nursery floor, so that there was no danger of being 'caught'.

I don't know what people used to pay to rent these houses for the London season – so correct, so necessary, so expensive and so silly. But I'll bet it was a pretty penny. They were all, any one I was ever in, in a bad state of repair, and the owners did nothing to them, because they knew that the flock of sheep which was Society would take them for the few weeks in the year which were so important, for any money.

And the front looked good; the drawing-room and dining-rooms were always lovely, so that was all that mattered. It was all the visitors ever saw. What the kitchen premises were like – whether they were fit for human habitation or not, whether they could reasonably be expected to cope with the work which would be demanded of them – none of it mattered.

I had the experience, a few years ago (in 1946), of working for one of the Ministries in a house close to Eaton Square near the one in which I had worked twenty years before, and identical in every way. I cannot describe the feeling, a kind of ghostly shiver as I walked in the front door and up to my office, which had once been the drawing-room. There was still the remains of the white fireplace, one or two white doors, tall and wide, and ornate ceilings.

It was a physical pain in my heart – *not*, I must hasten to add, a nostalgic pain – to go down to the basement where we kept rows and rows of files.

Here was the servants' hall, here was the butler's pantry, this dark little room was either the butler's room or the cook's.

And this, this dark dungeon, with the long dresser and this great ugly stove, and the now rickety wooden table, worm-eaten, had been the kitchen where I, and others like me, had quite literally sweated away an existence that was accepted as 'that station in life'.

If any of the girls came down with me to look for a file, I tried to say, 'Look, people used to work down here – this was the kitchen; look, this was the scullery,' they used to look at me as though I had two heads and one eye, then say with a shiver, 'God! What a dump! There's ghosts here, or something.' They just didn't believe me.

Yes, there were ghosts, and I was one of them. . . .

PART THREE

Skilled Workers

INTRODUCTION

1. No precise definition can be attached to the term 'skilled worker'. Usually he was regarded as synonymous with the craftsman, and in earlier times it was sufficient to make a simple distinction between the craftsman, who had learnt a specialized craft or 'mystery' by apprenticeship to a trade, and the unskilled labourer who had only muscular strength to sell. The rapid advance of industrialization and the factory system in the late eighteenth and early nineteenth centuries vastly complicated this traditional distinction by virtually creating a new category of manual worker – the machine-minder, or factory operative who, though intimately familiar with the particular, sub-divided operation of his machine, was able to exercise only limited judgement or discretion over its performance. For him – or for her, since a high proportion of such workers, especially in the textile factories, were female – a short period of training rather than a long apprenticeship was generally all that was necessary.

Thus, by the nineteenth century manual workers were generally divided into three groups: skilled, semi-skilled (often described as 'less skilled') and unskilled (usually known as 'labourers'). Each group shaded off into the next, and no sharp lines can be drawn between them. Yet, if it is not possible to define the skilled worker, it is possible to describe him, for his work and his style of life had certain characteristics which marked him off clearly from the rest. Most importantly, he possessed a degree of skill – a combination of manual dexterity and acquired knowledge – which gave him command over his materials and tools and a high degree of control over the quality of the finished product. This skill almost always entitled him to higher wages and to more regular employment than the unskilled worker, and released him from the drudgery of fetching and carrying, preparatory and rough work, to concentrate on the more exacting, and more creative, tasks. Historically, the craftsman's wage was approximately double that of the labourer, and although this differential probably narrowed somewhat during the nineteenth century the gap remained very wide: for engineering labourers in large provincial towns the weekly wage in 1867 was 15s. or 16s., while that of skilled men was 30s.[1] Socially and culturally, the gaps were even wider. Most skilled workers, well before the days of compulsory schooling, had received some elementary education, often supplemented by later attendance at evening classes or by extensive private reading: their diaries and autobiographies bear testimony to a high degree of intelligent observation, literacy and articulateness. Many were regular and ardent worshippers at chapel, and it is clear that, after the family, this provided the most important social institution in their lives; others had equally devout political convictions, often of a radical kind, and took a leading part in Owenite, Chartist and other reformist movements. Nearly all came under the sway of the 'new model' trade unionism of the 1850s and 1860s, forming powerful yet pacific organizations well ahead of the rest of labour; again, the 'self-help' agencies like Friendly Societies and co-operative stores were, at least until late in the century, largely the prerogative of the skilled worker. Economic circumstances generally allowed him to occupy better accommodation, to enjoy a more varied and nutritious diet, to devote more care to his children, to enjoy more leisure and to use it more constructively than other sections of the working population.

In these and other respects some skilled workers were no doubt closer to the 'petty bourgeoisie' than to the 'proletariat'. The Victorian working class was far from a single entity – rather, an infinite series of sub-classes shading imperceptibly one into another, but with almost nothing in common between top and bottom. Even within the skilled group there were many variations in earnings, conditions of work and social status, and even within a single skilled occupation a well-understood hierarchy, perhaps nowhere better exemplified than among the coachmakers. In 1837 it was reported that

[They] are not an equal body, but are composed of classes taking rank one after another . . . the body-makers are first on the list; then follow the carriage-makers; then the trimmers; then the smiths; then the spring-makers; then the wheelwrights, painters, platers, bracemakers and so on. The body-makers are the wealthiest of all, and compose among themselves a species of aristocracy to which the other workmen look up with feelings half of respect, half of jealousy. They feel their importance, and treat the others with various consideration: carriage-makers are entitled to a species of condescending familiarity . . . a foreman of painters they may treat with respect, but working painters can at most be favoured with a nod.[2]

Such hierarchies operated in many skilled trades. They may have been based on relatively small wage-differentials, on the length of apprenticeship, or on real or supposed differences of skill, but there can be little doubt that custom played a major part in their observance and perpetuation. The skilled worker was intensely proud, first of his own skill and, next, of the honour and tradition of his own craft. The medieval idea of the 'fraternity' still lingered – was, perhaps, encouraged – in the competitive conditions of Victorian industry, where the workshop could form a miniature community, protected from the harsh outside world by its own inherited lore and custom.[3]

A further, important characteristic of the craftsman was that he usually stood in a closer personal relationship with his employer than most other workers, and was nearer his equal in skill, intelligence and manners. This was necessarily much more true of the beginning of the period, in the 1820s and 1830s, than of a hundred years later, when the scale of almost all industrial undertakings had grown greatly, and when relationships had become depersonalized by the development of corporate organization. But in 1831 the average number of employees per employer throughout British industry on the whole was a mere eight and a half persons, and this included cotton-mills, iron-foundries and coal-mines where employees might be numbered in hundreds. In the craft trades the unit of production was still small-scale – typically the master–owner working alongside a handful of journeymen and apprentices – and this pattern survived into the twentieth century in those industries where hand-skills were more important than machinery. The 'new' skilled industries of the nineteenth century, like engineering, steel-making and ship-building, were necessarily larger in scale, employing more personnel, more sophisticated and costly machines, and were much more highly capitalized, usually on a joint-stock rather than individual basis.

Thus, the skilled worker in the period under review might be found in two very different types of industrial and employment situations – one, the surviving small-scale crafts, of which there were scores ranging from silversmithing and jewellery work to printing, wheelwrighting, tailoring and shoe-making; the other, large-scale and mechanized, based essentially on the manufacture and application of metals and machines. As the century progressed some of the old skills were overtaken and transformed by the new, with serious consequences to the earnings and status of those who, for one reason or another, could not adapt, but there can be little doubt that, in total, the numbers of skilled workers grew rather than diminished. The pessimistic accounts of the Industrial Revolution destroying craft skill and replacing it by unskilled machine operation ignore the creation of new skills by the self-same process: if hand-loom weaving was destroyed, power-mule spinning and powerloom weaving created new crafts, and the rise of mechanical engineering which accompanied that revolution called into existence a host of other new skills like fitters, turners, pattern-makers and boiler-makers. 'In 1850,' writes G. D. H. Cole, 'this process was in full swing, and, on balance, skills were coming into existence much faster than they were being destroyed.'[4]

Both types of skilled trades, the old and the new, offered their different opportunities. In the small-scale hand-trades the line between the craftsman and the master was often a thin one, and the natural ambition of many journeymen was to save up enough capital to enable them to start their own business. Mobility of the workman into entrepreneurship was a reality throughout the period in trades where skill and connection were more important than capital and machinery, and in building, printing, book-binding, tailoring, fur-niture-making and the host of country crafts which centred on timber and leather the ladder of opportunity could carry the am-bitious apprentice into the owning and employing class. In many skilled trades there was a good deal of retailing of finished products, of custom-work (for example, in the clothing and shoe-making trades) and of sub-contracting or 'buttying' (in the building trades, in ironfounding and railway-contracting), all of which provided opportunities to move out of wage-earning into retailing or mana-gerial functions. In the new, revolutionized industries the possi-bilities of entrepreneurial mobility were much more restricted. In the early stages of textile mechanization, the slippery ascent from weaver to factory-owner was not uncommon, and in mechanical engineering down to mid-century a man of initiative and intelligence could often launch his own concern.[5] But as the scale of new enter-prises grew it became more and more unlikely that a wage-earner would ever accumulate sufficient capital to break successfully into large-scale mechanized industry. Mantoux dated the virtual end of such a process in textiles at around 1830; in engineering it was un-doubtedly later, but in steel-making it probably never existed. In the revolutionized industries the vast majority of skilled workers were destined to remain wage-earners. They might raise their level of skill, become scarcer commodities in the labour market, and thereby command higher wages. They might move up the hierarchy – from trimmer to carriage-maker to body-maker, from bottom sawyer to foreman sawyer – and, if the business was large enough, achieve a supervisory or quasi-managerial function. But for most skilled workers the height of ambition would be to be numbered among the labour 'aristocracy' or élite, who, in the latter half of the nineteenth century, probably composed between 10 per cent and 15 per cent of the working class, increasing somewhat in proportion towards the end of the period as mechanization continued to create demands for new and higher skills. Many industries, both unrevolutionized and revolutionized, contained a proportion of such men, whose wage-base in mid-century may be taken as 35s. a week. In 1865 Leone Levi found wage-rates of 40s. or more among shipwrights, engine-drivers, book-binders, scientific-instrument-makers, cutlery-grinders, cabinet-makers, jewellers, forge-rollers, compositors, music-instrument-makers, watch-makers, wood-carvers and pottery-modellers and throwers; it is noticeable that so many of these were still hand-crafts, little affected by mechanization. Forty years later the position had changed markedly. In the Earnings and Hours Inquiry (Wage Census) of 1906, the occupations with the highest proportion of 40s. a week wage-earners are listed as shipbuilding platers and caulkers, cotton-spinners on eighty counts, engine-drivers, rivetters, engineering platers, steel-coggers and rollers, turners and fitters.[6] The predominance of the metal industries among the labour aristocrats was remarkable, while the skilled hand-crafts of mid-century had sunk relatively in importance and remuneration, and now generally failed to qualify for admission into the privileged ranks.

Enough has been said to illustrate the enormous diversity within the category of 'skilled worker'. At the upper end of the scale little masters and skilled journeymen intermingled in a complex series of economic and social relationships: at the bottom the tailor, the shoe-maker and the building craftsman shaded off imperceptibly into the 'less skilled' and even the 'labouring' categories. Neither contemporaries, subsequent historians or Census enumerators have been able to agree on a standard classification, for the good reason that in the last resort it was custom and precedent rather than logic that determined status. In their classic trilogy of studies of the condition of labour between 1760 and 1832 J. L. and Barbara Hammond included in their volume on *The Skilled Labourer* miners, cottonworkers, woollen- and worsted-workers, silk-weavers and framework knitters; no other traditional handicrafts were included, and no mention was made of the 'new' skills.[7] In the present volume, all the occupations which they listed have been transferred to the 'semi-skilled' chapter, not because there were no highly skilled cotton-spinners or coal-miners, but because predominantly these occupations were made up of people of a lower degree of skill (and, in the case of the textiles, of many women and children) who were conventionally not accorded 'skilled' recognition, at any rate in the period under present discussion. Such a classification may seem arbitrary, but it appears to accord better with contemporary observance.

An attractively simple route through this maze might be to take as the definition of 'skilled' any worker who had served a formal apprenticeship by indenture to a trade. Unfortunately, for the nineteenth century this would not be very helpful, for the practice of apprenticeship itself became exceedingly complicated and uncertain. Since the Elizabethan Statute of Apprentices (1563) the state had recognized a responsibility for the maintenance of skilled standards by seeking to enforce systematic apprenticeship in most trades for a period of seven years. In common with other aspects of mercantilism, the practice had decayed during the eighteenth century, partly through difficulties of enforcement in the growing towns and factory districts but, more fundamentally, because of a changed belief about the role of the state in relation to the economy.[8] In 1813 a number of masters and journeymen petitioned Parliament for the better enforcement of the Act, but a powerful body of employers responded by arguing for its abolition, and in 1814 Parliament decided in their favour. In line with the abandonment of wage-control in the previous year the state now removed itself from any concern with the recruitment of labour, firmly believing that this would be best ensured by leaving it to the free working of market forces.

The abolition of state responsibility did not, of course, abolish apprenticeship. In future it would be a matter between masters and men, and the evidence suggests that for some thirty or more years it continued to survive strongly, and especially in the handicraft trades. In 1842–3 the Commission on Children's Employment noted that while in textile-mills and mining there was no formal apprenticeship, in 'by far the majority of the [miscellaneous] Trades and Manufactures' apprenticeship was still the general rule. Some were bound legally for seven years, as in the past, before the Justices or by the Poor Law Guardians, but most were now bound without any prescribed legal forms, merely being required to serve their master until the age of twenty-one. The conclusion from the Report is that personal apprenticeship still usually accompanied handicraft and small concerns, but was practically dead in the textiles and in mining.[9]

Where apprenticeship survived, or grew up, in the latter half of the century, it did so either because the nature of the trade demanded some formal period of preparation or because the adult workers in the trade were organized sufficiently powerfully to be able to restrict entry to the occupation. The two factors might work in harmony, but in essence they were opposed – the first, the employer's prescription, the second, the employees' protection. In crafts with old-established Trade Clubs apprenticeship was often a privilege which allowed a father to bring in his own sons in priority to outside boys, a practice known as 'patrimony'; such was the case in the cutlery trades, among the coach-builders, the basket-makers, the coopers and the stonemasons. It was the new, essentially engineering, trades which presented the problem since they had no precedent to call on and were often still struggling to gain support and recognition for their union. Boiler-makers continued to enforce strict, legal apprenticeship to the master throughout the century, but in engineering, the Amalgamated Society of Engineers fought a losing battle to restrict entry down to the 1880s and eventually admitted to membership any man, apprenticed or not, who had worked for five years in an engineering establishment and had obtained the standard rate of pay.[10] Similarly, in printing, although the unions in theory required apprenticeship, and the best employers endorsed it, there were many small master printers, especially in country towns, who would take a man on his merits, and with sufficient experience such 'illegal' men could often gain admission into the unions. It was mainly a matter of size and location. The failure of the compositors' unions to carry out their apprenticeship regulations was due primarily to the rapid spread of the industry from a handful of towns to practically every village in the country; by contrast, the boiler-makers could make a reality of apprenticeship because ship-building was concentrated in a relatively small number of large establishments conducted, on the whole, by employers who had regard for high standards of workmanship. The other great enemy was machinery. The best cabinet-makers in London in mid-century had all been apprenticed men, but with the coming of machine-made furniture apprenticeship quickly declined and by the time of the Royal Commission on Labour in 1892 it was said to be extinct.[11] The judgement of Sidney and Beatrice Webb in 1920 was that

Notwithstanding a strong Trade Union feeling in favour of apprenticeship regulations, these cannot be said to be enforced today over more than a small fraction of the Trade Union world . . . Over by far the largest part of the limited field in which apprenticeship once prevailed, the system has gone practically out of use . . .[12]

2. Since the skilled worker cannot be precisely defined, he cannot be accurately counted. Nevertheless, statistics are available, mainly from the Census returns, which allow some approximate measurement and, at least, demonstrate the changes over time. It was not

until 1831 that the Census attempted any detailed return of the occupations of the people, and even then some very arbitrary classifications were adopted.[13] In that year, of all males in Great Britain aged over twenty years 31·5 per cent were engaged in agriculture, 39·6 per cent in trade and manufactures and 28·8 per cent in all other occupations.[14] We are, in 1831, therefore, discussing the skilled section of a class ('trade and manufactures') which numbered little more than a third of the whole population, and when it is remembered that in the same year only 25 per cent of the whole population was living in towns of over 20,000 inhabitants, it becomes clear that industrialization and urbanization had not yet profoundly affected the lives of the majority of people.

The trades of 1831 were, in fact, still predominantly pre-industrial handicrafts. Almost certainly, the largest of all was building, hardly touched by mechanization, new techniques or new materials (though the possibilities of cast and wrought iron for large-scale construction were just being discovered), but growing rapidly with the demands of an expanding population and mushrooming cities. The Census gave 203,000 men of twenty years and upwards engaged as brick-layers, masons, carpenters, slaters, house-painters, plasterers, plumbers and glaziers; boys, apprentices and labourers must have very nearly doubled the total.[15] It is clear that the various building trades offered the major outlet for skilled men in the early nineteenth century. Not only did the conditions of the market generally afford good employment prospects, but the small scale of the industry allowed a high degree of mobility into entrepreneurship. The term 'builder' (i.e. employing contractor) had come into common usage in the late eighteenth century, and the 1831 Census enumerated 871 in London, though only seven in Berkshire, twelve in Buckinghamshire and 147 for the whole of Wales. These were the respectable, substantial men erecting public buildings and the larger shops and business premises, but below them were thousands of 'speculative builders' as they were already called, the risk-taking brick-layers who rented land, secured materials on credit, mortgaged the house when it was half-built, and reverted to the ranks of the wage-earners if they were bankrupted. The same was true of all the associated trades. In the London of the 1830s there were about 1,000 master painters, with 3000–4000 regularly employed journeymen and another 6000–8000 employed for about seven months in the year;[16] among masons, carpenters and plumbers the pattern was the same – a proportion, perhaps around one fifth, of independent master craftsmen, a larger body of regular journeymen, some of whom were always moving into the masters' ranks, or falling back out of them, and a third group of seasonal workers, partly migratory and probably of a lower average degree of skill.

After building, it is likely that the clothing and footwear trades made up the second-largest category of skilled workers. In neither trade was there a sharp line between manufacturer and retailer, for many shoe-makers sold in their own shops and much tailoring was bespoke. The 1831 Census enumerated 133,000 adult male boot-and shoe-makers and menders in Britain, and 74,000 adult male tailors – an extraordinary total of over 200,000 to which has to be added boys and apprentices numbering perhaps half as many again. It would be unjustifiable to include the female branch of the trade – the milliners and seamstresses – under the heading of skilled workers since, although some of them were undoubtedly so, many had had little or no training and carried out essentially 'rough' work. What they numbered in 1831 is not clear, but twenty years later they were no less than 340,000, and this implies that the three great stitching trades – tailoring, shoe-making and seamstressing – were together employing something like three quarters of a million people. Many of the tailors and shoe-makers were in business on their own account, working with two or three other journeymen and a couple of apprentices: only in London and a few other leading cities were there any substantially larger units, and Stultzes tailoring firm, which was credited with 250 employees in the 1830s, was quite exceptional. In shoe-making, Northampton, Stafford, Kettering and Wellingborough already did a large ready-made trade organized on a capitalist out-work system, for supplying the shoe-shops of London and other cities, but in the smaller towns and villages bespoke work was the general rule.

A third important group of skilled men was those who worked in metals. In 1831 most of these were still old, pre-industrial crafts like the 58,000 adult blacksmiths, probably half of whom were strictly rural craftsmen, the workers in the 'Sheffield trades' (8,500 in 1824) who went under the various names of table-knife-forgers, hafters, grinders, spring-knife-blade-forgers, scale-forgers, the five distinct branches which made up the scissors trade and the four of the file trade, and the far greater number employed in the Birmingham hardware trades – the locksmiths, ironmongers, gunsmiths, toy-makers and nail-makers. The numbers in these are indeterminate, and not all were skilled trades: of the supposed 50,000 nail-makers, for example, many were women and children working in domestic shops and turning out a thousand nails a day for a merchant employer.[17] These were all pre-industrial, small-scale trades, but some branches of the metal industries exhibited very different tendencies and were essentially the creation of the Industrial Revolution. Even in the previous century Ambrose Crowley had organized a great hardware works at Winlaton, Durham, essentially on factory lines, and by 1831 there was a growing number of iron-founders, brassfounders and ship-builders whose large-scale enterprises could count employees in hundreds. The Carron ironworks were reputed to employ 2,000 men in the early nineteenth century, Crawshay's works the same number, Samuel Walker and William Yates at Gospel Oak, Staffordshire, 700, and Antony Hill at Merthyr 1,500. The history of the great iron-masters is well known, and needs no repetition here.[18] By 1831 they were providing employment for a small but important body of men of new skills – blast-furnacemen, puddlers and rollers of iron, casters, forgers, boiler-makers and so on, who were working in highly capitalized plants employing larger and more sophisticated machinery than had ever previously been known. The number of strict 'engineers' was, in 1831, still very small, since engines other than steam engines were still uncommon. The early textile machinery, mainly wooden, had been made by a variety of unprofessional 'mechanics' – loom-makers, clock-makers, millwrights and instrument-makers – but by the decade 1820–30 'the professional purveyor of machines made with the help of other machines, the true mechanical engineer, was just coming into existence – in Lancashire and London, where the demand was at its maximum'.[19] By then, Bramah, Maudsley,[20] Roberts, Fairbairn and others were developing a range of machine-tools – screw-cutting lathes, slide-rests, hydraulic presses, metal-planing and slotting machines – of vast potential importance to the progress of the engineering industry. As yet, the number of firms was tiny – two to three hundred 'master engineers' in London in 1824 of which the largest, Alexander Galloway, employed just over a hundred men – but flourishing industries were also growing up in Manchester, Glasgow and Birmingham which symbolized the important growth areas of the future. The year 1830 saw the opening of the first regular commercial railway from Liverpool to Manchester, and within the next twenty years Britain was to be covered by a network of some 6,000 miles of rail demanding the services of a host of new engineering skills.

But in 1831, and for many years to come, the 'typical' skilled worker was not in engineering but in the myriad of trades – 400 of them in London alone – which catered for the daily needs of the many and the luxuries of the few. The supply of food and drink required the services of something like 50,000 bakers and confectioners and 23,500 licensed victualler–brewers in addition to the

Table 4 The total number of persons in England and Wales occupied in the under-mentioned groups of industries (compiled from the Census Reports, 1851–1901)

Groups of industries	1851	1861	1871	1881	1891	1901
Agriculture	1,904,687	1,803,049	1,423,854	1,199,827	1,099,572	988,340
Building	398,756	472,222	583,019	686,999	701,284	945,875
Coal-mining	193,111	270,604	315,398	383,570	519,144	648,944
Cotton	414,998	492,196	508,715	551,746	605,755	582,119
Lace	61,726	54,617	49,370	44,144	34,948	36,439
Woollen and worsted	255,750	230,029	246,645	240,006	258,356	236,106
Linen	27,421	22,718	18,680	12,871	8,531	4,956
Silk	130,723	116,320	82,963	64,835	52,027	39,035
Iron and steel[1]	95,350	129,507	191,291	200,677	202,406	216,022
Machine-making and ship-building[2]	80,528	123,812	172,948	217,096	292,239	—[3]
Tailoring	139,219	142,955	149,864	160,648	208,720	259,292
Boot and shoe	243,935	255,791	224,559	224,059	248,789	251,143
Printing and book-binding	32,995	46,576	64,226	88,108	121,913	149,793
Furniture	47,958	64,148	75,202	84,131	101,345	121,531
Earthenware	46,524	53,611	65,478	68,266	82,760	92,556

[1] Including ironfounders.
[2] Excluding blacksmiths and ironfounders.
[3] In 1901 a different classification was adopted from that of previous censuses, which makes it impossible to state a comparative figure.

eleven great London breweries which were among the largest
business units in the country. Printers and compositors, goldsmiths,
silversmiths, watch- and clock-makers, jewellers, workers in hides
and skins, hat-makers, breeches-makers, wheelwrights, farriers and
furriers, working on their own account or as wage-earners in small
workshops unaided by elaborate machinery, made up the vast
majority of skilled workers at the beginning of our period.

No startling change in the pattern had occurred twenty years
later. The more detailed occupational Census of 1851, taken at the
time when the Great Exhibition was demonstrating to the world
Britain's clear industrial leadership, shows that the great majority
of skilled workers were still to be found in unrevolutionized handicrafts rather than in throbbing factories and engine-rooms. Table 4
shows the changes in principal occupations in England and Wales
from 1851 to 1901, during which time the population as a whole
increased from 18,000,000 to 32,500,000.

Though many of the craft industries survived strongly throughout
the century, the table illustrates the growth of the new skilled trades
like iron and steel, machine-making and ship-building, based on the
rapid progress of Bessemer steel, the machine-tool industry and
steam power applied to locomotion on land and sea. Equally noticeable, agriculture was now in rapid and absolute decline, as were the
silk and linen industries; woollen-manufacture had ceased to grow,
in terms of numbers employed, and the great staple, cotton, showed
only a small increase. Much of this was due, of course, to greater
labour economy by the use of more advanced machinery, but the
important fact is that throughout the second half of the century a
major occupational shift was taking place, away from agriculture
and textiles and predominantly into the metal trades. In 1851 the
proportion of men working in metals, including engineering and
ship-building workers was 15 per cent of the manufacturing population: already by 1881 it was 23 per cent.[21]

In 1867 a detailed attempt was made by the statistician, Dudley
Baxter, to categorize the whole population into classes, the division
being based partly on income and partly on occupation. Considering
England and Wales only, and taking ten million persons over twenty
years of age who were in receipt of independent incomes, his calculation was as shown on page 261.[22]

From his 'population' of 7,785,000 in the 'labour class' he placed
1,123,000 in two skilled groups – 'most highly skilled', earning about
35s. a week, 56,000, and 'highly skilled', earning 28s. to 30s. a week,
1,067,000. The details of the principal occupations and earnings
were as shown on page 261.

Class	Income per annum	Number of recipients	
Upper class	Over £5,000	7,500	⎫
Upper class	£1,000–£5,000	42,000	⎬ 49,500
Middle class	£300–£1,000	150,000	150,000
Lower middle class	£100–£300	850,500	⎫ 1,853,500
Lower middle class	Under £100	1,003,000	⎬
Skilled labour class	Under £100	1,123,000	⎫
Less skilled labour class	Under £100	3,819,000	⎬ 7,785,000
Agricultural workers and			
Unskilled labour class	Under £100	2,843,000	⎭

Men's weekly wage	Occupational group	Approximate number
35 shillings	Scientific-, surgical- and optical-instrument-makers	3,150
	Scale-makers	1,150
	Leather-case-makers	2,200
	Watch-makers	15,400
	Jewellery-workers	11,000
	Engine-drivers	9,300
28 to 30 shillings	Printers, binders, etc.	28,350
	Hat-makers	9,000
	Ivory-, bone- and wood-workers	13,600
	Earthenware-workers	20,300
	Glass-workers	9,700
	Arms- and tool-makers	44,250
	Iron-workers	91,700
	Cabinet-makers, upholsterers	39,000
	Musical-instrument-makers	2,200
	Building trades	387,600
	Ship-building trades	82,900
	Bakers' and butchers' men	70,000

However, in his third and fourth categories 'Lower skilled A and B' Baxter includes several trades which seem to belong more properly to the skilled, as follows:

Men's weekly wage	Occupational group	Approximate number
25 shillings	Coach- and harness-makers	30,000
	Hairdressers	8,000
	Gas-workers	8,000
	Tanners, curriers, skinners	19,200
	Rope-makers, etc.	11,300
	Blacksmiths and hardware workers	130,000
	Paper-workers	12,000
	Polishers, japanners	8,500
21 to 23 shillings	Boot- and shoe-workers	157,000
	Tailors	83,000

These would add another 470,000 or so, giving a total of around 1,600,000 skilled workers, or rather more than one in five of all manual workers.

The figures are interesting in a number of respects. In the most highly skilled, and best-paid, group only one occupation – that of engine-driver – appears as a representative of the 'new', Industrial Revolution occupations; all the rest are traditional handicrafts. In the second group only the arms- and tool-makers, the iron-workers and the ship-builders had been greatly affected by mechanization. In fact, it seems likely that the crucial period of change for skilled workers in this respect began to occur only in the 1880s, and that only thereafter were the handicrafts gradually overtaken by the new machine skills. Until then, the majority of skilled workers found their employment in customer work like that of the tailor or plumber (by 1881 there was one plumber in London for every 508 of the population) or in true handicrafts either as small independent masters or as journeymen working for small masters. In 1881 there were 132,000 blacksmiths in Britain, and even in London 'little masters' retained the bulk of the trade: down to 1871 blacksmiths continued to grow as fast as the population, but in the next decade there was, significantly, hardly any increase. Coach-builders, wheelwrights and saddlers were also still intact in the 1880s, though they were beginning to be threatened and were certainly experiencing change. When George Sturt took over his father's business as a wheelwright in Farnham, Surrey in 1884, his men had already forgotten how to make a wooden harrow, and were forgetting how to make a wooden axle for an old dung-cart.[23] What was happening in the wheelwright's trade, as in that of the saddler, the blacksmith, the plumber, the cabinet-maker and many more, was that materials were increasingly bought in partly made up or prepared form from a factory or other large-scale producer – iron axles, lead piping, sawn plank, prepared leather and so on – which in the past the craftsman had made for himself. And, at the other end of the process, he was increasingly selling, not direct to the customer, but to middlemen, dealers and retailers. Especially was this true of crafts like watch-making, where the skilled workers of Coventry and Clerkenwell now rarely made whole watches, but produced mainsprings or hair-springs for the 'watch-maker' whose name stood on the dial.[24] In cheap tailoring, furniture-making, boot- and shoe-making the same practice of sub-division was spreading – out-work craftsmen who made only chair-legs or trousers or linings for a master retailer: some worked on their own materials and preserved a degree of independence, others worked purely for the employer and were paid on a piece-work basis. By the 1880s the varied handicrafts of East London and East Leeds were beginning to be swollen by immigrants from the Polish ghettos, overstocking and very probably depressing conditions in those trades, particularly tailoring and furniture-making, into which they crowded.

But in several of these industries change was imminent, and the factory was already beginning to take over from the craftsman. In the 1871 Census there were listed 145 factories making boots and shoes, with an average of 125 workers in each: adaptations of the Singer sewing-machine of 1851 now made it possible to mechanically sew leather, while other innovations soon cut butts, stamped out soles and attached heels. By the 1880s Goodyear's 'sew-round machine' for the first time produced an exact replica of a hand-sewn welted boot, and a completely mechanized system was now, in theory, possible. Most 'factories' used only some of the processes, continuing to employ out-work craftsmen for some parts of the process, but in 1887 it was reported that 'there are now, even in the good class bespoke trade [of London] but four masters who get their tops cut out and closed in the primitive manner by men working in their homes'.[25] A very similar development was occurring in the mass production of cheap clothing, again based on the sewing-machine and its adaptations. Machining was first employed to any extent in Leeds in 1857, and by 1871 there were fifty-eight clothing factories in Britain employing an average of 136 workpeople each. Between them, however, they had only sixty-five horse-power of steam, used for cutting piles of cloth by a band-knife and for pressing: sewing-machines, running at up to 2,000 stitches a minute, were still usually hand- or treadle-driven. By the 1880s machinery was available for all the processes of low-grade tailoring, though for better-class work hand finishing, button-holing and so on was still done by skilled men and women in workshops or at home.

But as mechanization advanced, and some of the handicrafts began to decline in terms of numbers, status and earnings, the increased use of machinery itself demanded more men to make, operate and service it. In the Wages Census of 1906 the engineering, iron and steel and ship-building trades now dominated the labour aristocracy whose earnings exceeded 40s. a week, while even highly skilled carpenters, plasterers and masons with a daily wage-rate just before the war of about 6s. 6d. now failed to qualify for admission. The expansion of some of the new technologies, though not as impressive in Britain as in Germany, was sufficiently dramatic: the electrical industries alone grew eightfold between 1891 and 1911, and by the latter date were employing 100,000 men. If horse-cabmen and coachmen declined, railway workers continued to grow strongly, tramwaymen increased by 26,000 between 1901 and 1911 and in the same decade professional motor-drivers rose from 703 to 47,000.[26] The 46,500 pottery-workers in England and Wales in 1851 became 92,500 by 1901, the 48,000 furniture-makers 121,500, the 40,000 printers and book-binders 150,000 and the 139,000 tailors 259,000, and though, with the progress of mechanization, not all of these were increases of hand-craftsmen, it can scarcely be doubted that they represented a substantial growth in the numbers of skilled workers.

Though strict comparison of occupations is not possible, the evidence strongly suggests that the progress of industrialization continued to create a higher proportion of skilled jobs down to the end of the period under consideration. In 1867 Dudley Baxter had assigned 14 per cent of adult male workers to the skilled class, 49 per cent to the lower skilled and 36 per cent to the unskilled. For 1931 G. D. H. Cole's calculations are 30 per cent skilled, 40 per cent semi-skilled and 30 per cent unskilled, again for adult males: 'It is fairly safe to conclude that the proportion of unskilled workers has fallen, while that of highly skilled manual workers has risen, leaving the middle group of much the same relative size'.[27] Similar results are arrived at by Guy Routh in his study of occupation and pay in

Britain between 1906 and 1960.[28] By 1931 by far the largest occupations in the group were the metal-makers and metal-workers at
1,580,000; after them were building and contracting workers at
485,000, wood-workers 483,000, tailoring and shoe-making trades
249,000 and railway workers 129,000.[29] The number of self-
employed craftsmen had remained almost unchanged – 170,000 in
1911 and 200,000 in 1931, the principal categories being, in order,
builders, hairdressers, painters and decorators, shoe-makers, carpenters and cabinet-makers and bakers; by 1951 there were only
4,700 independent blacksmiths, as many photographers as watch-
makers, but twice as many motor mechanics as blacksmiths. Industrialization had unquestionably destroyed some old crafts and had
brought many formerly independent workers into the factory system, but, equally unquestionably, it had increased the total proportion of skilled workers.

3. The earnings history of the skilled worker can be conveniently
divided into three phases, each of which has well-marked characteristics – the first half of the nineteenth century, the 1850s to the
1880s, and from the 1880s to the 1920s. Although it is relatively easy
to assemble statistics of wage-rates, if not of actual earnings, for the
whole period, it is quite another matter to discover how they were
determined, especially in a period which witnessed a transformation
from conventional, customary rates to bargaining in a free market
economy. The ending of state control of apprenticeship and wage-
regulation by the repeal of the Statute of Apprentices in 1813 and
1814 ushered in a free labour market in which employers no longer
felt constrained to follow previous wage practices, and gradually
moved to the position of testing what the market would bear. Up
until 1814 qualified millwrights, for example, had been paid by
time; they were a highly organized society, which, presumably by
negotiation with the employers, had been paid on a standard time-
rate of about 42s. a week. In the new engineering workshops millwrights had successfully insisted on their standard rates, whatever
work they were put to, but the repeal of apprenticeship enabled
employers to bring in new men and 'to pay every man according to
his merit and to allow him to make his own agreement'.[30] The
growth of this payment by results, described as 'the engineers'
economy', appears to have spread rapidly in the 1820s, and to have
applied to other workers entering the industry, such as carpenters
and joiners. One leading employer, Alexander Galloway, now paid
his men from below 30s. a week up to 42s., depending on skill and
the nature of the work.

9*

Not all employers succeeded in so coercing the millwrights, and within a very few years the new engineers were busy establishing new time-rates on the old lines. The millwrights were in any case an extreme case of a craft threatened by mechanical revolution, and in most of the traditional handicrafts strong trade clubs and societies continued to maintain time-rates throughout the first half of the century. Francis Place described to the Committee on Artisans and Machinery in 1824 the 'perfect and perpetual combination' of the London tailors, and the powerful organizations of carpenters, plumbers, hatters and boot-makers, concerned to maintain agreed time-rates and to regulate the numbers of apprentices admitted to the trade even though there was no longer statutory sanction. Amongst the most powerful of all, it seems, were the Liverpool shipwrights and ship-sawyers, who successfully prevented the introduction of piece-rates as prejudicial to older workers, checked overstocking of the yards with apprentices, limited the day's work and made rules about the number of men required for particular jobs.

Professor E. J. Hobsbawm has put forward the view that in the first half of the nineteenth century both masters and men were only beginning to learn 'the rules of the game' of wage-determination. Workers were learning to regard their labour as a commodity to be sold in a free, capitalist economy, but where they had any choice in the matter, still fixed the asking price by non-economic criteria; equally, employers were beginning to understand the value of intensive labour utilization and incentives, but still tended to measure labour utilization by custom or precedent.[31] A skilled man's wage was, by long convention, approximately double that of an unskilled, which, at least in periods or localities of plentiful labour, was fixed at or near subsistence level: the base-line (as it were), of a skilled wage was, then, primarily determined by the maintenance of this differential, moving in line with movements in unskilled wages. Beyond this, the various skilled trades had their rank order, as previously described, again resting mainly on custom rather than on logical differences such as training-time or skill; higher status traditionally attached to some trades rather than others, and this was normally, though not invariably, reflected in wage-differences. One result of this, according to Hobsbawm's thesis, was that 'employers almost certainly got their skilled labour in the nineteenth century at less than market cost', and that 'ironfounders and engineers in Britain before, say, 1840, lived in a wonderful seller's market and could have demanded much more than the [provincial] rate of 30s. or so . . .'.[32] On the other hand, skilled workers like these had more discretion to adjust their work-load and 'productivity' to their earnings than had unskilled workers: a 'fair day's work' would be measured by social usage rather than crude market forces, and a less-than-market wage may well have been thought acceptable in return for more independence, leisure and respect.

The course of actual wages in the first half-century followed, usually with some short time-lag, the course of price movements:[33] a sharp rise during the period of rapid wartime inflation up to 1813, followed by a post-war fall, usually less, and then a period of relative stability up to 1850 is the general pattern. A London brick-layer's summer day-rate, which had been 3s. 9d. in the 1790s, rose to 5s. 6d. in 1813, subsequently fell only to 5s. and was 5s. 3d. in 1848; Manchester brick-layers were earning from 22s. 6d. to 24s. in the 1820s, only 18s. 6d. in a bad year, 1832, but 28s. in 1849. Francis Place reported (in 1834) that for his own trade of breeches-making wages had risen from 22s. in 1793 to 36s. at the end of the wars, and had never fallen since, and that this was typical of a very large body of skilled metropolitan workers. Compositors' standard time-wages had touched 36s. in 1810, falling to 33s. after the wars, while the very highly paid workers on morning and evening newspapers fell from 48s. to 43s. 6d. over the same period. In the new industry, engineering, there was less custom to guide wages, and as yet, less powerful unions to negotiate standard rates. The London millwrights' 42s. a week of 1813 was, as we have seen, broken by the introduction of 'the engineers' economy', and their earnings undoubtedly declined subsequently, Manchester ironmoulders earned 34s. 8d. in the dear year, 1816, 30s. in 1830 and 34s. to 36s. in the 1840s: turners followed the same trend, on a lower scale – 30s. in 1813, 26s. in 1820, then around 30s. throughout the 1830s and 1840s.[34]

One very important factor which must be borne in mind in any consideration of the earnings of skilled workers is that many trades contained an 'honourable' section working at full wages and a 'dishonourable' section employed at below – sometimes well below – standard rates. The London tailors are a good case in point. At the time when Henry Mayhew wrote his series of articles on London trades for the *Morning Chronicle* (1849–50) there were 23,500 London tailors, of whom 2,750 were in business for themselves and 20,800 operatives: of these, Mayhew believed that there were not more than 3,000 in the 'honourable' part of the trade, working on their own premises at 6d. an hour, and about 18,000 in the cheap, 'slop' or 'dishonourable' trade. Practically all the 'honourable' tailors were 'in Union', but twenty-five years previously there had been twice as many. Mayhew blamed the small 'sweating' masters who had crowded into the trade, had reduced wages, introduced payment in truck 'until the state of trade . . . appears to be approaching desperation'.[35] There had been an unsuccessful strike about 1834, and after this employers had gradually gone over from a time-rate of 6s. a day for twelve hours' work to piece-work in which the price paid for a garment was determined by the quantity of work in it, known as the 'log'. 'Honourable' employers, while in theory observing the new system, in fact kept to the old rates – for example, a pair of plain trousers would be estimated at ten hours' work and costed at 5s. (i.e. 6d. an hour), but 'sweating' masters would calculate a shorter time in order to pay a lower price without contravening the 'log'. One witness stated that fewer 'regular' hands were now kept, but the market was over-stocked with surplus journeymen who were forced to work a day and a half for a day's pay. A further result was that many journeymen now took work home to farm out to women and children at starvation wages: they, in fact, became middlemen or small 'sweaters' in their turn. Thus, there was now a wide range of earnings in the tailoring trade – from 39s. a week for a 'captain' in constant employment at an 'honourable' shop, to about 30s. for a regular hand on piece-work, also in a highly respectable shop, to a casual journeyman earning 25s. a week as an extra hand during the brisk season of May to July, but only 4s. to 6s. a week for the rest of the year at 'sank' work, making uniforms for soldiers, police and post-office workers; his total wages for a year were £21 16s. or 8s. 4½d. a week. In the East End 'slop' trade even worse conditions were discovered. One witness reported that he received 5s. for a Wellington 'surtout' which took twenty-six hours' work, but out of this he had to pay 1s. 6d. for trimmings, thread, candles and fire; his wife was dying of consumption, and a doctor had told him that if he did not apply for parochial relief he would be guilty of manslaughter. A young man who had just come out of a six-year apprenticeship for which a £7 premium had been paid declared that by working as hard as he could for eighteen hours a day he could earn only 12s. a week, out of which trimmings, thread, light and heat took 4s. Mayhew calculated that the average earnings in the 'respectable' slop-trade were 15s. 5d. a week, clear of deductions: in the 'dishonourable' slop-trade they were 8s.[36] By 1844 some three quarters (15,000 of the 21,000) of all London tailors were engaged in the East End, essentially slop-trade, and the now small number of 'honourable' masters was declining at the rate of 150 a year.

The plight of the tailors only exhibited in more extreme form a general trend in the earnings and conditions of many handicraft workers. Among the most highly skilled of all, the cabinet-makers, the official rate in the 1840s was 32s. a week, either by piece-work or by time-rate, calculated as ten hours a day for six days. Piece-rates were laid down in a 600-page book in which the piece-work price of every article of furniture was specified in great detail. But the 'Society' men to whom these rules applied were only 642 of the 5,208 London cabinet-makers:[37] the rest now worked for 'garret masters' and 'slaughter-houses', mostly in the East End, at greatly reduced wages. An old cabinet-maker who specialized in fancy tea-caddies and work-boxes reported that he had earned £3 a week twenty years ago, but now could only get 28s. a dozen at the ware-house, which, after materials, gave him 16s. a week. In the shoe-making trade also there were 'honourable' employers but many more small 'chamber masters' and 'slop masters' paying approxi-mately half the 'legal' rates, while in the baking trade there were 'full-priced' employers but many 'undersellers' and 'cutting bakers' who adulterated their loaves as well as over-working their men for reduced earnings.[38] The evidence is overwhelming that in many of the once-respectable skilled trades, in London especially but else-where to a lesser degree, competition had driven down the level of earnings to semi-skilled and even unskilled rates. Between the 1820s and the 1840s many employers in these trades were clearly learning 'the rules of the game' and discovering 'what the trade would bear', and customary rates were rapidly ceasing to apply.

Between the 1850s and the 1880s wages history begins to take on different characteristics. Some skilled workers, newly organized into powerful trade unions, were also beginning to learn the rules and to exact a higher price for a scarce commodity. One evidence of this was an increasing acceptance of, sometimes a strong preference for, piece-rates over time-rates, on the general argument that they bene-fited the efficient worker and were a defence against 'sweating'; although the engineers, the ironfounders and the building crafts resisted them, the boiler-makers, the shipwrights, the blacksmiths and other influential unions were, by the end of the century, firmly committed to piece-rates,[39] Again, it seems likely that skilled workers took advantage of their better labour organization to widen the differential between themselves and the unskilled, and that by the 1860s the ratio of average wages between skilled, semi-skilled and unskilled was of the order of 5 : 3·3 and 2·4.[40] 'Self-help' in this respect meant self-interest, and the New Model unions were in no doubt that the market value of their labour would be increased by scarcity and added skill – hence, the encouragement of closed-shop policies, restriction of entry, aid for emigration and for mobility of labour between areas of full and slack employment. Skilled workers also increasingly favoured the shortest hiring contracts, in place of the former long-term contracts, in order to facilitate bargaining for better terms with the least possible delay. In a period of increasing productivity, more 'intensive' use of labour and wide profit margins (at least down to the 'Great Depression' of 1873–86, and, even then, in most industries still), the skilled worker was in a position to test what benefits he could derive from a system which was clearly rewarding some handsomely.

These benefits were not wholly, or even mainly, in terms of wages: other factors such as working conditions, hours, holidays and status might be equally important. But so far as wages alone are concerned, it is likely that between 1850 and 1886 the skilled worker on average added about 30 per cent to his weekly or hourly rate of pay.[41] Trades already highly paid, like printing and engineering, did less well than this – printing perhaps only 16 per cent and engineering 25 per cent – but building-workers increased their rates by between 42 and 50 per cent, and this over a period when from end to end the general price-level had fallen slightly, and food prices steeply.[42] The contemporary economic statistician, Leone Levi, writing in 1885, was convinced that

With the enormous increase of wealth in the United Kingdom, the position of the working classes has likewise greatly improved. In a large number of instances working men of 1857 have become middle-class men of 1884 . . . Cases of rising from the ranks are by no means as rare as we might imagine. But working men of the present day are much better off than they were twenty-seven years ago, for all wages are higher . . . In 1857 a joiner got 27 shillings; now he gets 33s. 6d., or 36 shillings with piecework, showing an increase of 24 per cent . . . But even these wages fail to give a full view of the improved conditions of the labouring classes, for wherever piecework obtains, the wages average about one-eighth above day work, whilst all overtime is paid at varying rates. Taking a comprehensive view of the entire range of industries . . . I think I am justified in assuming that the working classes, as a whole, are in receipt of 30 per cent more in 1884 than they were receiving in 1857. . . .[43]

A mass of statistical evidence on wages in the 1880s then followed, of which the following earnings of skilled workers are representative: railway-engine-drivers 6s. a day, £93 a year; guards 4s. a day, £62 a year; London compositors 36s. minimum (the 'establishment' wage for a week reduced from sixty to fifty-four hours in 1872), readers 43s. 5d., and newspaper compositors 50s. to 70s.; London book-binders time-rates 32s. to 40s., engineering workers 36s. to 38s. in London, 31s. 6d. throughout the United Kingdom for a fifty-four-hour week (fitters at Sharp, Stuart and Company's Atlas Works, Manchester, 32s. to 38s., pattern-makers 36s., grinders 32s., rivetters 32s., planers and slotters 22s. to 27s.); Sheffield cutlers – a wide range from 20s. to 35s.; clock-makers' average 29s.; watch-makers' average 35s.; mathematical- and optical-instrument-makers, a wide range from 20s. to 70s., average 35s.; carpenters, joiners, masons, brick-layers 9d. an hour for a fifty-two and a half-hour week, plumbers 10d. an hour, painters 8d. to 8½d. an hour; cabinet-makers 7d. to 9d. an hour; carvers and gilders 34s. a week; upholsterers 40s. to 50s.; iron-puddlers 48s.; forge-rollers 50s.; silversmiths 30s. to 60s.; goldsmiths 1s. to 1s. 9d. an hour; diamond-setters 36s. to 80s.[44] Overtime could add substantially, though un-certainly, to many of these wages. George Barnes records how at Barrow-in-Furness in 1877 he was earning £3 a week as an engineer in the shipyards, by adding thirty-two hours a week overtime to the normal week of fifty-four hours.[45]

Between the 1880s and the First World War the earnings position of the skilled worker began to change in some important respects. For one thing, he no longer possessed the monopoly of labour organization, with the rise of trade unionism among semi-skilled and unskilled workers; in future, his differential would have to be guarded against groups who were increasingly able to bargain for wages above subsistence level. Second, by the 1890s both employers and employees had, in Hobsbawm's term, learned 'the rules of the game', and were in a position to conduct wage-determination by reference to market forces rather than custom and usage. Third, the continued development of technology was now beginning seriously to affect the fortunes of a number of traditional handicrafts and to produce a major shift from the old skills to the new. In total, it is likely that the proportion of skilled workers increased throughout the period, and that the proportion of 'aristocrats' within the skilled also increased.[46] But by 1906 craft workers once near the top of the labour hierarchy like hatters and tailors, cabinet-makers, coopers, saddlers and bag-makers found themselves with growing proportions of under-25s.-a-week 'plebeians', while the over-40 shillings-a-week 'aristocrats' were increasingly concentrated in the metal and engineering trades. It is also significant that with the exception of railway-engine-drivers and one grade of engineer, all these were occupations paid by piece-wage rather than time-wage. Their in-creasing use by skilled workers at this time was, perhaps, one of the means by which the differential of 2 : 1 between skilled and unskilled workers was maintained, and even increased in some trades.[47] Although unskilled wages fluctuated more widely than skilled, and gained ground in short periods, there is no evidence that the traditional differential narrowed from end to end of the period.

From the outbreak of war in 1914 pay structures began to take on new characteristics, and experienced more far-reaching changes in the next twenty years than in the previous hundred. Between 1914 and 1920 a period of rapid inflation saw prices outstripping the rise in wages, by which date the cost of living index stood at 266 compared with 100 in 1906–10; from 1920 onwards, both prices and wages fell, prices now more rapidly, so that by 1935 the cost of living index stood at 153. Average earnings in a selection of skilled trades for the three years 1906, 1924 and 1935 are given in Table 5.[48]

Table 5   Annual earnings of skilled men (occupational class 5), 1906, 1924, 1935

		1906	1924		1935	
		£	£	% of 1906	£	% of 1924
Coal-face workers		112	180	161	149	83
Pottery-turners		90	153	170	166	109
Pottery-throwers		110	198	180	203	103
Engineering fitters:	time	90	157	174	212	135
	piece	103	191	185	243	127
Boot- and shoe-clickers:	time	71 }	165	232	159	96
	piece	69 }				
Bakers		75	159	212	156	98
Carpenters		98	191	195	176	92
Bricklayers		94	191	203	176	92
Railway-engine-drivers		119	276	232	258	94
Railway guards		80	196	245	192	98
Compositors		91	209	230	218	104
Weighted average		97	182	188	197	108
Unweighted average		92	189	205	192·5	102

It is clear that skilled wages, in general, followed the direction of prices; four of the listed occupations showed further absolute gains between 1924 and 1935, even in a period of falling prices, while seven showed some small absolute falls more than compensated by price reductions.

For the regularly employed skilled worker the inter-war years therefore saw a continued advance in real earnings. What was noticeable, however, was that the traditional differential for skill narrowed considerably, especially during the period of inflation from 1914 to 1920. With labour now greatly in demand and unemployment at an all-time 'low', unskilled wages were no longer pegged to subsistence and, temporarily at least, made large gains. During the rapid deflation of 1920–24 the differential widened again and skilled workers recovered some of the lost ground, but it seems clear that since the First World War differentials have never been so wide or so rigid as they were in the nineteenth century, and that the general trend has been towards a narrowing.[49]

4. The previous section has indicated that even within the skilled trades the range of earnings was immense. Wages depended on the place of the particular trade within the hierarchy, the extent and effectiveness of trade union organization, whether a worker was a 'society' man employed by a 'regular' master or a 'non-Society' man in a 'sweating' branch of the trade, and so on. But, although the wage-levels so far quoted illustrate such variations clearly enough, it is important to remember that they represent the wages of men in full-time work, and take no account of unemployment, temporary or long-term. The distinction between 'constant' earnings and 'casual' earnings was, as Mayhew pointed out, of the utmost importance to the workman, since if he had only six months' regular work during a year his actual constant wages would be only half of his actual casual earnings.

The usual assumption has been that unemployment affected the skilled worker in the nineteenth century relatively little, and certainly much less than the unskilled; it is argued that his skill was a scarce commodity, strongly in demand, that he was less exposed to seasonal and cyclical fluctuations in trade, and that he possessed greater mobility than the unskilled man, tied down by ignorance and poverty. A closer examination suggests that such optimism was often ill-founded, that periodic unemployment, or under-employment, was much commoner than supposed and a major insecurity in the lives of even the highest paid wage-earners, Writing in 1850, Mayhew was in no doubt that such insecurity was increasing:

Constant employment, and consequently constant wages, are gradually passing into casual labour, and therefore casual earnings; for the economy

of labour is daily teaching capitalists to employ their labourers only when
they are wanted, and to get rid of them immediately the business in any
way declines; and as most trades are 'brisk' and 'slack' at various periods
of the year, a large number of workmen are employed only in the busy,
and discharged in the dull times.[50]

To quote only one of his many examples, the small London Cabinet-
Makers' Society, which in the decade 1840–49 had 452 members,
had an average of eighty-one unemployed (125 in 1848) for an
average of fifteen days a year (thirty-four days in 1848); the Society
paid out an average of £213 a year to the unemployed members.[51]
These, it should be stressed, were the most fortunate members of
the trade, with 'honourable' employers and a society to support
them, and it is clear that in many of the skilled workers' unions of the
day protection from unemployment was one of the principal objec-
tives. In 1844 the Spring Knife-Grinders' Protection Society of
Sheffield declared that 'the object to be accomplished is to grant
relief to all its members that are out of work; that none may have
the painful necessity of applying for relief from the parish'. The
Flint Glass-Makers had the same idea – 'Our wages depend on the
supply of labour in the market: our interest therefore is to restrict
that supply, reduce the surplus, make our unemployed comfortable
without fear for the morrow . . .'; and the Amalgamated Engineers,
in extending the period of benefit by a further nine weeks, asserted
that without this members 'would be compelled either to seek
parish relief, or take situations on terms injurious to the trade'.[52]
But, in Mayhew's estimate, non-Society men outnumbered Society
men in every main trade by about ten to one,[53] and for the vast
majority of these there was neither trade union protection nor state
unemployment benefit until after the First World War.

Of the real extent of unemployment, especially in the first half of
the nineteenth century, we can only catch occasional glimpses. Professor E. J. Hobsbawm's study of the tramping artisan revealed the
unsuspected volume of migration of skilled workers in search of
work, and the organized way in which many trade unions adminis-
tered the system.[54] The usual practice was to issue the unemployed
man with a 'blank' or 'clearance' which, on presentation to the local
secretary of a strange town at the 'club house' or 'house of call' entitled him to supper, lodging and a further tramp allowance if no
work was available: in this way, a man might follow a complete
circuit of all the branches – 2,800 miles for the compositors, 1,200
miles for the brush-makers. The practice was certainly not new in
the nineteenth century, though the indications are that it grew
rapidly, and by 1860 was in use among compositors, lithographers,

tailors, coach-makers, book-binders, smiths, engineers, steam-
engine-makers, stonemasons,[55] carpenters, ironfounders, coopers,
shoe-makers, boiler-makers, plumbers, brick-layers and other
crafts. A few statistics will reveal the extent of the practice. The
small society of Journeymen Steam-Engine Makers relieved 224
travellers out of its 695 members in 1837-8, 2,226 of its 994 members in the depressed year 1841-2. In 1840 the Ironfounders paid
out £11,500 on tramping for a total membership of 3,500, and in
1841-2 the four main printing unions relieved 7,200 travellers out of
their 3,400 members. In 1872 6 per cent of ironfounders took out
tramping cards; between 1873 and 1876 an annual average of 25
per cent of provincial printers. But by this time tramping was in
decline in most trades, and being replaced by static 'out-of-work
pay': only the compositors and the stonemasons preserved the
practice into the twentieth century. The important point is, however, that in the supposed 'golden age' of the mid-Victorian economy
such large numbers of skilled men had regularly to take to the road
in search of work.

Again, a good deal of scattered evidence is available about the
extent of unemployment during the cyclical slumps of the first half
of the century. During the severe depression of 1841-2 a contemporary estimate gave 36 per cent of Bolton iron-workers unemployed,
84 per cent of carpenters, 87 per cent of bricklayers, 66 per cent of
stonemasons and 50 per cent of tailors and shoe-makers; in Dundee
half the mechanics and ship-builders were out of work, in London
two thirds of the tailors, and in Liverpool half the brick-layers and
three quarters of the plasterers. The disastrous years 1841-2 were, of
course, abnormal, but they were only an abnormally bad instance of
what was normal in the early industrial economy – fluctuations between booms and slumps which recurred at frequent and fairly
regular intervals of four to eight years during the first half of the
century. They could be catastrophic to building workers, to tailors
and cabinet-makers who stood in a direct relationship with the
fortunes of their customers, but they could also disastrously affect
the standards of engineers and millwrights, ironfounders, compositors and other skilled workers in relatively 'safe' industries. We
know little about the average duration of this unemployment,
though in 1841-2 it affected some workers for a year and more. But
even if it were only for a few weeks or months it could spell ruin to
families whose standard of living was always frail, and who had few
savings or valuable possessions. No doubt a crisis of a few weeks
was surmounted by out-of-work pay, by credit or pawn, but if it
became extended, or recurred frequently, even the skilled man **could**

slip into poverty and destitution from which it might become impossible to escape.

From mid-century onwards it is likely that employment became more regular for the majority of workers, and that cyclical depressions were never again so severe. Statistics exist from 1851 onwards of unemployment among trade union members which indicate the general trends and these are useful for our purpose since, until the 1890s, they relate to skilled workers such as engineers, ship-builders, carpenters, joiners, wood-workers, printers and book-binders; they show serious peaks of unemployment, often at 10 per cent or more, in 1858, 1862, 1868, 1879, the mid-80s and 1908–9.[56] It is likely that the official statistics underestimated the true extent, since many men must have been unwilling to notify their union of their redundancy, at any rate immediately. Irregularity of work, even for the skilled, represented the major restriction on a secure standard of living up to the outbreak of war, and still reduced actual earnings by a significant proportion. Precisely what this proportion was is impossible to calculate, but Dudley Baxter wrote in 1867,

> None but those who have examined the facts can have any idea of the precariousness of employment in our large cities, and the large proportion of time out of work . . . I come to the conclusion that for loss of work from every cause, and for the non-effectives up to 65 years of age who are included in the census, we ought to deduct fully twenty per cent from the nominal full-time wages.[57]

After a period of practically full employment during and immediately after the First World War, unemployment on a massive scale began in 1921, to reach its highest point in 1931–2 when it exceeded 20 per cent of the insured population; only in one year, 1927, did it fall below 10 per cent. In this period unemployment was both widespread and long-term, affecting particularly those great staple industries on which Britain's wealth had been built in the previous century, and which often contained a high proportion of skilled workers. Iron and steel, ship-building and some branches of heavy engineering were especially affected by the fall in exports, and suffered much more than the newer industries based on the home market like the vehicle and electrical industries, food and tobacco. At its worst, in 1932, unemployment affected 62 per cent of ship-builders, 36 per cent of pottery-workers, 44 per cent of pig-iron-workers, 48 per cent of steel-smelters and iron-puddlers, 29 per cent of general engineers, 18 per cent of workers in tailoring and boot- and shoe-making, 30 per cent of builders and 22 per cent of furniture-makers and upholsterers, the national average for all insured workers being 22·5 per cent.[58] Many of these workers suffered catastrophic falls in their standards of living, heightened by the prosperity they had once enjoyed. An engineering fitter earning between £3 and £4 a week in 1924 would now be dependent on unemployment benefit allowing 15 shillings for a man, 12 shillings for his wife and half-rates for children, and in the depressed areas of Tyneside and Glasgow, Jarrow and South Wales, such reductions could continue for months and even years. In these years, some skills became a liability which the unemployed willingly exchanged for work of any kind.

Periodic unemployment, or under-employment, constituted, then, the chief limitation on the worker's earnings. But there were other significant deductions which could seriously reduce his wages, even for a full week's work. In many skilled trades the worker was required to find his own tools – to start with a complete set, and to replace them as need be – and these might vary from the cabinet-maker's elaborate tool-box, costing in the mid-nineteenth century up to £30, to the compositor's simple pair of tweezers costing a few pence. Large initial outlays would often have to be borrowed and repaid over the following months. But many workers faced regular weekly out-goings for fines or stoppages for inferior work, charges for the use of large implements (like the payment of 'pence' by sawyers), materials which they were expected to provide (like the 'trimmings' required of tailors in the 'slop-trade'), bonuses paid to foremen for obtaining work, commission to middlemen from whom orders were obtained; and stoppages for benefit or provident funds which a man often had to sacrifice on being discharged. 'Out-workers' carrying on their trade at home had, of course, to find their own heat, light and rent, and to pay for materials to be brought in and completed work delivered. In a number of trades, single men were often boarded with the employer, as in the case of the shoe maker reported by Mayhew who obliged ten men to lodge and work in a single large room at 2s. 6d. a week each.[59]

Workers of all sorts suffered from irregularity of payment, and from payment at the public house on Saturday night, where the need for change virtually obliged drinking.[60] Such forms of semi-truck, where the publican was a servant or agent of the employer, or where continuation in a job depended on spending so much on beer, were widespread and especially galling to the steady, sober worker with a wife and children to support. Payment of wages in public houses or beer-shops was at last illegalized by an act of 1883, but 'long pays' – intervals of a fortnight, a month, or even three months between pay-days – were not statutorily prohibited. 'Short pays' gradually became commoner, and were normal though not quite universal by the end of the century; it is worth noticing, however, that 'long pays' had sometimes accompanied long engagements, and had therefore guaranteed work for a month, or even a year. This kind of bondage, well known among the Northumberland and Durham miners, but also common among some Staffordshire potters until 1866, had been understandably unpopular, but its replacement by weekly hiring and weekly payment brought greater insecurity as well as greater freedom.

The close relationship in Victorian times between the public house and the means of obtaining work exerted a major influence on the 'take-home' earnings of workers of all degrees of skill. The 'houses of call' from which the trade clubs operated their primitive labour exchanges were almost always public houses at which the unemployed man would call three or four times a day in the hope of work. Trade union meetings were normally held in rooms provided free by publicans in the confident expectation of heavy sales of drink, at least until after mid-century when temperance came to be urged by some of the 'New Model' unions. More insidious were the practices, noted by Mayhew, by which a publican acted as go-between with employers, and would only negotiate for men who would immediately part with the bulk of their earnings over the bar-counter. The harrowing accounts of poverty-stricken wives and children dragging drunken men home on Saturday night who had already spent all but a shilling of their weekly wage are too common and too recurrent in the literature to be apocryphal. Excessive drinking was less common in the skilled than the unskilled trades, and as the century wore on it sank lower in the social scale, but it was part of the culture of working-class life which required an unusual effort of will to break. For the skilled worker, occasions which demanded drink included 'footings' when the new apprentice was compelled to 'stand treat' to his colleagues, to be repeated when his time was served, on his marriage, his promotion or his removal to another 'shop'.[61] Annual 'shop' outings, compulsorily saved up for by contributions over the preceding weeks, were occasions for general intoxication, as were occasional visits to wakes, fairs and the like. Such drinking was part of community life, of custom, camaraderie and good fellowship, and for a man to cut himself off from it was to assert an independence which labelled him as an odd, and probably uncongenial, workmate.

The return that the skilled worker made for his wage in terms of his labour for so many hours a week is impossible to generalize since it varied so much between individuals and trades. No act of Parliament in the nineteenth century legislated a maximum adult working day, nor was the skilled worker directly affected by the series of factories acts after 1833 which restricted the hours of children and young persons in textile factories and, in effect, those of adult spinners and weavers too. On the other hand, the skilled man earned a wage which, in normal times at least, permitted the enjoyment of some leisure, and he frequently belonged to a trade club or society which placed great importance on the negotiation and maintenance of reasonable working-hours and conditions. In pre-industrial crafts hours, like wages, were determined largely by custom; in the new trades, of which the classic example was engineering, they were initially fixed by reference to similar trades but, subsequently, by bargaining with the employers. Thus, in 1836 the London Engineers engaged in an eight-months' struggle with the employers for shorter hours, which ended in the establishment of a sixty-hour week and the penalizing of overtime by extra rates;[62] this, then, established the Normal Day (i.e. ten hours) which became the model for other crafts to emulate.

The concept of the Normal Day could, of course, apply only to those employed in factories, workshops or other establishments where routine work-patterns were observed, and many skilled workers, as we have seen, lay outside such a system. Where men worked for themselves, or were employed in their own homes on piece-rates, they worked for as long or as little as they chose; or, rather, as their financial state demanded. Similarly, the Normal Day had little or no meaning for the thousands of 'non-Society' men who worked for small slop masters and garret masters for incredibly long hours while work was brisk but for all too short ones when it was slack. Among the more fortunate, perhaps, were the 'slop' cabinet-makers, described by Mayhew:

> The labour of the men . . . is usually seven days a week the year through. That is – seven days, for Sunday work is all but universal – each of 13 hours, or 91 hours in all; while the established hours of labour in the 'honourable trade' are six days of the week, each of 10 hours, or 60 hours in all. Thus, 50 per cent is added to the extent of the production of low-priced cabinet work merely from 'over-hours', but in some cases I heard of 15 hours for seven days in the week, or 105 hours in all.[63]

At the other end of the spectrum were a few groups of very highly skilled craft-workers whose scarcity gave them an indifference to any idea of regular hours, and an independence which they were able to preserve throughout the century in spite of the advance of mechanization. Of such men, the best example is the members of the Amalgamated Society of Boot- and Shoe-Makers, who strictly maintained a Standard List of prices for piece-work, but kept to their privilege of coming in and out of the employer's workshop at any time, and never troubled to settle a Normal Day. Since a small but wealthy market for hand-made boots and shoes continued alongside the mass market for factory-made products, these workers were able to maintain what were, in effect, monopoly earnings, and to exercise complete discretion over their working hours.

Before 1836 the engineers had worked a ten and a half-hour day, together with uncertain overtime, and this seems to have been the norm for the skilled trades under 'honourable' employers. The House of Commons was told in 1825 that ten and a half hours in summer and less (down to eight and a half hours) in winter was the ordinary day's work for 'machine-makers, the moulders of the machinery, house-carpenters, cabinet-makers, stonemasons, bricklayers, blacksmiths, millwrights and many other craftsmen,[64] and this continued in most trades until the mid-century. Thereafter, it seems likely that factory legislation became the pace-maker, for the Ten Hours Act of 1847 brought down the working week for women and the under-eighteens in textile factories to sixty hours and introduced the Saturday half-holiday by ordering the cessation of work at 2 P.M. Through the 1850s and 1860s the protected factory workers stayed ahead of the skilled men, where a sixty-three-hour week was the average for compositors, building craftsmen and iron-workers, but as trade unions grew in strength and the demand for skilled labour increased, more concessions were made by negotiation, strike or the threat to strike. In 1872 the engineers were the first to achieve a nine-hour day after a long dispute had ended in a strike on the north-east coast; the building trades also established a fifty-four-hour average week in the same year. Thereafter, fifty-four hours remained typical of the fourth quarter of the nineteenth century, as sixty-three hours had been of the first and second quarters: it usually meant a nine and a half-hour day for five days a week, and a six and a half-hour Saturday, though there were many local and seasonal variations. The decade of the 1870s had, in fact, witnessed some of the most important gains of the century in working hours, including the Bank Holiday Acts of 1871 and 1875 which established four days in the year (Boxing Day, Easter Monday, Whit Monday and the first Monday in August) as national (though not yet paid) holidays.[65] Over the whole half-century 1836–86 it is likely, then, that average hours had been reduced by a fifth; and at the same time it seems certain that working conditions had generally become safer and less laborious. A series of enactments between

1864 and 1878 defined and enforced minimum standards relating to safety, ventilation and sanitation in the metal trades, blast furnaces, printing, paper-making and other trades which had escaped the earlier factory acts, and although in the mechanized trades the pace of work must have become faster than before, muscular effort was increasingly being replaced by skill, watchfulness and intelligence.

The Nine-Hour Campaign of 1871–2 was followed by a less widespread Eight-Hour Campaign in the late 1880s and early 1890s, in which only the gas-workers were immediately successful in reducing their shifts from twelve to eight hours. Coal-miners secured an eight-hour shift by Act of Parliament in 1908, becoming the first adult workers to win a statutory maximum working day. But skilled workers generally made little more advance in the period before 1914, when high unemployment combined with rising prices to weaken bargaining positions: a 50- to 52-hour working week was the most usual immediately before the war, and represented only marginal gains in the previous twenty years. The next major reduction came during the brief post-war boom of 1919–20, when many trades took advantage of their strong position to negotiate a shortening of the working week by about five hours, i.e. from 50 to 52 down to 44 to 48 hours, spread over five and a half days. Despite the ensuing depression and mass unemployment, the forty-eight-hour week was maintained (except by the coal-miners, whose shifts were increased) throughout the inter-war years.[66] Together with these shortened hours went a rapid extension of paid holidays. In 1925 the Ministry of Labour estimated that only $1\frac{1}{2}$ million workers received paid holidays under the provisions of collective agreements; by April 1937 the figure was about 4 million and by June 1939 about 11 million, the most usual amount being one working week plus recognized public holidays.[67]

No precise balance-sheet of gains and losses can be drawn up. Almost certainly, skilled workers formed a larger proportion of the labour force in the 1920s than they had done in the 1820s: they worked for shorter hours, had longer holidays, earned higher real wages and, by any of the measurable criteria, enjoyed a higher standard of life. On the other hand, fewer of them were now independent craftsmen or the fellow workers of small masters who had a personal and intimate relationship with their men; more and more worked at a specialized task in an increasingly sub-divided process where they might have little contact either with the employer or with the finished product. More of them worked to the rhythm of the indefatigable machine rather than the irregular note of their own tools, and their output, as well as their intensity of labour, was constantly being speeded up by further mechanical improvements. Even in the 1820s James Nasmyth had observed the effect of one of his steam engines on the workers at an Edinburgh foundry:

> The result of my labours was a very efficient steam-engine, which set all the lathes and mechanical tools in brisk activity of movement. It had such an enlivening effect upon the workmen that George Douglass afterwards told me that the busy hum of the wheels, and the active, smooth, rhythmic sound of the merry little engine had, through some sympathetic agency, so quickened the strokes of every hammer, chisel, and file, in his workmen's hands, that it nearly doubled the output of work for the same wages![68]

What these changes meant in terms of satisfaction from work is impossible to tell. Recent sociological studies, for example of the car-workers, would tend to suggest that earnings have become substituted for pride of work, and that satisfaction is increasingly looked for outside the work situation. But it would be quite wrong to suppose that nineteenth-century workers were indifferent to their wages, or that those who worked at sweated, repetitive, yet skilled tasks derived much satisfaction from their labour. Equally would it be wrong to imagine that modern highly sophisticated processes can bring no creative rewards, for the steel-maker, Patrick McGeown, can write as poetically and lovingly of his work in a steel-mill in the 1960s[69] as George Sturt did of his little wheelwright's shop of the 1880s.[70] What the two have in common are skill, judgement, discretion and responsibility; if these are present, the precise nature of the task, the degree of mechanization, the size of the organization and the nature of its ownership would seem to be largely irrelevant.

Charles Newnham
*carpenter and builder**

Charles Newnham was born in Rochester, Kent, in 1799, his father being a Freeman of the town. Educated at the Rochester Mathematical School, he was apprenticed to a local carpenter and went to work in London in 1817; although only eighteen, he was evidently employed as a journeyman carpenter at wages from £1 to 35s. a week. The extract covers the years 1817–20, a period of great building activity in London, when Newnham was employed mainly on the building of the Millbank Penitentiary. In later life he became a master builder in London, where he lived until 1870. He built and named after himself Newnham Terrace (now demolished) which was off Hercules Road, Lambeth, and part of Walcot Square, Kennington; for his own use he designed an Elizabethan-style cottage, which now stands as one of the entrances to Battersea Park.

On the 20th day of November, 1817, I arrived in town with my kit upon my shoulder, and the next morning found myself at work for £1 per week wages, and I was satisfied with it, as I was in good hands. I knew I should soon be worth, and have, more.

We all lived and lodged, together with our master (Mr Goff) and his family, at No. 16 Waterloo Place, St James's, which was then in course of being completed.

At that time Carlton House, the palace of the Prince Regent, stood in a line with the park side of Pall Mall, precisely opposite Waterloo Place, where the opening now is which leads into St James's Park, past his brother's (the Duke of York's) monument.

There was a screen running along Pall Mall in front of Carlton House, between the columns of which were lamps lit with gas. I believe they were the first lamps ever used for that purpose. At that time there were very few streets, if any, lit with gas . . . It is hardly possible for any one to imagine, who never saw, as I have, the difference in the effect produced in the shops and streets of London by using gas, instead of the old 'darkness made visible' oil lamps. We always knew when the 'Royal George' was at home by these lamps. When he was at home every lamp was lit up; when he was not, then only every other one was lit.

The family I was now located with were all of a moral caste, attending

* From *The Memoirs of Charles Newnham*, unpublished autobiography. The extract is printed by kind permission of Newnham's great-grand-daughter, Marjorie Newnham Brain, of Sidcup, Kent.

chapel regularly, no drinking, swearing or quarrelling. I was indeed happy in their company.

I remained at our job until it was finished, and immediately obtained employment in St Martin's Lane, through the recommendation of Mr Lee who kept the 'White Lion' in Market Street, afterwards St Alban's Place.

My new master's name was Hewitt. His business premises stood precisely where the northern fountain of Trafalgar Square now stands . . .

Two or three weeks afterwards, being recommended by Mr Goff to an old acquaintance of his who had just come up from Rochester to take charge of a job for a Mr Samuel Baker of that place, I gladly availed myself of the opportunity of being the first carpenter taken on as a London hand by that eminent builder; who is known as the builder of Lancaster Place, etc. in the Savoy precincts in the Strand, the Horse Barracks, Regents Park; the greater portion of the Penitentiary at Millbank; the difficult as well as dangerous job of underpinning the new Custom House, so as to cut out all the bad work and put in entirely new foundations; the Ophthalmic Infirmary, Moorfields, and the first and largest portion of the new British Museum.

I was now a full journeyman carpenter at 30s. per week besides overtime.

The Goff family having moved to Islington, I gladly availed myself of the opportunity of securing lodgings under the same roof as my foreman. He had a son about a year younger than myself, who had previously been a fellow pupil of mine under 'Old Joey' at Rochester Mathematical School, so that I felt myself quite at home. Never did a stranger behave better to a young and inexperienced hand than his father did to me.

Our lodgings were situated in Angel Court, nearly opposite Somerset House. Our landlord was a book-binder by trade, but did very little of it, his chief dependance being in his lodgers. He was a queer little old-fashioned man about five feet high. One of his legs being shorter than the other caused him to see many ups and downs in the world. He had never been out of London in his life but once, and that was to see a review on Wimbledon Common. The wonderful adventures he met with on that day served him as a topic to converse on for ever after. His good lady was a great stout burly woman about his own age, pretty clean in herself and her household generally; a pretty good cook, and of an exceedingly mild and willing disposition, never seeming to think it a trouble to cook or do anything for us, even if it happened to be out of the common way. So that we were quite at home here, although there were eight men lodgers in the house, six of the number working together with me.

The job I was employed upon being finished, and Mr Baker having no other in London for the time being, I was discharged, but not before even our benches were put on board a barge for the purpose of being taken back to Rochester where they were originally sent from.

The morning after I was discharged, myself and another being on the look-out for employment went into a public house for refreshment, when who should come in but my old master, Mr Mallett, who told me where to go for a job, with permission to use his name.

There was a new chapel building near Sloane Square, to be called the Ranelagh Chapel, and by a strange coincidence, a man I knew called Edmeades, who had been at one time in business for himself in Strood, was now foreman of the joinery work at this chapel. He at once recognized me, and not only set me to work, but my companion also. The job was in a hurry, the contractor's time expiring in three weeks. We made seven and a half days to the week at 5 shillings a day and beer twice a day . . .

Considerable jealousy was evinced by my new mates upon finding that Mr Edmeades had given me the very pick of the work. This determined me the more to do it so well as to prevent any fault being found with it.

I also received a communication from my old friend Mr Goff to bring my tools straight to his job whenever my present one was finished. This happened at the time alluded to, and then I again went to work and lodge with him and my companion Ned. Of course I now had full wages. Making all the extra time I could, I began to feel as if I had at last succeeded in placing myself in a position to live – if no more.

[Later, he is offered work on the Millbank Penitentiary.] Being informed that the job was to last three or four years and that Mr Baker my former foreman was there (he was no relation to Mr Sam Baker) I lost no time in paying him a visit.

I was flattered by his telling me that immediately he had arrived on the job, he had unsuccessfully endeavoured to find me, but he had got some of my old partners at work for him. I was told to bring my tools as soon as convenient . . . I took my tools for the first time inside the Penitentiary gates on the 29th September 1819, I found not more than four or five carpenters previously engaged upon the job, and felt that, barring accidents, I had made a good change . . .

It is always advisable for workmen to live near enough to their work to be able to go home to meals, not only on the score of comfort and economy, but also in order to elude the allurements of the public house. No person could be better aware of, or more ready and willing to carry out this arrangement than myself, but I was so comfortable in my new lodgings at Pimlico, that I could not make up my mind to leave them for some time to come.

My landlord's name was Jennings. He was shopman in a wholesale perfumer's establishment, where he had been from his boyhood. If called upon to give him a character, I should give it in these few words – 'I never knew a better man.' Mrs Jennings had been in service as cook in a gentleman's family. In order to improve their scanty income, she took in a little washing, and she also washed for myself and fellow lodger.

She, like her husband, took a pleasure in doing anything which was likely to please or benefit anyone she knew. I have many times felt sorry to observe that she had gone beyond her means in making a pie or tart, or perhaps a custard, merely for the satisfaction of asking me to have a bit.

I had not been long at the Penitentiary, when I was sent to make some extensive alterations and additions to Sir Robert Smirke's residence in Stratford Place, Oxford Street.

He had just taken to himself a wife, and was, of course, anxious to make the house as comfortable as possible before he introduced the new-made wife to her new abode.

Among other improvements, Sir Robert had a new office built at the back part of his premises, which abut upon Marylebone Lane. In order to get his clerks into it as soon as possible, he furnished me with three braziers and plenty of charcoal, with directions to keep up good fires all day long.

Now, as he intended eventually to warm this office by means of hot air pipes, it was built without a chimney in it.

The fumes of the charcoal making me feel very ill, I naturally put down one of the sashes in order to purify the air. Sir Robert, observing, directed me to close it.

I explained to him how the charcoal affected me, but I might as well have spoken to a statue. His answer was, 'I might as well have no charcoal fires at all, if you allow the heat to escape out of the window; besides, as it is frosty, I shall have the new plastering spoilt.' And out he went, without another word, seemingly indifferent as to what became of me, so long as his plastering went undamaged.

However, when my foreman paid me his next visit, I stated the case to him, and declared my inability to remain under the circumstances.

This alarmed him. For, as he said, Mr Smirke was such a curious man, he was fearful of being blamed if I left the work. As there was not much more to do, he so begged me to remain that I foolishly consented. It would have been better for me had I used a little of my usual firmness, and had thought a little less of his kindness towards me.

I remained a few days longer, every day getting worse, until one day I found myself coming over faint and giddy.

I went towards the outside door with the intention of opening it, but before I could do so, I fell to the ground.

I afterwards had a vague idea I turned myself so as to place my mouth towards the bottom of the door, but whether it was by accident or not, it was certainly this that saved my life.

I cannot tell how long I remained in this state, but I at length came to myself, cold and almost inanimate.

I got the door open and walked out of the cursed charnel-house (for I had very nearly made it such). Staggering along and occasionally supporting myself against walls or doors, after more than two hours of such suffering and labour as I never wish to encounter again, I tottered into my lodgings.

The good Mrs Jennings, alarmed at my appearance, was going for a doctor, when I stopped her and showed her that my flesh was all like putty. Whenever I pressed it the impression remained, showing clearly that my blood had stagnated in my veins.

She had one of those old-fashioned brass warming-pans, which I directed her to use in warming my bed, and also requesting her to make me some hot caudle; the house was for a short time in confusion, until, with assistance, I was in a hot bed, and well covered up with blankets.

With difficulty, I swallowed my caudle, and the doctor was now fetched. On his arrival, he found me in torture; being prickled with a thousand pins would have been a pleasant sensation compared with the pricking and shooting occasioned by the blood re-circulating. I was in such a profuse perspiration, I believe it might have been wrung out of the bedclothes.

The doctor said I had no doubt saved my own life by the means I had used. He sent me a little medicine and left time to give me strength.

At the end of a fortnight, I went to the foreman, fully expecting by that time my work had been finished by his sending someone else to do it. Not so, however, for, upon his making known my illness to the kind and considerate Sir Robert, and stating his intention to send another man in my stead, he was surprised to hear Sir Robert say 'he very much disliked strange men about the place' and would rather wait until I was well enough to finish the job.

I had no alternative but to leave Mr Baker's employ altogether, or go back to my hated job. I preferred the latter.

I had not been at work long, before Sir Robert came to me and seeing I looked like a ghost, he desired me to put down one of the sashes. I thanked him, and said as he refused to allow it to be done before, I abstained from doing it again for fear of giving him offence. I concluded with saying that I had had a fortnight's dangerous illness through working in the fumes of charcoal, and was but ill able to work then.

I cannot say whether there was, or was not, anything spiteful in my manner of uttering my words, but it is quite likely there was.

At any rate, as soon as the foreman came, he was ordered to go to Sir Robert. When he left him and came to me, he intimated that I had been insolent to Sir Robert.

I explained, and offered to go with him to my accuser and substantiate my innocence. This he clearly proved to me was the one way to make matters worse. He had already told Sir Robert that he attributed the offence to my blunt and sometimes uncouth way of speaking, not to any intention or idea of giving offence.

He offered to send someone in my place, but this was objected to. Sir Robert did me the justice to say no man could suit him better. If the foreman was satisfied that what I had said was not, as he had taken it to be, a studied insult, he would rather I should remain.

I did remain to finish my job, but I have never since that time recovered the same robust health that I possessed previously. I have always considered it would have been much more to the great man's credit to have made me a present of a pound note towards paying my doctor's bill, instead of accusing me, at the risk of throwing me out of employment, of being insolent . . .

During my residence here, my dear mother paid me a welcome visit. As I knew precisely when to expect her, I had got my landlady to make me a Kentish beef pie, according to my directions. Meeting my mother as arranged, as I came out of the Penitentiary gates at 12 o'clock, I took her home, delighted with the idea of having for dinner what I knew she preferred to anything else that could be offered to her. But, lo and behold, when we began to eat of it, it was as sour as verjuice; the confounded baker had placed a gooseberry pie over it, in such a position that I had got the juice of one, with the gravy of the other!

My mother intended stopping with me three or four days. As she dearly loved a good play, I took her to Astley's Theatre on the second evening . . .

To the intense delight of my mother, the play was *John Bull, or An Englishman's Fireside*. It was for the benefit of the celebrated Irish John-stone, who that night took his farewell of the stage. Of course, he played Dennis Brulguddery, Macready played Peregrine, and Liston and Emery also took part in the performance. The afterpiece was *Clare, or the Maid of Milan* in which the plaintive air of 'Home Sweet Home' was sung by the fascinating Ellen Tree.

My mother began to get uneasy, and wanted to go home on the morrow. I, with difficulty, conquered her inclination, and on the following evening took her to Drury Lane for the express purpose of putting home out of her head by enjoying the tricks and scenery of the splendid pantomime *Jack and the Beanstalk*, Jack being played by no less a person than the pretty Miss Poole.

It happened that, during the progress of the pantomime, the Clown and Pantaloon, after making a balloon, seated themselves in the car. Then a moving panoramic exhibition took place, very accurately showing the whole of the way from London to Paris. As the balloon was supposed to pass over the three towns, the home of my mother was most clearly depicted.

This settled her going there next day. I could keep her no longer. She and I have many times since laughed about this . . .

At an adjacent building, I had several times observed a plasterers' labourer at mealtimes, lower himself down by the single rope, which, passing through a block on the top scaffold, was used for hoisting up cement, sand, etc. instead of taking half a minute longer to come down the ladder.

Seeing him at his old trick one morning, I observed, 'You will one of these days take hold of the wrong part of the rope and come down by the run.'

'Oh, no I won't,' said he, 'I am not such a fool as that.'

Unfortunately for him, he was such a fool, for the very next time he attempted it, he did just what I had cautioned him about. He fell so close to me, that I narrowly escaped injury. The poor fellow, falling on to the pike heads of the iron railings, was impaled, the fence bar going through his side, completely into his body. We had great difficulty in extricating him. When his mates carried him to the nearest doctor, he pronounced him as quite dead.

He was a single man, and they carried him to his lodgings. An hour or two afterwards, two men went. Claiming to be the relations, they were allowed to take him away.

By and by, the real relations came. Finding the body had been surreptitiously removed, they proceeded to the Bow Street Police Office. Obtaining the assistance of a 'runner', they went in pursuit of the 'body-snatchers' as they were called. They escaped, but the body was found at the dissecting room of the celebrated Dr Brooks, near Blenheim Steps, Oxford Street. The body was reconveyed to the place where it was stolen from, to await the coroner's verdict, the relatives locking the door, and taking away the key, to make sure of the body being safe . . .

On the 12th day of October, 1820, I came of age, and had to go down to Chatham to receive my fortune, left me by my good Aunt Plaw.

I received my £30, one of the silver tankards always used in our dear old parlour, and on which my considerate aunt had had my name engraved, in conjunction with the original initials R.E.P. I also received from my uncle, the other executor, the old watch and appendage formerly belonging to my aunt, and which had been placed in his hands for safe keeping until I attained my majority.

Having made my mother a present, I returned to London, richer by far than I had ever been before.

Having only three or four years before been nearly able to wear at once all the clothes I had belonging to me, I had since gone to the other extreme. I now laid out a large portion of my £30 in clothes and tools, depositing the remaining £11 10s. in the Chelsea Savings Bank. . . .

Emanuel Lovekin

mining 'butty'[*]

Emanuel Lovekin was born in Tunstall, Staffordshire, in 1820, one of nine children of a skilled furnaceman who spent most of his earnings on drink. He became a 'trapper' in the pits at seven and a half years old, and was self-educated in his teens while recovering from a mining accident. Before marriage he became a tramping navvy, tunnelling for the new railways, and was an active Chartist acting as secretary of the local branch and standing trial in 1842. After marriage he became a 'butty' (contractor) colliery manager, or small master, starting many new pits in South Staffordshire; he

[*] From an unpublished autobiography, kindly brought to my notice by Lovekin's great-great-grandson Brian Daubney.

obtained the colliery manager's certificate of technical proficiency after the Coal Mines Act of 1872. Surviving several serious accidents and economic blizzards, Lovekin lived in moderate comfort, had fourteen children and visited some of them twice in America. He worked until 1899 and died in 1905. Throughout adult life he was a fervent Primitive Methodist, working as a Sunday School teacher and Superintendent.

At the age of seventy-five he started to write some memories of his life, altogether about 7,000 words of which this extract is approximately half; it is unedited, in his own spelling. It is the 'classic' story of self-education, hard work and religious faith rewarded by modest prosperity and peace of mind; the historian wishes that he had given more details of his Chartist experiences and financial transactions.

The original spelling and grammar have been retained.

> *Time as it is cannot stay,*
> *Nor as it was cannot be.*
> *Dissolving and passing away,*
> *Are the World, the ages and me.*

These are some notes of my life Emanuel Lovekin, Writtin by him, When he was nere seventy-five years old.

He says. I was born when Schooling was not thought very much of amoung the poorer people, and there was but very few Schools. I never knew but one with a man teacher. There was a few old Womens Schools; I was the forth Son. And there was no daughter when I was born. My Father was a furnace man, got very good wage. But spent a great part of it in drink, although Mother use to brew half a Measurer of Malt per fortnight for him which was alowed by his Master. My Mother was a big strong Woman, and not cast down with a little thing, but strugled through with a family of seven Sons and tow daughters, with a man that did not seem to take very little interest in home Matters, We were all under the controle of the Mother who held a Masterly hand. I was born in a house near the old yard at the back of the Bailiffs row, Danington Wood, on March 3rd 1820. But we removed from this house to one in the Dannington Barrick, where my Father died when I was about thirty years old. But Mother died at Tipton in South Staffordshire where my Brother Jonah was then living Somewhere about ten years after Fathers death, When quite young, I was Sent to an Old Lady's School, Whose name I know they called Tilly Wilson. I must be very young for I cannot remember any thing I learnt but a Song. She was a Primitive Methodist and She used to place us on a bench or form, and sing 'O ye young ye gie ye proud, you most die and ware a Sroud,' And that's about all I learnt, I was Small for

my age. Still at about Seven and a half years old, I was Sent to work in a
coal pit, it was little I could be exspected to doo except open a door for
waggons to pass through. After a time I was Promoted to drive a Donkey.
And a younger Brother of mine name Samuel, came to the door keeping
he was only seven and a half years old, So from one thing to another, I
got on to a young man. But when I was about 13teen, I had my thigh
broken and had to lei in bed thirteen weeks. And began to feel very
Strongley the desieries to learn to read. The young men I know came and
read to me and I begain to learn a little, and when I was able I went to a
nights School. And the little I learnt made me feel I was getting on very
nicely. But the School Master was a very good violin player. And I most
begain to learn *one* Which I Scratched on for many years, But never could
make much of it. I went to the Wrockmerdine Wood Primitive Methodist
Sunday School a good while learned a little knowlidge and truth, For
which I had great cause to thank God, Still by perseverence I got to read
fairly well and write a little and Somehow I was looked up to as Something
alien to the Common Class of young men. At this time things were very
bad, Little work and very little for it and the Condition of working people
espeically, from 1839 to 1842, was very discouraging, There was Sharp
and Strong Agitation going on with the Corn Law league and a Sect
called the Chartists, I was very favourable to the latter, And was Selected
Secy to a local Club, And got mixted up with Some of its great men.
Mersar Mason of Birmingham, and Hogg, Arthur O Nail, Thos
Alford, Thos Cooper, and Others and I even thought myself Somebody,
I felt very earnest in the work I had to do, Which was not very Small,
Meeting almost every night. And now and then very large gatherings,
We had one on the Wrekin. When over 30,000 were there, But in
1842 the riots begain in Several Counties, one very large one in North
Staffordshire, or the Potteries, And there was one with us in Shropshire,
not a very searious matter, Still it resulted in getting a few imprisoned.
And breaking up the Matter, I had a near chance of being imprision I
was tried and Set at Laberity, I formed an acquaintance with a man that
came from the Potteries and it was thought, he brought news of the doings
there, his name was John Nickholes, I very probaley learnt a lesson for
my after life, For I was more carefull in what Society I mixt up in, I was
twenty-two to twenty-three years old and was considered a moderate
workman in the pit But I could not bear the thought of working for about
2s. 6d. per day in a pit, Being a bit given to roaming about, I Set off with
a man much older than myself. We got Some very good jobs and got
plenity of money. But could not keep it as we did not stop long in one
place or at one job. Railway tunneling was very rife, at this time, But my
mate and I, had the getting of the quirry Stone for putting in the Locks
in the Severn reiver between Stourport and Woscester. We saved a bit
of money then wandered off again. Somewhere, But at last dropped in
Tunstall March 1843. I now begain to do as other young folks do which
ended in Marring Edna Eldest daughter of John and Martha Simcock,
Which I never repented the act, But we lived Happy together till death

parted us in 1881, After beening Married thirty-six years having fourteen children eight Boys and six girls, And there is now liveing six men and four Women, all Married and Some with familis of their own. Before I was married I went to the Tunstall Primitive Methodist Sunday School my wife went there to, And from then untill now I have been connected with School or Church or both, I am now Over seventy-four years old, I was about twenty-three or between twenty-three and twenty-four, When I began to go to the Tunstall Sunday School, But I belonged to the Primitive Sunday School in Shropshire when a youth, I was always very much enclined to them, and never went as far or as low in Sin and folly as Some do although I was bad enough, It took all I could get to keep myself before I was Married. But afterwards I had to keep many more, For we soon had children till there were 14teen of them. So I had always plenity of ways to spend what I got, Still, I was better off often than before I was Married, So with me at least Marriage was not a failure I Should Say. We lived in Williamson St Tunstall for many years after we were Married, And I worked for Mr H. H. Williamson, under the Management of Mr John Butterfield till we had five children, John, James, Mary, Martha, and Sarah Ann. Then I went to work for Merrs E. Challmor and F. Bomers at Turnhurst. Then we left Williamson Street and went to live at Pitts Hill not very far from Tunstall, Sarah Ann was very young when we removed there, Then I joined the Pittshill friends went to the Sunday School had a very good class of young men part of the time, Which I tried to teach the right way all I could, and have heard some of them speak well of me Since for which I felt well paid, I also had a young Women's Class although I never had the pleasure of hereing their praise I did what I could to teach them the truth and the way. It was a pleasure to me to be at School and I always tried to be there in time, Some time after I removed to Chell and was there till I came back to Tunstall again. Our William was born at Chell, We lived next door to Mr Henry Johnson, I had a moderate place at Turnhurst Colliery for some time, But the Manager Mr James Lindop left he went to South Staffordshire, Mr F. Bomers offered me the place after, But would not give me money enough, so I would not have it. Then there came one named John Skidmore and he know that the place had been offered to me so he wanted me out of his way, and he Set to injure me all he could. And at last Succeed in putting up a Gallows for me, But was hanged on it himself, They dismissed me, and I could not get my money from them to pay the men, and I had to put them in the county court for it, Which put them about very much. I gained my case. Then they put me in court and said I owed them Something. But they could not prove it, I afterward put them in the court of Exchequer in defence and got judgment therefor over £100 under the truck Act, And afterward they confessed themselves well beaten, I forgave them all but the expenses which would be very great. I was now out of place and my old Master Sent for me, and I went back to Scotia Colliery joined my wife's Father as a Butty, So I had to flit beck to Williamson Street Tunstall, and myself to the

Primitive friends at Tunstall again, There in school and Church, I joined
Mr Henry Binnell's Class that would be about 1856. After a time I left
Scotia Colliery and went to Mr Thomas Pearce's Colliery joined the
Hughes Brother's and was there some years. About this time I became
mixed up with the Odd fellowes M.C.U. joining through the General
Offices of the Tunstall St Martin's Lodge which I joined, and in the
Potteries and Newcastle District, and I am sorry to say it weakened my
connection at School and Church for a time. Still I lingered on but not
pressed forward, While I was at Mr Peake's colliery. I removed from
Williamson Street to Mount Street and was there till I went to South
Staffordshire. We had four children born in this Street, George, Thomas,
Sina, and Emanuel, and we buried two, Martha and George, While
there. Just now a change came again. They Hughe's and myself took a
little place from Mr James Lindop, Being over perswered by him and
Started a little colliery at the New invention's near Willinhall South
Staffordshire. It went on recovering the coal till nearly all the money was
gone. Mr Edward Hughes was managering it or rether mismanaging. So
there was a breaking up of us. I got two parties to Buy them out and I
went and managed it under the title of Lovekin, Tolley, and Hartshorn,
New envention colliery; While I had been at Mr Peake's I had made
many friend, and especially young Mr John Nash Peake. I had done
some good jobs for thim and risked my life very near at times, one time
I droped in eighteen yard of water, twisted through a place about five in.
in widh came up unconscious where I was, and was hurt very badly, Mr
J. N. Peake was very good to me. Nathail Turner was the Manager for
Mr Peake's colliery, But I had to leave aganst their wish to go to Manage
in the South, I had got to remove my family once again, We removed to
a large house on the Wolverhampton road from Bloxwich. Times were
very bad, and the coal we got had to be Sold very cheap. We Sold thousands of tons for 5s. 9d. per ton and it made it a Struling time for us,
Afterwards we Spent nearly all we had to try to recover another coal, But
when we got to it or the place the coal was gone Burnt up as hard as a
brick, and good for nothing, So we got the Land Lord to take over the
lease, and all there was on the place to release us, and came out as well as
we could. I lost about £500, While up there I joined the Primitives
methodist at Lane Head in the Darleston circuit, and I went to live at
Lane Head did all I could to help on the cause there, both Sunday
School and Church. I was Superintendent of the Sunday School Some
time leader of a class, and went nearly to every Quarter day . . .

We had three children Born while here, Edna, Richard, and Mary
Jane, But no I was in a fix, I had lost my money got a large family, and
no place, What to doo I did not Know, and it nearly got too much for me
to bear. I remember beening in a field, and scarce knew where I was and
what I was doing. I prayed to God, to open my way, And I had such a
manifestation of God's Mercies and goodness, That I felt certain that I
should see them all reared, and see them do for themselves a clear light,
And God as blessed me this far, For the youngest child is going in her

twenty-seventh year now; Married and one child doing Moderately well. As I write this; They are all married and gone. John, and James, with four children are in Philadelphia America, Sarah Ann, at Madeley, with eight children four Boy and four girls. But the eldest girl as gone to America and is married there. William is in Hanley somewhere, I dont know what to say about him, he is the black sheep, his wife is dead and has been some years, Two of his children my daughter Sina has. And he has has two with him, poor Lads, But he cannot look after himself or them. As we have had to cloth the elderest Boy for some time while he spends his money in drink, and other bad ways, I dont know, when he will, turn. Thomas lives at Derby, he has wife and three children and as buried one, Wife him and family are doing fairly well, Sina lives at Birmingham, and has only William two children a Boy and girl, Edna is liveing at Stafford. She as had two children, But as buried one, Emanuel, is liveing at Wigan he as one child a Boy. Richard is liveing at Shelton Harley he has three fine Boys, Mary Jane, as been liveing in London some time, But his now liveing in Tunstall She has a fine Boy; This is where they all are at the time I am writing. Begaining of 1895. But every year make a chang, and especially in some families, But I hope they all will do well, and live happy togather, and honner God, I had made a few friend while in the South. But I was very much enclined to come back to Tunstall again, So I came down; and Saw some I know here, and got a job soon; I joined Orlands Bawson, and we soon had some sinking to do, We sank the two ten ft coal pits at the Whitfield Colliery Compy, Mr Andrews, was the head manager, and Mr Joseph Mack under manager, We sank them althrough the ten ft rock, put a large lift in one pit to pump the water, Which has done for them every Since. That compy give it up, and Chatterley Colliery Compy took it off Mr Charles Homer, and it as done well for them, keep them on their feet, with the other colliery, Well now I most remove my family again, So I brought them down to Tunstall, in a house in Wedgwood Street, and I was soon with my Primitives friends again. The Rev John Gust the Superintendent, lived next door to me or me to him, I knew him and his wife very well, I did very well here, We had a Son Born here, Joseph, This is the last child we have had, and we think it is time for it, Rowson and I did a good bit of work together, But he kept a public house at Coleridge, he was to give it up, if I was to remain with him, But he would not leave it, and I left him, and got where I could. I met with Charles Shaw, and he and I took some pits at Newfields, under Merssr Challinor, and C. Leigh. Mr Kelker, was the head manager, and Mr D. Hancock under Manager. We were there soom time, and did Moderately well but could not see very far in the future, and especially for good, So we took a pair of pits to sink at the Racecourse Silverdale under Mr Benm Vickers and Co., So I went there and commenced the pits and left Chars Shaw at Newfields to finished there. We commenced the racecourse pit some time about 1870. There were three pits, I took George Clarke with me there and Charl Shaw, at Newfields So I was doing very well, I dont know how long I was there, I lodged with Mr

Clarke, during the week, and came home at the weekend. The pits were down about fifty yards each. We had a good deal of water, and look very likely to have a good deal more, I was coming home one weekend, and Met Mr John Nash Peake, and he asked me if I would come and work for him. He said he wanted a pit sinking, So I promised him to come and I did so. As soon as I could make arrangements at Silverdale, I got Mr Charl Shaw, to go to Silverdale, and I promised to get him with me as soon as I could at Mr Peake's, But I found very soon Mr Peake would not alow him to come, and Mr Tomkinson, was against him very much, and he put Elisha Webb, and Thomas Brunt with me, and it was in that way good time When every thing was above its value even labour. We got a lot of money for some time, Then Thomas Brown joined the Butties at the stone pits, when James Cooke left, and E Webb and I did as well as we could, Poor Brunt was killed in the Redshags, He was not long with them, two years or so. Mr Tomkinson never cared much for me beening there as Mr Peake me and he was the manager, Still I did very fairly well, for some good time, But he was a *Judas* to me, and when a convenent time came he tried to get out of me, I left for a few weeks, But Mr Peake, found it out, and would have me back again, after this I was put where I did very well, But about this time Mr J. W. Peake took a place at Silverdale, called the Rosemary Hill Colliery. There were a pair of pits to be sunk. I thought I should have to go, But the old *Fox* Put me in a very good place And said to me you would not care to go to Silverdale and leave your home if I could do well here, So I said I would reather stay at Tunstall if I could do very fairly well. Never thinking he had an axe to grind, as Franklin says. He had got James Cook ready to drop in the New place and that was filled up. He thought the time would come when I should be out altogather, But about this time there was an act in the House of Commons passed, That every colliery Manager Must hold a sertificate, given by Goverment. Mr Tomkinson trid to get one and could not, He trid twice at Newcastle Examining Committee and failed each time, In the meantime, I got a cetificate, So I was put on as the Manager; Both at the Tillieres colliery and Rosemary Hill, Silverdale, and Mr J. W. Peake found me a Pony and trap to go over with, Still he was So fixed by the family that he could not be removed very well, and I think Mr J. W. Peake could not well get out of him, as long as he chose to stop. So he had to be a kind of agent, went out to sell the mine a good deal, He now expressed himself to be very friendly with me and must be with him, or go everywhere with him, but I never feel very comfortable for I knew he was a very deceitful man, As I found out some years later. I did well for many years. But there came a time, when the colliery could not be made to pay very well, and was stoped for some time they lowered my salery and his 20s. per week. Then they wanted to take 20s. more off me. Just at this time he was put forward very much by the family, and he showed it very much with me, But I would not have it from him, and had to tell him what he was, In June 1886 I left and was out a good long time. I did not look after anything to doo, and in 1887 on the 20th April, I started to

America to see my two sons John and James wifes and familys. I got there
on May 3rd after being on the Water thirteen days. All this time I never
lost my conference in Him, that orders all thing well, Although I had
been doing very well as regurds this life I had many changes – Some time
dark and some time sunshine, But I trusted when I could not see very
clear nor very far before me . . .

After I came back from America, which was in September 1887, As I
landed at Liverpool on the 20th September, I was met there by Mrs
Lovekin and our Tom and his wife, as they lived at Rainhill near Liverpool. So we went there and stayed a day or two. Soon after I got home
Messrs R. Goodwin and J. Scragg, sent for me, they had started a little
colliery at Holly Wall, and they asked me to go and Manager it for them,
I went and was with them, till Mr J. Scragg died and the firm broke up.
In December 1891. Some time before this happened twelve month or
more, Messrs H. H. Williamson and Devenport of the Goldenndale Iron
works were starteing their colliery in the lowelands called the yeld hill
colliery. Engaged with me to Manager it for them and have continued
with them up to now 1895, and I hope to do so till I have done my work,
as I am now near or going in my seventy-six years old an age every one
does not reach too, But God has blessed me wonderfully. *Thank him* . . .

October 1902

We have a lot of rainy Weather and I dare not go out. I feel fairly well,
but very feeliby at times, we both are getting old Mrs is nearly seventy-
three, and me eighty-three. So we are fairly good for our time, and very
thankfull to God for his care to us all through the days that are past and
we will trust him for the further, we are in good hands. I dont get out to
the night meeting now and so done know very much as to how things are
going on. I am glad I did a bit when I was younger, for I have been connected with the Primitive Methodist for a good many years and have been
in church and schools for a good while, I first went in the Sunday School
about 1844, and was a member in Mr Henry Binnall class many years. I
went through most of the offices of the Sunday School, and was Supper-
entent two or three years, and was assistent to Mr H. Binnalls and the
Societeys Steward for twenty-five years, and when I retired the presented
me with an address. Which I have hung up for a family relict. But O
how little I have done for all the goodness God as done for me. I will
every give thanks and be glad and rejoyce in him who as been so good to
me all my days may I be worthey to ragin in the better world . . .

1904

I am now very feble. But still moderate taking all things togather. But I
am glad I did a bit when younger. I am now eighty-five years old. Bless
God for what I am. I will bless him and prease him for all his care to me.

An old potter*

The anonymous author was born in Tunstall, in the Potteries, in
1832, the son of a skilled painter and gilder in the pottery trade who
lost his well-paid job through victimization after a strike. The
author attended 'Old Betty's' dame school to the age of seven, when
he started work as a 'mould-runner' in a pottery works. In 1842, at
the age of ten, the family was unemployed and forced to enter the
workhouse: subsequently, he obtained work with a 'toy-maker' in
Burslem, making pottery figures of Napoleon, cats, dogs and so on.
He was a witness of the violent Chartist riots at Burslem and Tunstall. His later education was derived from the Methodist Sunday
School, from night classes with an old cobbler, and from the Young
Men's Mutual Improvement Society which he helped to found.
Politically conscious and deeply religious, he became a lay preacher
for the Primitive Methodists in 1854; his autobiography says
nothing about his later life and work, though he lived into the early
twentieth century.

The extracts describe his work as a boy potter between 1839 and
1842. Though not himself apprenticed, he was working in a skilled
trade, completely unrevolutionized by machinery; this, and the
strong influence of Methodism in the area, he blames for the lack of
effective labour organizations among the workers.

I began to work, but I could never see in what way my poor little bit of an
education could prepare me for such as came to my hand.

This began when I was a little over seven years of age, and it was in this
wise . . .

As no Factory Act applied in the district where I began to work, the
work of the children could be used as harsh necessity or harsher greed
determined.

We had an old neighbour, a kindly-disposed old woman, full of sym-
pathy for her poorer neighbours, suffering herself, perhaps, a little less
than those about her, and so willing to do what she could to help them.
She had a son, Jack, who was an apprentice in a 'pot-works' as a 'muffin-
maker'. His mother, knowing the poverty of my parents, suggested I
should become Jack's 'mould-runner'. It is necessary to explain that a
muffin-maker was one who made small plates less than seven inches in

* From *When I was a Child*, by an old potter, introduction by Robert Spence
Watson, Methuen, 1903.
10*

diameter. Such a workman needed a mould-runner. These moulds were a cast of plaster on which the clay was laid in something like the shape of a pancake. The clay was pressed by the wet right hand of the maker upon the plaster mould which was being spun round upon a whirling disc by his left hand. The plate-maker then got a wet tool which he pressed upon the clay, and by this gave the outer surface the required shape. By this tool, the foot-ring of the plate was formed on which it stands when used. When the plate had gone through these processes, the plaster cast on which it had been made had to be quickly carried away by the boy-help into a hot stove close by. Hence the term mould-runner. This stove was a room four to five yards square, shelved all round at regular intervals, on which the plaster moulds were placed by the boy so that the soft clay plate just made could be dried to a certain extent. In the middle of this so-called stove-room was placed an iron stove full of fire, with a sheet-iron pipe carried into the chimney. It was no unusual thing for this stove and the chimney pipe to be red with the intense heat of the fire. Frequently there was no light in this stove-room but such as came from the glare of the fire. It was the mould-runner's business to place the plaster moulds on the shelves on their edge, slightly leaning against the wall, so as to get full surface heat, and to avoid damage to the soft plate on the moulds.

To enable the boy to reach the higher shelves in this stove-room, a small pair of wooden steps was used. Up these he had to run for all the higher shelves, say one fifth of the whole number. He had to run to his 'master' with an empty mould, and return with a full one to the stove-room. This was properly called mould-running, for nothing less than running would do. A boy would be kept going for twenty minutes or half-an-hour at a time, the perspiration coursing down his face and back, making channels on both, as if some curious system of irrigation were going on upon the surface of this small piece of humanity. The latest developments of irrigation in Egypt would not surpass that of the 'sweat of the brow' and face and back of this boy. When so many dozens of the soft plates had been made, and had attained a certain dryness, the moulds were carried to the master to be tooled or 'backed' on his whirligig, so as to smooth the outer surface of the plate. They were taken back one by one into the stove-room to be still further dried, so as to shell off from the plaster mould, and then the 'green' plates were gathered in 'bungs', about two dozen in each bung, ready for 'fetling'. This fetling was the last process of the day's work, and a comparatively easy time for both master and boy, and very welcome, as both were exhausted by the long hard labour of the day. I should say there were regular intervals of change in the work when a 'set' of plates had been made, and this interval was filled up by the plate-maker and the boy 'wedging clay' or making 'battings'. This wedging clay was nominally the work of the boy, sometimes assisted by the plate-maker, and the latter made the battings, that is, from balls of wedged or refined clay he made the pancake-like shapes of clay which he had to use in making the next set of plates. Wedging clay, for a boy, was as common as it was cruel. What is now done by hydraulic pressure was then done by the bone and muscle of, perhaps, a half-fed boy. He had to take a lump of raw clay upon a plaster block, cut it in two with a piece of wire, lift one half above his head, and then bring it down upon the lower half, to mix them, with whatever force he could command. This had to be repeated till the clay was brought to the consistency of something like putty. Doing such work as this was 'rest' from the mould-running. Imagine a mere boy, running in and out of this stove-room, winter and summer, with its blazing iron stove, his speed determined by his master's speed at his work. Coarse oaths, and threats, and brutal blows in many cases followed any failure to be at the bench at the required moment. Thank God there is no mould-running or wedging now. Mechanical contrivances have done away with these cruel forms of child-labour. But such was the condition of life of thousands of youths 'when I was a child' and the great humane Parliament of England, composed of lords and gentlemen of kind and beneficent hearts, never once thought of the little Pottery slaves. Something was done for the children of Lancashire and Yorkshire, but for those of the Potteries, either in pot-works or brick-yards, nothing was done till many years after the time of which I write . . .

My wage was to be a shilling per week. For this large sum I had to work from between five and six o'clock in the morning, and work on till six, seven, or eight o'clock at night, just as Jack pleased. The earlier hour only applied to Monday night, as the potters had a devout regard for Saint Monday. This saint was the most beneficent patron the poor Pottery children then knew. On the other nights of the week work was rarely ever given up till eight o'clock, and it was followed until between five and six o'clock on Saturday. There was another part of a mould-runner's business, not the pleasantest, which should be mentioned. The poor lad had to get a fire lighted in the iron stove before-mentioned, so that work could be begun by six o'clock in the morning. Woe to the poor wretch who had not got his stove well heated by that time. If this were not so, words and blows fell thick and fast, and rarely did any employer ever trouble himself about this matter. The said employer thought it no part of his business to provide fire for the kindling of the stove fires. Boys had to go prowling about the 'bank', as the 'pot-works' was called, and pick up what they could of fire or wood. There were the ovens in which the pots were baked, one or more always firing night and day to bake the ware which they held. There were the 'biscuit' ovens, in which the ware was first fired, and then there were the 'glost' ovens, in which the glaze or enamel had to be burnt upon the pots. These ovens, with their fiery mouths, at regular intervals of space, were surrounded by 'hovels', broad at the base and tapering upwards in conical shape, so as to form a sort of chimney for the smoke from the ovens. Boys and girls stealthily peeped through the doors of these hovels, and if the 'fireman' was 'getting a nap', or absent for a short time, a dash was made with a shovel at an oven mouth. But if the fireman caught such an unlucky wight, the fire would be quickly spilled, and he would be helped further than he had bargained for by an ugly kick. The fireman got exasperated by such an intruder, because he was afraid any disturbance of his fire might endanger the proper firing of his ware, and this was a very responsible matter. His responsibility often made him brutal. There were, of course, instances of rare fun, where a boy's tact and audacity would beat the fireman's utmost vigilance. This fire-hunting went on in all seasons of the year, in sunshine and in pelting storms of rain and snow. Shivering or sweating this hazardous business had to be done, and was done, with mocking laughter in success, or with howling torture in defeat. Every morning brought its peril for the poor mould-runner. I have seen sights of sickening brutality inflicted upon mere children, and yet such was the social callousness of the time that neither masters nor men thought of measures to do away with these cruelties. I remember after I had been working for Jack, my master, for some weeks, he proposed one day that I should have a day's 'play'. This was the word used for a holiday. His reason for doing this was that he would save my day's wage of twopence. Poor Jack was no economist, or else he would have seen that if the thing answered for one day, it might just as well answer for every day. He looked simply at the twopence gained, and not at the pence lost by doing less work. So I was sent off to play. I was nothing loth, and leaped at the idea of a day's play. It was in the spring of the year, I remember, and in the free sunshine and with roaming friends I was happy. When Saturday night came I went, as usual, to Jack's home for my wages, for his mother always paid me out of what Jack brought home. He told his mother a very plausible story about my day's 'play', in his simplicity making it out, truly enough, that it was no fault of mine. Upon hearing this the kind-hearted old woman placed a shilling in my hand, saying: 'Here, lad, take the shilling; it was no fault of thine thou played.' Poor Jack! I shall never forget his face at that moment. More than sixty years have gone since then, but I shall never forget his confusion of face. What was worse for Jack was, that in my simplicity I told in the workshop that Jack's mother had paid me for my day's play. This brought upon him the laughter and banter of his shopmates. Jack took it all very quietly, and, to his credit be it said, he never blamed me for this, but I never got another day's play on such welcome terms . . . After working as a mould-runner for twelve months, and when eight years of age, I was sent to work at another pot-works as a handle-maker. This occupation was much lighter every way but in the matter of long hours. I had mainly to make tea-cup handles and porter-mug handles. These were made by two half moulds made to fit into one another by notches on one side and holes on the other. The piece of clay to form the handle was placed in the bottom half of the mould, then the top half was put on and pressed down by the boy's stomach, with a sort of wriggle. The clay for making handles, after being 'wedged', was put in an iron box, round in shape. At the bottom of the box was a metal die through which the soft clay was forced by a large iron plate at the top of the box, and which was worked down to the bottom by a screw, with a long handle to work it down. The clay came out like a tape worm, through the die, varying in thickness according to the size of the die, as required by the different sizes of handles to be made. The 'bank' I now began to work at was to open to me a new world, strange and sad and terrible in its revelations. So striking were those revelations that after sixty years I could go over the old ground and point out the places where the incidents occurred I am now going to relate . . .

I very soon found out that though I was required to be at the bank six days a week, that on Monday morning I was not required to be there before breakfast time. I found, too, that the place in which I worked bore a holiday aspect on Monday and Tuesday. This was the more noticeable from the size of the place I worked in. It was a long, narrow cellar, the basement of a five-storey building with a handsome frontage. At the lower end of the basement storey was the throwing-room, in which two throwers worked, and at the back of this was the stove, in which the ware was dried. No daylight ever directly penetrated this place, being built below the surrounding earth, and only lit by the stove fire.

On the line of the throwers' room there ran in front of the high road the turners' room, from thirty to forty yards in length, filled with lathes, and at the back of it another dismal dungeon, called a cellar, for the green ware brought from the thrower's stove or drying-room. Beyond the turners' room, still fronting the road, there were the handlers' rooms, connected by a dark, narrow passage, called 'The Purgatory', which ran underneath a grand entrance to the bank. The first handlers' shop was partly occupied by six young women who made 'stilts', or pot triangles, to put between pieces of flat-ware in firing, so as to prevent cohesion. There was another handler's shop in which a man and two boys worked; and 'the top hopper', a small dark den, with little light and no ventilation, sometimes used by stilt-makers and sometimes by handle-makers. All these latter shops were much below the high road, and were damp, dismal, stuffy holes, with little light even at midsummer. They always had a close, mouldy smell, as the only entrance to them was a deep, narrow staircase, some twenty steps deep. A similar entrance, some fifty or sixty yards away, led down to the turners' room.

When all the different workers were following their work, there was a busy hum from end to end of this long cellar. In the throwing-room were the two throwers, and four young women to turn the thrower's wheel, and to 'ball' for them. In the turners' room, there were about eight or ten lathes, with a turner and a lathe-treader for each lathe. These lathe-treaders were young women. The stilt-makers and the handlers in the rooms beyond made up a busy community of workers when work was going on. But on Mondays and Tuesdays, one or both throwers would be away drinking at a house properly called 'The Foaming Quart'. Sometimes half the turners would be away drinking too, and always one or both handlers. This course left the young women and boys very much to do as they pleased, and merriment and frolic were the order of those days. Sometimes the men would 'drink on the premises', and the drink was got by the most stealthy and ingenious methods, so as to elude the observation of the 'bailees' or overlookers . . . The drink was got by the top gate of the works, and women and boys were used to get drink in vessels which would have deceived a detective. Drinking away at the beer-shop was bad enough, and this was the commonest course taken, but drinking on the works was far more horrible, being accompanied by jollification and devilry unnameable. Then the young women were persuaded to join in the indulgence. Drink was forced upon them in many instances, if new to the business. Before night came some of these women were drunk, and didn't know where they were. Then the most lustful and villainous of the men – young men, generally – would scheme to stay all night. The boys were sent home. The decent and sober women fled before their usual time. The night was a revel of drink, lust and beastliness. Whoever came early next morning saw a veritable pandemonium.

Men were seen still stupefied with drink, and young women blear-eyed, dazed, with a stupid shyness dawning upon them, with woe-begone faces, and with tumbled and torn garments. The faces of all carried signs of besotment and weariness. No food was wanted, and little work was done. Some of the men stole away to the beer-house to get revived, and the many self-accusing women were languid and silent, and ashamed, till the closing hour released them from the scene they evidently loathed.

I know this is a grim picture, but I know it is true in every detail given, while many repulsive details, moral and physical, are suppressed. I am not sure whether the employers knew of these proceedings. One of them was rarely seen at the works. The other used to come about ten o'clock in the morning in a carriage and pair, and stay half-an-hour or an hour. I never saw him in a workshop. He may have been in one. I only speak that I know . . .

I have said there was generally little, if any, work done on Mondays and Tuesdays, and yet it was rare for any of the men to get on Saturday less than a full week's wage. From Wednesday to Saturday they worked themselves, and worked others, boys and women, like galley slaves. From four and five in the morning until nine and ten at night this fierce race for wages was run. There was no Factory Act then, nor for a quarter of a century afterwards. Women and children were then given up to the greed of employers, and to the drunken greed of many of their operative 'masters', as they were called. Many a time, after fourteen and fifteen hours' work, I had to walk a mile and a half home with another weary little wretch, and we have nodded and budged against each other on the road, surprised to find our whereabouts. No wonder ghosts were seen in the dark, gasless 'Hollow', with flashing lights of furnaces in the distance, and with noise of water from the flour-mill in the valley. Oh, yes, I have seen ghosts and heard their wailings on such nights, when my senses were dazed with weariness. Boys don't see them now, even in the 'Hollow', because the Factory Act sends them home at six o'clock, and because the road is lit up with gas lamps. These long hours were worked, too, on the poorest and most meagre fare. Bread and butter were made up in a hand-kerchief, with a sprinkling of tea and sugar. Sometimes there was a little potato pie, with a few pieces of fat bacon on it to represent beef. The dinner time was from one till two o'clock, and from then until nine or ten the weary workers got no more food. Weary for sleep, weak with hunger, and worn out with hard work, many wretched children, through summer and winter nights, had to make their way home at these late hours. Summer was no summer for them, except for warmth and light; while winter, dark and pitiless, always brought its full burden of horror and suffering . . .

As I have mentioned wages, I must describe the paying of wages on a Saturday night. We usually left the works between five and six o'clock. The custom was to pay three or four men, with their helpers, in one lump sum, say a five-pound note, and some odd sovereigns. It would have been just as easy for the employers to get silver or half-sovereigns, so that each worker could get his or her pay direct. No such thoughtful providence, however, existed. The wages were fastened up in one lump until loosened at some public house. Men and women and children had to go there for their wages. The publican took good care to be in no hurry in changing the money given him. Each one – man, woman and child – was expected to have a hot roll and cheese, to be paid for out of the wage to be received, however small the pittance. The roll and cheese were right enough, but the payment was arbitrary and unequal. Those rolls and cheese were devoured with rare gusto. Such shining crust, and such white flaky insides, were never seen in 'cottage loaves'. The eyes of the youngsters had a paradisaical vision before them, and the coy hesitation with which the crust was broken, the first dainty nibblings at the cheese, lest roll and cheese should get small too soon, were most amusing. It was something like the play of a cat with a mouse before she devours it. The boys would hold out the remainders of roll and cheese to show how much each one had left, and he was considered the hero of the hour who could seem to be eating all the time, and yet be the last to finish. The lad who finished, impelled by the strength of his hunger, was regarded with ironical compassion, and he regarded himself as a sort of victim, but couldn't tell who had victimized him.

The men, of course, soon ate their portion of food, and began the drinking, which, with short intervals, would not cease perhaps till the following Tuesday night. As the drinking went on they became talkative and effusive. Boys and women would be asked to drink and pressed to drink. In the case of the boys this sometimes meant semi-intoxication before the wages were received. Boys, I know, have been sent home drunk with the miserable pittance of two or three shillings in their pockets for working a week in the way I have described. Meantime the publican kept the change back. Apparently he was counting untold pound-piles of silver, and if asked for the change, replied he was getting on as fast as he could, and that other folks were before them. Not until he was assured of a fair return for his 'change', or until he saw his adult customers were settled for a night's booze, did he bring out the change. This may be said for the publican's honesty, I never remember a dispute about the change being wrong. When all were paid, the women and boys were sent home, the night's booze properly set in, and towards ten o'clock, poor wretched women would appear and entreat their husbands to go home. When this failed, they pleaded for money, as they had not a penny with which to pay the week's bills or to provide for the morrow ...

It came about that, after one of the box-rope floggings by the drunken 'handler' for whom I worked, I was sent to work at the lower bank, where china-ware was manufactured. Here I found circumstances as different as could be imagined. There was no trace of the drunken rowdyism which prevailed at the higher works. The atmosphere was a perfect contrast to the one I had left. Throwers, turners and handlers worked quietly every day, not doing as much on Monday as on other days, for Saint Monday always received some regard. But there was no drinking followed, either at the beer-shop or on the premises. 'The Foaming Quart' might have been a thousand miles away. 'Old Rupert', the handler I worked for, was kind and considerate. He never stormed, never swore, and certainly never flogged. On some fine spring days he would set himself and myself 'a task' to do so much work, and when done to go bird-nesting ... The old china bank to which I had removed was uplifting to me in another way. There were several men employed there who were really artists. They modelled specially beautiful figures in Parian. Occasionally they came across me, and sometimes I was in the places where they worked, though at times, when they were engaged on very special work, which the master did not wish to be known about until it arrived in the showroom, they were locked up. But when I met these men their gentleness and refinement brought a new strange influence upon me. In my two years of working life I had met with nothing but coarseness, even though it might, at times, be free from brutality. But now the speech of these men, and their looks and their ways, gave me a dim insight into another order of life. They came to their work as well dressed as the master himself. It was common in those days for 'Bailees' and painters and gilders, as well as these modellers, to go to work in tall hats and swallow-tailed coats. But there was something about these men felt to be more distinctive than their dress. I did not know what it was then. I know now it was their culture and its simple refinement ...

Thomas Wood
*engineer**

Thomas Wood was born in Bingley, Yorkshire, in 1822, the son of a handloom weaver earning 10s. a week, and grandson of a roadman who had once held Wesley's horse. An intelligent boy with a strong

* From *The Autobiography of Thomas Wood, 1822–1880*, privately published, 1956. Copyright © Miss Dorothy Wood, Brontë Hall, Beckett Park, Leeds, 6.

Methodist upbringing, he spent two years at the local Grammar School before beginning work in a woollen-mill at the age of eight. At fourteen the unusual step was taken of apprenticing him to a local 'mechanic' (engineer) manufacturing powerlooms, where he served his time until twenty-one. Unable to get work locally, he tramped through Lancashire and was eventually employed by Platts Brothers of Oldham, one of the very largest textile-machine-makers in the country with a work-force of nearly 2,000 men (in 1851 only fourteen engineering firms employed more than 350 men); here he worked on the latest machine tools and gauges invented by Whitworth, and was highly paid at 32s. a week until he and fifty others were dismissed in 1846. After further work in engineering his health began to fail, and he became a school attendance officer in Keighley; he died in 1880, aged fifty-nine.

His brief autobiography was written two years before his death during a fortnight at the Ilkley Convalescent Home; the extracts comprise about half of the original manuscript.

I was sent to a school taught by a man called Jim Lister. The mode of education was singular. I only remember one book in the room, which was his living-room. It was a big Bible, bound in leather. The little ones learnt letters out of it. Bigger ones learnt to read. I am not quite sure we ever read anything but the first chapter of St John. I could repeat a deal of this before I could read. The master always read a word or two ahead of the scholars. We went up to read in our turns once a forenoon and once afternoon . . .

Schools were few. There was one kept by the postmaster – that was a good school as things went, but it was 9d. a week. Only better sort of folk sent their children there. Then there was the grammar school, richly endowed, that taught Latin free. Anything else must be paid for. None were admitted till they could read the Testament and were over six years of age. And then some influence with the Vicar was necessary to secure admission.

Soon after I was six I was admitted here through the influence of grandfather . . .

I was at this school till about eight learning Latin grammar and writing. I don't remember ever being required to learn the multiplication table, or working a sum of arithmetic at school, or hearing or seeing one worked. It was a Latin school.

Working folk derided the idea of their children learning Latin, or, indeed, anything at all if it cost anything or entailed any inconvenience. I suppose grandfather thought learning was a great thing without stopping to ask about the quality or applicability of it to the practical purposes of life, for he, poor man, could not read a letter.

My schooldays would have been more pleasant but for one thing. I was the eldest of the family of four brothers and sisters. Father was a handloom weaver. Mother also worked at a pair of looms. Now weavers must have bobbins to weave. It fell to my lot to have to wind those bobbins full of weft from the hank, so between winding and nursing I had little time left for home lessons, still less for play. Moreover, winding bobbins is about as distasteful an occupation for a boy as could be conceived. It was usually done by old women, whose eyesight was tolerably good, but who were unequal to harder work, and whose age and circumstances rendered a light employment, where the prime quality was patience and perseverance, necessary to supplement the slender income of their household . . .

My school life came to an end when I was about eight years old. Perhaps I hastened the event for what with nursing and winding bobbins I had no time to con my lessons and was often on this account in trouble. I now went to work at John Sharpe's mill at the bottom of the town and quite close to the school I had left.

Going to the mill in those days was vastly different to what it is now. There were no inspectors, no public opinion to put down flagrant cases of oppression, or of cruel usage. Some of the overlookers were brutal beyond what would now be believed, while the master was feared and almost worshipped by turns. The usual hours of work were from 6 in the morning to 7.30 at night with forty minutes for dinner.

Breakfast and tea had to be taken at work, and by snatches, while standing or walking to and fro and receiving work. But when it suited the master he would run the mill till 9 o'clock. Mothers used on these occasions to come to meet or wait for their children coming out to take them home for fear of their falling asleep on the way. For these long hours, after about two or three weeks for nothing, I received 1s. 6d. per week. Small as it was it was a sensible and much needed acquisition to the family store. I worked at this mill over five years, and when I left I had 4s. 9d. per week, this point being reached by additions of 3d. from time to time as an advance . . .

The mortality among millhands was very great. Twenty or thirty years since I could reckon but few survivors, and in talking to one about it we could count whole families of children who worked with us who had gone to an early grave.

The memory of these things is passing away. Had a fair record been kept of the doings of some overlookers it would read more like the doings of a West Indian slave-driver than a sober record of English life. Poverty, keen want, made keener still by the ignorant thriftlessness of parents, upheld a system by supplying victims. Of the many prominent features which marked the last forty or fifty years none was so beneficial as factory legislation. It throws the protection of the law over those who cannot protect themselves. When that point is reached it ceases to interfere and a man may work twenty hours a day if so disposed . . .

My factory life, at least as a spinner, came to an end after five or six years' service. During those years any enjoyment, or freedom from work, or what was worse the fear of the overlooker, was on a Saturday night and Sunday. I was a fair attender at the Sabbath school (Independent). A few times in the year I played truant, the result of companionship with boys who often indulged in a country ramble or a hunt after birds' nests, or a visit to some spot such as the Druid's Altar whose charms were fresh the year through . . .

I was about fourteen when I went to learn the trade of mechanic under David Clayton. I can remember how ardently I longed to be delivered from the bondage of factory life. I wanted father to allow me to be a weaver or a wool-comber, the two occupations which at the time employed nine tenths of the population about here and required no apprenticeship as those trades, if they deserved such a name, were carried on at home mostly in the bedrooms or some outbuilding. They were to some extent their own masters, at least as to the hours they worked.

Father would not hear of it, so I was put to be a mechanic. Perhaps it caused as much remark among our neighbours as it would now if I put a son to be a doctor. I had 4s. 9d. per week when I left the mill, and after working in the shop a month or two for nothing, 1s. 6d. per week for the next three months, then 2s. 6d. to advance by 1s. a year. I am not quite sure how the arrangement was carried out, but in the last year of my apprenticeship I had 8s. per week.

My parents must have made a costly effort to get me a trade. Before I was twenty-one years old I was the oldest of ten children all at home. Usually there were four or five too young to work. Those who were working ranged from 1s. 3d to 5s. per week in their earnings. Father, as I have before said, was a handloom weaver, whose earnings did not average 10s. per week. He had the misfortune to enter the occupation rather late in life, so that he lacked the expertness which comes by an early training. But far more serious was it to cling to a doomed trade. Doomed to be crushed out by remorseless machinery.

I wonder if anyone thought of the anomaly of sending me to a power-loom-maker for my trade while powerlooms were slowly and surely drying up industrial life. Perhaps my father accepted the inevitable or, more likely still, I was sent there because there was no other opening. Mechanics, though so plentiful now, were rather scarce then; I am quite sure in saying there were not twenty in Bingley either in shops or factories.

Monster establishments like Prince Smith and Sons, where they employ 9,000 or 10,000 men, and manufacture both machinery and mechanics, had no existence. So I was to be a mechanic and have my heart's desire. As will be seen my parents paid dearly for it. Our food was of the plainest, the quantity seldom sufficient. I seldom satisfied my appetite unless I called at Aunt Nancy's after dinner to pick up what she had to spare. As to the luxury of pocket money, it was unknown . . .

There was no Mechanics' Institute in Bingley; indeed, in after years. I was one of six who met and decreed to have one. I only know one of the six living now, Sam Foster, a good man, living, I believe, at Cottingley. But there was an Institute at Wilsden, perhaps the best in the country then. It was only three miles off, so I resolved to enter that. I forgot the entrance fee. The terms were 1½d. per week; for the library classes extra. There was no reading room. Newspapers at 7d. each did not belong to working men and, I believe, there were none under that price. However the 1½d. was more than I could raise. I therefore got bundles of rotten sticks in the wood and sold them for firewood.

Turnip-tops and nettles when in season with mushrooms I collected, and whatever would sell. Well pleased was I when I had 3d. to meet my fortnight's contributions. Then, as to reading, in winter I had to read by firelight excepting when I could afford a ½d. candle, which I used to save to read with in bed. I have read perhaps scores of times till 12 or 1 o'clock. There were no curtains to fire. There were no interruptions. A house with seven or eight children on one floor is a fine opportunity for the display of patience on the part of a student or an earnest reader. Get into bed for warmth and then the luxury of an unbroken reading was a treat that compensated for any privations, and lifted me, for the time being, into another world . . .

I used to read at meal-times, and when I came home to dinner if it was not ready, Mother used to put the book I was reading quite handy, and then had to ask me to put the book down to eat my homely and frequently scanty fare. Three or four children rushing in from the mill at dinner-time, expecting to swallow their dinner and then rush out again for a short play before beginning work, were in no amiable mood when dinner was not ready . . .

When near my sixteenth year I began to join in some fashion at a newspaper. A man lent me his paper when it was a week old for a penny, I giving him the paper back when I had had it a week. The paper was the *Northern Star*, edited by Fergus O'Connor, a name at that time familiar as a household word throughout Yorkshire and Lancashire. In politics it was the extreme of Radicalism, or Chartism as it was then called, from advocating the People's Charter. It advocated six distinct changes which were deemed constitutional departures from the law and customs of the realm . . .

I served an apprenticeship to a mechanic for seven years to a master who was irritable, poor and wicked. The men among whom I worked were thoughtless, vicious and selfish. I suffered very much at times. Sometimes from fear of being out of work, and often from the negligence of the master. What made matters worse, I knew my parents could not get on without my wage. I knew that however they wished to sympathize with me they could not help me, or keep me one week if out of work. So I bore the burden as well as I could in silence, and looked with wistful eyes to the future . . .

In due course I was twenty-one (1843). I was called upon by the custom of the shop to provide a supper for the men to celebrate the occasion. In consideration of my poverty they agreed to have the supper in the shop instead of a public house. The master, or rather now the foreman, cooked it in his house hard by. It was a quiet, economical affair, but I had to borrow the money to defray the expense. Trade was bad in the extreme. Men were out of work or working short time. The roads swarmed with beggars. Families of six or eight persons were on the road together and esteemed themselves fortunate if they could obtain the shelter of an outhouse or a hayrick. I saw there was not work at the shop for the hands there were. I expected no favour such as staying and someone else leaving, so I was not surprised to receive my dismissal about two months after. I had only about 14s. per week as my first wage as journeyman, so the loss was small. The weekly wage of a good man was 20s. Perhaps I was not a good man, perhaps they wanted me to leave and not accept it. This is just what I would have done had it been possible without starvation for self and curtailing the comforts of mother.

I gave up my wage till I left home except some very small sums for needful purposes. I left home in search of work in the beginning of March and returned in the beginning of April. Having walked through Lancashire in search of work, I saw hundreds out of work and was regarded as an enthusiast in some places for seeking work when so many were out who were known to the masters.

I was accompanied by Edward Jackson, of Crossflatts, a fellow apprentice whose parents were rather better off and who all along had rather looked down on me. He was older, stronger and wealthier then me, but I derived no benefit from him in any form. He would frequently walk half a mile ahead of me.

When we approached a shop he would be the first to ask for work. The last day, in returning home, we walked over forty miles in the wet. I resolved never to tramp again with him or one like him. He got married soon after our return, and soon after that died. If I remember aright, it was hinted that he had over-exerted himself when on the road with me . . .

I had been at home about a week, when, meeting my old master, he asked me to go and do a piece of work that would take about a week's time. My very nature was glad and grateful for so small a mercy. I went the following morning. This was in April, 1843. Other work came in. I stopped about two years, then left of my own accord. My wages were advanced in the early part of the time, first 1s. a week, then 2s. and after a while another 2s. until I had 20s. per week. When I gave notice to leave I was asked if it was a wage question. I replied, 'No,' but the desire for improvement.

This was just the truth; I thought I was deficient in my trade, though I learned, and long practised, all I could learn there. But I heard about new tools, new machines, and new ways of working. I could never hope to see them in our shop, and if I was to learn, and improve, I would do so now before I either married or thought of it.

So one Friday in the summer of 1845 I left my old master for good and ever, and having arranged my little affairs, left home on the Monday following, for Lancashire. I walked to Hebden Bridge and took a train for Rochdale, my first railway ride. We were put into a truck worse and more exposed than cattle trucks now are. There were seats, or forms, to sit on, but they were swimming with rain. Not a bit of shelter from the driving rain, or sparks from the engine chimney, which then were very plentiful, and had a peculiar knack of falling down the back of the neck.

Sleeping at Rochdale I walked forward to Oldham, got work, started at dinner-time, and worked a half-day on the Tuesday after leaving home. After securing lodgings at night, I wrote home in a very hopeful strain. My wages at first were 28s. per week, increased afterwards at time and time to 32s. My parents shared my good fortune, particularly my sick mother. My only regret now is that more was not given, and, above all, that it was not given more cheerfully.

There was one little thing that sometimes irritated. Father never meddled with household matters. With the burden of debts that mother had to carry this was where help was needed and given. But, somehow, father thought more of a shilling given to him personally than a pound to the family exchequer. I missed many thanks, and much enjoyment, from not considering and humouring this feeling. It would have done no harm, and, would have promoted good feeling, and given pleasure in the retrospect which money cannot buy. On looking back I am ashamed that I neglected so plain and easy a duty . . .

I started work at Hibberts, Platts, now Platts Brothers, Oldham, one of the largest machine-shops in England. It was with a fear of an indefinite something that I commenced work for a firm who employed near 2,000 hands, whose tools were mostly Whitworth's make – I, who had never worked in a shop with more than eight or ten men and with country-made tools, the very best of which Platts would have thrown away as utterly useless. So I had cause for fear that I should not succeed and be found as efficient as other men in a place where no favour was shown – no paying a man what he was worth, but the ostensible rule was a fixed standard of wage, and if the man was not worth it he must go.

I saw many start that were paid off the first day, some at even a shorter trial. I determined to do my best, and if I failed there to try again elsewhere till I could stand conscious of a man's stature in the trade. I had youth and careful habits, and on general topics a mind better informed than any working men I knew. I soon dropped into my place.

Men in large shops are not troubled with a variety of work, but had one class of work and special tools. The men soon became expert and turned out a large quantity of work with the requisite exactness without a little of the thought required of those who work in small shops where fresh work continually turns up, but always the same old tools.

I learned quickness and accuracy, also that hard work and application were indispensable. Though I had left a wage of 20s. a week and was now with 28s., yet I was better placed at 20s. Superior tools and the method of working made the difference. The men among whom I worked were wicked and reckless. Most of them gambled freely on horse- or dog-races. Numbers brought a day's food with them and nearly all their breakfast, which was despatched with celerity when betting books were produced and bets made.

There were very few who took care of their money, fewer still who went to a place of worship, or regarded the Sabbath in any other light than as a holiday. Their mode of living was different to the homely manner I had been accustomed to. Flesh meat, as they called it, must be on the table twice or thrice a day. A rough and rude plenty alone satisfied them. The least pinching, such as I had seen scores of times without a murmur, and they were loud in their complainings about 'clamming'.

I began to attend chapel the first Sunday I was there. Soon after I began to teach in the Sunday School of Manchester Road Chapel. This was the best Sunday School I had seen, perhaps ever have seen. The discipline in the School was as near perfect as possible. While the teachers were held to their duty and punctuality by an iron hand, the hand was covered with velvet. Once every month each teacher's name was called over – if two minutes late it was read out . . .

After working here thirteen or fourteen months, I, along with fifty others, got stopped. I was told to come again in a few weeks and see if anything turned up. This was on the Saturday. On the Tuesday following I left Oldham and walked to Huddersfield. The day after I walked to Leeds, and for the second time in my life slept in a common lodging house. Such an abomination was a disgrace to the town, and the century. They are all under supervision now, and not before the need was felt.

The day following I walked to York. The day was wet, but after looking into lots of public houses without finding a fire I walked the streets till near bedtime. I then obtained a share of a bed for 1s. but got my jacket and waistcoat dried. I took the train the next morning at 5.45 for Darlington, and about 9 o'clock breakfasted on nearly black bread with a crust like a board and some skimmed milk cost 2d. . . .

I started here at 23s. per week. It was a small engine-shop with no proper order or economical way of working. My friends, if I may call them such, because they came from Bingley and Keighley, were here. I lodged with them at a place where there were six or eight lodgers. There was an abundance to eat. Though potatoes were 2s. per stone we had them twice a day. I often wished father and mother could have my supper instead of me.

I went to Stockton Methodist Chapel on two or three Sundays. I was living at South Stockton and had near two miles to go to chapel. Nobody noticed me. I stayed at prayer-meeting on Sunday night. No one asked me to come again. Very foolishly I ceased to go regularly and neglected to join the church, so I became a poor wanderer, unfit to take pleasure in wickedness, and my title to the joys of religion forfeited. I never joined the other lodgers in wicked conversation or flagrant wickedness . . .

I found father and mother suffering great want from the scarcity of work and the high price of the absolute necessaries of life. This was the year (1846) of the failure of the potato crop. They were 2s. per stone. Flour was usually 4s. 6d. and upwards – once it was 5s. Poor people did not get half enough of the plainest and most necessary food. Father would have died and seen his children die before he would have paraded his wants, or, I believe, asked for help. He was as poor as want could make him, but his independence was equal to a lord's.

I returned to South Stockton. Here at all events in my lodgings there was no stint. I and the rest, eight in all, boarded with the family, the head of which was a butcher, grocer and cattle-dealer. At my work I was gaining confidence, of which I was sadly deficient. Of course the class of work was something new to me, but I often saw men pose as good hands, 'clever', who I was persuaded owed their all to bounce and brag. These could give themselves airs and be supercilious to quiet observers who steadily plodded away. I have seen the destruction of many of these windbags in my time. The improved method of working and supervision has been the death of them.

[The autobiography ends.]

Henry Broadhurst
*stonemason**

Henry Broadhurst was born at Littlemore, near Oxford, in 1840, the 'eleventh or twelfth' child of a stonemason whose wage was 20s. to 24s. a week and hardly anything during two or three months of unemployment each winter. Henry left a private school (6d. a week) at twelve, and after a year in a blacksmith's shop joined his father and brothers at stonemasonry, in which trade he spent the next eighteen years. Meanwhile, he had become deeply involved in trade unionism and working-class politics. In 1872 he was the Stonemasons' Society delegate to the T.U.C., in 1873 Secretary to the Labour Representation League and in 1875 Parliamentary Secretary to the T.U.C. In 1880 he was only the third working man to be elected to the House of Commons, and in 1885 the first to hold office as Under-Secretary of State in the Home Office in Gladstone's government. He played an important part in many social and legal reforms for the improvement of working conditions.

The extracts describe his early life as a stonemason in London and 'on the tramp' in the 1850s and 1860s.

I am not conscious of ever having a goal for my ambition – that is, if I have at any time possessed an ambition. I have never burnt the midnight oil considering my next move. Each succeeding morning I have done the

* From *The Story of his Life from a Stonemason's Bench to the Treasury Bench. Told by Himself*, Hutchinson, 1901.

work nearest to hand. On the Saturday in November 1872, when I had done my last day's work as a stonemason, I should have thought the man beside himself who had then ventured to tell me that it was my farewell to my trade. I left the firm which then employed me, fully intending to obtain employment in some other firm the following week. That is now twenty-eight years back, and I have not yet sought the other firm. Even at this distance of time I constantly dream that I am working at my trade, and the sudden awakening to reality dispels the delusion almost with a shock. I still keep sufficient of my tools to make another start, though I fear I should not be a first-rate hand at it were I to try. Whatever positions I have occupied, I have blundered into them or stumbled upon them without thought or premeditation. With these explanations and apologies to those who may care to read these pages, I commit myself to the tender mercies and indulgence of the public . . .

My father's employers gave permission for me to enter the shop as a beginner, and thus opened out the new and broader life of a stonemason. As the youngest employee many duties besides the acquisition of a know-ledge of my trade fell to my lot. At eight o'clock in the morning I had to see that hot tea and coffee were ready for thirty or forty men. Then at ten I must start on my tour of 'the shop' to see how many pints of beer would be wanted at eleven, and this task had to be repeated at three o'clock. There were plenty of public houses close at hand, but I must fetch the beer from one nearly a mile away, because the landlord was foreman of the yard – a position invested with large authority. Therefore the duty of fetching the beer meant a long trudge twice a day for me. If a man did not drink beer he was regarded by his fellows as a muff or a 'Ranter'. Such men were, however, the exceptions. Most of us found it advisable to obtain our Saturday night and Sunday beer at the same house, so that the foreman must have found the custom from the shop a profitable affair. Such circumstances would be hard to find today; the trades unions have changed all that, as well as the once common practice of paying wages in the public house, which has now been made illegal.

About this time the second cholera epidemic broke out in England. Oxford did not escape the contagion, and our shop, being situated in a poor district by the river-side, became the centre of the plague's ravages. I can vividly recall the scenes of terrible wretchedness that took place round about the wharf where we were at work, as victim after victim was brought out of the houses by the plague authorities, and carried away to the temporary hospital on the outskirts of the town. Strangely enough, these scenes inspired me with no terror, and every day my father and I walked through the midst of the plague-stricken district to the scene of our labour. Amid such conditions I speedily passed through the stage of initiation into the stonemason's craft. My experience of those days con-vinces me that most lads will learn their father's trade quicker than any other; while a father naturally interests himself more in the advancement of his son than in that of one who is not related to him . . .

An incident which occurred during this period strongly impressed my mind with the necessity of some kind of technical instruction. I obtained employment at Wheatley some half-dozen miles from Oxford, where a new church was being built. By this time I had become fairly competent at my work, and greatly liked it. The first task set me was to work a huge block of stone, weighing probably a ton or more, into a base to carry one of the columns of the church. The design was a square tapering to an octagon and finishing with a circle. The square and the circle offered no difficulties, but how to obtain eight equal sides was utterly beyond my comprehension. To add to my distress my work lay at some distance from the men in my shop, and I was under the constant surveillance of a hard-hearted and uncouth foreman. I only realized my difficulty between the breakfast and dinner-hours, so that I would obtain no assistance from my mates. My perplexity reached the height of distress. I knew the foreman was no friend of my father, and therefore would give me but a short shrift if he found me in such a dilemma. I was also fully alive to the fact that if I took an undue time over the task my wages would suffer at the end of the week. How I prayed for the dinner-hour as the weary hours dragged by! But all things have an end, and at last my opportunity came. The persuasive power contained in a pint of beer soon induced one of the masons to describe the procedure, which I realized in an instant, with amazement that I had not intuitively discovered the simple process for myself . . .

With the completion of the church at Wheatley began what I may call the third phase of my life. As every student of political economy is aware, there is a certain percentage of the industrial life of the nation which must be migratory in character by force of circumstances. Just as when you look into a kaleidoscope, after taking your fill of one pattern you give the instrument a turn, and the pieces of glass fall away into new positions, some scarcely moving, others covering a wide area before they find a fitting resting-place – so in the sphere of labour the changes and chances of commercial life and the caprices of fashion keep a large army of working men in a state of motion, sometimes over short distances, sometimes from the southern counties to the western, or the eastern to the northern. Few men escape this experience; my turn now arrived, and for five years I was like Cain, a wanderer on the face of the earth.

As I have said, the church at Wheatley was nearing completion, and the discharge of the hands in the mason's yard began. My turn soon came, and I found myself – a hobbledehoy – out of employment. All my endeavours to get work in Oxford and the surrounding district failed. Business was slack, and masons were a drug in the market. So, as it happened in Robinson Crusoe's case, 'my head began to be filled with rambling thoughts'. I quickly made my decision to seek my fortune further afield, and from that moment I never again permanently resided under my parents' roof. I started on my venture into this new life one Monday morning with high hopes and a cheerful countenance. The night before my foot had kicked against something in the pathway, and a patient search in the blackness of a pitch-dark night had been rewarded by the discovery of a rough purse full of coppers. I took this treasure-trove for a happy omen; and, indeed, before the end of the week I had found employment in the town of Buckingham. My life there, and subsequently at Banbury and in Bedfordshire, where I stayed nearly a year, passed uneventfully in the exercise of my trade.

About this period I paid my first visit to the Metropolis, where I found employment for a short time in the firm of George Myers and Son. Like all country-bred lads, I was astounded at the life and movement of London. The teeming masses of humanity rushing in all directions, bent, as it appeared to me, on getting clear of their neighbours, yet never succeeding in shaking off their pursuers, the roar of the streets, the glare of the lamps at night-time, inspired in me a curious mingling of fascination and distaste. The same conditions were reproduced in the workshop. Above, below, and around me machines throbbed and whirled ceaselessly. The homely surroundings and social interests of country life had no existence here: life seemed a new thing, almost unearthly. I began to long for the sunlight on the quiet fields, the green hedgerows, and the music of the woods. Even the Houses of Parliament, with the great Clock Tower, my chief delight, could not compensate for the absence of the joys of rural life. A month's stay in modern Babylon was quite sufficient for me, and, gasping like a fish out of water, I set my face towards the open country.

After a week's wandering I found employment at a country house near Pangbourne, in Berkshire, a most delightful spot. The beauty of these new surroundings, and their contrast to the close air and grimy streets of London, inspired me with a strong desire to make a long stay here. Unfortunately, the work I was engaged upon was soon completed, and in a short time I found myself back in London. My return route lay through Reading and Windsor, and as I possessed a little money I made the journey by easy stages. In those days railway fares were much higher, and most working men, even though they had the means, regarded travelling by rail as an expensive luxury, only to be indulged in by the lazy and foolish.

On my arrival in London I found that a firm of builders, Lucas Brothers, were in want of masons at Lowestoft, and that they were paying the passage by sea to Great Yarmouth of employees engaged in London. Here was a chance offered which just suited me. I had never seen the sea, much less sailed upon its heaving breast. Accordingly, I found myself aboard a crazy old tub of a steamer pounding heavily down the Thames. Besides ordinary passengers, I found a number of other masons bound on the same errand as myself. In such company the day and night passed rapidly and jovially, and so liberally did I contribute my quota of the entertainment that when the steamer reached Great Yarmouth I had not a half-penny to bless myself with. My companions were in no better case, so we had perforce to tramp to Lowestoft, though this proved less of a hardship than we expected, as the distance turned out to be only ten miles.

After a stay of a few months I left the coast and found my way

Norwich, little suspecting that my wanderings were to cease for some six years. My employer was a Mr Lloyd, who had a thriving business in church erection and renovation and also in gravestones. He was a splendid master, and a bit of a character in his way. He insisted upon thorough accuracy and finish in all work done for him, with the natural consequence that in his 'shops' was displayed some of the finest mason's work I have ever seen. I well remember my first conversation with him. I had asked him, as is usual in the trade, if he were in want of hands. He asked me what I was, and I replied, 'A mason.' Turning a keen and searching glance on me, he suddenly rapped out in a grating voice, 'Are you a mason, or only a man calling yourself a mason?' Somewhat taken aback, I assured him that I had gained my livelihood as a worker in stone for some years; and after a few moments' consideration he consented to give me a trial. Apparently he found his startling question satisfactorily answered by the manner in which I handled the chisel, for after eight hours' work he readily complied with my request for an advance of half a sovereign (two and a half day's wages), of which I stood in sore need.

In Mr Lloyd's 'shop' I spent some of the happiest days of my life. The wages were only twenty-four shillings a week of sixty hours. If you were late in the morning you forfeited a quarter of a day's pay, not, as is now the case, simply half an hour's or an hour's wages, according to the time lost. On the other hand, there were many compensations. Frequently I have taken a half-holiday without any deduction of wages, and as frequently I gave a few hours' work late at night or early in the morning without putting it down as overtime. It was a give-and-take system, and I am not far wrong in saying that I took a great deal more than I gave, though always with Mr Lloyd's approval. I remember one autumn being in his yard six weeks without doing a stroke of really profitable work. Twice during this period I gave notice to leave, promising to return when work was found for me, but on neither occasion would my generous employer listen to my request. Fortunately, when matters were beginning to look desperate orders came in, enabling me to make up for the period of inaction.

A particular feature of this firm was the friendly and indeed familiar relations of master and men. Mr Lloyd was in special request for small repairs and rectifications in churches and country houses, which could only be carried out by a mason. Consequently, we were often obliged to drive a long distance to the scene of our labours. Many a score of miles did I travel with Mr Lloyd in his little trap on such journeys, taking our lunch together in roadside inns and enjoying our pipes while the pony was baited. Pleasant times were these. Jack was as good as his master, and his master scorned to be better than Jack. Times have changed since then, and manners with them. The struggle for a living wage has put an end to the friendly relations often subsisting between employer and workman, and today I fear it would require a long and exhaustive search to discover such conditions of employment as I have described.

During a period of terrible depression in trade – I think it must have been the winter of 1858-9 – I left the city of Norwich in search of work on what proved to be a disastrous journey. My time of setting out was not well chosen, but necessity knows no law. I started about the middle of December, only to return after nearly four months' absence, during which I tramped about twelve hundred miles without succeeding in finding a single day's work. I directed my steps in a southerly direction, making Southampton and Portsmouth my goal. My reason for steering in that direction was that I had heard of the construction of the Royal Victoria Hospital at Netley, and that many hundreds of masons had found employment on the works. Unfortunately for me, the same idea had attracted many others out of work by reason of the slackness of trade, and I found the road swarming with men imbued with the hope of finding employment on the Government buildings. Alike in our hopes, we were also destined to be alike in our disappointment. When I arrived, footsore and weary, at Portsmouth, my boots refused to be held together any longer by string, or any other device of the mechanical mind, and utterly collapsed – like the famous 'One-hoss Shay'. The hard and flinty southern roads had done their work, and through the holes in the leather the stony places had inflicted wounds and sores on my feet. Faint, weary, with spirit broken, I knew not where to turn. Happily, in my hour of need I met some good Samaritans. They were fellow masons who, tired of the weary search for non-existent work, had enlisted in the Militia Battalion of the Cheshire Regiment, called out for service at Portsmouth to replace the regular battalions decimated in the terrible Crimean War. Tolerably well fed, warmly clothed and securely housed, these militiamen appeared the picture of prosperity and happiness.

They lent a ready ear to my necessities, and at their suggestion I entered my name on the sick-list of my trades union, and obtained a week's lodging in its headquarters in that town. My militia friends generously guaranteed to provide me with food during that period. Accordingly, they proposed to their comrades in barracks that they should be allowed to introduce an old chum, fallen on evil times, to the mess, that he might share the bounties provided by the garrison commissariat. Tommy Atkins, true to his traditional character for good fellowship, agreed to the proposal with acclamation. I was at once installed in barracks, and, so far as meals were concerned, became a private in the Cheshire Militia. Discipline, especially in the militia, was much slacker in those days, and I had no difficulty in eluding the notice of the sergeants. For the time being I lived, as it seemed to me, like a lord, while the accumulation of my sick-pay (ten shillings a week) meant the possibility of new boots. With such a contrast as was afforded by my past destitution and misery and my present plenty and comfort, it was little wonder that the service of 'the Widow at Windsor' presented an alluring prospect . . .

I think my readers would be interested if I turned aside for a moment to describe the conditions under which such a long tramp was possible to a man with scarcely any means. Before I started on this unfortunate journey I had been out of work for a week or two, so that my entire capital amounted to less than ten shillings, and I finished the tour with the sum of sixpence in my pocket. At no time during my progress did I possess more than ten shillings, and on many occasions I was without even a penny. My trades union had relieving-stations in nearly every town, generally situated in one of the smaller public houses. Two of the local masons are appointed to act as relieving officer and bed-inspector. The duty of the latter is to see that the beds are kept clean, in good condition and well aired, and the accommodation is much better than might be expected. When a mason on tramp enters a town, he finds his way to the relieving officer and presents his card. On this card is written the applicant's name and last permanent address. In addition he carries a printed ticket bearing the stamp of the last lodge at which the traveller received relief. He was entitled to receive a relief allowance of 1 shilling for twenty miles and threepence for every additional ten miles traversed since his last receipt of relief money. Thus, if fifty miles have been covered the man receives one-and-ninepence. In addition he is allowed sleeping accommodation for at least one night, and if the town where the station is situated is of considerable size, he is entitled to two or three nights' lodging. Besides a good bed, the proprietor of the official quarters is bound to furnish cutlery, crockery and kitchen conveniences for each traveller, so that the relief money can all be spent on food. There is also no temptation to spend the small sum received on intoxicating drink, unless its recipient chooses to do so. The system is so perfect that it is a very rare occurrence for an impostor to succeed in cheating the union. Unfortunately, the stations did not exist everywhere, and when they were separated by forty or fifty miles – not a rare occurrence in the southern counties – the traveller's life became a hard one. I have frequently had to provide supper, bed and breakfast on less than a shilling, so it may be readily imagined that my resting-places were never luxurious hotels. When I look back on those days, and compare my condition and surroundings with the present time, it is like a peep into the Dark Ages. During the whole of that tramp, and over all those hundreds of miles, I do not remember more than one occasion upon which I got a lift on the road. Even an ordinary drayman little cares to pick up for ever so short a distance any person having the appearance which I presented at that period. But this was my last big tramp, and it was the longest lapse from employment that I have ever experienced in my life . . .

I think it was in 1865 that I removed to London. I quickly found work in a firm of sculptors, Farmer and Brindley. They were then engaged on the carving work in the block of Government offices adjoining Downing Street. I do not mean to imply that my engagement with this firm meant that I was in any sense competent to do carving work. My duty was to chisel down the rough blocks of stone as they were fitted in the building until they assumed the roughest outline of the intended decoration. Then the carver took up the work, shaping the stone in accordance with the artistic design until the finishing touches were given. The branch of masonry on which my energies were employed is called in the trade 'roughing-out', and was a higher class of work than I had hitherto experienced. Masons engaged on this kind of work received a halfpenny or a penny per hour more than the wages paid for the mechanical labour in the workshop, besides other little advantages of no interest to the public. Spurred by an ambition to improve my prospects, I conceived the idea of myself becoming a carver, and to this intent I bought some cheap books containing sketches of ornamental work in foliage and the like on one page, with a blank sheet opposite for copying. The study interested me greatly, and for some time I persevered in my intention; but ultimately I grew tired of the work, which involved considerable exposure to the weather, for nearly all the carving had to be done upon the building itself, and not in the workshop.

The last straw, however, which led to my final resolution not to continue in this branch of the trade was my employment on the Houses of Parliament. For a considerable interval I had been working in the 'shop' of my old employers, George Meyer and Sons, who were carrying out some decorative work on the Guildhall. Tempted by the superior rate of payment I returned to 'roughing-out' under Mr Herp, who had received the contract for the carving work on the Clock Tower and the new corridor which joined it to the main buildings of the Houses of Parliament. The time of year was November, and the north-east wind blowing up the river made my task a cruel one. At times the bitter blast would numb my hands until it was impossible to hold a chisel. My very bones would be penetrated with its icy edge until I felt as if clothed in a garment of lace. Little wonder that I gladly went back to the mason's shop, where some shelter, at least, was afforded . . .

Subsequently I was employed upon many of the best-known buildings in London, and traces of my workmanship might be found in Westminster Abbey, the Albert Hall, St Thomas's Hospital, Burlington House, the Guildhall, and the aristocratic residences in Grosvenor Place, Grosvenor Gardens and Curzon Street, Mayfair, though I am certain that the prolonged and minute search necessary to find such traces would not be rewarded by any startling artistic discovery.

The even tenor of my life was now broken by the first considerable labour dispute in which I had taken a part. In the spring of 1872 the men engaged in the building trades agitated for a reduction in the working hours and an increase of one penny per hour in their wages. The union officials had given the usual six months' notice to the employers, the period to expire in the month of May; but the employers decided to anticipate a strike, and locked the men out. The result was a month of enforced idleness. I was elected chairman of the lockout movement in my own trade. Rarely, I suppose, in the history of labour disputes was a lockout conducted on a more amicable basis. No breaches of the law occurred, and so quiet was everything that scarcely anyone save those interested in it was aware of its existence.

Ultimately, a conference was agreed upon, consisting of a committee of the Masons' Society (of which I was a member), and an equal number of representatives of the Master Builders' Association. The joint committee was presided over by Mr Hannen, the brother of the late Lord Hannen; and the chief figures on the employers' side were Mr Charles Lucas, and Mr Bird, the secretary of their association. After two meetings the conference drew up the conditions of the resumption of work. They consisted of an immediate advance of a halfpenny per hour, a further advance of the same amount to be conceded in the following year if trade was good, and the reduction of the hours of work from fifty-six and a half to fifty-two and a half per week for nine months in the year, and to forty-seven for the remaining three months. One signal advantage gained was that work should cease at noon on Saturdays. Under the system then in force work was continued on Saturdays till one o'clock, an hour after the usual dinner-hour. A serious consequence of this custom was that the men frequently celebrated the end of the week's work with a glass of beer, and, imbibing it on an empty stomach an hour after their usual meal-time, rapidly became intoxicated. Nothing succeeds like success, and the practical capitulation of the masters on the men's terms induced many employers who had hitherto refused to recognize the Masons' Society to change their policy; some firms even going so far as to instruct their fore-men to give the preference in taking on new hands to members of the Society . . .

George Sturt
*wheelwright**

George Sturt owned and managed a wheelwright's shop in Farnham, Surrey, from 1884 to 1920. The shop, originally established in 1706, had been bought by Sturt's grandfather in 1810; all five sons had entered the business, and Sturt's father, who inherited in 1865, had expanded considerably by adding a smithy and timber-yard. When he died suddenly in 1884 George, who was being educated for a profession, had to take control and learn the trade from his workmen.

His book is a detailed and deeply felt account of the skill required in making farm-carts, wagons and wheels in the days immediately before mechanization and motor transport. Chapters describe the buying and care of timber, the making of spokes, felloes and stocks, tyring and smithing, by a man who had education enough to stand back from the routine of work yet grew to love the beauty of the materials and the traditional skills that went into their manufacture.

* From *The Wheelwright's Sshop*, Cambridge Universiy Press, 1923, reproduced by kind permission of the George Sturt Memorial Fund.

When he sold the business in 1920 it was as a 'Coach and Motor Works' and 'the new machinery had almost forced its way in – the thin edge of scientific engineering'.

It was probably in 1885 that we left off on Saturdays at one o'clock instead of at four; and it may have been about the same time (but I have no recollection of it) that half-past five was substituted for six as the normal closing time. If the shop was 'making over-time' we took half an hour for tea and then went on again from six to eight. Including meal-times, this gave us a fourteen-hour day. The meal-times were, for breakfast half an hour (from eight to half-past); for dinner, from one to two. The ringing of Heath's bell across the street, was the signal. To see the shop empty at the first stroke for dinner was to know the source of that metaphor for quickness, 'To go like one o'clock'.

Though the normal hours were too long, the men were glad of over-time. In this connection it should be pointed out that in those days a man's work, though more laborious to his muscles, was not nearly so exhausting yet tedious as machinery and 'speeding-up' have since made it for his mind and temper. 'Eight hours' today is less interesting and probably more toilsome than 'twelve hours' then. But when men welcomed over-time it was because with their 24s. for an ordinary week they were under-paid and were glad to add to the money. The addition was at the rate of 6d. an hour, I think. One odd thing, which I could never understand, was that jealousy which caused the men to regard it almost as a right for all to have over-time if one did; so that however pressed the smiths might be I hardly dared ask them to work longer without giving the same treatment to the woodmen. A pack of children I sometimes thought these grown men, all older than myself.

To say that the business I started into in 1884 was old-fashioned is to understate the case: it was a 'folk' industry, carried on in a 'folk' method. And circumstances made it perhaps more intensely so to me than it need have been. My father might just possibly, though I don't think he would, have shown me more modern aspects of it; but within my first month he took ill of the illness he died of five months later. Consequently I was left to pick up the business as best I could from 'the men'. There were never any 'hands' with us. Eight skilled workmen or apprentices, eight friends of the family, put me up to all they could; and since some of them had been born and trained in little old country shops, while this of my father's was not much better, the lore I got from them was of the country through and through.

The objects of the work too were provincial. There was no looking far afield for customers. Farmers rarely more than five miles away; millers, brewers, a local grocer or builder or timber-merchant or hop-grower – for such and no others did the ancient shop still cater, as it had done for nearly two centuries. And so we got curiously intimate with the peculiar needs of the neighbourhood. In farm-wagon or dung-cart, barley-roller, plough, water-barrel, or what not, the dimensions we chose, the curves we followed (and almost every piece of timber was curved) were imposed upon us by the nature of the soil in this or that farm, the gradient of this or that hill, the temper of this or that customer or his choice perhaps in horseflesh. The carters told us their needs. To satisfy the carter, we gave another half-inch of curve to the wagon-bottom, altered the hooks for harness on the shafts, hung the water-barrel an inch nearer to the horse or an inch farther away, according to requirements . . .

Even the mixing and putting on of the paint called for experience. The first two coats, of Venetian-red for the underworks and shafts and 'lid colour' (lead colour) for the 'body' prepared the way for the putty, which couldn't be 'knocked-up' by instinct; and then came the last coat of red-lead for the wheels and Prussian-blue for the body, to make all look smart and showy.

Not any of this could be left wholly to an apprentice. Apprentices, after a year or two, might be equal to making and painting a wheelbarrow. But it was a painful process with them learning the whole trade. Seven years was thought not too long. After seven years a young man, nearly 'out of his time', was held likely to pick up more of his craft in the next twelve months than he had dreamt of before. By then too he should have won the skill that came from wounds. For it was a saying of my grandfather's that nobody could learn to make a wheel without chopping his knee half a dozen times.

There was nothing for it but practice and experience of every difficulty. Reasoned science for us did not exist. 'Theirs not to reason why.' What we had to do was to live up to the local wisdom of our kind; to follow the customs, and work to the measurements, which had been tested and corrected long before our time in every village shop all across the country. A wheelwright's brain had to fit itself to this by dint of growing into it, just as his back had to fit into the suppleness needed on the saw-pit, or his hands into the movements that would place a felloe 'true out o' wind'. Science? Our two-foot rules took us no nearer to exactness than the sixteenth of an inch: we used to make or adjust special gauges for the nicer work; but very soon a stage was reached when eye and hand were left to their own cleverness, with no guide to help them. So the work was more of an art – a very fascinating art – than a science; and in this art, as I say, the brain had its share. A good wheelwright knew by art but not by reasoning the proportion to keep between spokes and felloes; and so too a good smith knew how tight a two and a half-inch tyre should be made for a five-foot wheel and how tight for a four-foot, and so on. He felt it, in his bones. It was a perception with him. But there was no science in it; no reasoning. Every detail stood by itself, and had to be learnt either by trial and error or by tradition.

This was the case with all dimensions. I knew how to 'line out' a pair of shafts on a plank, and had in fact lined and helped saw on the saw-pit hundreds of them, before I understood, thinking it over, why this method came right. So too it was years before I understood why a cartwheel needed a certain convexity although I had seen wheels fall to pieces for want of it. It was a detail most carefully attended to by the men in my shop; but I think none of them, any more than myself, could have explained why it had to be so.

Some things I never learnt at all, they being all but obsolete even in that primitive shop. To say nothing of square-tongued wheels – a mystery I still think of with some awe – there was the placing of the 'tines' in a wooden harrow that remained an unknown secret to me. The opportunities of investigating it had been too few when cast-iron harrows, ready-made, banished the whole subject from our attention. I just learnt how the harrow was put together to be hauled over the field by one corner; but the trick of mortising the teeth – the 'tines' – into it so that no two cut the same track – this was known to one elderly man but never to me. The same man also failed to teach me how to 'line out' a wooden axle. Indeed, he forgot it himself at last. So it happened that when an ancient dung-cart arrived, needing a wooden axle for its still serviceable wheels, nobody was quite sure how to mark out the axle on the bone-hard bit of beech that was found for it. It was then that my rather useless schooling came in handy for once. With a little geometry I was able to pencil out on the beech the outlines of an axle to serve (in its clumsier dimensions) the better-known purposes of iron. Yet I have no doubt that the elderly wheelwright's tradition would have been better, if only he could have remembered it . . .

The skilled workman was the final judge. Under the plane (it is little used now) or under the axe (it is all but obsolete) timber disclosed qualities hardly to be found otherwise. My own eyes know because my own hands have felt, but I cannot teach an outsider, the difference between ash that is 'tough as whipcord', and ash that is 'frow as a carrot', or 'doaty', or 'biscuity'. In oak, in beech, these differences are equally plain, yet only to those who have been initiated by practical work. These know how 'green timber' (that is, timber with some sap left in it, imperfectly 'seasoned') does not look like properly dried timber, after planing. With axe or chisel or draw-shave they learn to distinguish between the heart of a plank and the 'sap'. And again, after years of attention, but nohow else, timber-users can tell what 'shakes' are good and what bad. For not all shakes, all natural splits, in seasoned timber are injurious. On the contrary it was an axiom in my shop that good timber in drying was bound to 'open' (care had to be taken to prevent it from opening too far) and that timber must be bad, must have lost all its youthful toughness, if the process of drying developed no shakes in it . . .

The coming of the sawyers at last – I think all the summer they worked in the woods, where the temporary saw-pits were without shelter, and where the men worked at cutting posts and rails and so on for landowners – the coming of the sawyers, towards winter time, when a roof over their heads became desirable, woke up the master wheelwright to a new interest in the timber he had bought. The proof was beginning, personal to himself. His judgement in buying those trees was put to its first test now. Its last was yet far ahead. Not until the seasoned timber was proven on the workman's bench in five or six years' time would the final verdict be given; but the first test began on the saw-pit, when the sawyers 'opened' the yet 'green' or sap-filled tree. What did it look like? The wheelwright was most eager to know how it looked, that heart of ash or oak or elm, of so many decades standing, which no eye had ever seen before. Lovely was the first glimpse of the white ash-grain, the close-knit oak, the pale brown and butter-coloured elm. Lovely, yet would it dry into hard tough timber? Was the grain as straight as had been hoped? And that knot – right through one plank – how far did it go into the next? Every fresh tree, as the sawyers cut out and turned over the planks, at last gave rise to questions like these.

The oaks under the saw had the fresh scent of the forest, nameless as their colour. Elm didn't smell nice – an unclean smell. Sometimes from the ash came fumes as of wood burning. Had the saw – it often grew too hot to touch – actually set something afire? But no. That penetrating odour, so disquieting in a woodshop until you knew its source, merely told that the ash-tree on the pit would probably turn out to be 'black-hearted'. A narrow band as if of ink-stain ran along the very core of the central planks. It was supposed to reduce their value slightly; but the wheelwright was thinking of use in his shop; and I, for my part, never grieved to see or to smell black-hearted ash. The texture of the grain told me more than the colour did.

Before ever the sawyers could begin, there was much for the owner of the timber to do, in deciding what they should cut it into. No doubt a builder or a shipwright would want different sizes and shapes, but no needs can have been more exacting or diverse than the old-fashioned wheelwright's. Length, thickness, 'turn' or curve, were all more or less fixed by traditions ever renewed, and even the sort of timber for different parts of wagon or cart or even wheelbarrow was not wholly a matter of indifference. Those portions which could not be easily replaced but might have to last for forty years or so had to be heart of oak. Nothing less durable would serve. Yet this limitation gave a sure guidance. It almost ear-marked the pick of the oak – the clean-run butts without bad knot or flaw – for the bottom framework of wagon or cart. And this gave the dimensions of the plank to be sawn, wagons taking the preference because the lengths required for them were none too easy to get.

Outside these limits there was indeed much opportunity for substituting one kind of timber for another (excepting in wheel-stuff). Tapering thicknesses of plank, to be sure, were set out for shafts ('sharps' we called them) usually in ash. But oak would do very well for this use, or even good elm, if some length or thickness or curve not prepared for in ash happened to be wanted.

Bearing in mind all the possibilities thus open, the wheelwright dealt carefully with each tree, deciding first the lengths it should be cut into, and perhaps altering his plans altogether if a bad knot after all turned out to be in the wrong place, or if the original intention would have involved too great waste in the total length. With a little pinching the measure here, and a little stretching there, it was usually possible to rescue odd and otherwise wasted inches and get them all together at the top into the two feet or so required for a 'felloe-block'. Lastly, the various points for cross-cutting the tree were scratched with a 'race' – a sort of knife with point turned back and sharpened at the bend for this especial purpose – and this done the wheelwright might pass on to the next tree. If he was really master of his timber, if he knew what he had already got in stock and also what was likely to be wanted in years to come, he kept a watch always for timber with special curve, suitable for hames, or shaft-braces, or wagon-heads, or hounds, or tailboard rails, or whatever else the tree-shape might suggest.

And when the sawyers had been instructed, still it was well to be near their work. Besides, the felloe-blocks, sawn down the middle, could often be profitably sawn again; and to pencil out the shapes on them gave the wheelwright much scope to exercise his ingenuity and his knowledge. It was in fact a fascinating task. I have spent hours at it beside the saw-pit. It must have been a cold job too. For it was always winter work; and sometimes snow lay on the felloe-blocks. It was cold, to handle them; cold to stand hour after hour trying the varying felloe-patterns on them. At least so I should suppose now; yet I have no recollection of feeling the cold at the time. The work was too interesting. The winter, the timber, the wheelwright's continuous tussle, the traditional adaptation, by skill and knowledge – all these factors, not thought of but felt, to the accompaniment of wood-scents and saw-pit sounds, kept me from thinking of the cold – unless to appreciate that too. Delightful? It was somehow better than that. It was England's very life one became a part of, in the timber-yard . . . Warm work, all this winter chopping of wheel-stuff was, and a good thing too. At six o'clock on a December morning the shop was raw cold. Men coming in out of the dark were glad of heavy work to warm them up before opening the shop to the winter day. As already explained, the windows were not glazed. As soon as the shutters were taken down – a little before breakfast at eight o'clock – the wintry air was free to come in, unless a piercing east wind or a driving snow were screened by putting up one of the shutters again. But of course this could not be effectively done during day-light; until it was dark once more the cold had to be countered by vigorous work. By half-past four or so the winter night allowed a more snug shuttering. The men kept on until six o'clock by artificial light.

'Twasn't much of a light. True, the cracks between the shutters or under the doors looked cosy enough to anyone passing outside, in the dark; but within . . . Fortunately men didn't want a very good light for felloe-chopping or spoke-dressing, for a good artificial light was not to be had in those far-off times. We worked by little hand-lamps of colsa oil. Flat wooden pegs made handles for these lamps. The pegs could be stuck into a movable stand – a 'dummy' as we called it – and the lamp set down close to the work shed a dim but sufficient light on it; otherwise the shop was not lit up . . .

I should soon have been bankrupt in business in 1884 if the public temper then had been like it is now – grasping, hustling, competitive. But then no competitor seems to have tried to hurt me. To the best of my remembrance people took a sort of benevolent interest in my doings, put no difficulties in my way, were slow to take advantage of my ignorance. Nobody asked for an estimate – indeed there was a fixed price for all the new work that was done. The only chance for me to make more profit would have been by lowering the quality of the output; and this the temper of the men made out of the question. But of profits I understood nothing. My great difficulty was to find out the customary price. The men didn't know. I worked out long lists of prices from the old ledgers, as far as I could understand their technical terms.

Commercial travellers treated me well – Sanders from Auster and Company, Bryant from Simpson's, Dyball from Nobles and Hoare. The last-named, I remember, fearing that I was in danger of over-stocking, could hardly be persuaded to book an order for four gallons of varnish, when he was expecting it to be for only two gallons. It was not until customers had learnt to be shy of my book-learned ignorance, my simplicity, my Ruskinian absurdities, that they began to ask for estimates, or to send their work elsewhere.

The steadiness of the men was doubtless what saved me from ruin. Through them I felt the weight of the traditional public attitude towards industry. They possibly (and properly) exaggerated the respect for good workmanship and material; and I cannot blame them if they slowed down in pace. Workmen even today do not understand what a difference this may make to an employer. The main thing after all (and the men in my shop were faithful to it) was to keep the business up to a high level, preserving the reputation my father and grandfather had won for it. To make it pay – that was not their affair. Certainly they taught me how to be economical, in 'lining-out' the timber and so on; but the time came when I found it needful to curb their own extravagance, scheming all sorts of ways, for instance, to get three shafts out of a plank, where a too-fastidious workman would have cut only two. It rarely happened the other way about, rarely happened that the condemnation of a piece of timber came from me; but it did happen, not infrequently, that a disgusted workman would refuse to use what I had supplied to him.

In this temper the shop, I feel sure, turned out good work. Especially the wheels which George Cook used to make were, I am bound to think, as good as any that had been built under the eyes of two experts like my father and his father. Cook, it is pretty sure, took his own time; but what a workman he was! There was another wheelwright in the shop whose wife used to take out garden produce in a little van, and when the van wanted new wheels, this man would not make them himself but asked that George Cook might make them. Truly, it was a liberal education to work under Cook's guidance. I never could get axe or plane or chisel sharp enough to satisfy him; but I never doubted, then or since, that his tiresome fastidiousness over tools and handiwork sprang from a knowledge as valid as any artist's. He knew, not by theory, but more delicately in his eyes and fingers . . .

There was no machinery, or at any rate there was no steam or other 'power', in my father's shop in 1884. Everything had to be done by hand, though we had implements to serve machine-uses in their feeble way. I myself have spent hours turning the grindstone. It stood under a walnut tree; and in sunny weather there might have been worse jobs. Only, sometimes the grinding lasted too long – especially for a new tool, or for an axe. Cook was a terror in this respect. Time seemed no object with him; he must get his edge. And he had a word I used to wonder at. For when a new plane or chisel proved over-brittle, so that a nick chinked out of it and needed grinding wholly away, Cook used to look disapprovingly at the broken edge and mutter, 'Crips.' What was that word? I never asked. Besides, Cook was too deaf. But after some years it dawned upon me that he had meant 'crisp'.

Another implement to be turned with a handle was a drill, for drilling tyres for the blacksmiths. To put this round, under its horizontal crank, was harder work than turning the grindstone. The shaft of it went up through the ceiling to a loft, where a circular weight – a heavy iron wheel in fact – gave the pressure on the drill. Men took turn at drilling, for it was often a long job. I don't remember doing much of this; yet I well remember the battered old oil-tin, and the little narrow spoon, and the smell of the linseed oil, as we fed it to the drill to prevent over-heating.

More interesting – but I was never man enough to use it – was a lathe, for turning the hubs of wagon- and cart-wheels. I suspect it was too clumsy for smaller work. Whenever I think of this, shame flushes over me that I did not treasure up this ancient thing, when at last it was removed. My grandfather had it made – so I was told. Before his time the hubs or stocks of wheels had been merely rounded up with an axe in that shop, because there was no lathe there, or man who could use one. But my grandfather had introduced this improvement when he came to the shop as a foreman; and there the lathe remained until my day. I had seen my father covered with the tiny chips from it (the floor of the 'lathe-house' it stood in was a foot deep in such chips), and too late I realized that it was a curiosity in its way . . .

But the want of machinery was most evident in the daily task of cutting up plank or board for other work, and of planing and mortising afterwards. We had neither band-saw nor circular saw. Most of the felloes were shaped out by adze and axe; the pieces for barrow-wheel felloes were clamped to a woodman's bench (for they were too short and small for an axe), and sawed out there by a boy with a frame-saw (I hated the job – it was at once lonely and laborious); the heavy boards were cut out (and edged up) with a hand-saw, being held down on the trestles with your knee (it was no joke to cut a set of one-inch elm boards for a wagon-bottom – your arm knew about it); but all the timbers for framework of wagon or cart, or harrow or plough or wheelbarrow, were cut by two men on a saw-pit . . .

Of the stock (the nave or hub) I hardly dare speak, such a fine product it was, and so ignorant about it do I feel. It is true that I learnt to buy stocks with confidence in my own judgement: I seasoned them, chopped them into shape, chose them at last even to satisfy Cook. Nay, he occasionally asked my opinion, if anything dubious was discovered in working. But, as I had never enough skill of hand and eye myself, I always entrusted the actual turning and mortising of stocks to a trusty man – Cook as long as he lived, and after him preferably Hole. These men, I knew, would sooner have been discharged than work badly, against their own conscience. So I left the stocks to them, only liking to look at each stock when it was brought from the lathe, and to 'weight' it (poise it) in my arms and hear the wheelwright say, 'Rare stock that.' His enthusiasm was catching. I felt a glow of pride in having ministered, however humbly, to so noble a tradition. Then I left the stock again to the workman.

A lumpish cylinder in shape – eleven or twelve inches in diameter and twelve or thirteen inches from end to end – a newly turned stock was a lovely thing – to the eyes, I thought, but more truly to sentiment, for the associations it hinted at. Elm from hedgerow or park, it spoke of open country. Well seasoned, it was a product of winter labour, of summer care in my own loft under my own hands. Long quiet afternoons it had lain there, where I could glance from the stocks across the town to the fields and the wooded hills. I had turned it over and over, had chopped the bark away, had brushed off the mildew while the quiet winter darkness had stolen through the shed, and at last I had chosen the stock for use, and put it into Cook's hands . . .

So, when I had had my look, the wheel-maker – Cook or another – carried the stock to his bench, there to mark on it with straddling compasses the place for the first auger-holes, preliminary to mortising it for the spokes. A tricky job this. One young man, I remember, marking out his stock, prepared for an odd number of spokes – eleven or thirteen; though, every felloe requiring two, the spokes were always in even numbers; which error he did not detect until he had bored his stock and spoilt it. Too big for the fire, and too cross-grained to be easily split and thrown away, it lay about for months, an eyesore to the luckless youth who had spoilt it and a plain indication that it is not quite easy to mark a stock correctly.

Likewise was it not altogether a simple thing, though the skilled man seemed to find it easy enough, to fix the wobbly stock down for working upon. It was laid across a 'wheel-pit' – a narrow trench with sills, about three feet deep – where iron clamps, themselves tightly wedged into the sills, held the stock steady back and front. Then the mortices were started, with auger-holes. How easy it looked! In my childhood I had heard the keen auger biting into the elm, had delighted in the springy spiral borings taken out; but now I learnt that only a strong and able man could make them.

The holes being bored, and before the actual mortising could begin, a gauge was attached to the front end of the stock, to be a guide for the

coming operations. This gauge was a slender bar of wood, almost a lath –
swinging round like one hand of a clock, but extending three feet or so
beyond the stock. At the outer end of it a thin sliver of whalebone pro-
jected just so far as the front of the spokes would come if they had the
right 'dish'. Note that. The spokes would have to lean forward a little
bit; and the gauge was set so that this might be attended to even in mortising the stock. Before ever a spoke was actually put in the wheelwright
tested the place for it, shutting one eye and squinting down with the
other to see that the front edge of the mortise was properly in line with
the whalebone sticking out from the gauge. The principle was very much
like a marksman's taking his aim by foresight and backsight. One mortise
having been cut, the stock was levered round with an iron bar so that the
opposite mortise could be cut, and thus it was done all round, splinters
or borings often dropping clear, right through the stock from one side
to the other into the wheel-pit. The uncut ribs of wood left between the
mortises were called 'meshes' – a word that will be wanted again. I do
not think we shall want again the word 'buzz' – the name for the strange
three-cornered chisel used for cleaning out the mortices of a stock and,
to the best of my belief, used for nothing else, unless for enlarging the
central hole in the stock. And now – how dare I go on to describe that
swinging drive of the wheelwright's action, fixing the spokes into the
stock? Prose has no rhythm for it – the spring, the smashing blow recurrent at just the right time and place. The stock is to be imagined, ready at
last, clamped down across the wheel-pit. From the front of it the gauge
slants up; the dozen or fourteen spokes are near at hand, each with its
tenon or 'foot' numbered (in scribbled pencilling) to match the number
scribbled against its own place in the stock. For although uniformity has
been aimed at throughout, still every mortise has been chiselled to receive its own special spoke, lest the latter should by chance have had any
small splinter broken away after all. The true wheelwright would not
take that chance. He intended that every spoke should really fit tight;
and there he has the spokes all numbered, to his hand.

He picks up one in one hand, and with sledge-hammer in the other,
lightly taps the spoke into its own mortise. Then he steps back, glancing
behind him belike to see that the coast is clear; and, testing the distance
with another light tap (a two-handed tap this time) suddenly, with a leap,
he swings the sledge round full circle with both hands, and brings it
down right on the top of the spoke – bang. Another blow or so, and the
spoke is far enough into the mortise to be gauged. Is it leaning forward a
little too much, or not quite enough? It can be corrected, with batterings
properly planted on front or back of top, and accordingly the wheelwright
aims his sledge, swinging it round tremendously again and again, until
the spoke is indeed 'driven' into the stock. It is battered over on the top,
but the oak stands firm in the mortise, to stay for years.

For an hour or so, until all the spokes had been driven into a wheel,
this sledge-hammer work went on, tremendous. I have seen nothing else
like it. Road-menders greatly smite an iron wedge into the road they are

breaking up; blacksmiths' mates use a ponderous sledge at some of their work; foresters, cleaving, make great play with beetle and wedges; but so far as I have noticed, these men (like the 'Try-Your-Strength' men at a country fair) do not really know how to use sledge or beetle. They raise it up above their heads and bring it down, thump, with all the force of strong arms; but a wheelwright driving spokes, though not necessarily a very strong man, was able, with knack, to strike more powerful blows, and many of them too, in succession. With one hand close under the head he gave the sledge a great fling, then slipped the same hand down the handle, to help the other hand hold it in and guide it truly round its circle. By the time it reached the spoke the sledge had got an impetus. With the momentum of a stone from a sling, it was so to speak hurled down on its mark, terrific . . .

Paul Evett
*compositor**

Paul Evett was born at St Peters, Jersey, in 1886, the son of a battery sergeant-major in the Royal Artillery. The family later moved to Dukinfield, Cheshire, where he attended school to the age of eleven, leaving to work in a rope-and-twine factory. Having acquired an interest in printing, he was apprenticed to a printing firm in Colchester for six years, and on becoming a journeyman compositor in 1906 began to move about southern England in search of experience and variety of scene. The extract describes his progress up to 1912, by which time he was becoming an active member of the Typographical Association and was involved in a strike in Newport, Monmouthshire in 1911 over the employment of a woman monotype-operator. After the war he became an assistant reader and took a correspondence course from Ruskin College, Oxford, in English grammar; after a spell of unemployment in the early 1930s, he became the reader of the *Law Times* and for the *Financial Times* until 1940.

The extract is an interesting comment on the printing trade at the beginning of the century. Although a long-unionized industry, only 40 per cent of printers were trade unionists in 1911, and outside the great cities the union had limited influence. The Typographical Association was trying to enforce the rule that there should not be more than three compositors' apprentices in any shop, however large, and for this reason Evett, like many others, learned

* From *My Life In and Out of Print:* unpublished autobiography.

his trade in non-union shops, in country towns. His memoir also illustrates the slow adoption of recent mechanical inventions – for example, the linotype machine which had come to England in 1889, though Evett did not see one until 1907. The extract may be compared with the important mid-nineteenth-century autobiography of C. M. Smith, *The Working Man's Way in the World*, 1853 (republished 1967).

My first introduction to the printing industry was in Stalybridge, Cheshire, in 1898 when I was about twelve and a half years old. We lived in Dukinfield. I had left school about twelve months before and had been working in a rope-and-twine factory. The reason for leaving school at so early an age was that I had reached the fourth standard and thus qualified to enter an examination entitling me to leave school and take up full-time employment. I passed this examination. I might mention that I am slightly lame, one leg being considerably smaller and a little shorter than the other, due to infantile paralysis, though in other respects I was then quite healthy and robust. The work in the rope-and-twine factory was proving somewhat too strenuous for me, for I had to run along the length of the rope-walk holding the ends of the newly made twine (or bant, as it was locally called), while my gaffer turned the frame on which the skeins were wound at a speed to suit himself rather than out of consideration for my lack of running power . . . Ever since a visit to a Stalybridge printer I had occupied my spare time in cutting type from cork and rubber, and bought myself a little rubber type-set and played about with these with very poor results, even by my own uninformed standards. I would put oil on newspaper pictures and obtain dim transfers therefrom. These occupations induced my parents to apprentice me to a printer.

We had now moved to Colchester and I was bound apprentice to Trinity Printing Works, for six years, to learn the art and mystery of the trade, and to keep out of taverns and houses of ill-repute, etc. The pay for the first six months was 2s. a week; for the second six months 3s. a week; second year 4s., third year 5s., fourth year 6s., fifth year 7s., sixth year 9s. A journeyman's wage was 6d. an hour; 25s. for fifty hours, 26s. for fifty-two hours. We worked fifty hours, and sometimes, when I grew a little older, I did surreptitious over-time.

At first, of course, I was the 'devil' in the machine room, and after learning the mysteries of washing-up and the art of becoming daubed with a variety of oily inks and stinking of paraffin and lye,[1] I learnt to use a lumbering treadle platen[2] without guards, now and again catching my fingers, without serious injury, for the platen seemed to be on springs, or was so loosely fitted that a slight squeeze was almost impossible. I did hurt my knee occasionally, if I kept my leg too straight, as then it got a bang on some underpart of the machine as the treadle reached its highest

[1] A caustic solution made from ashes, used for cleaning ink from type.
[2] A small printing press.

point. Later I was put on a power platen, with a guard, run by a pulley belt. I also ran errands, faster than the errand-boy, assisted one of the minders in melting gelatine and moulding rollers, and helped a comp in making stereos.[1] These two operations were done in a large and stinking cellar, which was also a hide-out when we boys were tired of work or wanted a spree.

I was, at first, fascinated with the working of the flat-bed machines: to see the paper fed and go round the cylinders and to be taken off by the flyers, almost unerringly, and I certainly got a thrill when I was allowed to feed one, which I did ever so nervously at first. One of the machines had no flyers, the printed sheets being taken off the cylinder by hand.

After about a year of this I was posted upstairs to the composing room. As was the case in the machine room so here there were as many apprentices as journeymen, sometimes more, as journeymen were occasionally stood off when work was slack. They were the times for all to join in sorting the huge pile of pie[2] that had accumulated, not always accidentally, I fear.

After some Egbertian experiences and a few times on the carpet, as was the lot of apprentices in those days, I settled down and learnt how to use a stick,[3] and became as good a display comp as the others – nothing special.

During the summer months itinerant comps would call in on us, some for a whip-round to help them on their way from London to Bungay or Beccles; some selling books, setting-rules, sticks, type-gauges, etc. It was said that some of these comps would augment their pay wherever they worked by selling tea, matches, collar-studs or bootlaces, or other knick-knacks.

During my apprenticeship I had learnt but vaguely about a Society for compositors, but had never been told its objects, and from the attitude of our journeymen it seemed to be something to be wary of. And so I bestowed little thought on the matter. I had never met a Society man. And so I went forth with all the effrontery of ignorance.

When the time came I reminded my boss – a kindly man to others, and more so, in a way, to himself – that my term of servitude had expired. He, with mock ingenuousness, expressed surprise that the time had flown so fast and that I had grown to man's stature so quickly, and said that he would keep me on and pay me £1 per week. On my objecting and pointing out that journeymen were paid 25s., he told me I was not a journeyman, but an improver – 'Was there not room for improvement?' he said. I agreed with that as sincerely then as I do now, but I also thought I had been deceived. I have often considered his words, sometimes with benefit, as I did when the first proof of the matter I had set for the *Clacton Times* was the subject of an inquest by the boss and the clicker.[4]

---

[1] Stereotypes, i.e. castings from original type.
[2] A jumbled mixture of type of various sizes and faces.
[3] The tool held by a compositor into which type is set.
[4] The charge-hand over a few men.

Disgruntled with my pay, and anxious to leave home – I had a good home but wanted to be independent – I took the first job offered, which was at —'s, Clacton-on-Sea, where the *Clacton Times* was printed. I was nervous, in a strange place, so different from the roomy, clean office I had left, and among silent strangers. Here I had set, from manuscript copy, three or four stickfuls in brevier[1] in the style of the parish magazine I had been used to. The case was terribly pied. The result was the dirtiest proof I have ever turned out and one which even now causes a blush of shame to mantle neck and cheeks. However, Mr — spoke kindly to me and told me to study the style of the paper and to take more care, in which the clicker acquiesced.

My engagement was for the summer season. My nervousness faded. I improved indeed, and I was put into the piece 'ship'[2] on the paper, where I can truly say I held my own, though I was no whip.[3] I certainly became friendly with the dis-hand, and no doubt gained a bob or two extra by his kindly help when sorts[4] were running short, and gratuitous information when a fat take[5] was next on the spike.[6] But as I often bought him beer I doubt if I benefited very much. The rate of pay was 6d. per thousand ens and my earnings were between 32s. and 38s. per week.

Though we had no whips in our 'ship,' on one occasion when we were extra busy a comp from London (on holiday, I suspected) was temporarily engaged. He was paid daily. I have forgotten his name, even if it were a false one. He proved to be the quickest comp I had come across so far, and his celerity filled me with envy. He was a whip! He was also artful. Too artful for us, simple provincials. During his first week with us he did his quota of dissing[7] as we did, but a good deal quicker. However, one morning he failed to show up. On drawing out the cases in his rack it was found that they were all practically empty. He had whipped up as many thousand as possible during the last day or two, taken his pay and left without doing his quota of dis, thus filching the firm of a nice little sum.

The summer season soon came to an end and so did my engagement. I had spent a very happy time in Clacton, both at work and in the social amenities – the theatre, the Opera House in the then new Palace by the sea, moonlight bathing, cycle rides round the countryside and to my home at weekends, often cycling from Colchester to Clacton on Monday mornings in time for work at 8 o'clock.

Now I had made up my mind that, as I was always likely to remain poor as a compositor, I would in very deed be a journeyman and stay

---

[1] A size of type, now 7-point (72 points = 1 inch).
[2] A 'companionship', i.e. group of men, on piece-work.
[3] A very fast-working compositor.
[4] Pieces of type.
[5] Copy with very short lines.
[6] A pointed wire document-file.
[7] Distributing used type into case.

in one job no longer than about two years, and so see as much of England as I could in this way. Motors were just being introduced, motor buses were few and were always breaking down and temporarily abandoned by the road-side, to be jeered at by us who cycled. Motor coaches had not been thought of. I was very fond of cycling and I loved the country, then so quiet and peaceful, with the pubs open all day and a quart, a pot of two beers costing 5d., bread and cheese (real bread and real cheese) always available at 2d. for as much as I could eat; and real ham sand-wiches, or real cold roast beef, and pickles in plenty. What more did a comp want on the road? Only a job in a country town.

I left Clacton and took a job at Ware with — and Son. The printing office was a small one at the back of a malting, in an overgrown garden, several yards from the river. A pleasant little place in a pleasant little town, where work was also pleasant and the three or four comps-cum-machine-minders a pleasant lot of chaps. But I had not met a Society man and still knew next to nothing of Society matters, and thought of them not at all. This was a seasonal job, chiefly on a local and a county directory, interspersed with bill-heads, pamphlets, posters, parish maga-zine and a series of interesting extracts from an original copy of Izaac Walton's *Compleat Angler*, set in long primer[1] old style with the use of the long 's', for which many pounds of l.c.[2] f's had been purchased so that the inside of the cross stroke had to be chipped off with a pen-knife . . .

Soon after the following Easter this job terminated and I straightway went to Portsmouth, to work in the office of the *Hampshire Post*. Up to now I had never seen a linotype, though, of course, I had heard and read of them. I used to take the *British Printer* regularly. Here I had to help in making up lino slugs[3] into pages, lay them down in sixteens, thirty-twos, etc., and generally do stone-hand's[4] work, set leading articles and ads for the paper, programmes for concerts, bills and posters – and winkle bags. This was the largest works I had so far worked in. I did not like it, but I stayed on to become acquainted with the town and countryside, both of which I thoroughly enjoyed . . .

[After dismissal, when the Workman's Compensation Act was intro-duced] The following Monday morning I started work in the same town in a little office behind a stationer's shop. Here I was engaged, on stab.,[5] on the July Voters' Lists, starting work at 6 A.M. and finishing at 10 P.M. Didn't my feet get tired! Tired of standing. After a few days of this I had to wear canvas slippers before breakfast, unlaced shoes between breakfast and dinner, older shoes in the afternoon and slippers again after tea, and then shamble to my lodgings to supper and welcome bed. On the first day I asked the O.[6] where I might find a 'perch'. He directed me

---

[1] A size of type, now 10-point.
[2] Lower-case type.
[3] Lines of type as cast from the linotype machine.
[4] Compositors who prepare type-pages ready for printing.
[5] The established, or ordinary, wage-rate.
[6] Overseer.

to the w.c. down the yard. He had never heard of a 'perch'. Nor could I
make one, for no old type-box or other material was available, not even
an empty case to turn on end. Anyway, I stuck it out and finished the job.
By the way, dirty post-cards were printed in this little office. The boss
was a member of the local Council or Board of Guardians, or some
official body.

I was fairly well-breeched after gobbling up all this over-time, so I
had a week's holiday in Pompey and roundabout, before taking a job
I had secured in Warwick town. This job, I feel, was my first introduction into the clan of real printers. I called on the boss as soon as I arrived
in the town in the late afternoon. He was a thick-set, round-faced, angry-
looking man. He had but one leg, the other had been amputated at the
thigh, high up. He told me where to go for lodgings, and said he would
not pay extra for over-time. But he did. The wages, if I remember
rightly, were 32s. per week.

The comps were friendly, and the snuff-boxes were freely passed
round. I was soon asked if I belonged to the Typographical Association.
As I did not, I was asked if I would join. I expressed my willingness, not
knowing exactly what I was letting myself in for. This was an 'open
house', but only a very few were not in the T.A. However, I filled in the
forms and duly attended the branch meeting (wet)[1] and was admitted as
a member on the 5th October 1907. I regularly attended chapels and
branch meetings (both of which were always wet), and learnt a lot, of
which I had been totally ignorant before. I was soon made to feel at home
with my fellow comps, an experience more strange than familiar (except
at Ware). I was happy at my work and in getting about that lush and
delightful countryside.

Several other fresh comps started work soon after I arrived. They
were of the travelling fraternity, who had learnt by experience where
seasonal work was to be found, and here they knew that the Autumn
County Voters' Lists were to be printed; also the Warwickshire County
Directory. T.A. Travelling Cards were then expiring.

And here, I would like to mention, was something the like of which I
have never seen elsewhere. The whole of this establishment was housed
in one wide and very long room with stone floor. At one end near the
entrance door were the machines, the one mono-caster[2] and the key-
board; then trestle tables at which folders and binders worked and on
which paper was stacked. The rest of the floor space to the other end was
the composing department. The boss's house was at the front of the
works and a little to one side. At the extreme end of the composing department was a sort of wooden gallery, elevated on baulks of timber and
reached by a fixed step-ladder. On racks all round this gallery were
hundreds of double-column all-metal galleys, quite new in appearance.
On these galleys were the pages of the whole County Voters' Lists, two

[1] Alcoholic drinks allowed.
[2] A machine casting single letters.

pages, close up, to each galley, with brand-new reglets[1] between each column dividing the address column from the name column, and so on. Most of the type was new, once-printed founders' type – Caslon long primer, I believe – a few were mono-set. All the galleys were numbered and the numbers corresponded to a MS. list indicating their contents. There was no difficulty in locating a specific galley.

So our chief job was to correct the pages according to the Registration Officer's up-to-date copy. Besides all these galleys was another series of hundreds of further galleys, single-column, bearing all the pages of type for the County Directory. I believe so many galleys of standing type in so limited a space is unique, to say the least.

Now, the boss, it was said, had been a schoolmaster, and had lost his leg through being kicked by a schoolboy whom he was chastising. He was certainly a temperamental old chap. He also suffered from an obvious rupture, which at times would confine him to his bed, where, it was also said, he throve on a bottle or two of whisky till he was well enough to get up again. He would spend hours on end sitting on a high stool peering into the mono-caster, with his hands and chin resting on his crutch. And he hated to be disturbed while thus engaged, and would wield his crutch at any would-be intruder, which once unluckily caught his wife and felled her. She at one time had been his servant or housekeeper.

During one of the bouts mentioned above, after I and the other imported comps had been there only a few weeks, we received a week's notice to leave. No reason was given. I was perturbed; but I need not have been, for at the weekend the notices were withdrawn. The old man was well again; and on the Monday following he issued a notice that on a certain date the whole firm would have the day off to attend the County Show at Kineton, travelling there in four horse-brakes, all expenses to be paid by him, including reasonable refreshment and meals. It was a glorious autumn day, a lovely ride, and a cheery crowd, and plenty of food and beer. The cavalcade of brakes was headed by the old man driving a high gig drawn by a first-class fast-trotting pony, his wife sitting beside him. This mode of travel round the countryside was a favourite pastime of his. And a smart turn-out it was. He was known to be a connoisseur of horseflesh, as well as of whisky. But print is really my theme.

In the works another pastime of his was to hop up the stairway to the gallery of racks, unbeknown to anyone (but not always) and to spy on us as we worked, and then, unexpectedly, to thunder at anyone he thought was miking. At one time one of the labourers in the machine room got into trouble and was spending a month in Warwick Gaol. The old man sent food to his wife and family and saw that they were cared for, and took the man back into his employ on release.

The Voters' Lists, of course, grew monotonous, though the Directory

[1] Strips of wood, not type-high.

was interesting enough, teaching me some interesting facts about the
county, some of which I verified on my cycle-rides through that delightful
county. Stratford-on-Avon and Leamington were of course favourite
haunts. I had to go to Leamington for my weekly bath – chalybeate
water 6d.; ordinary water 3d. I have tried drinking this spa water, but the
ordinary sort is better, and the local beer was better still. I did not worry.
I knew the job would not last long and I had, up to then, had no difficulty
in getting a new one. In the following spring I got the sack and went
home to Colchester, where my father was very ill. I got a job in the town,
in a small print-shop behind a stationer's shop.

Spottiswoodes were setting up their printing works there at the time
and I applied there for a job, and was told I would be notified when the
type arrived and would be given the job of laying the cases. But when the
manager found that I was a member of the T.A. he turned me down and
gave the job to a tram-conductor who had been a comp. Anyway, my
present job suited me for a time, and then I went to Chelmsford, to —'s
(an open house), where a variety of work was done, and a lot of council
minutes and the like, and the inevitable Voters' Lists set on piece. It
was a free-and-easy place, with a genial O. He was so genial that rather
than let me, or anyone for that matter, pop out to get a packet of Woodbines, he would get them himself. He was himself an inveterate cigarette-
smoker.

At 10 A.M. the boy collected our cans and went for our beer. If he happened to be late any morning, one of the comps would hit three times
with a shooting-stick[1] on a suspended chase,[2] at which we would cry at
the tops of our voices: 'Be-err!' and up would pop the O., saying, 'All
right, boys, he won't be long.' So long as we kept sober and did our work
it was not against the rules to bring in what beer or other refreshment we
wished to. This place was another converted dwelling-house, with cellar
for the machines, the two floors above being occupied by the composing
department. All was very cramped and the place rather dilapidated. But
I stayed on, chiefly because my father was still very ill. I would cycle
home nearly every weekend to see how things were there and to pay my
T.A. subs as there was no branch in Chelmsford.

When my father died and my mother settled, I applied for and got a
job in Newport, Monmouthshire, at —'s. This was another printing-
works behind a stationer's shop, where quite a good class of jobbing work
was done, and it was a full-Society house. Newport printers were very
well organized, under the very able leadership of Bill Humphrys, branch
secretary. The bosses were, as a rule, somewhat antagonistic to Society
activities.

The largest printing works in the town went so far as to employ a lady
mono operator, and paid her, as they said, 'within an ace' of the T.A.
rate. She was offered (it was alleged) T.A. membership, but refused it.
This encroachment the chapel and the branch, and the local Federation,

[1] A tool used to secure type in a chase.
[2] An iron frame surrounding type.

would not stand, and after fruitless conferences, all the employees (except apprentices) tendered strike notices and ceased work. All Federation members were organized into pickets, and we persuaded many would-be employees to return whence they came, often buying their railway tickets for the journey. We marched in noisy processions behind the blackleg O. from his work to his lodgings, and argued with those who had accepted employment with the firm, but mainly kept out of trouble with the police, who looked on without interfering. Tonypandy was not far away, where Mr Winston S. Churchill, then Home Secretary, had recently called out the military. So we were careful. Most of us were English, though there was a sprinkling of hot-headed Welshmen in our ranks who, when we received an offer of help from the Dockers' Union, clamoured for accepting it. Thankfully, they did not prevail, or arson, or worse, might have resulted. The 'Fair Wage Clause' was invoked in the Council Chamber, in local authorities governing public-utility undertakings, and others for whom the firm did the printing, and the firm felt the pinch.

Up till then I had met only two London comps, neither of whom had impressed me favourably. I was soon to see and talk to some more. These had been recruited in London, locked in 'engaged' compartments on the train and released at the station before Newport, to be brought by cars from there to their lodgings, which had been provided for them in a common lodging-house not far from their work place. How we learnt this information I don't now know, but it very likely was from the apprentices, who were very helpful in passing inside information to us. But it was sound. Some of us picketed the lodgings, in ones and twos, at a little distance, and when the conveyance arrived converged on them. A few of us (I was one) mixed with blacklegs and entered the house and into the room where their guide led them.

It was dusk and we had not been noticed. The guide left the room and we quickly and earnestly explained the position to these poor chaps, most of whom looked so down-and-out that it was hard to believe they were skilled craftsmen or other than poor street-gutter beggars.

We persuaded three or four of them to come to the branch secretary, much to the chagrin of the guide when he returned to the room. Out of branch funds we bought their tickets and packed them back to London, with an extra bob or two in their pockets.

It took a long time, but eventually the firm came back into the fold, after their former employees had dispersed themselves far and wide. Oh what trouble one woman can cause! . . .

However, two years were up and I wanted a change. I inserted an ad in the *Printers' Register*, which I knew the boss read, for it was through that periodical that he had engaged me. The week my ad, appeared I received notice, but had received no replies. After hanging about Newport for a week or two I jumped on my bike and rode as far as Reading (barring the journey from Portskewit to Pilning through the Bristol Channel tunnel). Next day I rode to Gravesend, the only time I have ridden through London, and the only part of the ride I did not enjoy. I had always fought shy of London, whether for work or pleasure. It could then offer me neither. I am not a real countryman, but a provincial who loves the country and country towns rather than cities with their 'fretful stir unprofitable and fever of the world'.

It was now 1912. I applied personally for a job at Harmsworths (later the Amalgamated Press, now Fleetway Printers Ltd) at Rosherville, just outside Gravesend. I was laughed at. No comps had been employed there since the 1911 London comps' strike (except a stone-hand or two). The branch secretary, the jovial, rotund, snuff-taking Freddy Newton, sent me off to Chatham, to —'s, where the *Chatham Observer* was (and still is) printed. Here my chief work was the setting of an Esperanto dictionary, six different founts of type being used. I very soon learnt Esperanto, and was made a sort of clicker of the small 'ship' of two or three comps. Other work was the *Esperanto Journal*, the usual small display jobs, and the *Sapper* and other R.E.s work dealing with the part the R.E.s had taken in the Peninsular War and in which I found a deal of interest. This job lasted longer than expected owing to a type-founders' strike holding up deliveries of necessary sorts for the dictionary. This was a full-union shop and Bill Cable the able T.A. branch secretary. He was a good chap and did all he could for the branch members. The district sections of the T.A. were coming into full swing with beneficial effects on members seeking work, as was exemplified in my own case when this job finished. Bill Cable got in touch with the district secretary, who fixed a job for me right away at the Salvation Army Printing Works (The Campfield Press) at St Albans. My railway fare was paid, but I cycled from Gravesend on the Sunday and started work on Monday, in what I consider the best printing works I have ever been in. It was a six weeks' job on a catalogue for Garstins of London, bag- and trunk-makers. At 8 A.M. all employees were gathered in the entrance hall for a religious service conducted by the Works Chaplain, whose place was occasionally taken by other S.A. officers. A Salvation Army comp wielded a concertina to lead the hymns, and the flourishes and arpeggios he introduced into the tunes delighted us by their variety and the skilful abandon with which he executed them. He was a master of the instrument. During the services, which usually occupied about ten minutes, frequent exhortations were made to those at the rear of the hall to desist from reading their newspapers and attend to the Word as expounded by the elect – but with little avail, I am afraid. On special occasions the service lasted a good deal longer, but no one minded that. We had both morning and afternoon tea-breaks, providing our own milk and tea and sugar, and the mid-day break was one hour and a quarter. The place was painted white or cream throughout, was light, airy and clean.

The catalogue finished, I was given notice, but at the same time was informed by the clicker of the room, honest Albert Bolton, that should I wish to come back again I was to keep in touch with his brother Bill. Brother Bill was the hard-working, conscientious T.A. district and branch secretary. He was also the reader on our floor, and a very likeable

man. If Brother Bill knew where to find me he would let me know when a
vacancy occurred. He did more: he sent me straight to Redhill, giving
me my Removal Card to Mr Fitch, the branch secretary there, who
worked with his father-in-law in the office in which the vacancy had
occurred...

Arthur Gill
*gold-beater and ticket-writer**

Arthur Gill was born in a back-to-back house in Claro Place, Leeds,
in 1887, which was still standing when the autobiography was
written in 1969; he was the second of eight children, four of whom
died when young. His father was a boot- and shoe-repairer, though
he had served his apprenticeship as a teazle-setter of superfine
cloths, which were out of fashion by the time he had qualified.
Arthur's education was at the Meanwood Road Board School and
the Primitive Methodist Sunday School; he left school at thirteen,
having shown marked ability at drawing and painting, and began
work with a gold-beater. From here he moved to a sign- and ticket-
writer, becoming a highly skilled hand eventually earning 35s. a
week. By 1914, when he married, the hand-written-ticket trade was
beginning to decline and he was working increasingly on advertisement slides for use in the cinemas. During the slump of 1930 he set
up his own business at home, producing showcards, tickets, church
posters and, occasionally, illuminated addresses at £10 each. He
was Superintendent of the Sunday School for many years, and continued to draw, paint and work part-time until he retired at eighty
in 1967.

The extracts describe his work as a gold-beater, a craft which had
remained basically unchanged since at least the Middle Ages, and as
a commercial artist in the once-flourishing trade of ticket-writing.

My working days from 1900

I started my working life in November of the year 1900. My first job
was a very unusual one. Fortunately this job had been kept open for me,
for my brother Will had told Mr Barnes a week or two before my thir-
teenth birthday that he had a brother nearly ready for leaving school. As
Mr Barnes was wanting a boy, he said he would keep the job open for me.

* From *I Remember: Reminiscences of a Cobbler's Son,* unpublished autobiography.

Mr Wallace Barnes was a gold-beater; his premises were situated in Bramley's Yard, Lowerhead Row, Leeds . . . Wallace Barnes was a tall elderly man with a white beard, jovial and very well read. Folk round about used to consult him now and again when they had problems or wanted information.

He had a son and a daughter working for him at the time: Gilbert and Madeline. My first duty was to sweep the floors every morning – and to sieve the sweepings into a large barrel. These sweepings (about twice a year I think) were sent to the smelters, for which Wallace Barnes received remuneration. I don't know how much, but it was evidently a worthwhile proposition. The actual beating of the gold was done on a huge stone slab in the basement. I think about two 'beatings' of gold were done each week. A beating consisted of an ingot of gold about three inches long, one inch wide and about a quarter-inch thick. Wallace Barnes got his gold from various sources. He used to buy little nuggets of gold, sometimes old jewellery and trinkets, and what was called gilders' skewings. In those days huge ornamental gilded picture frames were very fashionable and high-class picture-framers used to gild these frames with genuine 23-carat English gold leaf (loose gold – not transfer). The result was that quite a lot of loose bits of gold leaf used to fly about and settle on their benches and on their floors. The gilder had what was called a gilders' rubber; with this he just touched the bits of gold leaf lying about, the bits sticking to the rubber. Once the rubber had got the gold on to it – it stuck! When the gilder thought his rubber had picked a good quantity of gold bits, he took it to the gold-beater who immediately put a match to it, and set it alight (for the rubber was inflammable); he then weighed the residue in very fine scales and paid the gilder in cash according to the weight of the residue. Occasionally the gold-beater couldn't procure enough gold for a beating, and I remember on one occasion old Wallace Barnes putting his hand into his pocket and pulling out one or two golden sovereigns and putting them into the melting pot to make up the weight required. Gold sovereigns were currency in those days. All the same I don't think it was strictly legal to deface the coin of the realm.

The process of beating gold is very interesting. First of all, the gold is put into a small melting-pot, a certain amount of silver or copper added, according to the shade of gold required. It had to be one part metal to twenty-three parts gold to make it 23-carat. Pure 24-carat gold could not be used, as pure gold is too soft for beating – it would break up into pieces before it was beaten to the required thinness (which my old boss once told me was 250,000th part of an inch). If one puts a gold leaf up to the light, it can be seen through – it is a blueish-green colour. It had to be beaten thin, otherwise it wouldn't be a paying proposition. When the gold was melted in the furnace, it was poured into a mould, making the ingot (before-mentioned). This was then put through a steel roller, constantly increasing the pressure; this lengthened it without increasing the width. I've often helped to twine the rolling machine (it reminded me of when I helped mother to twine the wringing-machine on washing days). The gold eventually came out in a long ribbon a few yards long, and about as thick as the tin on an ordinary tin can. This was then cut with scissors into small squares (approximately one inch square). These squares of gold were placed in the centre of pieces of vellum about four inches square (there would, I think, probably be sixty or seventy pieces of vellum); they were then bound together by slipping a parchment band round each side, thus enclosing everything. This was called a 'kutch'.

The kutch was now ready to be placed on the slab to be hammered. This was done with the gold-beater's heaviest hammer (about twenty pounds in weight). The beating went on till the little gold squares spread to the edges of the kutch. The pieces of gold were taken out separately and laid out on a cushion of smooth leather and cut into quarters (these quarters would be approximately two inches square); these squares were then put between gold-beaters' skins (same as in the kutch). These skins were about six inches square; these were fastened with parchment bands again. This lot of skins was called a 'mould'. The beating of the gold started again, but now with a lighter hammer. This went on until the gold spread to the edges of the mould. Again, the gold was taken from the skins with small wooden tweezers and laid on the cushion and cut again into quarters with a gold-cutting knife. These quarters were again laid in the middle of skins. The gold leaves by now were getting thinner – and about a thousand of these skins, with the gold between them, was only about one inch in thickness . . . The beating started again, but now with the gold-beater's lightest hammer. The beating was not now continuous; it had to rest while the gold-beater 'ventilated' it to keep the skins and the gold cool. Continuous beating would make the skins and the gold too hot, and the leaves of gold would break up into pieces. So it went on until the gold spread over the whole skins. The gold was now taken out of the skins with the tweezers and very gently blown flat on to the cushion and cut with special wooden reeds; two reeds parallel to each other, the width of the gold leaves (which are three and a quarter inches square) and fastened together by what I would call a 'bridge handle'. The leaves were cut square-shape by slicing vertical and then horizontal, thus leaving a gold square leaf in the middle. This square was then put in a special gold 'book' between each page, with the aid of the tweezers. There were twenty-five leaves in a book. These books of gold at that time cost 1s. 3d. per book (I think the price in these days of 1969 would be nearer £1 per book). After each beating of gold the skins had to be brushed with brine, back and front, to clean them, and take away any stickiness. All surplus gold, after the squares for the books had been cut, was melted up again for the next beating. I worked at Wallace Barnes for about eighteen months or thereabouts. I left, as I wasn't sure I wanted to be a gold-beater all my life. Also there were only two gold-beating firms in Leeds: Wallace Barnes and Charles White (there are no gold-beaters at the time I'm writing these memoirs in Leeds) . . .

I had now to look out for another job. I got one, and this turned out to be a 'job after my own heart'. A firm of ticket- and showcard-writers, gold-blockers and dealers in advertising novelties called F. Mitchell and Company of Gascoigne Street, off Boar Lane, Leeds, advertised for boys to learn the trade. I applied, and got a job in the ticket and showcard department. Mr Mitchell had four or five really good craftsmen and three or four boys working in this department. I remember the thrill it gave me as I watched these craftsmen wielding the fine sable writers and pens on the cardboard and producing beautifully written showcards and tickets. Most of the lettering on these showcards and tickets was done in outline and our job as boys was to 'fill-in' with sable brushes of differing sizes with the colours required.

Mr Mitchell was a very good boss, and very encouraging to his boys. I remember, after about six months, going to his office to ask for a rise. He said, 'Ask the foreman (Johnny Rider) to give you a few pieces of card and ticket ink to take home, and then show me a sample of your work, and if it's satisfactory, I'll give you a rise.' I put my best into my effort, and he was pleased with my work – and he gave me a rise. Mr Mitchell was a very good businessman, very good-looking, tall, and a fresh complexion. He did quite a lot of travelling himself, and employed two or three other travellers. They were all smartly dressed, with frock-coats and top hats, and among their clients were well known firms who required first-class work. Thus, the firm of F. Mitchell and Company had a reputation for good-class work. He also specialized in advertising novelties.

He also had a gold-blocking department and some of the showcards and tickets were done in this department. This class of work was done by hot presses which stamped the gold-leaf lettering into the showcards and tickets and also for making gold bevelled-edge cards and such-like. It was quite distinct from the handwritten work in the department in which I worked. I was lucky to be working among real good craftsmen, as it gave me the *chance* of eventually becoming one myself. All was going well, when quite suddenly there was a sad calamity. Mr Mitchell had been round the departments, as was his custom on Saturday mornings. He looked as well as ever on this particular Saturday and one could have taken a lease on his life, but when we came to work on Monday morning we were greeted with the sad news that Mr Mitchell was dead. We were all stunned and couldn't take it in for quite a time. And that was a turning-point in the business, which was never again quite the same. Mr Mitchell had a brother Tom (who knew very little about the business) who, along with Mrs Mitchell (who had been separated from her husband), took charge of the business which slowly declined. But more of this later . . .

I wanted to get on as quickly as I could, and get on writing tickets and showcards in addition to filling in and shading. One of the other boys (who lived near Johnny Rider and who was a favourite of his) was given the chance of *writing* small tickets and I seldom got a ticket to *write*, although I knew I could do them as good as this other boy. Soon after this my chance came. Johnny Rider, for some reason or other, left Mitchells. I'm under the impression he got the sack! The outcome of this was the arrival of a new foreman for the ticket-writing department. He was a Mr Smith from Newcastle. He was a very fine craftsman who specialized in designing high-class showcards, and was an expert in stencil-cutting for aerograph work. I once saw him cut two stencils, then with the aid of the aerograph (which is a high-powered spray) he produced a beautiful reproduction of the old-fashioned ginger-beer bottle, showing the glass marble in the neck of the bottle – I was simply fascinated – it looked so realistic.

He also designed beautiful floral aerographed showcards of nasturtium flowers and leaves, lovely work indeed. Strange to say, he wasn't expert on actual lettering, but passable. His talent was designing and he stuck to that. Now to relate how my chance came about. In the first place, he was a stranger to us all, he had no favourites among the boys, but he kept his eyes open to find out what we were capable of doing. He gave me a chance of writing a few small tickets, then gradually larger ones. Then he let me have a shot at a bit better work. He soon found out I was very keen and he seemed well satisfied with my work. The result was – I was given better and better-class work to do, and larger showcards to write. I was in my element! Besides using fine sable-hair writers, the pen was used a great deal for doing small lettering on tickets. In those days many high-class jewellers had neat gold bevelled-edged small tickets which were hand-written to put in their windows with the articles they sold. Also high-class tailors and outfitters used (as well as large showcards) what were called 'Mottoes'. These were small tickets about six inches by one inch (often with gold bevel edge) with wordings such as 'Made To Measure', 'As Now Worn', 'Very Fashionable', etc. These mottoes were often written in fine copper-plate script or engrossing. One of the fine craftsmen who worked at Mitchell's at this time was a Mr Crum; he was a little round-shouldered man who looked rather 'crummy' and, to look at him, no one would have taken him to be an expert in penmanship, but he was. He was the most beautiful script copper-plate-writer I have ever come across; in fact, for small lettering of any type he was expert. Whenever I had the chance of watching him wield the pen. I did so, and was fascinated.

My ambition was to emulate him to the best of my ability, and I practised and practised, and eventually my penwork improved more and more until I felt 'quite at home' with the pen, and even now, in my latter years, long after my retirement. I write my own Christmas cards, some with original ink sketches and some with original water-colour sketches, to send to our family and friends year after year, as I have been told they are much appreciated. There was another young man who was married, called Joe Nicholson; he could do some nice work at times, but he was a bit too fond of the booze, especially at weekends. Often on Monday mornings, when his hands were shaky, he would curse and swear as he was trying to control his hands and would ask the foreman to give him

some 'knock off' work that wasn't so particular. I used to feel sorry for
him, as, when sober, he was a nice chap and very friendly. The firm did a
certain amount of poster work, which wasn't as tedious as writing showcards, and Joe came in for most of that. I eventually took up a certain
amount of poster work, in addition to showcard work.

I continued to work at Mitchells for round about four or five years,
and before I left was writing many of their first-class tickets and showcards. I must mention that when Mr Mitchell was living, he introduced
a new class of work. This was sets of 'fashion model' showcards. These
sets usually incorporated two large bevelled-edged stout cards about
twenty-four by eighteen inches, illustrated with figures of fashionably
dressed men, women, boys and girls – and twelve small cards with individual figures dressed in the latest styles.

Mr Mitchell must have been in touch with good printers of these
fashion plates, and he bought them in large quantities. Our job was to
cut them out with scissors. Preparatory work had to be done first. Mr
Mitchell employed a beveller who cut these thick cards with a beautiful
bevelled edge. He then had delicately coloured landscapes painted as
backgrounds for these cards, then came our job of sticking on the cut-out
figures – probably eight to twelve figures on the large cards, and just one
figure on the small ones. They looked beautiful when finished and hundreds of sets were sold.

If I was asked, '*When* was the time of your life?' my answer would be,
'When working for Mr Mitchell!'

It was in the year 1906 when I started work for B. Roberts and Company, advertising contractors and sign-, poster- and ticket-writers. I had
a room of my own to work in, and found myself the boss of my own
department, as the only other person in it was a young chap called
Arthur Spink, who was about a year older than myself. He was a bound
apprentice, and had about a year to go before his time was up at the age of
twenty-one. Unfortunately for him, he was absolutely hopeless at the
job, and should never have been bound to it. This was well known
throughout the Works, and he had become the 'errand-boy' and general
'mug-about' for anybody who wanted him. I had charge of all the work
that came to my department. I remember on one occasion giving him a
small card to write (about twelve by ten inches) which I could have done
in about half an hour – it took him practically all day, and it was only fit
for the waste-paper basket when finished. After that he was quite pleased
just to 'fill up' any poster or ticket I outlined for him. A few months
after I started work for B. Roberts, he wanted an 'Agreement' with me to
stay till I was twenty-one years of age. This Agreement Form (or rather,
a copy of it) I have saved, and have it before me now as I write in the
year 1969. It is rather amusing to read again this 'Agreement' which is
couched in 'legal jargon' thus:

Between Henry Arthur Gill, of 4, Wharfedale Street, Meanwood Road, Leeds,
of the first part, Arthur Gill, a minor of the age of 19 years and upwards, son of
the said Henry Arthur Gill, of the second part, WITNESSETH that in consideration

of the services of the said Arthur Gill, he the said Henry Arthur Gill, doth for himself, his heirs, executors and administrators COVENANT, promise and agree with the said B. Roberts and Co., their executors and administrators in manner following, that is to say: – that the said B. Roberts and Co. etc. . . .

All this tripe, when it's only an Agreement – *not* an Indenture where a promise is made to teach one a trade – and, by the way, the legal scribe who made out this Agreement couldn't even spell the word 'administrators'. The word is used four times in the Agreement, and in every case is spelled 'adminstrators' (leaving out the letter 'i'). So much for the 'learned'!

However, the Agreement promised me 12s. per week up to December 31st, 1906 – then to June 30th, 1907, 15s. per week – then to December 31st, 1907, 17s. 6d. per week – then to June 30th, 1908, £1 per week – then £1 2s. 6d. until I reached the age of twenty-one years, namely the 24th day of November, 1908. 'B. Roberts & Co. agree to pay for all Bank Holidays, Good Friday and Christmas Day.' Not a vast amount of wage, but one has to remember that this period was *before* the First World War, when money values were not the same as now, in 1969. I soon found out that B. Roberts and Company was a far larger firm than I had ever anticipated. They were advertising contractors as well as sign-writers and poster- and ticket-writers. By far the most important part of the business was the making, designing and writing of theatre advertising curtains. He supplied these to a vast amount of theatres, music-halls, empires, hippodromes, etc. to many towns in England, and Scotland and some in Ireland and Wales. He had a large staff of sign- and curtain-writers, and a goodly number of travellers on the road, getting orders for 'spaces' for advertisements. Large concerns such as Dewars Whisky, W. D. and H. O. Wills, and many other big business people as well as smaller businesses used the theatre curtain medium to advertise their commodities. He also had the programme rights of many theatres, and his travellers canvassed for orders for advertising spaces on these programmes. Ben Roberts was also the Managing Director of Waddingtons, Printers of Camp Road, Leeds (not associated at that time with John Waddingtons, Printers) and all the printing of the programmes was done there. When the pantomime seasons came along Roberts and Company were, for a few weeks before Christmas, very busy indeed preparing special curtains for the panto season and his staff were often working all night during the week or so before Christmas; Ben Roberts used to buy his men fish-and-chip suppers and beer to keep them at it! Mr Taylor was the foreman of the sign and curtain department. (He was another of those very fine craftsmen it has been my good fortune to be associated with.) Many of the curtain spaces required (in addition to the lettering) illustrations of all kinds, for instance, many of the publicans who advertised would have their photograph reproduced on their curtain space. On occasions, some of these publicans would send a 'stamp-size' photo of themselves, and I have been amazed at the fine enlarged reproductions Mr Taylor painted on the curtain space, which were a perfect replica of the original, the resemblance being almost uncanny. Whatever illustrations were required, large or small, intricate, original or any other kind, he could always produce them in the appropriate colouring, and I never knew him to be stuck . . .

T. R. Dennis
*cabinet-maker**

T. R. Dennis was born in Preston, Lancashire, in 1910, and was educated at the Church of England Elementary School from 1915 to 1924. He then began work as an apprentice cabinet-maker, but was sacked in 1931 during the depression and then became self-employed as a joiner until the outbreak of war. He left the Army in 1945 as a staff sergeant, being mentioned in despatches and having attended a Clerk of Works course. After the war he became a Clerk of Works with private architects, with Preston Corporation and with Lancashire County Council, retiring as Chief Clerk in 1971. He has three children, all of whom are university graduates.

The extract describes his early work in a still unmechanized cabinet-maker's shop in the 1920s.

The subject of work now began to come up at home. My father being an Army man had no trade; he was keen on me having one even though this would be a hardship to them as apprentices had little pay, and they may have tools to buy. Of course the G.P.O. was a good body to work for, maybe Bobby Hudson could put a word in; if you started off as a telegraph boy and behaved well, then you may become a postman or even a sorter; a boy had to be four feet eight inches, I was just that. A few weeks before I was due to leave school Mum saw an advert in the *Post* for an apprentice cabinet-maker. I had no idea what one of these was until I was told they made furniture. The following morning quite early I was at Mr Robinson's with Mum. What an ugly man he was; he wore thick glasses, he had a scar on his top lip, partly hidden by a very untidy moustache, he was a thin man. At Mr Robinson's feet sat an airedale dog; I think it fancied my bare knees, several times I thought it was going to stick its teeth in. I could start Easter Tuesday, and think myself lucky, he didn't really need me as he had already started Tom Jackson. I would get 7s. 6d. a week.

On our way home Mum planned how she would put money away each

* From unpublished autobiography. This extract is reproduced by kind permission of the owner, Dr D. Melville, Southampton.

week so I could buy tools. Of course I would need a 'brat'. Mum had to ask what this was, she was surprised when she found out it was an apron. We called at the market for the material, and before long I was trying my brat on. In seven years I would be a fully qualified journeyman; this was something to look forward to (I came out of my time in the depth of the worst depression known). I had planned the night of the interview that I would make my mother a piece of furniture long before I was twenty-one; I knew she would see I got the tools I would require. I stood outside Robinson's well before 8 A.M. on the day I started work, I had clean shoes, a nice white brat, a new dinner-basket for my lunch, and a tin can for my tea. I pictured the workshop to be like the woodwork class; it wasn't quite as I expected.

Tom had started work some week or so before me, and he had the job of showing me around. I was taken to Rushton's the wood-turner; I had to go here for water needed for drinking, and of course the glue-pots. Drinking-water was kept in a bucket at the end of a bench with a piece of ply over to keep dust out. Sam East was the main man; he had been in the war and sometimes could be very depressed. He had no teeth (there was no N.H.S. then, and teeth were about £20 a set). Ben Cooper came next; he had been too young to go to the war, a fiery-tempered individual. Then there was Charlie Green, again too young for the war, he was a nice person; Geoffrey the boss's son was a very weak character of a man, and weak in body. He also had no teeth. He was supposed to be a wood-carver. Bill Shanks and Arthur Small were about eighteen years old, then there was Tom Jackson. I had always been taught to say 'Sir' to older people; Tom took me to Sam East and said, 'This is Jimmie.' I said, 'Hello, Sir.' Imagine my surprise when he said, 'Don't bloody well call me Sir.' I then said, 'Very good, Mr East.' 'And don't call me Mr,' said Sam. This rather shattered me. I had played tricks, etc., but swearing was not so far one of my failings.

We had no fuel other than the shavings and off-cuts of wood, but a big stove had to be kept alight to keep the glue-pots warm, and at mid-day to brew the tea with. This was the youngest boy's job, as was the delivering of furniture to several shops, all carted on a truck. Time seemed to stand still that morning. I had put the kettle on the stove at 11 A.M. as instructed. I had gone to one and all to ask what they required from the shops, first collecting their brew and putting it in the cups or cans ready. What a mess some of it looked, tea, sugar and condensed milk all mixed in a little mustard tin. Mr Robinson had Horlicks. It was ten minutes past 12 when I returned with the dinner shopping. I had had to wait for chips; no tea was brewed, people sat about. When I had brewed Sam's tea and taken it to him I said, 'Sorry I'm late.' The reply was if it occurred again I would get my arse kicked. I then brewed Mr Robinson's milk; he had just come into the room. I went to Bill, the nearest one to me, and asked if he had a spoon to stir the milk with. I was told to stir it up with the glue-stick out of one of the pots, and to make sure that there was plenty of glue on the stick, glue makes weak milk look richer.

I now went for my own dinner. That and my new basket had gone. At this stage I was near to crying, and so hungry. Everyone sat on their bench to take their meal. I had no bench and sat on a box near the fire. Robinson before he started eating blew his nose in the shavings. My, I would have to be careful. In fact, I was not caring if I ever got my dinner, and my word didn't people swear, the four-letter word being the favourite. This to me was a sacred word; I had learnt about babies with this word. My dinner and basket were eventually shown to me on the roof of a lean-to shed. I had little time to get to them before it was 1 P.M.

'Get t'truck out, Tom; first make sure there is a good fire on to keep t'glue hot, and you can take this wardrobe to Brown's.' The shop I had to call at was described and located to me, the robe wrapped and tied to the truck. I was told it should not take me more than three quarters of an hour to get there and back; I would get a lift unloading at the other end. It is a long way to Brown's. I was afraid of being late and I began to run. There is quite an incline near the Parish Church. I had found that the truck was heavy on my arms; I was able to run quite nicely down the hill, I just needed the weight to the back a bit more. So, I lifted the shafts up. Of course the whole lot went up, me as well. There was a clattering of bells, and the tramcar behind me came to a halt. With running, the tipped-up truck had skidded on, and turned into the tram-track. I was helped to get the truck on even keel by passers by, and I heard someone say, 'Someone thinks t'lad's a bloody donkey.' I began to think I was.

When I returned to the works I was asked to get some clean water from Rushton and while there would I ask Joe for some strap oil. I did just that. Never ask any one bigger than yourself for strap oil. If you do you are bent tight over their knee and hit with the flat side of a cutcross saw. What a day; thank goodness it was over. Little did I realize more and worse was to follow.

After the war there had been a bit of a boom. Mr Robinson had done quite nicely out of it all, but things were getting a bit tighter in 1924 when I started work. Robinson himself only did a short day; he started at 10 A.M. and finished at 3.30 P.M. Tricks on us boys were played in his absence. My second day at work I was shown how to make glue-brushes out of cane, to clean the glue-pots and break up cake glue and soak it ready for heating and using the following day. Brushes made from canes are excellent. The cane we used was bought in long lengths and was solid; we cut this to the length required, nicked it about one inch from the end and peeled a thin layer off. After boiling the end for about an hour we would beat the cane and split the fibre, and this could be done again as the brush wore away. Clean glue is essential at all times, and clean pots for it to go in.

I remember I was told on this day about standing about. I had swept up, gone all errands, made glue and brushes, and taken some furniture to the polisher's. When I asked what should I do I was told to clean the drinking bucket out. To do this I was given a piece of sandpaper to scout with; it is surprising what a lot of slime collects. I soon had it bright. I rinsed it well with my hand and cold water, and for my reward I was told to keep it like that.

My third day, till 3.30 more or less as usual, then Robinson went. 'Tom! Come here,' called Sam. I duly obeyed. 'Hold that still while I plane it,' says Sam. I pressed on the wood even harder, only to be told it was still moving. 'Sit on it,' said Sam. This I did. I wondered why I needed to sit on the wood – I had seen them plane it before. I found out. A brawny arm went around my neck and I was pulled flat on the bench. Ben, Bill and Arthur ran across to where Sam had me held. I was of course struggling. When overpowered my trousers were taken down and shirt lifted up. God knows how a girl must feel when molested, I felt awful. My ears were getting wet with the flow of tears running from my eyes as I lay on my back. I was telling them they were rotters, the strongest language I used then. Taunts were being used about my undeveloped body, such as, 'What a little tosser; there is no hair on it.' Then it was agreed that glue was a good thing; the pot was brought and my privates painted. This was not enough, saw-dust was also rubbed in. What a plight to be in. We had no water in the building, or room to hide in. I was also physically hurt as the glue had been quite hot. I sulked and remained uncomfortable until home time. I also wondered what my Father would say and do. I did not tell Mum what had happened – it would be rude; she of course guessed something had taken place and no doubt wondered why I had dashed up to the bathroom, something I never did then without a reminder. Dad did nothing. All apprentices got tricks played on them; if fathers went complaining then boys would be called 'cissies'. I wasn't even asked what had been done to me. But there are tricks and tricks.

Being glued happened to Tom and myself several times in the first few months, but it was also a harder job for all concerned. I was not taken by surprise again and I had started to lash out, and to hurt if I could. 'Tom tells me he can fight you,' I am told. Tom is of course not there. I say, 'I don't care if he can.' The reply to this is that I am a marred arse. Tom is also told when I am not there that I said I could fight him; Tom is not amused, he is older than myself. Eventually we were paired up for the amusement of others; we were egged on to fight and give no quarter, and we did, and I won. I did get a cut or two, but I felt quite proud of the first-aid meted out – a clean pine shaving was used as a bandage, stuck to each side of the wound. I never saw a first-aid box for several years at Robinson's. I think, in fact we all knew, that a law was passed that first-aid boxes had to be available, and kept full. Other jokes that were played on me as time went on were (these were always done from behind) to press about half a pound of putty into your hair; this did make Mum cross, I had to use paraffin to get it clean. On another occasion I had some venetian red powder put on my head. I could not brush it off easily so I went to Rushtons and washed under the tap. This was a mistake – venetian red is a fast dye, and I don't suppose I held my head under the tap long enough to wash the powder out. I had lovely red hair, that is till it grew out. Mother was wild about this and threatened to come to see Robinson. I asked her not to – I would be called soft and they might take it out of me. Tom's mother did come, after he had broken out in a bad rash.

This was the finish of many tricks and work was getting short. Robinson could talk about sackings; also about the competition that was now being felt as his competitors installed machinery and cut him in price. Robinson thought all this out and decided it would be cheaper to do without machines and employ boys instead of men. Hard times were to follow and soon I would be told to start buying tools, I would be going on the bench. Going on the bench and only fourteen and three quarter years; the next apprentice would go errands for me, we would play tricks on them, but not glueing, it's dirty . . .

My parents were quite thrilled to be told I would have to buy some tools. I was to ask Sam East to go with me, he would know what was best. Iron tools like Stanley were not in use then; tools were made out of beech and it was the practice to stand them in oil for a week before using them. This I did. I took particular care in sweeping the bench clean and standing the tools neatly on it for use the day after I had taken them out of oil. The following day when I arrived at work I was amazed to find all my tools missing except the jack plane, and this was glued and nailed to the bench. What was worse, it appeared to have a six-inch nail through it. I learnt that glue is no good in contact with oil, and the six-inch nail was not in the plane – the head of a nail had been cut off and stuck to look as if it had been knocked in.

Tools and you need breaking in. It took some time and I got plenty of practice at first doing the work of a planing machine. One day Robinson came to me and said, 'Here, get on with this oak dressing-table and washstand.' There seemed to be a pile of wood, all oak. I did not know where to start, and when I went to Sam East he told me, 'F— off, you kids will put me out of work one day.' Tom was in the same boat. I eventually went to Charles, the nice man. He said he would help but I had not to be like the rest, cut swearing out, and go with him one night a week to blow the church organ at St Marks where he was the organist . . .

Ted Waters was the apprentice to follow me. He had worked elsewhere, and was a little older than myself and bigger, a serious sort of chap. Not long after his arrival Sam East was sacked. I remember on his last day at Robinson's how he swore and recalled his service to the nation, now his reward. Robinson really bullied us apprentices at work. He played one against the other on how long we took to make similar things. We were even sworn at if he knew we played football at night; he contended if we worked hard we would be too tired for play. On one occasion we were all whistling 'God save the King' when Robinson came in one morning, flew into the room in a rage and said, 'For Christ's sake, if you must whistle, whistle something that makes you work faster.' He then visited each of our benches to examine our work. Being of poor sight his nose touched the wood, and a volley of abuse starting with the four-letter word would follow should there be the slightest thing at fault. If there was nothing to find fault with, you were not doing it fast enough. Work became harder to get, another apprentice was started. Charlie was sacked. Ben worked harder to keep his job, he was the hardest-working man I ever met in my life. He also tried to impede us others – after all we were doing the same type of work as he, and our pay was, starting at fourteen years, 7s. 6d. increasing by 2s 6d. per annum. Labour was easy to get, so many were coming out of work; the labour exchange had great strings of men queueing up; I looked down on the unemployed men. Robinson was a Tory and most dinner-times he would lecture us on a decaying nation – people were lazy, unions were a curse, etc. My father having been a soldier had never during his service been allowed a vote. He was a Tory also, he had just been taught that only Tories were loyal, others were reds; this outlook of course still prevails.

With my other friends we began to saunter around the town at night. We would go around the market when the stalls were taken down, and we were unkind to the children we saw collecting cabbage-leaves and part-bad fruits that had been thrown away. Often they were without shoes or clogs. We were unkind in the way we spoke of them – they were referred to as dirty little bastards, and we bet that their idle father was on the dole. Bob Saunder's father had a tailoring business. They were of course feeling the loss of business; this, however, was put down to the Jews and Burton the tailor. Bob's greatest pleasure was to get us to stand looking into a Burton shop window; he had found out that an assistant when not otherwise engaged stood on a ladder to look over the back of the window and if he saw anyone looking interested he would come outside to try to get them into the shop. Bob would waste his time by making all types of inquiries, then insult him. The poor chap only got a pittance of a wage and had to rely on commission. I began to feel more softhearted. At home my sisters were only doing poorly at work; Louise had now only two looms as against four previously, and she was not lazy. I have seen her cry on a Friday night when she has handed her earnings to Mum. My grammar-school friends also got me into some rough 'do's'. More than once I was landed in to fight some stranger they had picked a fight with, and then backed out. I began to see less of them and more of the boys who went to work.

The effort at work and the energy I had to use made me look very tired when I went home at night-time; I also had a thin face, and was inclined to be pale. This worried my mother. She thought I could be helped if I did not have to walk to work, so I was given a bike. It was bought on the 'never-never', but it suited me and did not worry when I took the 2s. 6d. each week to G. Moss. They were glad of the business.

I could dwell on the hard work I had to put in as an apprentice, but it would bore you. I will record, however, that Robinson used me for making anything that was new in design; I was never given a drawing – a sweep of the hands, a swear word or two to impress that he was only doing this to keep us in work. The first kidney dressing-table that was ever made at Robinson's was described so. 'You know what a bloody kidney-bean looks like in shape. Well, I want you to make a dressing-table that shape. It wants to be four feet six inches long and about twenty-one inches wide, two feet six inches high. Queen Anne legs, two drawers each side of the knee-hole, to be veneered in figured walnut.' Robinson himself had never used tools. I often lay awake at night working out problems of construction, and worrying. I cut my hand one day at work and had to go to the hospital to get it stitched. I had to walk there on my own, about a mile. I had four stitches put in by a young doctor; there was nothing to ease the pain, and the needle hurt going in and out. I had gone to the hospital without a proper dressing or recording the accident, something that must be done today. I still had to work with my hand bandaged. You can imagine how mucky the bandage was when I got home at night. I had had a gruelling time at work. I had solved the problem of the kidney dressing-table, and could make it in forty-eight hours. Remember we had no machines. I was now asked to make a serpentine sideboard. Hard work and worry had me looking thin in the face and black under the eyes. Mother was worried, and so when I reported with a cold one day she packed me off to the quack . . .

I made my mother a sideboard before I was sixteen years. I had no bench or vice, it was difficult. I made a fine sideboard for sister Phil for her wedding present; I was then eighteen. Mother felt a little outshone with this, so I made a new one for her; it is now at home forty-two years later; Mrs Swalwell bought the one I made first. I used to build trellises, sheds, etc., for neighbours and any payments I would get I gave to Mum; she treated me back well in return. I spent hours on the garden at No. 6. Dad did a lot of digging but I did the lawn-laying, and with Mum most of the gardening. I planted the fruit trees under Mum's supervision, and those now huge poplar trees, all before I was twenty-one. I often got told off by Robinson for using energy at home – he needed mine for work. I never let Robinson see me take my tools home to work with, he was against that and had made it clear. There are many things that happen in seven years. I speed over most. I condemned the miners when I was six-teen for the General Strike. I have grown and learned since of the great injustice society and state did towards them, and later to all working-class people. Shame is on many. Unemployment was making great inroads to the security of working people by the time I was twenty-one, and one by one my sisters left home to work in mental hospitals or in other work in the favoured south. Robinson found it harder to find work and we had to work faster so things would be cheaper. This was a great benefit to those in secure jobs, but it was a disaster to all others; when a man cannot work he cannot spend, and this throws others out of work. We grumble now at taxation when we are affluent, we grumbled then at rates and taxes to pay a pittance of dole to our fellow men. It was even said, 'They do not want work.' It was even said of me.

Robinson had got down to a staff of two, Ben and myself. The rate of pay then should have been 1s. 4d. per hour; Ben got 1s. 2d. and myself

10½d. per hour. We finished up enemies by trying to beat each other in production, we would not go to the toilet for fear of losing time. We did the shop-fitting to the Gift House in the Arcade. I think it is still there. The owner was so disgusted with my boss just sitting there and bullying that she told Robinson off, stating she had never seen anyone work so hard. When he went I was given 10s. My twenty-first birthday was a quiet affair, a couple of cards and a very cheap watch from my parents; I also received a tie-press from a friend who in turn had had it for a present. I saved it for a similar occasion. My mother's health started to give some trouble and she was often in great pain. Even my youngest sister was now away from home. Dad had a job that was seven days to the week, and twelve hours a day if others were sick or on holiday, and fifty-two weeks to the year, hence I had a lot to do for Mum. We had a specialist to her; with working families they had to have their fee first. All we got to know was, 'I confirm your doctor's findings, £5.' I will skip my mother's illness and my father's sorrow. She died at forty-eight years in 1931. God bless her, but not the doctor.

'You will have to lay off for a fortnight,' I am told by Robinson. 'You are single.' This meant signing on – not me! Men who signed on were lazy. I was a true blue and other true blues had told me so. Just about this time I had been asked by a shopkeeper if I could make a bureau like he had seen in another shop at £4 10s. I said I could. To do this I had to collect my tools from work. Robinson saw me, and went into me left and right for working at home; I answered back and got the sack. What now? I had an idea. I would go round the shops that Robinson dealt with. The only money I had was 15s. I was promised credit from a 'do-it-yourself' shop – that is bad buying, so I could only do small things at first. My father, on a wage of £2 10s. with a mortgage of £1 per week and rates on top, would keep me and Mabel who had now come home for house-keeping, I had not to worry about the board. I did however put up the cost of housekeeping as I needed gas to keep glue hot, and flat-irons to use when veneering. I also had to buy sundry items – this was out of poor Mabel's allowance, and at times a cut in rations, often toward Fridays.

I had saved £4 10s. when I went to Liverpool to buy timber at a timber-yard on the docks. I bought one-inch oak and mahogany board, and for carcase work I bought floor board from Preston Dock, ten pieces at a time ten feet long, and I would carry these home. This was 'unproductive time' as Robinson would say, so I used to run. Ripping wood up I would count as unproductive time even though it was graft cutting strips of oak out of twelve boards. I allocated any time between 6 P.M. and midnight for this sort of work. I did some very good-class work for Browns in the High Street, I did a bedroom suite for £21; it had a six-foot robe (shaped-front) dressing-table and tall-boy and bed to match. It was sold for £65. Making does not pay, you must sell. When I had made furniture I had to get it to the shop. To do this I would go to Peel Hall Street to borrow a hand-cart, take it home and load up, with help from sister Mabel if Dad was at work, then I would run with my load. I would have three journeys to make for a full suite, it was 'non-productive' time. I was getting work only because I was under-cutting. Cutting one-inch hardwood I would do for a farthing a foot, or I would form rebates for the same price. I was not better off than working for old R.

I now had an idea – if only I had a shop to sell my off-cuts of wood. I found a shop; I had to pay a month's rent in advance – what a blow – but Dad out of his little helped however, as he did for the electric that also had to be paid in advance. What a feeling of expectancy opening a shop! I had dreams of customers wanting to buy and me, ever ready to help them with their wood-working problems. Two hours after opening the shop and no one appearing interested, I made excuses that it was Monday. Then I felt things were starting to improve – a man came in, he wanted me to advertise in the local Catholic magazine. He told me it was foolish not to do so, but I did not. I could not afford to. I closed the shop at 8 P.M., the normal time in those days, and went directly back to No. 6 and started work on making furniture for the shops in town. At the end of my first week as a shop-owner I took 3d. To keep up with my cabinet-making I worked each night till 12; Saturday and Sunday I worked till 4 P.M. Eventually the shop did pay, even though poorly, but working to midnight most nights was hard going, and with all this I had yet to earn £3 in any one week. I had also lost all right to claim sick and unemployment benefits; I could not afford to pay toward them . . .

REFERENCES

PREFACE

1. James Aitken, ed., *English Diaries of the Nineteenth Century, 1800–50*, Penguin Books, 1944, p. 7.
2. Arthur Ponsonby, ed., *More English Diaries*, 1927, p. 234.
3. ibid., Extract from the diary of Charles Russell, p. 234 et seq.
4. Among the best-known are: Joseph Arch, *The Story of My Life*, Frances, Countess of Warwick, 1898; reprinted McGibbon and Kee, 1966.
Samuel Bamford, *Passages in the Life of a Radical*, 1844 and *Early Days*, 1859.
James Dawson Burn, *Autobiography of a Beggar Boy*, 1855.
William Reitzel, ed., *William Cobbett: The Progress of a Ploughboy to a Seat in Parliament*, 1933 (collected from autobiographical elements in Cobbett's writings).
The Life of Thomas Cooper, written by Himself, 1872.
John Hodge, *Workman's Cottage to Windsor Castle*, 1931.
George Jacob Holyoake, *Sixty Years of an Agitator's Life*, 1892 and *Bygones Worth Remembering*, 1905.
Charles Knight, *Passages of a Working Life*, 1864–5.
The Life and Struggles of William Lovett, 1876.
Thomas Mann, *Tom Mann's Memoirs*, 1923.
James Nasmyth, *Autobiography*, 1883.
Robert Owen, *The Life of Robert Owen, written by Himself*, 1857–8.
Alexander Somerville, *Autobiography of a Working Man*, 1848.
5. Valerie E. Chancellor, ed., *Master and Artisan in Victorian England. The Diary of William Andrews and the Autobiography of Joseph Gutteridge*, Evelyn, Adams & Mackay, 1969.
Garth Christian, ed., *A Victorian Poacher. James Hawker's Journal*, Oxford University Press, 1961.
George Ewart Evans, *Ask the Fellows who Cut the Hay*, Faber, 1965. (Based on farm workers' oral memories.)
Jocelyn Baty Goodman, ed., *Victorian Cabinet Maker. The Memoirs of James Hopkinson, 1819–1894*, Routledge & Kegan Paul, 1968.
Fred Kitchen, *Brother to the Ox: The Autobiography of a Farm Labourer*, J. M. Dent, 1940; reprinted Aldine, 1963.
Margaret Penn, *Manchester Fourteen Miles*, Guild Books, Cambridge University Press, 1947.
C. M. Smith, *The Working Man's Way in the World*, W. & F. Cash, 1853; re-issued Printing Historical Society, 1967.
Guida Swan, ed., *The Journals of Two Poor Dissenters, 1786–1880*, Routledge & Kegan Paul, 1970.
Dorothy Wise, ed., *Diary of William Tayler, Footman, 1837*, St Marylebone Society Publications Group, 1962.
6. William Matthews, *British Autobiographies, Bibliography of British Autobiographies Published or Written Before 1951*, Berkeley, California, 1955; reprinted Hamden, Connecticut, 1968.

British Diaries 1442–1942, Berkeley, California, 1950; reprinted Gloucester, Massachusetts, 1962.

7. J. Goldthorpe *et al.*, *The Affluent Worker*, Vol. I, *Industrial Attitudes and Behaviour*, 1969. Cambridge University Press.

8. E. J. Hobsbawm, 'The Tramping Artisan', in *Labouring Men. Studies in the History of Labour*, Weidenfeld and Nicolson, 1964, pp. 34 et seq.

9. Patrick McGill, *Children of the Dead End: The Autobiography of a Navvy*, 1914.

10. Chancellor, op. cit.

PART ONE – THE LABOURING CLASSES

1. E. H. Phelps Brown and Sheila V. Hopkins, 'Seven Centuries of Building Wages', *Economica*, New Series, Vol. XXII, No. 87, August, London School of Economics and Political Science, 1955, p. 202.

2. J. F. C. Harrison, *The Early Victorians, 1832–1851*, Weidenfeld and Nicolson, 1971, p. 35.

3. J. H. Clapham, *An Economic History of Modern Britain*, Vol. II, *Free Trade and Steel, 1850–1886*, 1932, p. 24.

4. ibid., Vol III, *1887–1914*, pp. 63 and 531.

5. Frank A. King, *Beer Has a History*, Hutchinson, 1949, p. 154.

6. Guy Routh, *Occupation and Pay in Great Britain, 1906–1960*, Cambridge University Press, 1965, p. 34.

7. R. D. Baxter, *The National Income of the United Kingdom*, 1868.

8. Geoffrey Best, *Mid-Victorian Britain, 1851–1875*, Weidenfeld and Nicolson, 1971, p. 100.

9. Routh, op. cit., Table 1, pp. 4–5.

10. Clapham, op. cit., Vol. I, pp. 66 and 113.

11. John Burnett, *Plenty and Want. A Social History of Diet in England from 1815 to the Present Day*, Penguin Books, 1968, Table 9, p. 153.

12. Labourers' Wages. Report from the Select Committee on the Rate of Agricultural Wages, and the Condition and Morals of Labourers in that Employment, S.P., 1824, (392).

13. James Caird, *English Agriculture in 1850–51*, 1852.

14. For fuller details of the agricultural labourer's standard of living, see Burnett, op. cit., chs. 2 and 7.

15. Joseph Arch, *The Story of My Life,* ed. Frances, Countess of Warwick, MacGibbon and Kee, 1966, pp. 30–33.

16. Fred Kitchen, *Brother to the Ox: The Autobiography of a Farm Labourer,* 1940.

17. Frank Wensley, *My Memories, 1890–1914*, unpublished autobiography, privately communicated, MSS. p. 47.

18. G. R. Porter, *The Progress of the Nation*, 1847, p. 166.

19. W. W. Rostow, *The Stages of Economic Growth*, Cambridge University Press, 1960, p. 53.

20. J. A. Schumpeter, *Business Cycles*, Vol. I, 1939, p. 271.

21. For a sociological analysis of the early cotton industry in terms of structural differentiation see Neil J. Smelser, *Social Change in the Industrial Revolution*, Routledge and Kegan Paul, 1959.

22. Edward Baines, *History of the Cotton Manufacture in Great Britain*, 2nd ed., Frank Cass, 1966, p. 238.

23. *Life in East Lancashire, 1856–60.* A newly discovered diary of John O'Neil

(John Ward), Weaver, of Clitheroe. Mary Brigg. *Transactions of the Historic Society of Lancashire and Cheshire for the year 1968*. Vol. 120, p. 92.

24. Phyllis Deane, *The First Industrial Revolution*, Cambridge University Press, 1965, pp. 88–9.

25. ibid., p. 94.

26. S. G. Checkland, *The Rise of Industrial Society in England, 1815–1885*, Longmans, 1964, pp. 56–7.

27. William Ashworth, *An Economic History of England, 1870–1939*, Methuen, 1960, pp. 76–7.

28. Checkland, op. cit., p. 131.

29. Valerie E. Chancellor, ed., *Master and Artisan in Victorian England: The Diary of William Andrews and the Autobiography of Joseph Gutteridge*, Evelyn, Adams and Mackay, 1969.

30. Clapham, op. cit., Vol. II, 1932, p. 87.

31. W. Cooke Taylor, *Notes of a Tour in the Manufacturing Districts of Lancashire*, 1842, p. 36.

32. Leon Faucher, *Manchester in 1844*, 1844, pp. 105–7.

33. Andrew Ure, M.D., F.R.S., *The Philosophy of Manufactures*, 1835, p. 301.

34. William Dodd, *The Factory System Illustrated*, 1842, pp. 108–10.

35. Frederick Engels, 'The Condition of the Working Class in England in 1844', in *Karl Marx and Frederick Engels on Britain*, 1953, p. 182.

36. The standard accounts of the history of factory regulation are contained in B. L. Hutchings and A. Harrison, *The History of Factory Legislation*, 3rd edn, 1926, and J. T. Ward, *The Factory Movement, 1830–1855*, David and Charles, 1962.

37. Leone Levi, *Wages and Earnings of the Working Classes. Report to Sir Arthur Bass, M.P.*, 1885, pp. 121–9.

38. S. and B. Webb, *Industrial Democracy*, 1920, p. 200.

39. Ellen Gill, unpublished autobiography, privately communicated, MSS, p. 5.

40. J. B. Cumberlidge, unpublished autobiography, privately communicated, MSS, p. 5.

41. W. A. Abram, 'Social Condition and Political Prospects of the Lancashire Workman', *Fortnightly Review*, Vol. IV, new series, July–December 1868, p. 431.

42. ibid., p. 432.

43. Margaret A. Pollock, ed., *Working Days. Being the Personal Records of Sixteen Working Men and Women Written by Themselves*, 1926, pp. 234–5.

44. C. R. Fay, *Life and Labour in the Nineteenth Century*, 3rd edn, Cambridge University Press, 1945, p. 184.

45. Clapham, op. cit., Vol III, 1951, p. 531.

46. Emanuel Lovekin, unpublished autobiography. See this volume, pp. 289–96.

47. Clapham, op. cit., vol. II, p. 165.

48. Geoffrey Best, *Mid-Victorian Britain, 1851–1875*, 1971, Table, p. 112.

49. Thomas Mann, *Tom Mann's Memoirs*, 1923, pp. 11–12.

50. *Our Coal and Our Coal-Pits; The People in Them and the Scenes around Them. By a Traveller Underground*, 1853, p. 152.

51. ibid., p. 186.

52. ibid., p. 157.

53. ibid., p. 158.

54. ibid., p. 166.

55. J. C. Symons, *Arts and Artisans at Home and Abroad*, 1839, quoted in Clapham, op. cit., Vol. I, p. 558.

56. A. L. Bowley, *Wages in the United Kingdom*, 1900.

57. Leone Levi, op. cit., pp. 136–7.

58. Clapham, op. cit., Vol. II, pp. 467–8.

59. Routh, op. cit., Table 38, p. 88.

60. B. L. Coombes, *These Poor Hands. The Autobiography of a Miner working in South Wales*, Gollancz, 1939, p. 88. For extract, see pp. 107–15.

61. Fay, op. cit., p. 194.

62. See the autobiography of Thomas Jordan on p. 99–107.

63. Clapham, op. cit., Vol. II, p. 24.

64. For numerous examples of sweated trades from the 1830s to the 1850s see *The Unknown Mayhew: Selections from The Morning Chronicle*, ed. by E. P. Thompson and Eileen Yeo, Merlin Press, 1971, Penguin Books, 1973.

65. Quoted in Henry Hamilton, *History of the Homeland*, Allen and Unwin, 1947, p. 323.

66. Margaret Stewart and Leslie Hunter, *The Needle is Threaded. The History of an Industry*, Heinemann and Newman Neame, 1964, pp. 60–61.

67. Leone Levi, op. cit., p. 132.

68. ibid., p. 131.

69. Charles Booth, *Life and Labour of the People in London*, Vol. IV, 1893. Report by Miss C. E. Collet, 'Women's Work', pp. 259, 295. The wage statistics relate to 1888.

70. Louise Jermy, *The Memories of a Working Woman*, 1934, pp. 41 et seq.

71. Margaret Penn, *Manchester Fourteen Miles*, Guild Books, Cambridge University Press, 1947. The whole autobiography is an unusually perceptive evocation of Lancashire village life at the beginning of the century, and deserves to be better known.

72. Olive Christian Malvery, *The Soul Market*, 1906.

73. Mrs Carl Meyer and Clementine Black, *Makers of Our Clothes. A Case for Trade Boards*, 1909. This contains the findings of an independent inquiry into women's tailoring and dress-making, with many case studies and wage statistics.

74. Stewart and Hunter, op. cit., p. 144 et seq.

PART TWO – DOMESTIC SERVANTS

1. Census of 1851. Ages and Occupations, 1852–3, Vol. LXXXVII, Parts I and II.

2. J. H. Clapham, *An Economic History of Modern Britain*, Vol. I, *The Early Railway Age, 1820–1850*, 1939, p. 568.

3. The early censuses are known to have been inexact, and the 'count' of domestic servants must have been particularly difficult. More important, the classifications changed over time, making strict inter-census comparisons impossible.

4. Table compiled from J. A. Banks, *Prosperity and Parenthood. A Study of Family Planning among the Victorian Middle Classes*, Routledge and Kegan Paul, 1954, pp. 83–7.

5. ibid., p. 135.

6. 'Modern Domestic Service', *Edinburgh Review*, Vol. CXV, April 1862, pp. 409 et seq.

7. David C. Marsh, *The Changing Social Structure of England and Wales, 1871–1961*, Rev. edn, Routledge and Kegan Paul, 1965, p. 118.

8. Marsh, op. cit., p. 126.

9. Arthur Marwick, *The Deluge: British Society and the First World War*, Bodley Head, 1965, pp. 91–2.

10. ibid., p. 303.

11. Ministry of Labour, Report of the Committee Appointed to Inquire into the Present Conditions as to the Supply of Female Domestic Servants, 1923, p. 6.

12. ibid., pp. 15–16.

13. ibid., pp. 33–4.

14. Marsh, op. cit., p. 147.

15. For a description of the Tudor organization and domestic officers of the great household, see John Burnett, *A History of the Cost of Living*, Penguin Books, 1969, pp. 74 et seq.

16. Dorothy Marshall, *The English Domestic Servant in History*, Historical Association, General Series G.13, George Philip, 1949, pp. 6–7.

17. ibid., p. 7.

18. For details of the organization and duties of an eighteenth-century household staff, see *The Housekeeping Book of Susanna Whatman, 1776–1800*, Ed. Thomas Balston, Geoffrey Bles, 1956.

19. The first edition (1861) of Mrs Beeton's *Book of Household Management* devotes many pages to recipes for home-made cleaners and polishes, though proprietary brands were becoming common by the 1880s and 1890s.

20 J. A. Banks (op. cit.) lists twenty-eight books on domestic economy (as distinct from cookery) published during the Victorian period, and this is by no means exhaustive. In addition, there were many journals and periodicals on the same subject.

21. J. H. Walsh, *A Manual of Domestic Economy*, 1857.

22. Samuel and Sarah Adams, *The Complete Servant*, 1825. Samuel had been successively groom, footman, valet, butler and house-steward, his wife maid-of-all-work, house-maid, laundry-maid, under-cook, lady's-maid and housekeeper. They were, therefore, extremely well-informed about domestic management and practices in the period immediately before the Victorian age.

23. See, for example, William Lanceley, *From Hall-Boy to House-Steward*, 1925 and John James, *The Memoirs of a House Steward*, Bury, Holt & Co., 1949.

24. For further details of French chefs and their influence on English cuisine, see John Burnett, *Plenty and Want: A Social History of Diet in England from 1815 to the Present Day*, Penguin Books, 1968, pp. 85 et seq.

25. Ref. his best-known work, *The Cook's Oracle*, 1817.

26. Isabella Beeton, *The Book of Household Management*, etc., 1861, p. 963.

27. ibid., p. 977.

28. Charles Booth and Jesse Argyle, 'Domestic Household Service' in Charles Booth, *Life and Labour of the People in London*, Vol. VIII, 1896, pp. 227–8.

29. Beeton, op. cit., pp. 976–7.

30. *A New System of Practical Domestic Economy: Appendix of Practical Estimates of Household Expenses*, 1824.

31. Walsh, op. cit., 2nd edn, 1873, p. 673.

32. *The Lady's Maid*, Houlston's Industrial Library, quoted in E. S. Turner, *What the Butler Saw. Two Hundred and Fifty Years of the Servant Problem*, Michael Joseph, 1962, p. 124.

33. *Quarterly Review*, Vol. 84, p. 176.

34. For a detailed description of nineteenth-century governesses, see Wanda Fraiken Neff, *Victorian Working Women: An Historical and Literary Study of Women in British Industries and Professions, 1832–1850*, 1929, Ch. V, pp. 151 et seq. For an early-nineteenth-century governess's autobiography see *Elizabeth Ham, by Herself*, ed. Eric Gillett, Faber, 1945.

35. *A New System of Practical Domestic Economy; Appendix of Practical Estimates of Household Expenses.*

36. For example, *The Economist and General Adviser*, No. 36, 22 January 1825, p. 57.

37. *Economy for the Single and Married, etc.*, by One who 'Makes Ends Meet', 1845.

38. Walsh, op. cit., 1857, p. 606.

39. ibid., 2nd edn, 1873, pp. 221, 369 and 677.

40. Beeton, op. cit., p. 8.

41. W. T. Layton, 'Changes in the Wages of Domestic Servants during Fifty Years', *Journal of the Royal Statistical Society*, Vol. LXXI, 1908, p. 516.

42. Walsh, op. cit., 1st edn, 1857, p. 226; R. K. Philp, *The Practical Housewife* . . . 1855, p. 8.

43. Walsh, op. cit., 2nd edn, 1873, p. 224.

44. Booth and Argyle, op. cit., p. 230.

45. Thea Holme, *The Carlyles at Home*, Oxford University Press, 1965.

46. *Diary of William Tayler, Footman, 1837*, ed. Dorothy Wise, St Marylebone Society Publications Group, London, 1962.

47. Beeton, op. cit., p. 8.

48. 'Modern Domestic Service', pp. 426 et seq.

49. Leone Levi, *Wages and Earnings of the Working Classes. Report to Sir Arthur Bass, M.P.*, 1885, p. 80.

50. Report on the Money Wages of Indoor Domestic Servants (by Miss C. E. Collet), Vol 42, Parliamentary Papers, 1899, p. 111.

51. Layton, op. cit., pp. 515 et seq.

52. See p. 234.

53. See p. 226.

54. Herbert Llewellyn Smith, *The New Survey of London Life and Labour*, 1930.

55. Marshall, op. cit., pp. 10 et seq.

56. Turner, op. cit., p. 98.

57. 'Modern Domestic Service', pp. 411 et seq.

58. Turner, op. cit., p. 243.

59. Booth and Argyle, op. cit., Vol. VIII, p. 225.

60. 'Modern Domestic Service', p. 414.

61. Jessie Boucherett, 'Legislative Restrictions on Woman's Labour, *The Englishwoman's Review*, Vol. LXXVIII, 1873.

62. William Clarke, 'The Social Future of England', *Contemporary Review*, Vol. LXXVIII, December 1900, p. 867.

63. 'Modern Domestic Service', pp. 415–16.

64. Anon., *Etiquette*, 1857. Quoted in Turner, op. cit., pp. 218–19.

FURTHER READING

Domestic service as an occupation has received little attention from historians, and there are few major secondary sources. Among the more useful are Dr Dorothy Marshall's pamphlet *The English Domestic Servant in History* (Historical Association, London, 1949), D. M. Stuart's *The English Abigail* (Macmillan, 1946), which gathers together much descriptive material from literary sources such as novels and plays, and E. S. Turner's *What the Butler Saw: Two Hundred and Fifty Years of the Servant Problem* (Michael Joseph, 1962), whose elies some wide research in contemporary sources. J. A. Banks's seminal study into the middle-class standard of living in Victorian England, *Prosperity and Parenthood* (Routledge and Kegan Paul, 1954), contains much on the numbers and wages of domestic servants in the middle of the century. L. M. Salmon's *Domestic Service* (1901) is a detailed historical account of the institution of domestic service, based mainly on American experience, but containing useful comparative data on European practice. The place of domestic service in the social and occupational structure is examined briefly in David C. Marsh, *The Changing Social Structure of England and Wales, 1871–1961* (rev. edn, Routledge and Kegan Paul, 1965) and census material is summarized in B. R. Mitchell and Phyllis Deane, *Abstract of British Historical Statistics* (Cambridge University Press, 1962). A valuable chapter on the work and recruitment of governesses is contained in Wanda Fraiken Neff's *Victorian Working Women: An Historical and Literary Study of Women in British Industries and Professions, 1832–1850* (1929).

Beyond these, reference must be made to original sources. For statistical and wage data much information is contained in the numerous editions of G. R. Porter's *The Progress of the Nation* (e.g. new edition, 1847), in Leone Levi's *Wages and Earnings of the Working Classes* (1885), in Charles Booth and Jesse Argyle's article 'Domestic Household Service' in Charles Booth's *Life and Labour of the People in London*, Vol. VIII (1896), and in W. T. Layton's article 'Changes in the Wages of Domestic Servants during Fifty Years' in the *Journal of the Royal Statistical Society*, Vol. LXXI (1908). Parliamentary Papers were little concerned with domestic servants, almost the only useful ones being Miss C. E. Collet's Report on the Money Wages of Indoor Domestic Servants (Parliamentary Papers, Vol. 42, 1899) and the Ministry of Labour Report on the Present Conditions as to the Supply of Female Domestic Servants, 1923. Much valuable information on the duties and wages of servants is to be found in the many nineteenth-century publications on domestic economy and household management: among these are *A New System of Practical Domestic Economy* (1824), Samuel and Sarah Adams, *The Complete Servant* (1825), J. H. Walsh, *A Manual of Domestic Economy* (1857) and Mrs Isabella Beeton, *The Book of Household Management* (1st edn 1861 and many subsequently). Many articles on the 'problem' of domestic service appeared in the periodical press, some of the more revealing being 'Human Progress' (*Westminster Review*, October 1849), 'Modern Domestic Service' (*Edinburgh Review*, April 1862), 'Household Service' (*Fortnightly Review*, January 1868), 'Domestic Service: a Social Study' (*Westminster Review*, February 1891), 'A Reformation of Domestic Service' (*The Nineteenth Century*, January 1893), and 'The Social Future of England' (*Contemporary Review*. December 1900). Journals such as *The Englishwoman's Review*, *The Englishwoman's Domestic Magazine*, *The Lady*, *The Queen* and similar women's magazines contain many references from a middle-class employer's viewpoint.

PART THREE – SKILLED WORKERS

1. G. D. H. Cole, 'The Social Structure of England. Part I: The Working Classes', *History Today*, February 1951, p. 66.
2. W. B. Adams, *English Pleasure Carriages*, 1837, pp. 188–9.
3. See Thomas Wright, *Some Habits and Customs of the Working Classes, by a Journeyman Engineer*, 1867, particularly the chapter 'On the Inner Life of Workshops'.
4. Cole, op. cit., p. 63.

5. For examples, see S. G. Checkland, *The Rise of Industrial Society in England, 1815–1886*, Longmans, 1964, ch. 4, sections 4 and 6. James Nasmyth, the engineer, describes his own ascent in *An Autobiography*, ed. Samuel Smiles, 1883.

6. E. J. Hobsbawm, 'The Labour Aristocracy in Nineteenth-Century Britain', *Labouring Men, Studies in the History of Labour*, Weidenfeld and Nicolson, 1964, p. 288.

7. J. L. and Barbara Hammond, *The Skilled Labourer, 1760–1832*, Longmans, 1919.

8. T. K. Derry, 'The Repeal of the Apprenticeship Clauses of the Statute of Apprentices', *Economic History Review*, 1931.

9. Royal Commission on Children's Employment, second Report: Trades and Manufactures, 1843. Quoted in J. H. Clapham, *An Economic History of Modern Britain*, Vol. I, *The Early Railway Age, 1820–1850*, 1939, pp. 571–2.

10. Sidney and Beatrice Webb, *Industrial Democracy*, 1920 edn, p. 470. Chapter 10, 'The Entrance to a Trade', contains a detailed discussion of apprenticeship in relation to trade unionism.

11. Clapham, op. cit., Vol. II, *Free Trade and Steel, 1850–1886*, p. 470.

12. Webb, op. cit., p. 476.

13. For detailed statistics of occupations, and comment on the Census returns, see Charles Booth, 'Occupations of the People of the United Kingdom, 1801–1881', *Journal of the Statistical Society*, Vol. XLIX, 1886, pp. 134 et seq.

14. G. R. Porter, *The Progress of the Nation*, new edn, 1847, p. 53.

15. Clapham, op. cit., Vol. I, p. 72.

16. ibid., p. 165.

17. biid., p. 175. For an autobiographical account of the Birmingham trades of this period, see G. J. Holyoake, *Sixty Years of an Agitator's Life*, 2 vols., 1892.

18. T. S. Ashton, *Iron and Steel in the Industrial Revolution*, 1924; and references in Checkland, op. cit.

19. Clapham, op. cit., Vol. II, p. 152.

20. See Nasmyth, op. cit., for a description of Maudsley's workshop.

21. Checkland, op. cit., p. 218.

22. Table compiled from R. Dudley Baxter, *The National Income of the United Kingdom*, Appendix IV, 1868, pp. 88 et seq.

23. George Sturt, *The Wheelwright's Shop*, Cambridge University Press, 1923. For an extract from the work, see pp. 320–30.

24. Clapham, op. cit., Vol. II, p. 126.

25. ibid., p. 131.

26. ibid., p. 471.

27. Cole, op. cit., p. 66.

28. From Guy Routh, *Occupation and Pay in Great Britain, 1906–1960*, Cambridge University Press, 1965, Table 1, p. 5.

29. ibid., p. 29.

30. Select Committee on Artisans and Machinery, 1824, pp. 27 et seq.

31. E. J. Hobsbawm, 'Custom, Wages and Workload in Nineteenth-Century Industry', *Essays in Labour History*, ed. by Asa Briggs and John Saville, Macmillan, 1960, pp. 114 et seq.

32. ibid., p. 118.

33. For an examination of price movements throughout the nineteenth and twentieth centuries, see John Burnett, *A History of the Cost of Living*, Penguin Books, 1969, chs. 4 and 5.

34. A. L. Bowley, *Wages in the United Kingdom*, 1900, p. 122.

35. *The Unknown Mayhew. Selections from The Morning Chronicle, 1849–1850*,

Ed. and intro. by E. P. Thompson and Eileen Yeo, Merlin Press, 1971, p. 183.
Penguin Books, 1973.

36. ibid., p. 206.

37. ibid., p. 368.

38. John Burnett, 'The Baking Industry in the Nineteenth Century', *Business History*, Vol. v, No. 2, 1963.

39. Webb, op. cit., p. 287 et seq.

40. Checkland, op. cit., p. 232, based on R. Dudley Baxter, *The National Income of the United Kingdom*, 1868.

41. Clapham, op. cit., Vol. ii, p. 451.

42. Burnett, op. cit., pp. 199 et seq.

43. Leone Levi, *Wages and Earnings of the Working Classes. Report to Sir Arthur Bass, M.P.*, 1885, pp. 30–31.

44. ibid., pp. 73 et seq.

45. George N. Barnes, *From Workshop to War Cabinet*, 1924, p. 21.

46. Hobsbawm, 'The Labour Aristocracy in Nineteenth-Century Britain', p. 290.

47. ibid., pp. 290 et seq.

48. From Routh, op. cit., p. 88.

49. ibid., ch. 3, 'The Time and Circumstances of Pay Changes', pp. 109 et seq.

50. Thompson and Yeo, eds., op. cit., 'Conclusion: Low Wages', p. 471.

51. ibid., p. 361.

52. Webb, op. cit., p. 163.

53. Henry Mayhew, *London Labour and the London Poor. The Condition and Earnings of Those That Will Work, Cannot Work and Will Not Work*, Vol. iii, 1861, p. 231.

54. Hobsbawm, 'The Tramping Artisan', *Labouring Men*, pp. 34 et seq.

55. See Henry Broadhurst, M.P., *The Story of his Life from a Stonemason's Bench to the Treasury Bench. Told by Himself*, Hutchinson, 1901. Extract on pp. 312–20.

56. B. R. Mitchell and Phyllis Deane, *Abstract of British Historical Statistics*, Cambridge University Press, 1962, pp. 64–5.

57. R. Dudley Baxter, *The National Income of the United Kingdom, 1868*. Quoted in William Ashworth, *An Economic History of England, 1870–1939*, Methuen, 1960, p. 23.

58. Mitchell and Deane, op. cit., p. 67.

59. Thompson and Yeo, eds., op. cit., p. 257.

60. See the extract from *When I was a Child*. By an old potter, Methuen, 1903, on pp. 297–304.

61. John Dunlop, *Philosophy of Artificial and Compulsory Drinking Usage*, 6th edn, 1893.

62. Webb, op. cit., p. 340.

63. Thompson and Yeo, eds., op. cit., pp. 392–3.

64. Clapham, op. cit., Vol. ii, p. 448.

65. J. A. R. Pimlott, *The Englishman's Holiday*, Faber and Faber, 1947, pp. 147 et seq.

66. A. L. Bowley, *Wages and Income since 1860*, pp. 18 et seq.

67. Pimlott, op. cit., pp. 217–21.

68. Nasmyth, op. cit.

69. Patrick McGeown, *Heat the Furnace Seven Times More*, Hutchinson, 1967.

70. George Sturt, *The Wheelwright's Shop*, Cambridge University Press, 1923. For extract see pp. 320–30.